BATTLEFIELD GUIDE TO THE
WESTERN FRONT
- NORTH

WW1 100th Anniversaries/GPS Edition

Mons • Le Cateau • Notre-Dame de Lorette, Artois
• The Yser • 1st Ypres • Neuve Chapelle • 2nd Ypres
(Gas Attack) • Aubers Ridge • Festubert-Givenchy •
Loos • Fromelles • Vimy Ridge, Arras • 3rd Ypres
(Passchendaele) • 4th Ypres (The Lys)

TONIE AND VALMAI HOLT

Pen & Sword
MILITARY

Cover illustration: *Preserved trenches at Sanctuary Wood near Ypres*

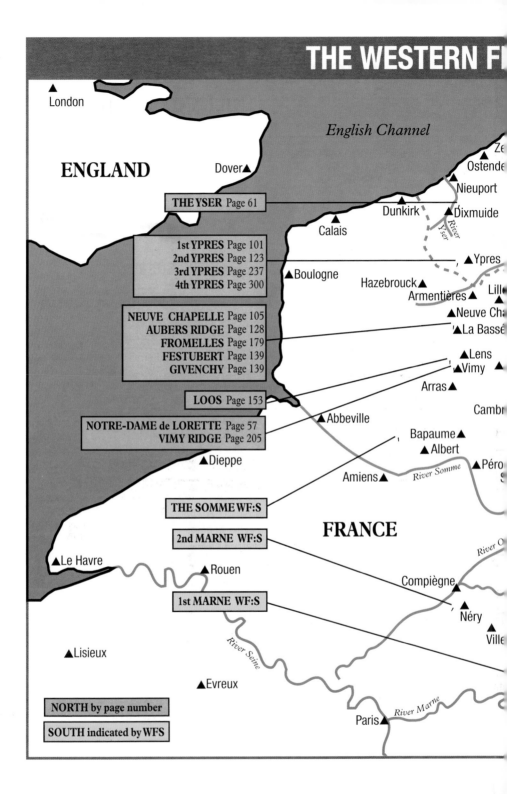

London

English Channel

ENGLAND

Dover

Ze
Ostende
Nieuport

Dunkirk **Dixmuide**

Calais

River Yser

Boulogne

Hazebrouck **Ypres**

Armentières **Lill**

Neuve Cha
La Bassé

Lens
Vimy

Arras

Cambr

Abbeville

Bapaume
Albert

Dieppe

Péro

Amiens *River Somme*

FRANCE

River O

Le Havre

Rouen

Compiègne

Néry

Ville

Lisieux

River Seine

Evreux

NORTH by page number

SOUTH indicated by WFS

Paris *River Marne*

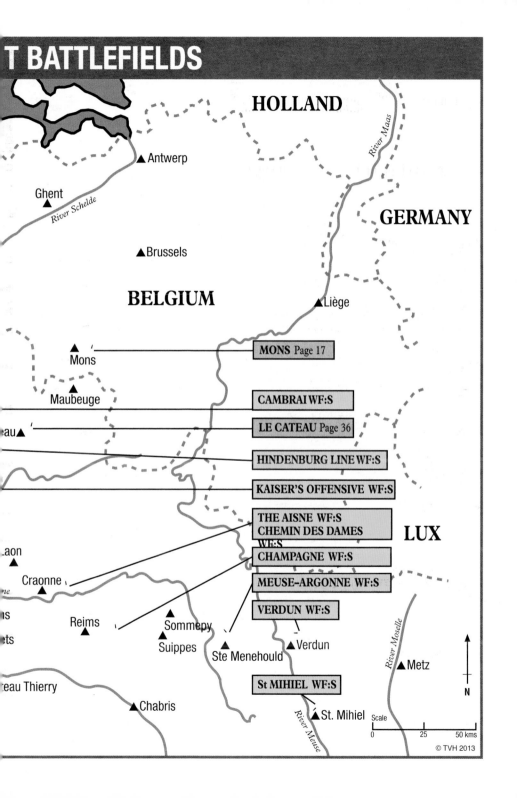

HOLLAND

River Maas

Antwerp

Ghent

River Schelde

GERMANY

Brussels

BELGIUM

Liège

Mons

MONS Page 17

Maubeuge

eau▲

CAMBRAI WF:S

LE CATEAU Page 36

HINDENBURG LINE WF:S

KAISER'S OFFENSIVE WF:S

THE AISNE WF:S
CHEMIN DES DAMES WF:S

LUX

Laon

CHAMPAGNE WF:S

Craonne

MEUSE–ARGONNE WF:S

ne

VERDUN WF:S

s

Reims

Sommepy

River Moselle

ts

Suippes

Verdun

eau Thierry

Ste Menehould

Metz

St MIHIEL WF:S

Chabris

River Meuse

St. Mihiel

Scale

N

0   25   50 kms

© TVH 2013

By the same authors:

Battlefield Guide Books

Holts' Battlefield Guidebooks: NormandyOverlord/
Market-Garden/Somme/Ypres, 1982-1988

Visitor's Guide to the Normandy Landing
Beaches, 1989, 1990

Battlefields of the First World War: A Traveller's
Guide, 1993, 1995, 1998, 1999

Major & Mrs Holt's Concise Battlefield Guide to
the Ypres Salient, 1994, 1995, 1996

Major & Mrs Holt's Battlefield Guide to the
Somme + Battle Map, 1996, 1998, 1999, 2000,
2003, 2007, 2008

Major & Mrs Holt's Battlefield Guide to Gallipoli
+ Battle Map, 2000

Major & Mrs Holt's Battlefield Guide to
MARKET-GARDEN (Arnhem) + Battle Map,
2001, 2004, 2013

Major & Mrs Holt's Battlefield Guide to
Normandy D-Day Landing Beaches + Battle
Map, 999, 2000, 2002, 2004, 2006, 2008, 2009

Major & Mrs Holt's Definitive Battlefield Guide
to the Normandy D-Day Landing Beaches, 2012

Major & Mrs Holt's Concise, Illustrated Battlefield
Guide to the Western Front – North, 2004, 2007, 2012

Major & Mrs Holt's Concise, Illustrated Battlefield
Guide to the Western Front–South, 2005, 2012

Major & Mrs Holt's Pocket Battlefield Guide to
Ypres and Passchendaele, 2006, 2008, 2010

Major & Mrs Holt's Pocket Battlefield Guide to
The Somme 1916/1918, 2006, 2008

Major & Mrs Holt's Pocket Battlefield Guide to D-
Day Normandy Landing Beaches, 2009

Biography

Violets From Oversea: 25 Poets of the First World
War, 1996, reprinted as Poets of the Great War,
1999, 2010

My Boy Jack?: The Search for Kipling's Only Son,
1998, revised and reprinted 2001, 2007, 2008, 2009

In Search of the Better 'Ole: The Life, Works and
Collectables of Bruce Bairnsfather, 1985, revised
and reprinted, 2001

Picture Postcard Artists: Landscapes, Animals and
Characters, 1984

Military History

Till the Boys Come Home: the Picture Postcards of
the First World War, 1977, revised 2014

I'll Be Seeing You: the Picture Postcards of World
War II, 1987

Germany Awake! The Rise of National Socialism,
illustrated by Contemporary Postcards, 1986

General

Picture Postcards of the Golden Age: A Collector's
Guide, 1971, 1978

The Best of Fragments from France by Capt Bruce
Bairnsfather (Editors), 1978, 1983, 1998, revised
edition, with authors' royalties to 'Help for
Heroes', 2009

Stanley Gibbons Postcard Catalogue: 1980, 1981,
1982, 1984, 1985, 1987

Battlefield Maps

Major & Mrs Holt's Battle Maps: The Somme/The
Ypres Salient/Normandy/Gallipoli/Market-Garden
(Arnhem), 1986-2013

First published in Great Britain in 2004,
2nd Revised Edition 2007, this 3rd Revised Edition 2014

PEN AND SWORD MILITARY

an imprint of
Pen & Sword Books Ltd
47 Church Street
Barnsley, South Yorkshire S70 2AS

Text copyright © Tonie and Valmai Holt, 2014

ISBN 978 178159 397 4

Typeset by LS Menzies-Earl, Chic Graphics

Printed and bound in India
by Replika Press Pvt. Ltd

Pen & Sword Books Ltd incorporates the imprints of Pen & Sword Aviation, Pen & Sword Family History,
Pen & Sword Maritime, Pen & Sword Military, Wharncliffe Local History, Wharncliffe True Crime, Wharncliffe
Transport, Pen & Sword Discovery, Pen & Sword Select, Pen & Sword Military Classics, Leo Cooper,
Remember When, The Praetorian Press, Seaforth Publishing and Frontline Publishing

For a complete list of Pen & Sword titles please contact
PEN & SWORD BOOKS LIMITED
47 Church Street, Barnsley, South Yorkshire, S70 2AS, England
E-mail: enquiries@pen-and-sword.co.uk   Website: www.pen-and-sword.co.uk

CONTENTS

Legend for Maps

Bunkers	●	Place names	▲
Demarcation Stones	◉	Sites of Special Interest	○
Memorials	◌	War Cemeteries	●
Museums	●		

LIST OF MAPS

ABBREVIATIONS

Abbreviations and acronyms used for military units are listed below. Many of these are printed in full at intervals throughout the text to aid clarity. Others are explained where they occur.

A/	Acting		L/	Lance
ASH	Argyll & Sutherland Highlanders		Mia	Missing in action
BCA	*Battaillon de Chasseurs Alpins*		MC	Military Cross
BCP	*Battaillon de Chasseurs à Pied*		MiD	Mentioned in Despatches
BEF	British Expeditionary Force		MM	Military Medal
Brit	British		MoH	Medal of Honour
CAP	*Chasseurs à Pied*		OP	Observation Point
C-in-C	Commander-in-Chief		OR	Other Rank(s)
CO	Commanding Officer		ORBAT	Order of Battle
Comm	Communal		POW's	Prince of Wales/Prisoners of War
Coy	Company		Pte	Private
CWGC	Commonwealth War Graves		RF	Royal Fusiliers
	Commission		RE	Royal Engineers
Ger	German		RI	*Régiment d'Infanterie*
GHQ	General Head Quarters		RIDG	Royal Irish Dragoon Guards
Gnr	Gunner		RIR	Royal Irish Rifles
HAC	Honorable Artillery Company		RoL	Regiment of Line,
HLI	Highland Light Infantry		RWF	Royal Welsh Fusiliers
IWGC	Imperial War Graves Commission		SGW	Stained Glass Window
K	Kitchener (as in Division)		SMLE	Short muzzle Lee Enfield
Kia	killed in action		T/	Temporary
KOYLI	King's Own Yorkshire Light Infantry		VC	Victoria Cross
KRRC	King's Royal Rifle Corps		WFA	Western Front Association

ABOUT THE AUTHORS

Respected military authors Tonie and Valmai Holt are generally acknowledged as the founders, in the 1970s, of the modern battlefield tour.

Valmai Holt took a BA(Hons) in French and Spanish and taught History. Tonie Holt took a BSc(Eng) and is a graduate of the Royal Military Academy, Sandhurst and of the Army Staff College at Camberley. They are both Fellows of the Royal Society of Arts and Science and have made frequent appearances on the lecture circuit, radio and television. They are founder members of The Western Front Association and Honorary Members of the Guild of Battlefield Guides.

The authors.

Their company, Major & Mrs Holt's Battlefield Tours, gradually grew, at first through their consultancy with Purnell & BCA Book Clubs, to cover battlefields as far afield as the American Civil War, Arnhem, the Crimea, El Alamein, Monte Cassino, the Normandy Landing Beaches, Vietnam, Waterloo, the WW1 Gallipoli, Italian and Western Fronts, the Falkland Islands, South Africa and other destinations.

In 1984 they acted as consultants to the cities of Portsmouth and Southampton, The Département of Calvados, Townsend Thoresen and British Airways to co-ordinate the first great commemoration of the D-Day Landings, the 40th Anniversary. In that same year they were appointed as ADCs to Congressman Robert Livingston of Louisiana for services in support of American veterans. Also in the 1980s they were asked to take over the organisation of the Royal British Legion Pilgrimages and greatly improved the standard for the benefit of the widows and families. They also acted as consultants to the Accor group as they began to receive more British groups in their hotels.

Their tours soon established a sound reputation for the depth of their research, which was then transferred to their writing. their *Major & Mrs Holt's Battlefield Guides* series comprises, without doubt, the leading guide books describing the most visited battlefields of the First and Second World Wars. They have a unique combination of male and female viewpoints allowing military commentaries to be linked with the poetry, music and literature of the period under study and can draw upon over 30 years military and travel knowledge and experience gained in personally conducting thousands of people around the areas they have written about. In the early days they were privileged to be able to record the memories of veterans of the Great War and then of World War Two, which have been incorporated into their books.

In December 2003 the Holts sponsored and unveiled a memorial to Capt Bruce Bairnsfather (the subject of their biography, *In Search of the Better 'Ole*) at St Yvon near 'Plugstreet Wood' and worked with the local Commune on the new Plugstreet '14–'18 information Centre where they are mounting a major exhibition of Bairnsfather items from their collection and giving a lecture in September 2014.

In 2007 an updated edition of their biography of John Kipling, *My Boy Jack?*, was published to coincide with the ITV drama, *My Boy Jack*, starring Daniel Radcliffe and they acted as consultants for the IWM Exhibition of the same name.

In 2008 they celebrated their Golden Wedding Anniversary.

In 2009, the 50th Anniversary year of the death of the cartoonist Bruce Bairnsfather, they updated their 1978 published collection of 140 of his most enduring cartoons, *The Best of Fragments from France*, and this, together with tribute cartoons freely donated by some of the world's leading cartoonists, was sold at a Charity Auction for 'Help for Heroes'. Bairnsfather would have approved. All authors' royalties from the sale of the book go to the Charity. For more information and latest news VISIT THEIR WEBSITE:

www.guide-books.co.uk

INTRODUCTION

The Next War

The long war had ended.
Its miseries had grown faded.
Deaf men became difficult to talk to,
Heroes became bores.
Those alchemists
Who had converted blood into gold
Had grown elderly.
But they held a meeting,
Saying,
    'We think perhaps we ought
    To put tombs
    Or erect altars
    To those brave lads
    Who were so willingly burnt,
    Or blinded,
    Or maimed,
    Who lost all likeness to a living thing,
    Or were blown to bleeding patches of flesh
    For our sakes.
    It would look well.
    Or we might even educate the children.'
But the richest of these wizards
Coughed gently;
And he said:
    'I have always been to the front
    – In private enterprise –,
    I yield in public spirit
    To no man.
    I think yours is a very good idea
    – A capital idea –
    And not too costly...
    But it seems to me
    That the cause for which we fought
    Is again endangered.
    What more fitting memorial for the fallen
    Than that their children
    Should fall for the same cause?'
Rushing eagerly into the street,
That kindly old gentleman cried
To the young:
    'Will you sacrifice
    Through your lethargy
    What your fathers died to gain?
    The world *must* be made safe for the young!'
And the children
Went...

              Osbert Sitwell, 1931

The tombs were indeed put up, the altars erected, the children were educated and continue to be as the Great War features in school syllabi to this day. And not once, but many times again, the children 'went'. The idea that we should learn from history that war was too terrible ever to countenance again after the Great War has been dispelled many and many a time. Yet still we strive to make sense of the greatest conflict that the world had ever seen before 1914.

After some thirty-five years of studying that war, travelling thousands of miles over its battlefields, leading thousands of people around them, talking to scores of local experts and, above all, interviewing veterans and reading personal accounts, we are convinced that the closest we can ever come to understanding what it may have been like to take part in it and what it was in aid of, is to walk its haunted sites while studying the accounts of those who were there.

For wars are fought by human beings, not arrows and blue and red lines on maps. Their currency is human lives, of boys of 14, of men of 68. Their blood and bones, their memories and experiences impregnate the ground they fought for, in the shallow zigzags of trenches and the grassy or water-filled hollows of mine craters, in dank underground tunnels and chambers and musty bunkers – even below peaceful townships and rolling hills and beautiful thick woods. There we may occasionally glimpse a hint of their pain, hear echoes of the humour that sustained them, feel their longing for home and loved ones, sense their fear and patriotism.

THE WESTERN FRONTS NORTH AND SOUTH

Hence this guidebook, which, with its companion volume, *The Battlefield Guide to the Western Front – South*, is the culmination of our years of involvement in the Great War. The books are written as a tribute to those special people of '14-'18, so different from us today because of their culture, their mores, their attitudes of a truly bygone age, and in the hope that it will help you, the reader, to get nearer to an understanding of what it was all about by getting to know where it all happened. They are written from personal experience and are designed to be simple to use, practical and informative. If we mention a bunker we have explored it, a trench we have walked through it, a memorial we have seen it, a cemetery we have visited it...

This **North** volume closes the gap left between our detailed guidebooks to the Ypres Salient (also included in more concise form in this book) and The Somme (where the **Second** volume begins geographically). It visits the areas of the briefer, smaller-scale but highly significant battles at Mons and le Cateau (both fought over at the very beginning and end of the war), the desperate efforts of the Belgians on the Yser, the battles of Neuve Chapelle, Aubers Ridge, Festubert, Givenchy, Loos and Fromelles and the long struggles of the French in Artois at Notre-Dame de Lorette and Vimy Ridge.

The significant contribution of the old 'Dominions' - Australia, Canada, India and New Zealand - is well acknowledged here and it is increasingly marked by their own countries.

Each battlefield has its own fascination and sites where one can still relate to the conflicts that took place on them.

The **South** volume covers the Somme battlefields, moves eastwards and southwards through Cambrai, the Marne, the Aisne, Champagne, the Meuse-Argonne and St Mihiel to Verdun, covering American, Commonwealth and French campaigns. Together they form a comprehensive guide to the major battlefields of the Western Front and hopefully lead the reader to visiting new, extremely interesting areas where, in several cases, recent developments have opened up sites that have remained 'dormant' for many years.

Since our first group tour in 1977, when no other post-WW2 organised tours existed for the general public, the battlefield scene has changed beyond all recognition. Then we would stand alone with the faithful buglers at the Menin Gate, be the sole signatories in remote cemetery registers, place our poppy tributes on rarely visited memorials. It was a very privileged time.

Gradually the interest and momentum rolled on. Local authorities realised that battlefields could equate to tourism. Designated routes were devised and signed, sites were refurbished, made safe for visitors, car parks were constructed, small museums with superb personal exhibits but little professional curatorship skills were expanded and 'modernised'. Perhaps a little of the 'soul' was lost in the process but now, as battlefield touring has moved from the exclusive realms of the 'buff' or the 'pilgrim' to that of the 'student' and the 'tourist', the benefit is that so many more people are able to be exposed to the lore of the Great War and who can contribute to keeping the memory alive.

THE WW1 CENTENARY AND REMEMBRANCE TOURISM

The ever-continuing research by armchair historians and energetic local enthusiasts alike has led to a flood of new information and the discovery and opening up of new sites to visit. The universal availability of information via the Internet has led to the sharing of such knowledge on a scale previously unimaginable via websites and chat rooms. The widespread use of 'sat-navs' has led to simpler navigation. The significant milestone **100th Anniversary** of successive battles of the Great War has led to a flurry of new build, updated and expanded Visitor and Interpretation Centres and Museums (see Fromelles, Lijssenthoek, Mons, Nieuwpoort, Ors-Wilfred Owen House, Passchendaele, Ypres) the erection of new regimental and personal memorials, with millions of Euros being invested in new projects by the European Community, National Governments, Ministries of Defence and Culture, Regional Departments and Communes, various private sponsors and old Dominion Governments making National Statements.

UNESCO is recognising a huge Franco-Belgian project submitted by the *Association des Paysages et Sites de Mémoire du Front Occidental de la Grande Guerre* (www.heritage-grandeguerre. fr www.paysages-et-sites-de-memoire.fr to identify and log all the major sites of the 1914-1918 war along the old Western Front, from the North Sea to Switzerland – cemeteries, memorials, museums, craters, bunkers, fortifications, trenches. Research by individual Departments and Communes will be collated according to UNESCO specifications.

The Project **'14-18 Remembered'** is another cross-border enterprise (Nord Pas-de-Calais, Westhoek, Comines-Warneton, Somme, Aisne etc) whose main aim is to promote **Remembrance Tourism** by joint publicity and marketing, updated news items, the improvement of facilities of existing sites etc and a smart-phone App. This is a phrase which is heard with increasing frequency as the old veteran/pilgrimage market gives way to both more general tourism and heritage tourism for families researching family connections with the war. See http://www.1418remembered.co.uk/

The major investment of Australia and Canada in sites where their soldiers fought and fell has led to a huge increase in remembrance tourism from Down Under and N. America – as the war cemeteries' Visitors' Books in the area bear witness.

The Westhoek WW1 site - http://www.wo1.be/ continues to be an exceptional mine of information about the War in Flanders and its main sites.

Many sites are creating audio-guided routes using i-phones and i-pads. The Canadians have erected many Plaques to their VCs in the Ypres Salient and in the Nord Pas-de-Calais and Picardy. The Australians are funding new Museums in Fromelles and other sites...

Extensive underground archaeology (by expert official archaeologists in the Salient and around Arras and experienced investigators such as Peter Barton, Franky Bostyn, the Durand Group, Johan Vandewalle and many other well-qualified workers, has led to the opening up of many vast 'souterrains' and bunkers. An unprecedented, completely new war cemetery has been created by the Commonwealth War Graves Commission at Fromelles following the discovery of a mass grave at Pheasant Wood. The incredible story of the identification processes undertaken are described in the Fromelles chapter.

THE BRITISH GOVERNMENT'S PLANS FOR THE CENTENARY

Formally announced on 10 June 2013, these are detailed on www.gov.uk/ww1centenary. Highlights are:

- On 4 Aug 2014: Ceremonies in Glasgow & St Symphorien CWGC Cemetery, Mons (qv)
- Candlelit vigil at Westminster Abbey, extinguishing at 2300
- Re-opening of IWM after £35 million refurbishment of WW1 Galleries.
- The Museum also has a full programme – see IWM Centenary Partnership Programme www.iwm.org.uk
- National acts of Remembrance on 24 April in Gallipoli 2015, 1 July 2016 (Somme), Battle of Jutland and the 1st day of the Passchendaele Offensive in 2017 and 11 November 2018 (Armistice)
- £5.3 million project to take 2 pupils from each state secondary school on a battlefield Tour
- A good summary of many national plans is to be found on www.greatwar.co.uk
- The CWGC also has some remarkable plans (see WAR GRAVES Section, Page 320).

PARDON FOR EXECUTED MEN

A major development in August 2006 was the announcement that UK Defence Secretary, Des Browne, had agreed to apply to Parliament for the blanket pardon of the 306 Allied servicemen (although the New Zealanders have already been pardoned by their Government) executed during WW1 for desertion, cowardice and other offences. This follows years of campaigning by families such as that of Pte Harry Farr, who is commemorated on the Thiepval Memorial. Although there is immense sympathy for the families who have lived under the cloud of stigma for ninety or so years and there are indubitably many cases of horrendous miscarriages of justice in the sentencing of men, often badly represented and/or suffering from shell-shock and other nervous diseases, there is not universal approval for the action. Historian Corelli Barnett, for example, has warned of the danger of applying modern morals and ethical values to the past and the fact that a blanket pardon would include cases of real criminality, dereliction of duty etc. (Consult 'Shot At Dawn' in the Index of this book for the graves of executed soldiers visited on various itineraries.)

THE FLAME OF REMEMBRANCE

What is important is to keep alight the flame thrown to our hands by John McCrae in the best-known poem of the Great War: *In Flanders Fields*. In writing this book – the fulfilment of so many years of studying and visiting the battlefields – we have endeavoured to hold it high and now pass it you.

Tonie and Valmai Holt,
Woodnesborough, 2014

HOW TO USE THIS GUIDE

This book may be read at home as a continuous account, used en-route as a guide to specific battles and battlefields, dipped into at any time via the Index as a source of fascinating detail about the First World War or kept as a reminder of past visits to the sites described.

The most significant WW1 battles of the Western Front fought to the north of the Somme and Paris are included in chronological order. Each battle is separately described under the headings 'A Summary of the Battle', 'Opening Moves' and 'What Happened' to remind readers of its historical significance, so that the details may be more readily understood and to provide a framework upon which the accounts that follow may be hung. Each battle described is accompanied by an especially drawn map and the conduct of the battles can be more easily followed by constant references to the appropriate map.

At the front of each chapter are one or more quotations from people who were involved in the war and these have been chosen to give a relevant personal flavour to the detailed accounts. Those already familiar with the First World War will find the chapter quotations apposite before reading further, while those less familiar may well find it worthwhile to read the quotations again at a later stage.

MILES COVERED/DURATION/OP/RWC/
TRAVEL DIRECTIONS/EXTRA VISITS/N.B.s

The battlefield tours cover features that during our many years of guiding parties across them and writing about them have been the most requested, as being the best-known, the most important, the most emotive... Added to them are the new sites that have recently been opened up. None is exhaustive – this is a condensed battlefield guide – but in combination with the specially drawn maps for each battle they provide a compact and hopefully illuminating commentary upon the events of the time, from glimpses of the Grand Designs, through individual acts of heroism to the memorials that now mark the pride and grief of a past generation.

A start point is given for each tour from which a running total of miles is indicated. Extra Visits and 'N.B.s' are not counted in that running total. Each recommended stop is indicated by a clear heading with the running total, the probable time you will wish to stay there and a map reference to the relevant sketch map and, in the case of Ypres, to *Major & Mrs Holt's Battle Map of Ypres*. A new important addition to the heading is a GPS location for each stop. The letters **OP** in the heading indicate a view point from which salient points of the battle are described. **RWC** indicates refreshment and toilet facilities. Travel directions are written in italics and indented to make them stand out clearly. An end point is suggested, with a total distance and timing without deviations or refreshment stops. 'Base' towns or cities are suggested which can provide convenient and comfortable accommodation and restaurants.

In addition **Extra Visits** are described to sites of particular interest which lie near to the route of the main itineraries. These are tinted light grey and boxed so that they clearly stand out from the main route. Estimates of the round-trip mileage and duration are given.

Boxed sections headed **[N.B.]** point out further sites of interest which you may wish to stop at as you pass or make a small deviation from the route to visit

It is absolutely essential to set your mileage trip to zero before starting and to make constant reference to it. Odometers can vary from car to car and where you park or turn round will affect your total so that it may differ slightly from that given in this book. What is important, however, is the distance between stops. Distances in the headings are given in miles because the trip meters on British cars still operate in miles. Distances within the text are sometimes given in kilometres and metres as local signposts use these measures.

Stout waterproof footwear and clothing, binoculars and a torch are recommended. Make sure you take adequate supplies of any medication that you are on. Basic picnic gear is highly recommended for remoter areas where restaurants are virtually non-existent or which close for lunch on unexpected days (and there is no greater pleasure than a crusty baguette filled with creamy cheese washed down with a drop of the beverage of your choice consumed on a sunny bank in a quiet corner of a battlefield). The boutiques in motorway stops can provide the wherewithal for a picnic if you are unlikely to pass a local supermarket or village shop (many now sadly permanently closed). It is also important to make sure that you have a full tank when you leave the motorway. Petrol stations are very rare in some localities. A mobile phone is a reassuring accessory.

MAPS/CHOOSING YOUR ROUTES/PARTICULAR VISITS

There are recommended commercial maps for each tour and it is suggested that the traveller buys them, or their nearest updated equivalent, and marks them before setting out. These maps, used in conjunction with the sketches in this book, make it possible not only to navigate efficiently but also to understand what happened where - and sometimes 'why'. For the battlefields of The Four Battles of Ypres reference is made to the very detailed *Major & Mrs Holt's Battle Map of The Ypres Salient*. The sketch maps which accompany each battle described in the book use the same colour coding system of mauve for war cemeteries, yellow for memorials, blue for museums, pink for bunkers and craters, orange for demarcation stones.

For an excellent overall view of all the battlefields in this book the **Michelin 236 Nord Flandres-Artois Picardie 1/200,000** – 1 cm : 2kms is highly recommended.

The battles are arranged chronologically and their descriptions are self-contained so that any individual battlefield may be visited in any order. An approximate distance from Calais is given to the start point of most battlefields. If they are to be visited in geographical sequence, then the large sketch map on pages 2 and 3 will help you plan your route. The nearest Autoroutes linking the battlefields are indicated.

There are many options for the visitor in choosing his or her itinerary, depending upon interest, time available etc. For practical reasons the geographical constraints will probably have to take precedence over the chronological order of the battles and it would obviously take several weeks thoroughly to tour in one long journey all the battlefields described. Studying the campaigns in any sort of meaningful order is further complicated by the fact that many of the battlefields overlap and were also fought over at several different periods. This particularly applies to the area covered by the Four Battles of Ypres, Mons and Le Cateau, the battles of Neuve Chapelle, Aubers Ridge, Fromelles and Festubert. Specific places to be visited may be found by reference to the Index and if a particular grave is to be located you should consult **the Commonwealth War Graves Commission Debt of Honour website** or the **American Battlefield Monuments Commission website** before you set out (see below).

At the end of the book the 'Tourist Information' section gives tips on how to prepare for your journey, where to eat or stay, and where you will find information and help.

Hotels/Restaurants/Tourist Offices en route are distinguished by a distinctive typeface.

The 'War Graves Organisations' section describes in brief the dedicated associations which tend and administer the war cemeteries and memorials that you will visit following the tours. Other Commemorative Associations are listed.

GPS REFERENCES – LATITUDE AND LONGITUDE – TRENCH MAPS

In view of the increasing use of 'satnavs' for navigation and for the convenience of readers who wish to go directly to specific locations, we have added GPS references to all major stops on the Battlefield Tours for this edition. We have used the digital form of GPS as it is the simplest. It can be directly typed into most modern sat nav devices and into Google Maps. The references refer to the closest parking place to the site. Though a satellite navigation system can be a great help, we do not recommend that you rely exclusively upon it as it may direct you away from a route that is integral to an understanding of the 'shape' of a battle.

A splendid device: **Great War Digital** has released a searchable DVD set containing 750 British trench maps for France and Belgium called LinesMan. This innovative software permits navigation on screen between modern IGN French maps and trench maps, and when used with a GPS receiver the user's real-time position is shown over a moving map display. The software has to be registered by internet or phone to obtain full functionality and some patience and application are needed to become familiar with the system, but for the enthusiast this facility will become a must. Details can be found at www.greatwardigital.com

PLACE NAMES

Note that there is considerable and often confusing variation in place names created by the disparate Flemish and French versions of the same place name, e.g. Mesen and Messines, Ieper and Ypres, Kortrijk and Courtrai, Rijsel and Lille, Doornik and Tournai, Nieuwkerke and Neuve Eglise, Waasten and Warneton etc. Also the names of CWGC Cemeteries tend to employ the French version of place names used in the war. Thus we have 'Wytschaete' Mil Cemetery in Wijtschate, and 'Westoutre' Cemeteries in Westouter. During the war Elverdinge, Geluveld, Hooge, Poperinge, Vlamertinge had an 'h' after their 'g'. Nieuport was Nieuwpoort, Diksmuide was Dixmude, the Ijzer was the Yser - and so on.

TELEPHONING

When calling Belgium from the UK the '+' indicated in the phone number = 00 32.
When calling France from the UK the '+' indicated in the phone number = 00 33.

COUNTDOWN TO WAR

*'The lights are going out all over Europe,
we shall not see them lit again in our lifetime'*
Edward, Viscount Grey of Fallodon

On 28 June 1914 Archduke Franz Ferdinand and his wife were assassinated at Sarajevo in Bosnia. The Archduke was the heir apparent to the throne of the Austro-Hungarian Empire, then ruled by the Emperor Franz Josef. He had gone to Austrian-occupied Bosnia on a tour designed to bolster up the Empire which was cracking under a rising tide of ethnic nationalism. The assassins were Serbs and the Austrians immediately accused the Kingdom of Serbia of harbouring the killers and others like them, and determined upon revenge. It also seemed an opportunity to crush the growing strength of the Serbs.

Erzherzog-Thronfolger Franz Ferdinand
und Gemahlin Herzogin Sophie von Hohenberg
gefallen durch Mörderhand am 28. Juni 1914 in Sarajevo.

Memoriam postcard of the Archduke and his wife.

On 23 July the Austrians sent an ultimatum to Serbia demanding that anti-Austrian propaganda should be banned in Serbia and that the man behind the assassination be found and arrested. To these points the Serbs agreed, but they did not agree to having Austrian officials in their country to supervise the proceedings. On 28 July the Austrians, considering the response to be unsatisfactory, declared war on Serbia.

Now the dominoes began to fall as old loyalties, tribal relationships and treaties toppled country after country into one armed camp or the other. Germany sided with Austria, Russia with Serbia. The French, still hurting from their defeat by Prussia in 1870 and determined to regain from Germany their lost provinces of Alsace-Lorraine, saw a victorious war as a method of achieving that objective.

On 31 July Russia ordered general mobilisation followed that same day by Austria. The British Foreign Secretary, Sir Edward Grey, asked both France and Germany if they would observe Belgian neutrality. France replied 'Yes'. The Germans remained silent and the Belgians ordered that mobilisation should begin the following day.

On 1 August the French ordered mobilisation, Belgium announced her intention of remaining neutral and Germany declared war on Russia. On 2 August German troops invaded Luxembourg and made small sorties into France. Belgium refused to allow German forces to cross her soil with the object of 'anticipating' (as the Germans put it or as in the case of Iraq in 2003 making a 'pre-emptive strike') a French attack and the King of the Belgians appealed to King George V of Britain for help.

On 3 August, Bank Holiday Monday, Germany declared war on France, while in Britain bright sunshine warmed the holiday crowds and Sir Edward Grey told Parliament, that 'we cannot issue a declaration of unconditional neutrality'.

On 4 August, just after 0800 hours, German forces crossed into Belgium. The British issued mobilisation orders and the British Ambassador in Berlin told the Chancellor that unless Germany withdrew her troops by midnight their countries would be at war with one another.

The Germans did not withdraw. It was war.

THE SCHLIEFFEN PLAN

The German plan for the conquest of France began to evolve in the early 1890s under the direction of the chief of Staff, Field Marshal Count von Schlieffen. France and Russia were allied against possible German aggression under the Dual Alliance of 1892 and so Schlieffen had to devise a plan that avoided fighting both enemies at the same time. According to German military intelligence estimates the Russians would be unable to mobilize fully for six weeks after the beginning of a war. Therefore, reasoned Schlieffen, if France were to be attacked first and defeated within six weeks, Germany could then turn around and take on Russia. That logic, however, only moved the goal posts to uncover another challenge: how to defeat France in six weeks?

Schlieffen had the answer to that too. The key element to a quick victory was surprise and simplistically the plan aimed to convince the French that they should maintain their major forces in the area of Alsace-Lorraine to counter an invasion directly from Germany around Metz, while the actual assault descended on France from the north via neutral Belgium.

General von Kluck, Commander Ger 1st Army, wounded 1915, retired October 1916, died 1934.

Ten German divisions were nominated to keep an eye on the Russians, while 62 were assembled to take on the French. Of these latter, five armies were assembled in a line facing west and stretching northwards from Metz (**see Map 1, page 18**) to form a door hinged upon Switzerland. This door was to swing in a massive anti-clockwise movement through Belgium. At the top of the door was von Kluck's 1st Army and von Schlieffen had enjoined that the very last soldier at the end of the swing should 'brush the Channel with his sleeve'.

Von Schlieffen died in 1912, saying on his deathbed, 'Above all, keep the right wing strong'. His successor was Helmut von Moltke, nephew of the von Moltke of the 1870 War and made of different stuff to his eminent ancestor. A cautious man, lacking the ruthlessness upon which Schlieffen's plan depended and frightened by the possibility of a strong counter-attack by the French in the area of Alsace-Lorraine, he strengthened the hinge end of the door, weakening the force that was planned to sweep through Belgium.

Nevertheless, when the invasion began, von Moltke had almost 1½ million men forming his door and at the far end of his extreme right wing, there was the 1st Army, commanded by General von Kluck, who saw himself as Attila the Hun. On 4 August 1914 the door began to swing and Attila invaded Belgium.

MONS

23 AUGUST 1914 – 11 NOVEMBER 1918

'Our men have come to believe that every one of you
carries a portable Maxim with him'
A German officer to an 'Old Contemptible'.

'I suppose that in the first place it was to comfort myself that I thought of the story of "The
Bowmen" and wrote it in the early days of September. And perhaps I had better go into the
box for the last time and answer once more that the tale is mere and sheer invention.'
Arthur Machen whose story in the Evening News of 29 September 1914
gave rise to the legend of 'The Angels of Mons'.

SUMMARY OF THE BATTLE

This was the first battle of the war for the British Expeditionary Force (BEF), which faced the invading German armies along a defensive line based upon the Condé Canal running through the northern outskirts of the Belgian town of Mons. The German attack began at 0830 on the 23rd of August 1914 from the north, and by mid-afternoon the British were forced to withdraw with an estimated 1,600 casualties. German casualties are variously numbered at between 3,000 and 15,000.

OPENING MOVES

On 4 August 1914 the Germans invaded Belgium and headed for Liège, expecting only a token resistance. They were wrong. The forts around Liège held out until 7 August, the same day that advance parties of the BEF began to land in France en route to Belgium.

On 20 August the Germans marched through Brussels and headed onward towards Mons and the Franco-Belgian border, less than 40 miles away. Early on the morning of 23 August their artillery came within range of the Mons-Condé Canal, which lay between them and France, and they began shelling the crossing points. Along the canal, unknown to the Germans, waited the men of the BEF.

Following the order to mobilize on 4 August, the British knew exactly what to do, because everything was written down in the 'War Book'. In anticipation of future conflicts, political and radical thinkers had envisaged as many different scenarios as they could and recorded in millions of words of instructions just what was to be done when any particular prediction came to pass. Thus, in August 1914, the section of the War Book entitled, *In the Event of War with Germany,* was opened and its instructions concerning the BEF were followed.

The Expeditionary Force (EF) was one of the three elements of the Army that came out of the Haldane Reforms of 1906/7. The other two elements were the 'Forces Overseas' and the 'Territorial Force' designated for Home Defence. The EF was made up of a core of Regular units stationed at home, but trained and prepared to move overseas to any trouble spot. Militia battalions of men having six months' training formed a 'Special Reserve' to fill out the EF in the event of general war, 70,000 Special Reservists being recalled in August 1914.

The Allied plan required the British to take up a position at the extreme left of the French line and to assemble in the area of the old fortress of Maubeuge, some 12 miles south of Mons. Following the War Book instructions, training and equipping (only one pair of boots) of militia reinforcements began immediately and in Britain on 9 August the main bodies of the BEF marched to their local train stations early in the morning to catch the evening boat from

Southampton to Boulogne, Le Havre or Rouen. The movements of one battalion over this period were:

9 AUG:	7 am March to station
	Afternoon. Arrive Southampton
	Evening. Sail from Southampton
10 AUG:	Afternoon. Arrive Le Havre
	March to rest camp
11 AUG:	Midnight. March to station
	Slow trains north for the next five days
17 AUG:	7 mile march to Maubeuge area
20 AUG:	15 mile training march
21 AUG:	18 mile training march
22 AUG:	11 mile training march
23 AUG 0100 hours:	14 mile march to Mons to take up defensive positions.

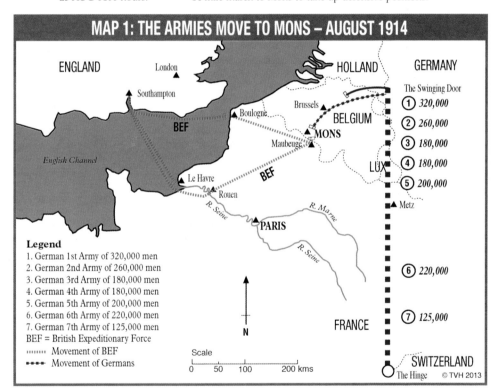

MAP 1: THE ARMIES MOVE TO MONS – AUGUST 1914

Legend
1. German 1st Army of 320,000 men
2. German 2nd Army of 260,000 men
3. German 3rd Army of 180,000 men
4. German 4th Army of 180,000 men
5. German 5th Army of 200,000 men
6. German 6th Army of 220,000 men
7. German 7th Army of 125,000 men
BEF = British Expeditionary Force
••••••• Movement of BEF
◆◆◆◆ Movement of Germans

Some amongst those en route to Maubeuge may have been aware that they had passed through the 1709 battlefield of Malplaquet, where Marlborough's army beat the French and went on to take Mons. This time the French were our allies, if not always co-operative friends.

The promised strength of the BEF was six infantry divisions and one large cavalry division, but Lord Kitchener, appointed Secretary of State for War on 5 August, mistrusted the French plan and kept back two divisions so that, when concentration of the BEF was complete at Maubeuge on 20 August, the force under Sir John French's command totalled about 80,000 men divided into two corps of two divisions each, plus an independent brigade and a cavalry division.

Early on the morning of 23 August, the BEF made its final moves into its defensive positions along the Mons-Condé Canal. I Corps, under General Douglas Haig effectively detaching itself and moving well to the east of Mons, and II Corps, under General Smith-Dorrien, a survivor of the massacre at Isandhlwana in the Zulu War, covered the canal west from Mons to Condé on the Escaut, Mons itself and the canal to Obourg in the east, (a total of some 17 miles as the crow flies) (see Map 2, page 20). Then they waited for von Kluck's legions to arrive. It wasn't a long wait.

WHAT HAPPENED

Von Kluck's troops were moving, fast. The II (Ger) Corps at the top end of the swinging door had marched 140 miles in 11 days. Just after first light on the morning of 23 August German divisional cavalry were tapping at the British II Corps forward positions. At 1030 hours the IX (Ger) Corps artillery opened up in the area of Obourg and together with the III (Ger) Corps artillery quickly dominated the British line through Nimy along the canal towards Jemappes in the west.

At 1100 hours a massed infantry attack was made towards the canal bridges at Nimy, held by the 4th Royal Fusiliers and at Obourg, held by the 4th Middlesex (the 'Diehards', a name derived from the exhortation of their dying CO at Albuhera in 1811), both of the 3rd Division. This frontal assault by the 18th (Ger) Division, coupled with a flanking movement by the 17th (Ger) Division which had crossed the canal at an undefended spot east of Obourg, forced a British withdrawal to begin at around 1300 hours to intermediate positions in and around the town of Mons.

Along the canal to the west the Germans made multiple small crossings and at mid-afternoon another major attack developed, forcing further withdrawal along the whole British line. It was the beginning of the **'Retreat from Mons'**.

THE BATTLEFIELD TOUR

• **The Route**: The tour begins at the 4th RF & VC Memorial at the Canal at Nimy then visits the plaque to 4th Royal Fusiliers, 4th Middlesex, 2nd RIR and 56th Coy RE at Maisières; the Memorials to the first and last British actions of the war at Casteau; the sites of the actions of the 4th Royal Fusiliers and the 4th Middlesex at Obourg; Mons General CWGC Cemetery; the Memorials at the Binche (la Bascule) crossroads, the Saint Symphorien CWGC Cemetery and ends at Mons Town Memorials & Museum.
• **Extra Visits** to Villers-St-Ghislain to Gen Allenby 1914 HQ; Ville-sur-Haine Memorial to Pte Price.
• **N.B.** The following sites are indicated: Monument to 7 executed members of the VSR; 'Big Red One' 1944 Monument, Mons.
• **Total distance**: 17.00 miles
• **Total time**: 4¼ hours
• **Distance from Calais to start point** 126 miles. Although it is motorway all the way to Mons note that there are **No Tolls**.
• **Base town**: Mons
• **Map**: IGNB M736 Sheet 45. 1:50,000
    From Calais take the A16/A26 direction Paris, then A16/E40 direction Dunkerque/Lille. Take Exit 28 to Lille/Ypres on the A25/E42. Note that navigation is tricky around Lille and take the A1 direction Villeneuve d'Asq, then the A27/E42 direction Bruxelles/Tournai.
At approx 79 miles the border into Belgium and Wallonia is crossed and the road number changes to the E42.

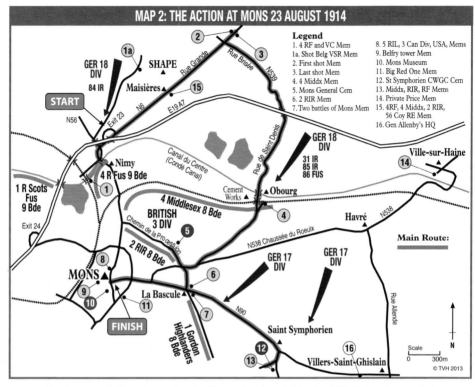

MAP 2: THE ACTION AT MONS 23 AUGUST 1914

Legend
1. 4 RF and VC Mem
1a. Shot Belg VSR Mem
2. First shot Mem
3. Last shot Mem
4. 4 Middx Mem
5. Mons General Cem
6. 2 RIR Mem
7. Two battles of Mons Mem
8. 5 RIL, 3 Can Div, USA, Mems
9. Belfry tower Mem
10. Mons Museum
11. Big Red One Mem
12. St Symphorien CWGC Cem
13. Middx, RIR, RF Mems
14. Private Price Mem
15. 4RF, 4 Middx, 2 RIR, 56 Coy RE Mem
16. Gen Allenby's HQ

Continue round Tournai, crossing the Escaut Canal, and join the A7/E19. Continue to Exit 23/23bis from the E19/E42 and take the Exit N6 SHAPE/Nimy.
Set your mileometer to zero. *Follow signs to Mons/Nimy on the N6 straight over the traffic lights. Cross the Canal (now called the Canal du Centre and on which there is a sign 'Point 1' on the 'Mons Battlefield Tour', a local signposted route) and immediately turn right into the square in front of the Town Hall. Take the small road to the right of the Town Hall (ignoring the No Entry sign) and turn left along the Canal to the railway bridge. Stop.*

NOTE. For many years the historically important Mons Battlefield, its Museum, Memorials and signs were in a progressively sad state of neglect. The town of Mons has undertaken an ambitious and exciting programme in time for the Centenary of the '14-'18 War, the highlights concentrating on the momentous events that took place here in August 1914 and in November 1918 – The First and Last Shots of the War'.

Memorials will be cleaned and Signs and Information Panels at all the major sites (existing and new) will be replaced or updated with QR codes and a booklet in French and English will be available from **The Tourist Office** (qv) which will supplement the information, with maps, GPS locations etc.

• The Nimy Canal Bridges/4th RF & VC Memorial/1.3 miles/15 minutes/Map 2/1/OP/Lat & Long: 50.47543 3.94542

Stand on the bank to the west of the bridge with your back to the canal. You are facing away from the enemy who approached from the other side of the river.

The railway bridge and the road bridge up the canal in the direction from which you came were the responsibility of the 4th Royal Fusiliers to defend and were given to C Company commanded by Captain Ashburner. Following some casualties from the Germans' early shelling, the Company had a brief encounter with a German cavalry (Uhlan) patrol and took prisoner Lieutenant von Arnim, son of the general commanding IV (Ger) Corps.

Shortly after the skirmish with the patrol the German infantry attack began. A solid mass of soldiers in columns of fours came on towards the canal from the north. The Tommies were astounded. Their opponents moved as if on parade, as if taking part in some Napoleonic war game. They were ducks in a shooting gallery to the riflemen of the BEF who were trained to fire fifteen aimed rounds a minute and capable of almost double that with such a target. Although their first attacks failed, the Germans came on, pausing to direct machine-gun fire on to the Fusiliers' positions and to co-ordinate their attack with artillery fire. The two machine guns commanded by Lieutenant Dease, sited on the top of the embankment where you are standing at the southern end of the bridge, wreaked terrible havoc among the grey horde, but the Fusiliers were suffering too.

Captain Ashburner was wounded in the head and, despite reinforcements brought up from the battalion reserve in the Nimy Square, by midday the situation was becoming serious. Only one machine gun was now operating and that was being fired single-handed by Lieutenant Dease, despite his having been hit three times. Inevitably Dease died (he is buried in St Symphorien cemetery, which is visited at the end of this tour) and Fusilier Private Frank Godley volunteered to take over the weapon. For a whole hour he held off the German attack as the Fusiliers began a withdrawal down the road to Mons. He too was wounded and just before being overwhelmed by the Germans he dismantled the gun and threw it into the canal. Three months later, while in POW camp, **Frank Godley** learned that he **and Lt Dease had each been awarded the Victoria Cross (VC)**, the first ones of the Great War. On 19 July 2012 Godley's VC was sold by Spinks to an anonymous buyer for £276,000. After the war Godley, who had a large 'walrus' moustache, dressed as Bairnsfather's 'Old Bill' and raised funds for the Royal British Legion.

At the end of the day the Fusiliers had some 250 casualties, about half the number of Germans they had killed.

Below the bridge on the southern side of the river is a **Plaque** (made of resin, replacing the original bronze plaque which was stolen for its metal value) commemorating the action and the VC awards. It is Point No 2 on the Mons Tour. The French blew up the bridge in 1940 damaging the Plaque which was recovered by a villager from Nimy, who looked after it until the end of the war. The bridge was blown up again in September 1944 and the bronze Plaque was placed on the present bridge on 12 November 1961.

Look east to the road bridge you crossed (Point No 1). This was a swivel bridge around which there was a desperate battle and the German Pte Niemayer is fêted as a hero for jumping into the water under fierce British fire to operate the bridge's mechanism, closing it to enable the first German troops to cross, an action which cost him his life.

By walking 100yds to the bend in the Canal west of the railway bridge, the Belfry Tower of Mons can be seen in the distance (visited at the end of the tour) and to its right some slag heaps. The large expanse of water is the lake and pleasure port formed in 1970 when the Mons-Condé Canal was closed to make way for the motorway.

Return to the main road and turn left back over the Canal. Continue on the N6 direction Maisières.

N.B. by turning first left on the N56, Route d'Ath and forking right on Chaussée Brunehauult you will pass on the right, just as the road changes its name to Rue des Fusillés, the 4-star **Hotel Mercure Mons** (Nimy). Tel: + (0) 65 72 36 85 E-mail: mercuremons@cgmhotels.com 53 rooms, outdoor pool (strictly summer only), good restaurant, quiet forest setting.

(By continuing on the Route d'Ath instead of forking right, you will come to the 3-star **Hotel-Restaurant Monte-Cristo**. Tel: + (0) 65 40 37 10 E-mail: lemontecristo@hotmail.be 12 rooms, attractive restaurant.)

By continuing along Rue des Fusillés to the rear entrance to SHAPE to the right, there is a grey stone obelisk **Monument to 7 members of the VSR** (Volunteer Intelligence Service) shot on 2 March 1916. Their names are on the back of the Monument, Map 2/1a **(Lat & Long: 50.50091 3.95371).**

Nimy Railway Bridge with Road Bridge just visible beyond.

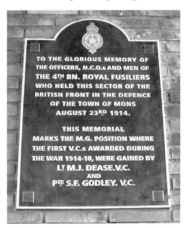

Plaque under the Nimy Railway Bridge to the 4th Royal Fusiliers and 1st VCs of the War, Lt Dease and Pte Godley.

Tribute from UK Personnel at SHAPE on Maisières Plaque.

Plaque to 4th RF, 4th Middx, 2nd RIR & 56th Coy RE, Maisières Church.

Continue on the dual carriageway to the second of double traffic lights and turn right immediately past the church. Park behind it. On the church wall is

• Plaque to 4th RF, 4th Middlesex, 2nd RIR and 56th Coy RE, Maisières/3.0 miles/10 minutes/Map 2/15/Lat & Long: 50.48809 3.96515

The stone Plaque bears the legend in French, 'This plaque was erected with humble respect and thanks by the British and Belgian Veterans and their families in memory of the British Officers and Soldiers who were killed here in battle 23 August 1914 in the Battle of Mons and who were buried in the cemetery of Maisières. Their bodies now rest in the Military Cemetery of St Symphorien but their memory will always be honoured in this place. 56 Coy Royal Angineers [sic], 4th Battallon (sic) R Fusiliers, 2nd Battalion (sic) RIR, 4th Battallon (sic) Middlesex Regt.' Indeed a wreath is still laid here every 11 November by local authorities and members of SHAPE.

*Continue on the N6 through Maisières following signs to **SHAPE** (which you will pass on your left). After **SHAPE**, and immediately following a crossroads controlled by overhead traffic lights, is a rise with a large building on the right, the old Restaurant le Medicis (currently closed). Stop beside it and carefully cross the busy road to the memorial opposite.*

• The First and Last Shots Memorials, Casteau/4.9 miles/10 minutes/ Map 2/2 and 2/3/Lat & Long: 50.50493 3.99760

This is Point No 3 on the Mons Tour. It was near this spot that Corporal E. Thomas of C Squadron 4th Royal Irish Dragoon Guards (4th RIDG) fired the first British shot of the war, an event commemorated by the Monument which was unveiled on 20 August 1939, less than 2 weeks before Germany invaded Poland thus beginning WW2. Not since Waterloo had the British fired a shot on the Continent of Europe. The Memorial, by Mons architect Bertiaux, stands where the 4th RIDG began their charge upon the enemy. Too often British visitors come away from this spot with the idea that the first shots of the war were fired here. Not so: the first British shots were indeed sounded here but by 20 August Belgium had essentially been over-run and in a series of encounters generally known as the Battles of the Frontiers the French had already suffered some 300,000 casualties.

General Allenby's cavalry had crossed into Belgium on 21 August and at about 0700 hours on 22 August while riding out from Mons the RIDG, an element of the division, part of 2nd Cavalry Brigade, made contact with the enemy along this road. Two troops of the Dragoons were involved – 1st Troop who engaged with sabres and 4th Troop who used their rifles. Corporal Thomas, who was in 4th Troop, described what happened:

'I saw a troop of Uhlans coming leisurely down the road, the officer in front smoking a cigar. We were anxiously watching their movements when, quicker than I can write here, they halted, as if they had smelt a rat. They had seen us! They turned quickly back. Captain Hornby got permission to follow on with the sabre troop and down the road they galloped.'

Hornby's 1st Troop charged into the middle of the Germans, who included three cyclists, Hornby himself running a German lieutenant through with his sabre. Meanwhile, as the enemy dismounted and scattered, 4th Troop came up and dismounted too. Corporal Thomas's account continued:

'Bullets were flying past us, and possibly because I was rather noted for my quick movements and athletic ability in those days, I was first in action. I could see a German cavalry officer some four hundred yards away standing mounted in full view of me, gesticulating to the left and to the right as he disposed of his dismounted men and ordered them to take up their firing positions to engage us. Immediately I saw him I took aim, pulled the trigger and automatically, almost as it seemed instantaneously, he fell to the ground, obviously wounded, but whether he was killed or not is a matter that I do not think was ever cleared up.'

In all eight Germans were killed. There were no British casualties and **Captain Hornby** was awarded the **DSO**.

Cross the road back to the plaque on the Medicis wall.

The Plaque commemorates the place where, at 1100 hours on 11 November 1918, an advanced post of the 116th Canadian Infantry Battalion welcomed the cease-fire. The Canadian Corps had liberated Mons earlier that day and had continued their advance to this spot where Corporal Thomas had fired the first shot four years before.

Return to your car. Drive back to the first traffic light junction and turn left on Rue Brisée direction Obourg and then take the fourth turning to the right on the Rue du Bois d'Hayon, signed Obourg. Continue downhill and turn sharp right following the road under the motorway on Rue St Denis signed Obourg. Continue through Mons-Borinage to Obourg. Continue into the village on a section of cobbled road and at the crossroads turn left on Rue de l'Yser to Obourg Centre and then right on Rue de Portugal. Continue straight through and over the roundabout and follow signs to Mons on the N539. Drive over the canal and the railway and take the first left sharply backward to the railway station. Stop. Walk over the footbridge (and because of its good vantage point the account of the action here is best read from the bridge) to the centre platform. The cement works is on the canal to the west of you from the footbridge. Go down the steps to what seems to be an isolated square brick wall. There is a plaque on the northern face.

• Plaque to the 4th Middlesex Action at Obourg Railway Station/8.3 miles/15 minutes/Map 2/4/Lat & Long: 50.46954 4.00756

The plaque was unveiled on 9 September 1951 on the old railway building, erected in 1849 and demolished in 1981 when the line was electrified. It was then moved to this brick Memorial which is Point 4 on the Mons Tour. It commemorates the stand of the 4th Middlesex here and the bravery of a lone British soldier who held the Germans at bay from the roof of a building which once stood on this spot. The area has changed greatly since 1914 but the line of the old houses on the northern bank and the line of the road on which you have parked give a clear indication of the position of the original bridge.

The Middlesex had taken up fire positions all around the village on 23 August. D Company commanded by Captain Glass covered the bridge and B Company in the station was commanded by Lt Wilmot-Aliston following the death of the company commander and his second in command in the storm of German artillery fire that began around 0800 hours. It was probably in this area that Private J. Parr (qv), the first British soldier to be killed, met his fate. He is buried in St Symphorien cemetery (qv). Lt Wilmot-Aliston became the first British soldier to be taken prisoner by the Germans.

The Middlesex machine guns and rapid fire caused appalling casualties in the thickly packed grey ranks of the six assaulting battalions. As at Nimy, the Germans paused and regrouped, adopting tactical movements co-ordinated with machine gun and artillery fire. Despite support from two companies of the 2nd Battalion RIR at around midday, the Middlesex were forced to withdraw shortly afterwards. Latest reports of Captain Henry Glass were that, despite two legs shattered by machine-gun bullets, he remained propped up against a wall of the railway station overseeing the withdrawal of his men. The unknown soldier on the roof covered his comrades as they moved out until he was killed by the advancing Germans. The Middlesex had suffered badly. At the beginning of the day they had been almost one thousand strong. At evening roll call under three hundred answered their names.

Return to the N539, turn left and continue into La Sablonnière. Turn right at the junction, signed Centre, on the N538 and at the next traffic lights turn right on Rue de la Procession, signed Crematorium. Continue to the large cemetery on the right and stop in the parking space. Walk to the entrance.

Site where 116th Can Inf Bn welcomed the cease-fire on 11 November 1918, Casteau.

Monument to 7 Shot Belgian Intelligence Volunteers, Rue des Fusillés.

Detail of the Plaque.

Monument to the First British shot of the War by Cpl Thomas of the 4th RIDG, Casteau, with detail of plaque.

Plaque to commemorate the stand of the Middlesex at Obourg Station.

CWGC Plot, Mons General Cemetery.

Detail of Plaque.

Monument to First and Last Battles, la Bascule, with detail of Plaque.

Celtic Cross to 2nd Royal Irish, la Bascule.

• *Mons General Cemetery, Belgian Mil & CWGC Plots/10.1 miles/30 minutes/Map 2/5/Lat & Long: 50.45908 3.97558*

To the right of the entrance is a **Plaque to 241 Heroes of the Resistance, (of the clandestine Press) 1940-1945** and to the left the CWGC sign. The cemetery is open 1 March-15 November 0800-1700 and 16 November-29 February 0900-1600. Beware – you will be locked in if you don't make closing time! We just made it to the amusement of the Guardian.

The CWGC plot (P1) is signed to the left inside the entrance and leads one upwards by a series of signs to the plot at the top of the cemetery (a good steep 5 minute walk). A plan of the cemetery may be obtained from the office to the right of the entrance.

At the top the Belgian Military plot is first reached to the left and now also extending to the right for new burials, for this is a cemetery like many American ones (such as Arlington in Washington) where ex-servicemen have the right to be buried with their comrades and the burials are in date order. The majority bear a touching photograph of the soldier, often in his wartime uniform. There is a Memorial with a fine bust of King Albert at the top of the plot on the left.

The CWGC plot was designed by Sir Edwin Lutyens in a unique and imaginative style. Between the Cross of Sacrifice and the Stone of Remembrance is a row of splendid gold-topped flagpoles and a ceremony takes place here on 11 November each year. The Cemetery Report and Visitor's Book are set in a circular stone seat to the right. There is a fascinating mixture of nationalities (e.g. Russian and Rumanian) and dates of burial here – from 1914-1919 (although the majority seem to be from 1918 and 1919). The later dates were of casualties from the appalling flu epidemic which swept through civil populations and servicemen mal-nourished from four years of deprivation or from men who died as prisoners of war. There are 393 Commonwealth, with 11 unidentified, a Special Memorial to 3 men and 1 WW2, 72 Russians with 2 Unknown, 16 French, 8 Romanian and 1 German with 2 Unknown. They range from **Pte E.B. Quinton**, Norfolk Regt, 28 September 1914 and **Cpl R. Richardson**, RFA, 4 October 1914, age 28, to **Maj H.H. Robinson, MC + Bar**, RAMC, 3 May 1919, age 29 'on active service from August 1914'. **Sapper Clifford Lawrence Cashmore**, 4th Can Div, 1 December 1918, 'age 26 years and 11 months', has a distinctive, non-standard headstone. The burials are from the various military hospitals, CCS and Field Ambulances in Mons and include **Major John Southern Maidlow**, 49th Bty, RFA, age 39, one of only two fatal casualties from the burning of the first aid post in Gendebien Château (qv), la Bascule on 23 August 1914.

Very few visitors' signatures appear in the Visitor's Book, only a small number from the UK. This remarkable plot deserves more visitors and the caring CWGC gardeners should have more proof that their dedicated work is seen and appreciated.

Return to the traffic lights, turn left and take the first right turn on Chemin des Mourdreux. Continue to traffic lights at a crossroads. This is la Bascule. Turn left onto the N90 and stop as soon as you can safely do so. Walk back to the large memorial.

• *The La Bascule Memorials/10.7 miles/10 minutes/Map 2/7 and 2/6/ Lat & Long: 50.45211 3.98055*

As the BEF fought their way back from the canal line they made a stand here around the crossroads. The keystone of the defence was a small group of some 40 men gathered together by RQMS Fitzpatrick of the 2nd Battalion Royal Irish Regiment and this key crossroads position, so important to the safe withdrawal of the BEF, was held until nightfall. At midnight RQMS Fitzpatrick and 18 survivors continued the withdrawal, thus completing an action for which Fitzpatrick was later awarded the DCM.

The Memorial was inaugurated in 1952 by Field Marshal Lord Alexander of Tunis and commemorates the two battles of Mons: 1914 and 1918. The architect was Edmond Bertiaux, Director of Mons Municipal Works, who had designed the First Shots Memorial. It consists of a memorial panel flanked by two Tuscan pillars. It claims that 'here' the forces of the British Empire fought the first and last battles of Mons. It was originally in the Belfry garden in the centre of Mons and was moved here in August 1986 when there was another unveiling ceremony.

German Memorial to Royal (sic) Middlesex & 46 British Graves, St Symphorien Cemetery.

Headstone of Belgian Veteran, Joseph Duperrois, complete with photo in uniform, who died 1964, Mons General Cemetery.

Headstones of Lt Dease, VC, Pte Parr, Pte Price, St Symphorien Cemetery.

Differing German Headstones, St Symphorien CWGC Cemetery.

The junction is sometimes referred to as the 'Binche crossroads' because the N90 leads east to the village of Binche.

Cross the road to the other memorial.

This Celtic cross was unveiled by Sir John French on 11 November 1923. It commemorates the actions of the 2nd Royal Irish (18th Foot).

On the corner diagonally opposite are the grounds of Gendebien Château, now the residence of the C-in-C at SHAPE. At the time of the battle the building was used as the first aid post of the 2nd Royal Irish under the command of their medical officer, Major Long. It was set alight by German shelling, but all save two of the wounded were evacuated safely. One of the fatalities, Major J.S. Maidlow of 49th Bty, RFA, is buried in Mons Communal Cemetery *(qv)*.

Return to your car and continue into St Symphorien and at the roundabout go straight over and take the next turning right. Follow the signs to the CWGC and German cemeteries. There is a further sign to the left. The cemetery is then on the right.

• Saint Symphorien CWGC Cemetery and Memorials to Middx, R. Fusiliers, R. Irish/12.8 miles/25 minutes/Map 2/12 and 2/13/Lat & Long: 50.43271 4.01109

It is here that one of the first commemorative events of the WW1 Centenary will take place on the 100th Anniversary of the outbreak of the war on 4 August 2014 - a Service of Anglo-German Reconciliation. This is one of the, if not the, most unusual and lovely cemeteries on the Western Front. It was begun by the Germans immediately after the battle in the remains of an old potash mine and the layout of the cemetery follows the contours of the spoil heaps, with trees and bushes forming leafy glades connected by small paths. The land was the gift of a local resident, Jean Honzeau de Lehaie, and the architect was W.H. Cowlishaw who, among many other works, also designed the Pozières Memorial and worked on the world's first Garden City at Letchworth.

At one side of the entrance is the bronze box which contains the visitors' book and the Cemetery Report listing all the British soldiers buried here and on the other side is a box containing German information, for men of both sides lie in this cemetery – true 'comradeship in death'. After the Armistice there were 245 Germans and 188 Commonwealth burials. Further graves were then added to make a total of 284 German and 229 Commonwealth (of which 65 are unidentified).

The British have the standard white Portland stone headstone. (Harder Italian Carrera-style stone is now used when headstones are replaced.) The German graves have grey granite markers grouped regimentally, often with different headstones for the various Regiments and for officers and men.

Among the British are some graves of particular note: **Lt Maurice Dease, VC,** generally accepted as having won the first **VC** of the war, though four **VCs** were won on the first day of the battle; **Pte J. Parr,** said to be the first British soldier killed in the war [there is considerable argument about the date of his death: whether it was 22 or 23 August, the date on the headstone having been altered as two RFC men buried in Tournai CWGC Cemetery, 2nd Lieutenants Waterfall and Bayley, were killed on 22 August 1914 - Bayley was a distant relative of Gordon of Khartoum and a friend of Lanoe Hawker] and **Pte J.L. Price** (qv), the last Canadian soldier to be killed in the Great War. He was shot by a German sniper at 1058 hours on 11 November 1918 while holding flowers given to him by Belgian civilians grateful for their liberation; **Pte G.E. Ellison** of the 5th Royal Irish Lancers, who was the last British soldier to be killed in the War, also on 11 November 1918 and whose grave is almost directly opposite Parr's.

The Germans erected a number of distinctive memorials in the cemetery – to the 'Royal' Middlesex Regiment (a column surmounted by a sphere), to the Royal Fusiliers (a curved stone seat), to the Royal Irish Regiment, and an obelisk to the dead of both armies. Details and locations of all of these are given in the Cemetery Report.

Extra Visit to Villers-St-Ghislain (Gen Allenby 1914 HQ), Map 2/16/Ville-sur-Haine Memorial to Pte Price (Map 2/14) Approximately 5.1 miles. Approximate time: 20 minutes

Return to the junction with the N90, turn right signed Binche and continue on the N90 to Villers-St-Ghislain.

In the school and teacher's house of this village, No 334 Chaussée du Roi on the right (which remain much as they were in 1914) **Gen Allenby had his HQ in August 1914 (Lat & Long: 50.43183 4.042219).**

Continue through the village and at the first crossroads turn left to Havré. In the village continue downhill to the church and turn right. Continue over the railway line and two canals, turning left into the village of Ville-sur-Haine. Turn left at the crossroads just before the Town Hall on the right and drive down towards the canal.

On the right is a red brick Memorial with a bronze Plaque 'To the memory of 256265 **Private George Lawrence Price**, 28th North West Bn, 6th Can Inf Bde, killed in action near this spot at 10.58 hours, November 11 1918. The last Canadian soldier to die on the Western Front in the First World War. Erected by his comrades on November 11 1968.' **(Lat & Long: 50.47440 4.0640)**

The Memorial was originally erected on the wall of a house on this spot but moved to this brick frame when the house was demolished.

Return to St Symphorien Cemetery and pick up the main Itinerary.

Return along the N90 to La Bascule and that point pick up the signs 'E-19 E-42' and 'Mons 1km'. Continue into Mons Centre.

Note that there is now no parking in the Grand' Place but there are several well-signed parking areas within easy walking distance. Park as near as you can to the Square.

• Mons: Walking Tour of Battlefield Interest including new Museum/90 minutes/Map 2/8, 9, 10/Lat & Long of Tourist Office: 50.45456 3.95263/ R/WC

MONS (see also **Tourist Information** Section, page 333)

As stated above, for many years the important 1914/1918 battlefield that surrounds the City and relevant sites within it were woefully neglected.

The creation of Mons as the **European Capital of Culture** for 2015 will have a great effect on restoring Mons to its former glory and in engendering new cultural and historic projects. A series of Centenary events is planned from August 2014 which include a Charity Parade by WW1 re-enactors; a free guided tour of the new Museum on 23 August (this will be an annual event); celebration of 50 years of twinning with Sefton; 'Crisis 1880-1914' Exhibition at the Mons Fine Arts Museum; in 2015-2017: Photographic Exhibition; Carillon Concert of British Military Music; in 2018 (mainly around November) many events to commemorate the Armistice and the last few days of fighting in Mons.

It is hoped that these projects will re-instate Mons – such an emotional name to British and Canadian visitors in particular - as an unmissable WW1 site.

New Mons Museum (approx Lat & Long: 50.45020 3.95714)

Mons boasted what was once a fascinating War Museum which included an interesting WW2 section, founded in 1930, based on the collection of M. Georges Licope who, as a 14-year-old, had witnessed the Lancers entering Mons in August 1914. It was sited in the grounds of the Town Hall but was later relegated to the rue de Houdain and its iconic exhibits depleted.

Memorial to Pte Price, Ville-sur-Haine.

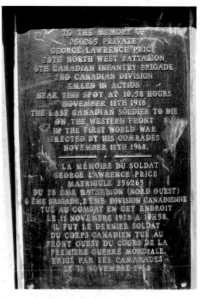

Detail of Plaque.

Gun which fired the last shot of WW1, Mons War Museum.

Cover of Harold Begbie's book on the Angels of Mons.

Artists's impression of the new Museum, Mons.

The School in Villers-St-Ghislain, Gen Allenby's HQ, August 1914.

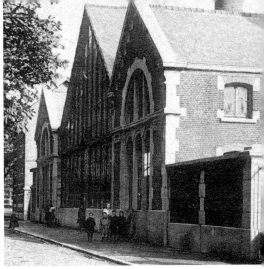

The old Water Works, Mons, whose facade is being used in the new Museum.

Germans in Grand' Place, Mons, 28 August 1914.

The Angels of Mons - a 1915 oil painting.

Contemporary View, Gran' Place, Mons.

In anticipation of the 100th Anniversaries of the First World War from August 1914 onwards, the Museum was closed while a new Museum, **The Interpretation Centre for Military History of the Town of Mons** (CIHM) was constructed in the extended old **Machine à Eau** (Water Works) building at the junction of Bvd Dolez and Ave Frère Orban, just off the ring road. The 2,500m construction has been designed by architects Pierre Hebbelink and Pierre de Wit and will examine the relationship between the citizens of Mons and the forces which fought over its territory during the War.

Due to open on 23 August 2014 and with a possible name change to **'Mons Memorial Museum'**, it will devote 20% to the French Revolution and early battles, 40% to WW1 and 40% to WW2. The story of the **'Angels of Mons'** will be strongly featured, especially in the inaugural exhibition, with many artistic representations of the legend. During the evening of 23 August 1914, bowmen 'angels' allegedly appeared in the sky over Mons and prevented the Germans from annihilating the British. Sworn affidavits from highly respectable 'witnesses' were produced verifying the heavenly intervention, Arthur Machen, a journalist with the *Evening News*, which published the story on 29 September 1914 had amalgamated earlier versions. He wrote it to relieve his despair at the retreat of the British Army. Later he admitted that the stories of the angels were 'every one of 'em lies, sir'. However, this did not deter the believers. Harold Begbie wrote a book, *On the Side of the Angels*, maintaining that they had indeed appeared and offering various 'eye witness' accounts. By Christmas 1915 the book was in its third edition.

Many of the old favourite exhibits will find a new home here – such as the magnificent collection of Regimental drums and the gun which fired the last shot of WW1. The WW2 section covers the Occupation, the Resistance and the Liberation by the Canadians on 2 September 1944.

NB. At the junction of the Boulevard Dolez and Avénue des Guérites is a grey granite obelisk to the **'Big Red 1' (Map 2/11, Lat & Long: 50.45038 3.95757)** similar to that overlooking OMAHA Beach in Normandy, commemorating the Liberation Battle by the US Division of 2-4 September 1944.

For your walking tour of the town centre, it is thoroughly recommended that you go first to the **Tourist Office** (which is at No 22 between the magnificent theatre building and the fine Gothic 15th Century Town Hall, Tel: + (0) 65 33 55 80, e-mail: info.tourisme@ville.mons.be website: www.monsregion.be) to pick up a town plan and lists of **restaurants/hotels** etc. Also available is a well-written leaflet, *Battlefield Guide Mons August 1914*, describing numbered Points around the battlefield. It is planned to modernise/replace these signs for 2014 with information markers and to update the booklet.

There is a variety of **restaurants** around the beautiful typical Flemish square – from the cheap and cheerful to the gourmet – and it makes a good lunch stop.

Walk to the Town Hall.

Mons Town Hall Plaques (Map 2/8). In the archway of the entrance porch of the Town Hall are Memorial Tablets to the **5th Royal Irish Lancers** who fought in both battles of Mons, unveiled in November 1922, with a fine *bas relief* at the bottom and to the **Canadian Corps** who liberated Mons on the morning of 11 November 1918 and the firing of the Last Shot. This was unveiled in 1926. There is also a bronze Plaque to the **United States of America**, sculpted by Gustave Jacobs. This is in thanksgiving for the food brought to Belgium from the USA during WW1.

Inside the *Salle de Mariages* is a small **Memorial Plaque** to the **US 3rd Armd Div**, June 1944-May 1945. Elements of the Division took part in the Liberation of Mons in September 1944.

To the left of the archway is an iron monkey, known as the 'Grande Garde' which dates from the Middle Ages but whose origins are shrouded in mystery. Its smoothed surface bears witness to the fact that is considered good luck to touch it (see Tourist Information below).

Walk on to the corner of the square and follow signs uphill via the Rue des Clercs to the Belfry (Beffroi). It is a five-minute puff up a steep hill to the area of the Belfry tower, which stands on the Castle Hill behind the Town Hall.

The Belfry Tower and *Château* **Gardens (Map 2/9)**. The 87m high seventeenth century flamboyant baroque style belfry and the area around it have been undergoing extensive renovations for many years. In 1999 UNESCO classified the area as a site of world-wide historical heritage. The exterior renovation was finished by 2012 and it is planned that it will once more be possible to visit the top of the tower with its unique view over the battles of 1914, 1918, 1940 and 1944. The delightful carillon will play some WW1 tunes during the 100th Anniversary period.

In a cavity at the base of the tower was buried some soil taken from graves of British and Canadian soldiers killed at Mons in the First World War. During the ceremony, on 3 November 1935, a small silver replica of the tower was given to the British Ambassador as a gift for HM King George V.

Face north beyond the tower.

The overview of the battlefield depends upon the foliage on the trees and general ambient visibility. On the horizon is the east-west motorway that runs from Liège to Valenciennes. At this point it runs parallel to and just behind (north of) the line of the canal defended by II Corps.

The beautifully renovated Belfry Tower, Mons.

Straight ahead, i.e. at 12 o'clock, a pool beside the canal may be visible. That is the area of Nimy defended by the Fusiliers where you were at the beginning of the tour. To the right, at 2 o'clock, a cement factory on the horizon marks the canal site defended by the Middlesex.

In the grounds the British and Canadian War Memorial, now moved to the Binche crossroads (qv) because of all the renovation work, was unveiled in 1952 by Lord Alexander of Tunis in a ceremony attended by King Baudouin and many other dignitaries. Alexander was then the British Minister of Defence but he had served as a Lieutenant in the 1st Irish Guards at Mons in August 1914.

The only remnant of the Castle complex, the residence of the Counts of Hainault, is the Saint Callixtus Chapel, built in 1051. **Open** daily 1200-1800 – the park is open 1000-1800.

Return to the rue des Clercs and follow signs to Place du Chapitre and
St Waudru's Church. This historic 15th Century church (which has a fascinating and valuable collection of treasures and relics relating to Saint Waudru) contains one of the series of over 30 **Commemorative Tablets**, designed by Lt Col M.P.L. Cart de Lafontaine, FRIBA, executed by Reginald Hallward and with an inscription by Rudyard Kipling, that were erected in cathedrals and important churches in Belgium and France, with replicas at CWGC HQ at Maidenhead, in Westminster Abbey and at Delville Wood on the Somme.

End of Mons Tour

OR Continue to follow the path of The Retreat to Le Cateau *by taking the A7-E19 west from Mons, then at Exit 23 following the D659-D649-D934-D932-D955 south to the International Cemetery and pick up the Le Cateau Itinerary from there.*

Plaque to US 3rd Armd Div, 1944-45, Mons Town Hall.

Detail of Plaque to the 5th Royal Irish Lancers, 1918, Mons Town Hall entrance.

Plaque to American generosity, Mons Town Hall entrance.

Plaque to the Canadian Corps, 11 Nov 1918, Mons Town Hall entrance.

LE CATEAU-ORS

26 AUGUST 1914/OCTOBER-NOVEMBER 1918

*'Early on that memorable day the Cornwalls, after a
wretched night, stood to arms.
It was still dark and their clothes were sodden with rain:
many had not slept at all. Stand To was the worst hour
of the day: chilled through and drowsy.'*
DCLI Regimental History.

'When men are too tired to march, they must lie down and fight.'
Gen Sir Horace Smith-Dorrien, GCB, DSO, Commanding II Corps.

SUMMARY OF THE BATTLE

Following its defeat at Mons on 23 August 1914 the BEF fell back to the south, pursued by the Germans. Just after dawn three confused days later, on the anniversary of the Battle of Crécy, von Kluck's army caught Smith-Dorrien's tired II Corps at Le Cateau from where, after a morning's battle, the retreat continued. British casualties were about 8,000 men and 38 guns. German casualties are estimated at 9,000.

OPENING MOVES

The plan of the French Commander-in-Chief, General Joffre, to counter the German invasion was known as 'Plan 17'. Its essential idea was that of a massive counter-attack through the German centre to the south-east of Belgium. What came out of Plan 17 was a series of four major engagements known as 'The Battle of the Frontiers'.

In three of the battles in Lorraine, the Ardennes and on the Sambre, the French, following their tactical doctrine of *l'attaque à l'outrance* (attack to the extreme), threw themselves forward into the maelstrom of German machine-gun and artillery fire without apparent regard to tactical caution.

The French offensive stopped in bloody confusion with over 300,000 casualties and the armies began to withdraw.

The fourth 'Battle of the Frontiers' was the stand of the BEF at Mons on 23 August and as night fell Sir John French, the British Commander-in-Chief, had in mind to continue the defence the following day.

The French 5th Army to the immediate right of the BEF was under the command of the 62-year-old General Lanrézac who, believing that the security of his whole army was threatened, that same night of 23 August gave the order for a general retreat without telling Joffre – or the BEF. Fortunately there was a British liaison officer with the 5th Army who brought the news of the withdrawal to Sir John in his HQ at Le Cateau just before midnight. Orders were sent immediately for the BEF to retire.

General Haig's I Corps, which had not been in action, received its orders by wire at 0200 hours on 24 August and was underway before dawn. General Smith-Dorrien's II Corps HQ was not in telegraphic contact, having been in battle all day at Mons, and its orders did not arrive until 0300 hours. As II Corps began to move it was once more under fire.

Sir John French oscillated between innocent optimism and extreme pessimism about the

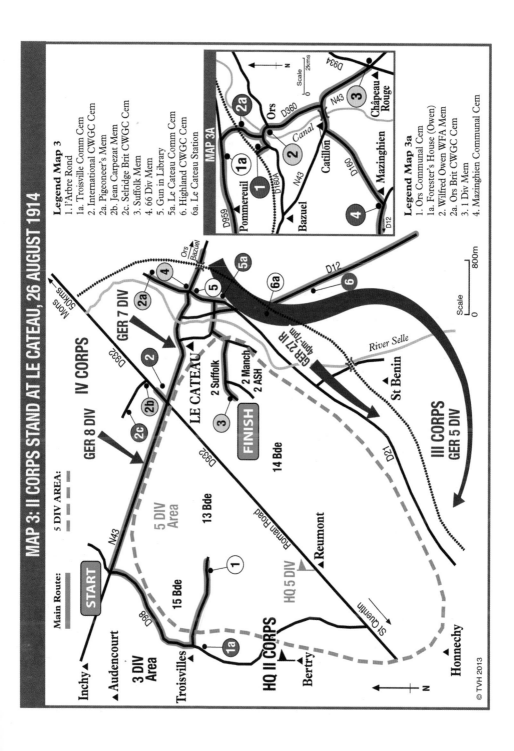

MAP 3: II CORPS STAND AT LE CATEAU, 26 AUGUST 1914

Main Route: ▬▬▬▬

5 DIV AREA: ▬ ▬ ▬

Legend Map 3

1. l'Arbre Rond
1a. Troisville Comm Cem
2. International CWGC Cem
2a. Pigeoneer's Mem
2b. Jean Carpezat Mem
2c. Selridge Brit CWGC Cem
3. Suffolk Mem
4. 66 Div Mem
5. Gun in Library
5a. Le Cateau Comm Cem
6. Highland CWGC Cem
6a. Le Cateau Station

Legend Map 3a

1. Ors Communal Cem
1a. Forester's House (Owen)
2. Wilfred Owen WFA Mem
2a. Ors Brit CWGC Cem
3. 1 Div Mem
4. Mazinghien Communal Cem

MAP 3A

© TVH 2013

military situation. The British High Command did not trust the French and Lanrézac's retreat reinforced that attitude. When Lord Kitchener had briefed the British C-in-C on the responsibilities of the BEF he had said that it was 'to support and co-operate with the French Army' but had added 'You will in no case come in any sense under the orders of any allied general'. Sir John had met Lanrézac on 17 August, a week before Mons. Neither spoke the other's language and the meeting ended uncomfortably. Thus nation to nation there was hardly accord in the adjoining allied forces.

Yet things were just as bad within the BEF. Douglas Haig, commanding I Corps under Sir John, wrote in his diary, 'I know that (Sir John) French is quite unfit for this great command', while Sir John was not at all pleased at the appointment of Horace Smith-Dorrien to command II Corps. He had named General Plumer to take over after the original Corps commander died, but Kitchener chose Smith-Dorrien, who himself wasn't the greatest fan of the C-in-C. These antipathies laid reins over the course of the coming battle and led to unpleasant post-war altercations as to whether the battle of Le Cateau need ever have been fought.

At 2025 hours on 24 August Sir John French issued 'Operation Order No. 7'. It said in part:

'The army will move tomorrow, 25th inst, to a position in the neighbourhood of Le Cateau, exact positions will be pointed out on the ground tomorrow.'

It was a long march. I Corps was to take the eastern half of the position and II Corps the western. On average the troops had to march between 20 and 25 miles. I Corps routes were very complex, crossing and recrossing the River Sambre, and they were also occupied here and there by the retreating French. Thus I Corps fell behind II Corps and communication between the Corps was lost.

At 2100 hours on 25 August Smith-Dorrien received orders from GHQ to continue the withdrawal on the following day and not to make a stand. Yet II Corps did not withdraw but actually stood and fought. The reader is invited to consider the circumstances in which the decision to fight was made and for that purpose should now assume the identity of General Smith-Dorrien. Imagine that it is 0200 hours on the morning of 26 August. Your Corps has been on the move for 24 hours, marching along roads thick with refugees. It is dark. It is raining. You have no communications with I Corps but you have heard rumours that they are behind (to the north) of you and that they are under pressure from the Germans.

Your troops are tired and are now approaching the town of Le Cateau, which offers a certain solidity for defence and some comfort from the elements. You may get an idea of the conditions from this account by Frank Richards, a soldier in the Royal Welch Fusiliers, who described in *Old Soldiers Never Die* how he got to the town from Mons:

'We marched all night and the greatest part of the next day and dug trenches. We were only in those trenches a few hours before we were on the march again... We marched all night again and all next day. We arrived in Le Cateau about midnight, dead-beat to the world. I don't believe any one of us at this time realised that we were retiring, though it was clear that we were not going in the direction of Germany. Of course the officers knew, but they were telling us that we were drawing the enemy into a trap. Le Cateau that night presented a strange sight. Everyone was in a panic, packing up their stuff on carts and barrows to get away south in time. The Royal Welch camped on the square in the centre of the town. We were told to get as much rest as we could. The majority sank down where they were and fell straight asleep.'

Then General Allenby, who was commanding the Cavalry Division, suddenly arrives at your HQ and says, in effect,

'The high ground before Le Cateau that I planned to hold to cover your retreat tomorrow has been taken by the enemy. I cannot contact General French and in my opinion the Germans will attack you at first light unless you can get away now and in the dark.'

You are also out of contact with GHQ which has moved back to St Quentin. The rest of the Corps is stretched out to your left over a total frontage of around 13 miles. It is up to you alone to decide what to do – to stand or not to stand. You call in your divisional commanders to report to you. They virtually say, 'Many men are separated from their units', or 'The men are too weary to move before the morning', or 'The roads are jammed with refugees', or 'Some roads have been washed out by the storm.'

What would you decide to do? Would you obey your order to continue to retreat? Smith-Dorrien decided to disobey his orders and to stay and fight on the ridge which runs behind the town and roughly parallel to the Le Cateau-Cambrai road.

WHAT HAPPENED

Shortly after dawn on 26 August, German troops of the left hand column of III (Ger) Corps entered Le Cateau and came up against elements of 5th Division – the Duke of Cornwall's Light Infantry (DCLI) and East Surreys – near the railway bridge on the Bazuel road about a mile east of the town, when after a short fire fight conducted from the windows of the houses the British withdrew to the high ground behind the town.

Realising that the British meant to stand and fight, von Kluck decided to mount a frontal attack with IV (Ger) Corps behind an artillery barrage on the main British line behind the Cambrai-Le Cateau road, and to send III (Ger) Corps to the east to outflank the BEF (see **Map 3**). The British line consisted of 5th Division on the high ground astride the Roman road covering from Le Cateau to Troisvilles, 3rd Division to the west up to Caudry and the newly arrived 4th Division beyond that.

An early German cavalry attack on the extreme left of the BEF, mainly against 4th Division, was checked, and German small arms activity then focused upon the 5th Division area through the morning, with infantry pressing forward tactically across the broken ground with machine guns, and using the spire of Le Cateau church as an Observation Point (OP). By mid-morning the Germans controlled the high ground to the east of the River Selle and had uncovered the end of the British position.

The morning had been an artillery battle above all else, with some 230 Royal Artillery pieces ranged against about 550 of the enemy along the total frontage of about 13 miles. The 5th Division area from the Le Cateau spur to Troisvilles was about 3.5 miles and consisted mostly of cut cornfields with patches of beet and clover, dramatically different to the houses and slag heaps of Mons. With the exception of the broken ground behind the railway station the general aspect was one of gently rolling Atlantic waves of open fields. There was little opportunity to find cover for guns or for men.

The Germans continued to concentrate their efforts upon the Le Cateau spur across which the Roman road struck straight through to St Quentin. A breakthrough at Le Cateau could divide and perhaps destroy Smith-Dorrien's Corps. The main strain of the attack fell upon the King's Own Yorkshire Light Infantry (KOYLI) and the Suffolks and an attempt to reinforce them by the Manchesters and two companies of the Argylls failed. Nevertheless, at midday the British line still held.

Inexorably von Kluck's forces built up against the open right flank and by 1300 hours the British on the exposed spur were under artillery fire from three German divisions and under frontal and flank attacks by a dozen infantry battalions. It was time to get out.

Smith-Dorrien decided to withdraw by divisions from right to left, i.e. 5th Division would be the first to move. His order was issued at 1340 hours but much of the line communication had been destroyed by the artillery bombardments and the message had to be delivered by runner. 5th Division HQ received the order at 1400 hours, forward units got it at 1500 hours. 2nd KOYLI and 2nd Suffolk never got it at all and by 1600 hours they were surrounded and virtually wiped out.

The Royal Artillery had suffered badly. Not a single Battery left on the ridge was capable of sustained action, being damaged or without horses or ammunition. But some guns could be saved – had to be saved – and, in volunteering to return to the ridge and recover the remaining two guns of 37 (Howitzer) Battery, **Drivers Fred Luke and Job Drain, as well as their officer, Captain Douglas Reynolds, won the VC**. Luke survived to serve with the RAF Regt in WW2. Drain also survived and formed part of the Honour Guard at the burial of the Unknown Soldier at Westminster Abbey on 11 November 1920. Both he and Luke attended the VC Reunion Dinner given at the House of Lords on 9 November 1929. On 9 September Reynolds silenced a battery which he had discovered while reconnoitring, was severely wounded on 15 September and killed at Le Touquet on 23 February 1916. He is buried in Etaples Mil Cemetery.

Thus II Corps withdrew from Le Cateau, having stopped the German advance for half a day in a battle that many, including Sir John French, said should never have been fought. Others believed that the fight had saved the BEF and even the C-in-C in his Despatch dated 7 September 1914 wrote, 'I cannot close the brief account of this glorious stand of the British troops without putting on record my deep appreciation of the valuable services rendered by General Sir Horace Smith-Dorrien. I say without hesitation, that the saving of the left wing of the Army under my command on the morning of August 26 could never have been accomplished unless a commander of rare and unusual coolness, intrepidity and determination had been present to conduct the operation personally.'

Later French was to vilify the II Corps Commander (who was extremely popular with his men and whose cheery smile was recorded as being a great morale-raising factor during the Retreat) and accuse him of disobeying orders at Le Cateau. In 1915 he had Smith-Dorrien recalled to England.

However, contact with the Germans had been broken. They did not immediately pursue and the BEF was able to breathe a little more easily as it fell back towards Paris and the Marne. Le Cateau cost over 8,000 casualties and 38 guns.

In 1918 Le Cateau once again featured in the fighting when, in the final months of the war, the Allies chased the Germans northwards following the breaking of the Hindenburg Line (see our *Guide Book to the Western Front – South*). Thus on the suggested tour that follows below, the visitor will see many casualties from 1918.

THE BATTLEFIELD TOUR

• **The Route:** The tour begins near the 'Arbre Rond', then visits the International Cemetery, continues through Le Cateau to the Memorial to Shot Pigeoniers, 66th Div Commemorative Horse Trough, British Plot, Le Cateau Communal Cemetery. It then visits Owen's Commemorative Forester's House, Bois l'Evequeue; Ors British Cemetery; Ors on the Sambre-Oise Canal where the poet Wilfred Owen was killed – his grave in the CWGC Comm Cem and the WFA Memorial; the 1st Div Memorial at La Groise; the Highland Cemetery and the Suffolk Memorial on the Le Cateau Ridge.
• **Extra Visit** to 5th Div Battle HQ, Reumont.
• **[N.B.s]:** The following sites are indicated: Troisvilles Communal Cemetery; Carpezat 1944 Memorial & Selridge Brit CWGC Cemetery, Montay; British field gun in Le Cateau Library; Le Cateau Station; Mazinghien Communal Cemetery
• **Total distance:** 30 miles
• **Total time:** 4 hours
• **Distance to Calais from start point** via Cambrai: 107 miles. Motorway Tolls
• **Base town:** Cambrai
• **Map:** IGN 2607 Est Le Cateau 1:25,000 and 2707

If continuing from the end of the Mons Tour, take the A7-E19 west from Mons, then at Exit 23 follow the D659-D649-D934-D932-D955 south to the International Cemetery at Le Cateau and pick up the Itinerary from there.

In this way you will have followed the general path of the Retreat of 11 Corps. However it should be remembered that the movement involved thousands of men, horses, pieces of artillery and multiple items of general stores stretching over many miles both north and south, east and west. Central control of such a movement was almost impossible once it had been set in motion given the limited means of communication of the period – runners, liaison officers, wire (not much use on a retreat!), aeroplanes and even pigeons. General Gough, Commanding 3rd Cavalry Brigade later wrote, 'We often groped about in the fog of war'.

If coming from Calais take the A16/A26/E15 direction Paris/Arras/Reims, then keep left at the junction with the A1, following Cambrai/Metz/Nancy and take Exit 8 signed to Cambrai on the D939. Keep following signs to Cambrai to the roundabout and take the D643 with a prominent sign to MUSEE MATISSE, Le Cateau. Continue over the St Quentin Canal and several roundabouts.

On the right in Beauvois en Camb. is the excellent **Restaurant La Buissonière**. Tel: +(0) 3 27 85 29 91 (Lat & Long: 50.14161 3.37867). It has an elegant Gourmet restaurant and an attractive Brasserie with a choice of menus.

Continue on the D643 (the area to the right of the road was held by the French 84th Territorial Division) through Caudry. After Caudry, to the right, about a mile away, was the extreme left hand area of 11 Corps on 26 August, held by 8th Brigade including the 4th Middlesex who had suffered so much at Mons and who prided themselves on being 'first in and last out of Le Cateau'. Continue towards Inchy.

As the Roman road rises to a crest after Inchy you are effectively in No Man's Land with the German assaults coming from your left towards 5th Division positions on your right.

*Turn right just before the restaurant on the left on the D98 signed Troisville. (**Restaurant 'Le Pendu'**, Neuvilly, Tel: 08 99 78 60 77. Open: 0900-2000).*

Set your mileometer to 0. *Continue to Troisvilles to the large brick calvary in the village. Keep left (ignoring the No Entry sign) and continue to a crossroads with another calvary.*

N.B. In the **Troisvilles Communal Cemetery** (Map 3/1a Lat & Long: 50.10275 3.47535), straight over and some 200 yards on the left, are 30 British WW1 burials, over half of whom are Unknown and which include 5 Special Memorials to men who fell on 26 August 1914, 7 named graves from August 1914 and 10 from 1918. The Cemetery was first used by the Germans in August 1914 and by British units in 1918. The white CWGC headstones, with a Cross of Sacrifice, are in an immaculate enclosed grassy plot which stands out amongst the predominantly dark grey local graves with their many personal tributes.

Turn left along a track which is driveable if reasonably dry. Continue some 1,200 yards to the lone tree to the right of the electricity pylons.

• *L'Arbre Rond/1.7 miles/5 minutes/Map 3/1/Lat & Long: 50.10273 3.48923*

This is Point 138, l'Arbre Rond, on the IGN map. At the time of the battle trees were few and far between in the

Headstone of 14 Unknown Soldiers, Troisvilles Communal Cemetery.

area and the tree that stood here was about 40 ft high. It was marked on the maps that the Germans had and they used the tree as a marker on which to range their artillery.

The 15th Brigade of 5th Division held this area with Brigade HQ nearby in the cutting. The 1st Norfolks were tasked to prepare the defences – and they wanted to cut the tree down so that the German guns could not range upon it. They set about sawing it through but never quite finished the job.

There are various accounts about the fate of the tree and the reported planting of a sapling in the late 1950s, but the romantic can scrutinise the gnarled trunk and be convinced that healed saw cuts can still be discerned.

The tall thin wireless mast at Le Cateau Station (it is a useful marker throughout the tour in the same way as the mast at Pozières on the Somme) is visible in the distance to the right of the tree. Thus, from where you are to the mast represents the approximate frontage of 5th Division – about 3 miles.

L'Arbre Rond, Troisvilles.

Return to the D643 and turn right. Continue to the roundabout and turn left signed to Le Cateau Mil and German Cemetery on the D932. Continue to the cemetery on the right.

• Le Cateau CWGC International Military and German Cemeteries/5.5 miles/20 minutes/Map 3/2/Lat & Long: 50.11057 3.52731

This is known as the International Cemetery because of the considerable number of British, German and Russian burials. The ground was laid out by the Germans in February 1916 with plots for their own and for the British dead which have separate entrances and visitors' books. There are over 5,576 Germans buried here (most in a mass grave) including some females. There are a number of large German Memorials including a pyramid structure on which is embossed *See Getreu bis den Tod* (Faithful unto Death). Curiously a very similar pyramid is to be found on the 1942 battlefield of El Alamein to commemorate German fighter pilot Captain H. J. Marseille. Also in this cemetery is a Memorial column erected by the Leibkurassier Regiment which names its casualties on the day of the battle. Thirty-four Russian prisoners lie together in a separate plot under French style crosses.

The burials in the British Cemetery number some 640, buried in sections representative of 1914 and 1918 and include 3 UK Navy, 473 UK Army, 1 UK Airforce and 182 UK Unknown, 6 Australians, 2 Canadians and 1 Unknown, 2 New Zealanders, 24 South African and 4 Unknown and 2 German. The CWGC Plots were designed by Charles Holden. Here is buried **Lance Corporal John William Sayer, VC**, 8th Queen's R W Surreys, who won his award for an action on 21 March 1918 at Le Verguier where he held on to his post under heavy fire until nearly all the garrison was killed. He was captured and died of wounds incurred on that day on 18 April 1918. Also buried here is **Capt the Hon Robert Bruce**, 34, 2nd ASH, 26 August 1914, 'Master of Burleigh' and **Capt Archibald Kennedy**, 2nd ASH, 26 August 1914, brother of Capt P. A. Kennedy, who has a Private Memorial (qv) in Fromelles.

This general area formed a focus for the attacks of the 7th (Ger) Division and from here the German artillery had clear views over the British positions.

Walk between the British and German sections of the Cemetery to the wall at the back. On a clear day the station mast beyond the town is visible, once again providing an idea of the frontage of 5th Division, with the Arbre Rond, though not visible, being the same distance away to the right.

German Pyramid Memorial, International Cemetery, Le Cateau.

Headstone of L/Cpl Sayer, VC

Memorial to the Leibkurassier Regt, Russian burials behind, International Cemetery, Le Cateau.

The view to the south, along the D932 an old Roman Road, at times here obscured by trees, is directly towards the high ground of the Le Cateau ridge beyond the town on which 5th Division made its stand.

N.B. Memorial Carpezat & Selridge Brit CWGC Cemetery. By continuing on the D932 and taking the 1st turning to the left, signed to Selridge British Cemetery, a stone Memorial to 21-year old Jean Carpezat may be seen immediately on the left **(Map 3//2b Lat & Long: 50.11366 3.53219)**. Carpezat was shot by the Germans on 3 September 1944 (and a Square in Le Cateau is named Place 3 Septembre in his memory), two weeks before he was due to be married. The touching inscription translates, *Passer-by bow down. It is here that the soul of Jean Carpezat, 21 years, FFI, flew towards God. Dead so that France should live!! Never Forget. 3 Sept 1944.*

The metalled road continues to the tiny **Selridge British Cemetery, Montay (Map 3/2c Lat & Long: 50.11988 3.52130)** which is enclosed by a hedge. It contains 141 burials, including 6 Unknown. Montay was reached in the Pursuit to the River Selle on 10 October 1918 and on the 28th and 29th the Cemetery was made by the 33rd Division and named Selridge (Selle Ridge). The river is about three quarters of a mile to the right. Originally the cemetery had 60 graves, dating from 10 October to 1 November, the majority belonging to the 6th or 12th Lancashire Fusiliers or the 2nd Argyll and Sutherland Highlanders. Eighty seven more graves were added after the Armistice of which 86 came from Neuvilly Cemetery No. 2.

The Glasgow Highlanders (9th H.L.I.), eleven of whose men are buried in the Cemetery, like so many regiments put up a memorial of their own – a wooden cross – but also like most it no longer exists.

Return to the D643.

*Memorial to Jean Carpezat,
3 Sept 1944, Montay.*

Selridge Brit CWGC Cemetery, Montay.

> • *Extra Visit to 5th Division Battle HQ, Reumont/Lat & Long:*
> *50.08386 3.48321 Round trip: 4.5 miles. Approximate time: 20 minutes*
> Go straight over on the D932 Roman road. Drive into Reumont and stop at the second building
> on the left – a pair of semi-detached cottages.
> **5th Division Battle HQ.** This house (No 41, much renovated and under repair at the
> time) was used by the divisional commander, General Sir Charles Fergusson, as an HQ.
>
> Until over a decade ago the building
> was marked with a Plaque (see
> picture) which has been stolen.
> General Fergusson, by climbing up a
> ladder being used in the works,
> watched most of the battle from the
> roof of this house, from where he
> could clearly see the parlous state of
> our right flank as the Germans
> worked forward along the Selle Valley.
>
>
>
> *The stolen 5th Div Plaque, Reumont.*
>
> At noon Smith-Dorrien arrived
> here and the commanders discussed
> the possibility of retirement. One
> hour later General Fergusson sent a
> message to II Corps HQ at Bertry
> saying that 5th Division could not hold out much longer and at 1320 hours added that he
> ought to begin to move unless reinforced.
>
> General Smith-Dorrien ordered the move of two reserve battalions to Bertry, some 2
> miles west of here, to come under Fergusson's command and told the divisional
> commander to withdraw when he thought fit, after which 3rd and 4th Divisions would
> follow. Fergusson issued his orders around 1400 hours. Forward battalions did not get
> them until 1500 hours. Some never got them at all, in particular the KOYLI of 13th
> Brigade who, despite an heroic stand by **Major Yate** for which he was awarded the **VC**,
> were overwhelmed, only eight officers and 320 men answering the roll that evening.
>
> By 1700 hours the whole of II Corps was in retreat - but in good order with flank
> guards established. At 1800 hours darkness and rain settled over the long moving column
> and the German pursuit lost contact.
>
> *Return to the D643 and pick up the main Itinerary.*

*Turn left and continue into Le Cateau, uphill to the important Matisse Museum on the left with
some parking.*

Opposite it is the **Tourist Information Office** of 'Le Pays de Matisse' **(Lat & Long: 50.10548
3.54286)** (Tel: + (0)3 27 84 10 94) with extremely helpful staff, where leaflets listing the town's
hotels and restaurants (of which there are several) may be obtained. Sadly the **Hotel Mouton Blanc**,
where the patronne hid several wounded British officers in August 1914, is no more.

During the first part of the Retreat, Sir John French had his advance HQ in the *Mairie* at Bavay
(about 20 miles north-east of Le Cateau) but visited Le Cateau (where his main GHQ was
situated) briefly on 24 August 1914 when he was gratified to see the leading elements of 4th
Division 11 Corps. He then moved GHQ to St Quentin on the evening of the 25th.

*Continue uphill past the splendid Mairie on the left and follow the road left and right to the traffic
lights. Turn left on the D643 signed Toutes Directions. Continue to the first traffic lights at a
crossroads. Turn left on Fontaine à Gros Bouillon and continue .4 miles, bearing right uphill on rue
des Fusillés Civils to the Memorial on the right.*

• Memorial to Shot Pigeoniers, Le Cateau/7.3 miles/5 minutes/Map 3/2a/ Lat & Long: 50.10980 3.54883

The Memorial is to 5'Innocent Civilians shot by the Germans on 24-27 November 1914 for keeping pigeons'. There was a strict prohibition by the Germans for keeping carrier pigeons for obvious reasons. The Memorial was funded by the Town of Le Cateau and the Commune of Catillon. [There is also a Memorial to the pigeons and a similar martyr in Lille.]

Turn round and continue to the Parking des Remparts on the right. Stop and Park. Walk to the horse trough on the left at the corner with the traffic lights.

• 66th Division Commemorative Horse Trough/7.7 miles/5 minutes/Map 3/4/Lat & Long: 50.10459 3.54615

At the corner on the left as you walk up is a horse trough with a Plaque in memory of the members of the 66th Division of the BEF who'fell in the liberation of Le Cateau from German occupation in October 1918'. The town was entered late on 10 October 1918, after four years of occupation, by the 5th Connaught Rangers.

Return to your car. Continue straight over onto Rue du Marché aux Chevaux.

Memorial to Shot Pigeon Keepers, Le Cateau.

66th Division Commemorative Horse Trough, le Cateau.

> N.B. On the left is the town Library (with large blue wrought iron gates by a pedestrian crossing). In it may be found a **British field gun (Map 3/5. Lat & Long: 50.10351 3.54501)** which was donated to the town in 1932 by the 93rd Bty RFA in memory of the Battles of Le Cateau 1914 and 1918 and reputed to have been used in the 1914 action.

Continue to the road junction and turn left on Rue de Fesmy, signed to Le Cateau Communal. Continue to the cemetery on the left.

• British Plot, Le Cateau Communal Cemetery/7.9 miles/20 minutes/ Map3/5a/Lat & Long: 50.10152 3.54688

Incorporated into the local cemetery, on the top right hand corner, is the CWGC plot, which was used by the Germans to bury British dead in August and September 1914 and by the British in the last three months of 1918. In it there are some 150 burials including thirteen Australians. The

CWGC Plot, Le Cateau Communal Cemetery.

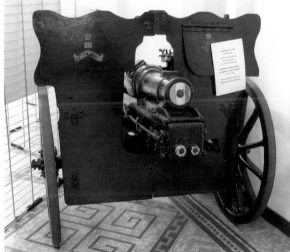

93rd Bty RFA Memorial Gun, Le Cateau Library.

Germans used Le Cateau as a railhead and had a major hospital in the area. In 1922 sixty five German graves were removed. It is likely that the British also had medical facilities here too as many of those buried in the cemetery died after the Armistice, including **Chaplain 4th Class Ernest Edward Johnson** on 1 December 1918 and **Shoesmith J. Smith** of the RFA, 15 December 1918. There is a large German Memorial in the Plot to 178 British, French and Germans originally buried here.

> *Return to the crossroads with the traffic lights and turn right on the D643, rue de Landrecies/Ave Mal. Leclerc and fork left on the D959 direction Landrecies. Continue for some 3 miles to the striking white house on the right. Park behind the building.*

Wilfred Owen Tribute Maison Forestière, Bois l'Evêque.

• Wilfred Owen's Commemorative Maison Forestière, Bois l'Evêque/11.9 miles/30 minutes/Map 3a/1a/Lat & Long: 50.11533 3.62322

The Cellar, Maison Forestière.

Recognising that Owen had become a cult figure and that more and more visitors came to the area to find his grave and the site of his death, as well as to enquire about the cellar in which he wrote his last letter home the night before he was killed, M. Jacky Duminy, the *Maire* of Ors decided to create a permanent site of commemoration to the poet. With the support of the local community, the Wilfred Owen Association (contact@wilfredowen.fr), the Département de Le Nord-Pas-de-Calais and other cultural organisations, he commissioned the imaginative English artist and sculptor Simon Patterson and the renowned French architect Jean-Christophe Denise, to design this exceptional work of art – which is not described as a memorial, an exhibition or a museum – from the existing, somewhat derelict but original, Forester's House where Owen passed his last night.

The outcome has the appearance of a large sculpture. The house and its closed front door and shutters have been rendered in stark white, the roof remodelled to represent an overturned open book, with space below it which illuminates the completely bare single room of the house. It is approached by a circular path on whose white walls are inscribed the words of Owen's last reassuring letter to his beloved mother, '...*There is no danger down here, or if any, it will be well over before you read these lines...*' Before she read the lines, her son was already dead.

Inside the spiral of the path is a small open-air amphitheatre where live literary and musical events are held.

The path leads to the small 'smokey cellar' in which Owen and his platoon, his *'band of friends'*, laughed and created a fire with damp wood. It has been left in its original red brick state.

Stairs then lead to the large room, with simple benches around the walls. As the words of several of Owen's poems are read (in English or in French), the text, either in Owen's own hand, showing the many amendments he made, or in the printed version, are projected onto the high walls. The English version is read by Kenneth Branagh. His rendition of Owen's most famous poem, *Dulce et Decorum Est,* has an extraordinarily emotional impact, surely the finest possible interpretation of this searing rebuttal of the cliché that it is sweet and fitting *pro patria mori*, written as a rebuttal of the blithely insensitive poetess Jessie' Pope's jingoist summon to arms, entitled *The Call*. Owen's poem was written whilst he was in Craiglockhart War Hospital in 1917 pronounced 'unfit for General Service for six months' with 'neurasthenia' after his experiences on the Somme. There he was influenced by the poets Siegfried Sassoon and Robert Graves who inspired him to produce his finest and most memorable work.

The Forester's House was inaugurated on 1 October 2011 in the presence of Owen's nephew, Peter Owen, the British Ambassador, the French Minister of Culture and many local dignitaries and members of the Wilfred Owen Association – witnessed by a reported 900 people.

Open: Mon, Wed, Thurs, Fri, Sat 0930-1230 & 1400-1800 and Sun 1000-1200. Contact: **Cambrai Tourist Office,** Tel: +(0)3 27 78 36 15.

Continue on the D959.

To the left is the charming **Estaminet de l'Ermitage,** Tel: +(0)3 27 77 99 48. Open for lunch Mon-Fri. and for groups on Fri & Sat evenings by appointment. [See Tourist Information.]

Continue on the D959 to the turning to the right on the C6 signed to Ors British Cemetery and continue on it to the Cemetery sign on the left. Park by the iron gate.

• Ors British CWGC Cemetery/12.9 miles/20 minutes/Map 3a/2a/Lat & Long at gateway: 50.10822 3.63879

NOTE: The CWGC sign does not state that the cemetery can only be approached by going through the side gates of 3 iron gates and crossing some 300 yards over 2 fields which could be marshy when wet. It is not accessible by wheelchair. The gates may well be locked by the farmer if there is a bull in one of the fields! The Cemetery will then be seen on the left (Lat & Long: 50.10755 3.64281).

The Cemetery was started in November 1918 and contains 107 Commonwealth graves, 58 UK, 1 Australian, 41 S. Africans and 6 Unknown. There are several HLI and RE graves from the crossing of the nearby Sambre-Oise Canal on 4 November 1918.

Continue on the C6 to the junction with the D160 and turn right past the church. Continue to the right turn onto the rue de la Gare on the D160B following green CWGC signs to Ors Communal Cemetery. Stop at the local cemetery on the right. Walk through the local graves to the hedge-enclosed CWGC plot at the rear.

Ors British CWGC Cemetery.

Headstones of Lt Wilfred Owen, MC and 2nd Lt James Kirk, VC, Ors Comm CWGC Cemetery

WFA Plaque to Crossing of the Sambre-Oise Canal.

Detail of Plaque.

• Grave of Wilfred Owen, Ors Communal Cemetery/14 miles/15 minutes/Map 3a/1/Lat & Long: 50.10280 3.62835

In the back row is a headstone inscribed 'Lieutenant W.E.S. Owen, MC, Manchester Regiment, 4th November 1918. Age 25.' A somewhat reluctant soldier – he didn't join up (in the Artists' Rifles) until 15 October 1915 – Owen was commissioned in the Manchester Regiment on 4 June 1916. He arrived in France in January 1917 and saw action near Serre on the Somme. In March he was concussed but rejoined his battalion in April at Savy where he was shell-shocked. Then followed the famous episode at Craiglockhart War Hospital near Edinburgh where he met Siegfried Sasson and Robert Graves and wrote some of his most searing war poetry. He rejoined the 5th Manchesters in November and the following month was promoted to full Lieutenant. In August 1918 he arrived at Etaples and subsequently rejoined the Manchesters at Amiens. For his part in an action at Beaurevoir-Fonsomme Owen was awarded the MC. The reluctant soldier had become a fine regimental officer. In October his battalion took over the line west of the Sambre-Oise Canal and by 2 November they had cleared the west bank at Ors of the last enemy. Owen was detailed to lead his company in the dangerous canal crossing by raft with orders that there should be 'no retirement under any circumstances'. At 0545 on 4 November the Manchesters pressed on despite murderous fire from the heavily defended German bank. At 0700 hours, under swirling mist and gas, the attack was aborted. Among the dead were Owen, 2nd Lt James Kirk and A/Lt Col John Neville Marshall, CO of the nearby Lancashires. Both the latter were awarded the VC for their gallantry and cool leadership during the costly crossing and their graves are in the same row as Owen's.

In one of the war's tragic ironies, his beloved mother, Susan, received the telegram informing the family of his death as the Armistice bells were ringing in his home town of Shrewsbury.

Owen's short military career provided him with the material for the unforgettable poetry, such as *Anthem for Doomed Youth, Dulce et Decorum Est* and *Strange Meeting*, that make him probably the most read of all the Great War poets.

The D160B on which you are parked is a no-through road. Beyond in the forest is the old military camp (marked on local maps) where the Manchesters gathered before the attack on the canal. At the far end of the forest, approached from the D959 Le Cateau-Landrecies road, is the 'Forester's House' visited earlier. An audio-directed 'Wilfred Owen' walking trail through the Forest frrom the Forester's House to the Canal was opened on 2 June 2013.

Turn round, return to the main road and turn left into Ors, passing the Mairie on the right. Drive over the canal and park immediately on the right. Walk back over the bridge to the memorial on the left as you walk.

• Wilfred Owen WFA Memorial, Ors/14.5 miles/10 minutes/Map 3A/2/ Lat & Long: 50.09937 3.63545

The handsome black WFA Plaque was unveiled by the Chairman of the Wilfred Owen Association in 1991. It commemorates the crossing of the Sambre-Oise Canal by 32nd Division on 4 November 1918 during which four VCs were won and amongst whose casualties was the poet Wilfred Owen, killed on the towpath about one kilometre to the north of the bridge.

The surviving VCs were Res Maj Arnold Horace Santo Waters (later Sir Arnold) and Sapper Adam Archibald.

Return to your car and continue to the next turn to the right on the D360 signed Catillon/La Groise. Continue to the junction with the D643 and turn left signed La Groise. Follow signs to Guise and continue to the traffic lights. Turn sharp left on the D934 and stop immediately on the left opposite the memorial on the right.

• 1st Division Memorial, La Groise/18.1 miles/5 minutes/Map 3a/3/Lat & Long: 50.05908 3.67344

This handsome Memorial was erected 'To the Glory of God and to the abiding memory of the 1st Division of the BEF which from August 1914 to November 1918 served and suffered in France and left there close upon 160,000 dead'. It bears the quotation 'Who [sic] stands if freedom fall, Who dies if England live?' from Rudyard Kipling's 1914 poem, *For All we Have and Are*. It shows the figure of St Michael.

A plaque bears the ORBAT of the Division and a further plaque records that the Memorial was re-erected by 32nd Eng Regt and blessed in the presence of the Mayor and Citizens of La Groise and Maj-Gen Alexander-Sinclair, officers and men of the 1st Division based in Germany on 28 August 1977. At that time it was moved back from the roadside where it had been hit several times by passing cars. Since that time the Memorial has been maintained by the CWGC for the MOD. It stands at the crossroads where at noon on the 26 August 1914 the Division was first attacked and compelled to fall back and where on the morning of 4 November 1918 those crossroads formed the centre of its line of consolidation seven days before the Armistice. It is, therefore, rather like the 'First and Last Shots' Memorials at Mons (qv). The original Memorial was sculpted by R. Goulden in 1926 *1st Division Memorial, la Groise.* and cast by A.B. Burton. It was inaugurated on 17 April 1927 in the presence of Marshal Foch, Lt-Gen Sir Arthur Holland and Sir Peter Strickland.

Opposite is the handily-placed **Le Chapeau Rouge Restaurant Routier** with attractive décor. Tel: + (0)3 27 77 23 39. Open: Mon-Fri 0500-1500 and Sat 1100-1500 and 1800-2300.

Return to Catillon and continue on the D643, over the Sambre-Oise Canal and turn left to Mazinghien on the D160. At the crossroads in Mazinghien turn right on the D115 signed Le Cateau.

Mazinghien was captured by the **American 27th and 30th Divisions** on 19 October 1918. They were the only American forces to remain under British command throughout the war and were taking part in the pursuit following upon the breaking of the Hindenburg Line some 20 miles south-west of here. The 117th Regiment of 30th Division has a Memorial at Brancourt-le-Grand some 13 miles south-west of here commemorating their capture of the town on 8 October 1918.

N.B. On the right is the local Mazinghien cemetery with a green CWGC plaque (**Map 3a/4**) on the wall. **Mazinghien Communal Cemetery CWGC Plot (23.2 miles, Lat & Long: 50.05213 3.59259)** is at the rear of the Cemetery. It contains a total of 23 identified graves, including a line of headstones from the Sambre-Oise Canal crossing of 4 November 1918, including 7 Loyal North Lancs buried shoulder to shoulder and 1 Unknown German from the same date.

Continue and at the crossroads turn right on the D12 to Le Cateau. Continue to the cemetery on the left.

• Highland CWGC Cemetery, Le Cateau/26.8 miles/20 minutes/Map 3/6/OP/Lat & Long: 50.08593 3.54790/OP

At the back of the Cemetery look right along the wall to a tall wireless mast. This is the area of Le Cateau Station where the first German attacks began. Just on the left of the mast, behind it in the

Highland CWGC Cemetery, le Cateau.

middle distance, the Suffolk Memorial, which marks the effective end of the battle, may be visible if the vegetation is co-operating. The station can be visited next.

Further left is a factory complex which indicates, to a first approximation, the route of the valley of the Selle and left again a large single bushy-top tree on the skyline indicates the village of Reumont where 5th Division had its HQ. Given reasonable visibility it is readily seen from here how the German 5th Division's advance from the railway station area up the Selle River Valley outflanked the Suffolk's position. The skyline running right to left is the route of the Roman road and indicates the centre line taken by the British 5th Division as it retired on the afternoon of 26 August.

Rudyard Kipling called these military cemeteries 'Silent Cities' and an examination of a number of graves here shows the diverse nature of some of them: **Pte James Osborne Kemp,** age 26, served with the 4th Bn AEF, was twice wounded in Gallipoli, was MiD, invalided out with the rank of Captain, rejoined in the Argyll & Sutherland Highlanders and was then killed on 10 October 1918; **Rfmn Bernard William King**, KRRC, age 30, a deacon, the son of a priest, who had to obtain his Bishop's permission to enlist; **Lt A.E. Skemp**, Gloucesters, age 36, Professor of English at Bristol University, 1 November 1918; **Pte Supple**, a 19-year-old boy, Worcesters, 20 October 1918; **Pte Torgerson**, an American from Minnesota who served with the Canadian Lord Strathcona's Horse, age 29, 9 October 1918.

Seven of the Highlanders who gave the Cemetery its name.

The Cemetery was begun by the 50th (Northumbrian) Division in October 1918 and the name comes either from the high ground on which the Cemetery stands or the 32 graves of the Black Watch that are contained within it. Altogether there are some 624 burials.

Continue on the D12 towards Le Cateau under the railway bridge and then some 50 yards to a small turning to the left.

N.B. At the end of this road (about 300 yards) is the rebuilt **Railway Station (Map 3/6a, Lat & Long: 50.09140 3.53986)** and the tall radio mast which can be seen from several places on the tour. By standing with one's back to the Station entrance and looking between the buildings and trees ahead it is possible to see the Suffolk Memorial 1,400 yards away.

Continue to the crossroads and go straight over on rue de la République following signs downhill to J. Rostand College and turn first left on the D21 signed Pole Sanitaire de Santé. Continue uphill to the traffic lights and turn left, still following signs to the College. Continue past the hospital on the right and bear left and then right until you reach the College. To the right of the parking is a bumpy track leading uphill. This can be negotiated by car if dry (if wet 4-wheel-drive would be advisable) and you have good ground clearance. Keep to the right at the fork at the top of the hill and continue to the Memorial in the clump of trees.

• The Suffolk Memorial/29.0 miles/15 minutes/Map 3/3/Lat & Long: 50.09833 3.52330

You are now on the high ground of Point 139. This marks the centre of the Suffolks' position, one of the four infantry regiments that made up 14th Brigade, part of 5th Division. The other regiments were the 1st East Surreys, the 1st Duke of Cornwall's Light Infantry and the 2nd Manchester Regiment.

The original II Corps order issued from Corps HQ at 2215 hours on 25 August, just over an hour after Sir John French's withdrawal order arrived, envisaged the retreat continuing on 26 August and early that morning the Suffolks had already started to withdraw when, at 0600 hours in thick morning mist, they were stopped and told to hold the spur. Half of the Brigade did not receive that order and were in the skirmish action near the railway station. The Suffolks, therefore, had no choice of position and had to scratch shallow trenches where they stood, taking up thin firing lines on the forward slope of the feature you have just climbed and facing in an arc generally to the north and north-east.

The supporting artillery, 11th, 52nd and 37th (Howitzer) batteries of 15th and 8th Brigades Royal Field Artillery (RFA), was lined up some 200 yards behind the Suffolk's trenches but in front of reserve troops so that the guns were actually sited among the infantry. As you can see the position is totally exposed. The only camouflage available to the gunners were stooks of corn which they lashed to the gun wheels.

To the north is the area of the International Cemetery 1400 yards away and to the east the skyline marks the high ground beyond the valley of the River Selle, ground that the Germans occupied very early in the morning and thus opened II Corps' right flank. The initial forward movement of von Kluck's forces was towards you from the north and German forces worked their way east and then south along the valley of the River Selle. German machine guns were sited in the area of le Cateau church tower.

Lt Col Stevens commanding 15th Brigade RFA told 52nd Battery, 'We will fight it out here and there will be no retirement', and before the guns could be properly dug in they came under rifle fire. Soon after 0600 hours German artillery opened up causing considerable casualties among the gunners and the drop-shorts fell on the Suffolks in their shallow trenches.

At about 1000 hours a German infantry attack began to develop from the area of the River Selle (see **Map 3** for orientation) just south of Le Cateau and 52nd Battery inflicted considerable damage on the enemy despite having several limbers set on fire by a German HE shell. Another infantry attack began at noon from the north. Once again it was discouraged by the artillery. The gunners' fire controller had his OP well forward in the front line of the Suffolk trenches and his instructions to the guns were relayed back by a chain of orderlies lying out in the open because all telephone wires had been destroyed.

The volume of noise beating down on the trenches was horrendous. German HE shells from some one hundred guns were bursting overhead and our own guns, between 100 and 200 yards away, added their own cacophony as they returned fire.

Despite attempts at reinforcement by the Manchesters, and Argyll and Sutherland Highlanders sent forward from 19 Brigade, the courageous tenacity of the gunners and the steady marksmanship of the Suffolks, the German effort gradually built up against this flank, moving ever closer and at mid-morning an aerial observer reported that a 6-mile long column of German infantry was moving down the Roman road towards the crossroads (near the International Cemetery which you visited earlier).

As targets appeared the artillery engaged them but, of the four British batteries supporting the positions on the ridge, only one remained intact at the end of the morning and most of the ammunition in the lines had been used. The 52nd Battery fired over 1,100 rounds in the action. At 1330 hours a

The Suffolk Memorial, le Cateau.

message was received ordering the guns to withdraw, but heavy casualties among the horses, let alone both men and guns, made this no easy task.

'One of the saddest things I have seen was the wounded horses trying to keep themselves on their legs by leaning against the stooks of corn', said one Sapper officer.

Lt Col. Stevens who had earlier told 52nd Battery that there would be 'no retirement' (the word 'retreat' had not yet come into use in the BEF) decided that he needed confirmation of the order to withdraw before acting upon it and it was not until 1400 hours that the guns of the Brigade were told to move. There was no escape for the 52nd, however, because their CO, Major A. C. R. Nutt, did not receive any order at all.

German infantry were attacking to the right of the Suffolks and working clear round them. A hail of machine gun fire poured down from the guns to the north. The British field guns fired singly as best as they could, most of the men being dead or wounded, and the last minutes were described by Lt Col Stevens as follows:

'About 2.40 pm some cheering was heard on our right about 300 yards away and over the crest. About five minutes afterwards we heard 'Stand Fast' and 'Cease Fire' sounded and whistles blown. Then it was shouted down the line from the right, 'You are firing on friends'. All firing stopped at once. On standing upright and looking just over the crest we found everyone standing up and the firing line being rounded up by Germans. The position was lost, considerable numbers of the enemy being round our right and right rear.'

The fight had lasted eight hours. The Memorial, a cenotaph, commemorates the actions of the 2nd Suffolks, the Manchesters, the Argylls and the supporting batteries of the Royal Artillery It bears the names of the Officers, NCOs and Soldiers who were casualties of those regiments on 26 August 1914, many of whom are buried in the International Cemetery, such as Capt the Hon Bruce (Master of Burleigh), 2nd ASH. There are 3 Drummer Boys: L. C. Hill, D. Yeatsley and A. Offley. It was unveiled in 1924 by Gen Smith-Dorrien and despite its name it is essentially one to 14th Brigade of 5th Division and the attached Divisional Artillery.

ANOTHER MYTH OF THE RETREAT:

The Stirrup Charge of the Scots Greys and the Black Watch. 28 August 1914

As the story of 'The Angels of Mons' (qv) supposedly inspired the tired British soldiers at the beginning of their Retreat from Mons (and later discovered to be a fabricated news story), so did the stirring exploits of the Scots Greys and Black Watch on 28 August 1914 as they reached St Quentin after the Battle of Le Cateau.

This time the story originated in *The Illustrated London News* and was reinforced by that publication a week later with a drawing by Richard Caton Woodville that went on to be instantly famous. It depicted the Scots Greys charging the Germans with foot soldiers of the Black Watch clinging on to their stirrups (a similar story had been told, set on the Waterloo Battlefield). Once near the enemy the Black Watch detached themselves and made a furious bayonet charge.

The Greys had indeed made a brave attack near St Quentin, but in his account 'The Black Watch', Scout Joe Cassells of the Regiment maintained, 'In the newspaper accounts of the campaign this incident was described as 'The Great St Quentin Charge', in which, it was asserted, the Black Watch (foot soldiers) participated, holding onto the stirrups of the Scots Greys. This bit of colouring was inaccuracy. We aided the Greys and the Lancers with rifle and machine-gun fire only.'

Just as few chose to believe that the Angels of Mons was a fabricated story, the tale of the famous Stirrup Charge refused to wither. It inspired Countess Feodora Gleichen to sculpt a wonderful depiction of the action in bronze – a statue that takes pride of place in the private collection of the authors. It also inspired a poem by Arnold F. Graves in his anthology, *The Long Retreat*, published in 1915. Entitled *The Highlanders'* it describes the charge in some detail...

...We couldn't fight 'em, wouldn't run,
We thought for certain we were done,
When suddenly upon our right
I saw a flash of sabres bright –
The cavalry! It was the Greys;
And just in time; a cheer we raise.
I saw as past me they went clanging,
A tartan to each stirrup hanging...

The Stirrup Charge at St Quentin.

Another interesting 'fact' that we have been unable to verify was that soon after the Greys arrived in France on 17 August 1914, 'staff of the B.E.F. issued a directive ordering the Scots Greys to dye their horses. The reason was partly because the grey mounts made conspicuous targets, but was also partly based on the fact that the all grey mounts made the regiment distinctive and therefore easier to identify. For the rest of the war, the grey horses of the regiment would be dyed a dark chestnut.' Whether this directive had been carried out before the famous charge we cannot ascertain. But a further account states, 'For a while there were unhappy experiments to dye the horses with permanganate solution.' There are also reports of the grey horses being dyed 'khaki' during the Boer War.

• *End of Le Cateau Battlefield Tour*
OR return to Le Cateau or Cambrai for RWC.

NOTRE-DAME DE LORETTE, ARTOIS

5 OCTOBER 1914-OCTOBER 1915

'She must become the voice which weeps for her youth cut down in its flower,
the voice which prays for the eternal rest of their souls, the voice which talks of
hope to the widows, fiancées, parents, the voice which calls tomorrow's
generations to pilgrimages of remembrance and pity.'
Monseigneur Julien, Bishop of Arras
writing about the Monument at Notre-Dame de Lorette.

SUMMARY OF THE BATTLES

There are three distinct French actions around Notre-Dame de Lorette which can be identified as the battles of Artois though their precise dates and results differ according to the French or British accounts. We give a median interpretation.

The **first** began on **26 October 1914** following the German threat to Arras and the occupation of Notre-Dame de Lorette and the Ablain St Nazaire heights by the Bavarians. It ended in French losses of some 125,000 and no gains.

The **second** began on **9 May 1915** (the British Aubers Ridge and Festubert attacks were part of the same overall offensive) and lasted until 24 June with estimated losses of 140,000. The French re-took Ablain St Nazaire and the heights of Notre-Dame de Lorette and Neuville St Vaast but not Souchez or the ground commanding it.

The **third** battle was launched on **25 September 1915** (the British Loos attack was part of the same overall offensive) and lasted for about three weeks. The French gained a foothold on Vimy Ridge, took the Labyrinth (qv) and re-captured Souchez at a cost of 135,000 casualties. German losses were estimated as 178,00. There the lines stayed until the Arras offensives of April 1917, by which time the battlefield 'resembled a furious sea, a veritable chaos, the image of the earth after the flood' (Galthier-Boissière).

OPENING MOVES

The war was barely two weeks old when in the middle of August 1914 General Galliéni began building barricades in Paris against the rapidly approaching invader and at the end of the month advancing German forces reached Arras, plundering it on 6 and 7 September but leaving a day later. French resistance before the Marne was stiffening and as Moltke urged on his troops around Arras to push on to the French capital, Galliéni and Foch launched surprise attacks against the Germans. The invader recoiled and thus began the 'Race to the Sea' as the Germans were pushed back north. But here they held on to Notre-Dame de Lorette, Ablain St Nazaire, Souchez, Givenchy, Thélus and Vimy – just about all the high ground before Arras – though not Arras itself. That high ground held the key to the Douai plain, its coal mines and industry, and in the next twelve months the French would make three desperate attempts to take it back.

MAP 4: NOTRE-DAME DE LORETTE, ARTOIS 5 OCT 1914–OCT 1915

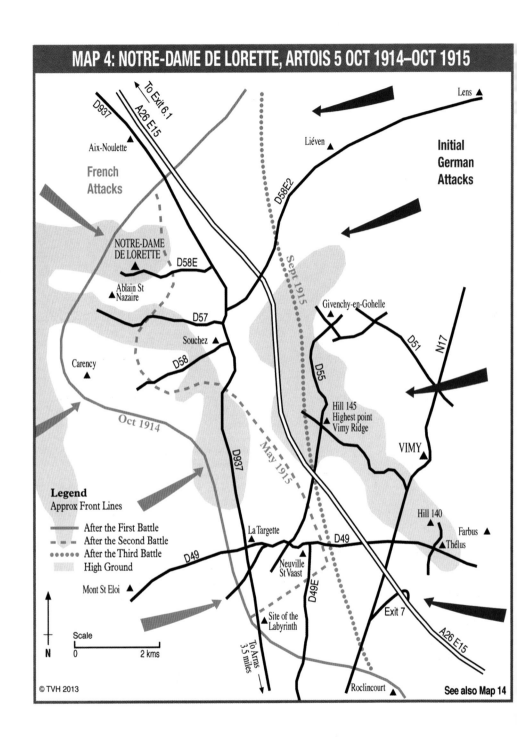

Lens

To Exit 6.1

D937

A26 E15

Aix-Noulette

French Attacks

Liéven

D58E2

Initial German Attacks

NOTRE-DAME DE LORETTE

D58E

Ablain St Nazaire

D57

Souchez

Sept 1915

Givenchy-en-Gohelle

D51

N17

Carency

D58

D55

Oct 1914

Hill 145
Highest point
Vimy Ridge

VIMY

D937

May 1915

Legend
Approx Front Lines

――― After the First Battle
– – – After the Second Battle
•••••• After the Third Battle
░░░ High Ground

Hill 140

Farbus

La Targette

D49

Thélus

Mont St Eloi

D49

Neuville St Vaast

D49E

Exit 7

A26 E15

N

Scale
0   2 kms

Site of the Labyrinth

To Arras
3.5 miles

Roclincourt

See also Map 14

© TVH 2013

WHAT HAPPENED

The progress of the three battles may be more readily followed by reference to **Map 4.**

The first battle, a series of German attacks and French counter-attacks, followed the advance of the Crown Prince of Bavaria's 62nd Army moving down from the direction of Armentières, which headed for Arras intending to take both the town and its road and rail network as well as the high ground around it.

On 16 September, after the massacre of General d'Amade's territorials at le Transloy on 27/28 August (commemorated there by a significant memorial and which we cover in detail in our guide book to the Somme), the first French troops moved in to defend Arras and some two weeks later, on 2 October, von Arnim's IV Corps moved towards Arras from the east along the Cambrai road, causing many civilians around Givenchy to flee to the west. On 5 October, after a number of cavalry engagements with the French, the Germans occupied Ablain St Nazaire, Aix Noulette, Givenchy, Liévin, Lens, Monchy le Preux, Souchez, Notre-Dame de Lorette and Vimy, effectively cutting Arras off from the north and east. They immediately set about preparing defensive positions with strongpoints and trenches. At about the same time at Feuchy, just below the River Scarpe and some 3 miles due east of Arras, General Barbot and his Alpine troops of 77th Division held the German advance, forcing it to swing to the north and thus saving Arras from immediate occupation. The city then came under the care of General d'Urbal with a defensive force of General Fayolle's 70th Infantry Division (Fayolle would command the French 6th Army on the Somme on 1 July 1916) plus General Barbot's command (Barbot moved into Arras from Feuchy) and the Zouaves of the 45th Division. Throughout the whole of this period the French mounted counter-attack after counter-attack, suffering heavy losses.

On 5 October plans were being made to evacuate the city but General Foch, who the night before had been made Commander-in-Chief of the French forces, arrived and forbade it. General Barbot, despite the fact that his Alpine Division had been reduced to a quarter of its full strength, is reported as having said with great élan, 'While I still live there will be no retirement!'

Taken aback by the stubborn defence of Arras the Germans began to bombard the city at 0930 on 6 October, an artillery offensive that continued day after day including the use of big 210mm and 280mm guns. The attacks intensified. Between 21 and 23 October they were particularly virulent and were watched by the Kaiser, the Germans taking as a target the Belfry tower in the middle of the city. At 1120 on 21 October the 69th shell found its target and to paraphrase a French account, 'The Belfry's cry of agony echoed around the whole town like a plaintive scream of a soul leaving its body.' On the 22nd a determined attack on Arras through St Laurent Blangy, barely a mile and a half north-east of the city, was held by Barbot's Zouaves and Chasseurs so once again the General saved the city.

Arras did not fall and the opposing sides settled down to face the cold wet winter in trenches, much as was happening at Ypres and just like that city Arras, although under siege, would never fall, defended and held by the French (under Pétain who replaced d'Urbal) until March 1916 and thereafter by the British.

The second battle, an attack by the French, was prompted by the fact that the Germans on the high ground were able accurately to direct their artillery fire upon Arras and the French lines. Between Arras and Notre-Dame de Lorette General Foch assembled five Corps of the 10th Army, all full of enthusiasm for the affray despite the formidable German defences of fortified villages, shelters, barbed wire and re-inforced machine gun positions. On the Notre-Dame de Lorette hill were five lines of deep trenches with multiple rows of barbed wire while the old chapel itself (on the site of today's basilique) had been turned into a fortress with machine guns, sand bags and metal plates.

At 0600 on 9 May 1915 the preliminary bombardment began and four hours later the infantry attacked. Between Souchez and Neuville St Vaast XXXIII Corps under Pétain made rapid progress and the Moroccan Division reached the heights of Vimy, where their memorial now stands. In Lille the Germans of Prince Rupert's 4th Army prepared to evacuate but Pétain had gone too far too fast, nearly three miles in one hour, and his exhausted troops were stopped and then pushed back by German reinforcements brought up in lorries.

At Notre-Dame de Lorette, where XXI Corps under General Maistre had been repeatedly attacking and encroaching upon the hill since December 1914, the area of the chapel was finally gained on 12 May after hand to hand fighting in the ruins, but it was ten more days before all of the Germans were pushed off the hill. On the first day French troops reached the Labyrinth, an especially constructed and formidable fortress of underground works, trenches, and wire, heavily armed with machine guns, but not until 17 July, following a French bombardment said to consist of 300,000 shells, would the whole position be cleared. Two days later the second battle came to an end after fighting whose intensity was matched only at Verdun. Souchez remained in German hands.

The third battle, which began on 25 September, was in conjunction with a British attack at Loos (qv) to the north. The French 10th Army was tasked to take Vimy Ridge but first it had to take Souchez below Notre-Dame de Lorette. The artillery preparation, more calculating than previous efforts and re-inforced with weapons brought up from Verdun, lasted for five days with particular concentration upon road junctions and any features that might represent fortifications. The Germans, however, replied with fierce fire upon the forward trenches, filling parts of them with the dead and churning up the ground over which the French planned to attack. The infantry of Fayolle's XXXIII Corps (he had taken over from Pétain) went in at mid-day on the 25th, the men weighed down in clothes soaked from heavy rains of the night before. Captain Humbert in *La Division Barbot* described their passage thus, 'Our own artillery roared behind us, the shells flying above our heads and bursting everywhere. One could see nothing, understand nothing ... the men went blindly on'. Souchez, the objective of 77th Division, cost many French lives and it was not fully cleared until the following day while at Cabaret Rouge Humbert records, 'Each night ... the dead were loaded on carts while the companies going up the line passed by long rows of other dead awaiting their turn to be removed.'

Meanwhile little else was achieved though parts of Vimy Ridge were reached as far as the Arras-Lens road (now the N17) but these advances were temporary, furious German counter-attacks forcing the French back into their own trenches. Souchez had been taken, Vimy had not and once more the front settled into trench warfare. Vimy Ridge would not be taken until April 1917 and then by the Canadians

THE BATTLEFIELD TOUR

• This is made in conjunction with Vimy Ridge, Arras – see page 205 and Map 14, page 207.

THE YSER

16-29 OCTOBER 1914

'The fate of Europe, up to the time of Waterloo, has always been
decided in Belgium. It is difficult to escape from this idea.'
Marshal Foch. 19 November 1914.

Ce n'est qu'un bout de sol dans l'infini du monde...
Ce n'est qu'un bout de sol étroit,
Mais qui renferme encore et sa reine et son roi,
Et l'amour condensé d'un peuple qui les aime...
Dixmude et ses remparts, Nieuport et ses canaux,
Et Furnes, avec sa tour pareille à un flambeau
Vivent encore ou sont défunts sous la mitraille.
Emile Verhaeren.

It's only a piece of earth in the infinity of the world...
It's only a narrow piece of earth,
But which still contains its king and its queen
And the concentrated love of a people who love them...
Dixmude and its ramparts, Nieuport and its canals,
And Furnes, with its tower like a flame,
Still live or are slain by the machine gun.

[**Emile Verhaeren**, born on 21 May 1855, was Belgium's best-known French language poet. Original, vital, lyrical, his three main themes were the improvement of humanity's lot, love of his wife, and of Flanders. Deeply moved by the outbreak of war, yet too old to fight, he lectured extensively throughout France on Belgian's cause. He was accidentally killed boarding a train after a rally in Rouen on 27 November 1916. After the Armistice his remains were transferred to his native town of Adinkerke.]

SUMMARY OF THE BATTLES

This is the story of a river and a railway. By the end of October 1914 following the struggles around Liège, Namur and Antwerp the exhausted Belgian army had fallen back onto a ten miles long line of defence based on the Yser River between the North Sea at Nieuport and the town of Dixmude. On 21 October the Germans crossed the Yser at Tervate (**see Map 5**) and a probable German advance to the Channel Ports was only prevented by the flooding of vast tracts of land and the adoption of a defensive line based on the Dixmuide to Nieuport railway embankment which ran behind the river. After 15 days of continuous struggle the front held. The lines would hold for four years.

OPENING MOVES

Closely involved in their nation's bitter struggle were King Albert and Queen Elisabeth of the Belgians. Albert was a monarch of the old school, seeing himself as a conscientious and active Head of State and Head of the Armed Forces. Born in Brussels on 8 April 1875, the younger son

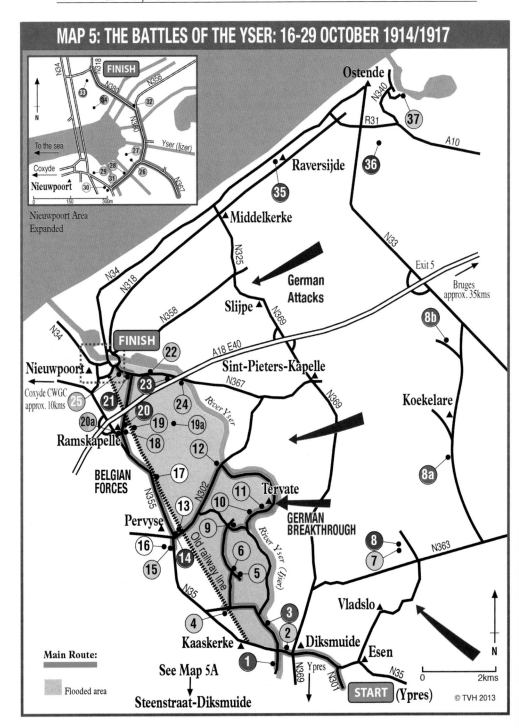

MAP 5: THE BATTLES OF THE YSER: 16-29 OCTOBER 1914/1917

Nieuwpoort Area Expanded

FINISH

To the sea

Coxyde

Nieuwpoort

Yser (Ijzer)

Ostende

Raversijde

Middelkerke

German Attacks

Slijpe

Bruges approx. 35kms

Exit 5

FINISH

Sint-Pieters-Kapelle

Nieuwpoort

Coxyde CWGC approx. 10kms

Ramskapelle

River Yser

Koekelare

BELGIAN FORCES

Tervate

GERMAN BREAKTHROUGH

Pervyse

River Yser (Ijzer)

Old railway line

Vladslo

Kaaskerke

Diksmuide

Esen

Main Route:

Flooded area

See Map 5A

Steenstraat-Diksmuide

START (Ypres)

© TVH 2013

LEGEND: MAP 5: THE BATTLES OF THE YSER: 16-29 OCTOBER 1914/1917

1. Yser Tower Museum & Mem
2. Admiral Ronarc'h & Marines Mem
3. Trenches of Death Museum, Mem, Marker Stone
4. Albertina Marker
5. Vrouwekerke chapel, Mems, Marker Stone
6. Albertina marker, Heron stream
7. Käthe Kollwitz Mem
8. German Cem Vladso
8a. Kathe Kollwitz Tower Mus
8b. Lange Max Mus, Koekelare
9. Albertina Viconia Château
10. Albertina marker Tervate Bridge
11. 2nd Bn 1st Grenadiers Mem
12. 3rd/23rd Infantry Regt Plaque
13. Pervyse old station house
14. Flying Officer Robertson grave
15. Albertina Marker Pervyse
16. Observation tower Pervyse
17. Bunkers in railway embankment
18. 16th French Chasseurs & 6th Belg Regt Mems
19. 14th Inf Regt & old station Mems

19a. Mem to Halifax 1944 Crash Site Mem, Ramskapelle
20. Belgian Cem, Ramskapelle
20a. Marker Stone/Fr 16th Chas à Pied, Ramskapelle
21. Ramskapelle Road CWGC & Comm Cems
22. 3rd Carbiniers & Lt Gen Baron St George Mems
23. CWGC WW2 graves
24. 14th Inf Regt & 7th Inf Granite Soldier Mems
25. Demarkation Stone, Wine Brug
26. Lt Calberg Mon
27. Yser Mon
28. Albertina Marker, Sluizenbrug
29. 1942 WW2 Mem
30. Taverne de Gansepoot
31. Bust of H Geeraert
32. French 81st Div Mem
33. Brits Mem to the Missing
34. King Albert 1 Mem &'De Ganzepoot' Mus
35. Raversijde WW1/WW2 Museum
36. Ostende New Comm CWGC Cem
37. HMS *Vindictive* Mem

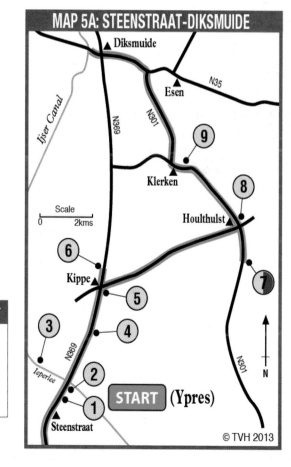

LEGEND: MAP 5A: STEENSTRAAT-DIKSMUIDE

1. Gas Mem, Steenstraat
2. Belg 3rd Regt Mem, Kippe
3. Bros Raemdonck Mem, Kippe
4. Belg 3rd Div Mem, Kippe
5. Albertina Marker, Kippe
6. Armand Van Eecke Mem, Kippe
7. Belg Cem + Albertina Mem, Houthulst
8. Belg 22nd Inf Regt Mem, Houthulst
9. Pilot W. Coppens Mem

of Philip, Count of Flanders, and brother of Leopold II, he succeeded to the throne on 23 December 1909, through a series of premature deaths. A graduate of the Brussels *Ecole Militaire* he served as an officer in the Grenadiers. In 1900 he married Elisabeth, second daughter of the Duke of Bavaria and they had three children: Leopold, Duke of Brabant (the future Leopold III), Charles, Count of Flanders, and Marie José.

On his accession, Albert was particularly concerned with social reforms, the patronage of arts and literature and, especially, the organisation of the Army. In May 1913 he consented to the raising of the Belgian Army to a strength first of 190,000, and then to 350,000, but in July 1914, when World War I was moving inexorably to its outbreak, Belgium was still dangerously unprepared for war. She depended for her survival on the treaties signed by Great Britain, France, Prussia, Russia and Austria to preserve her neutrality – notably the 1839 Treaty of London, the famous 'Scrap of Paper'. It had been tested, and held firm, in 1870 during the Franco-Prussian War. But Leopold II mistrusted the strength of the protective treaty and reinforced the forts of Liège and Namur as a failsafe. Neither the treaties nor the forts were to save Belgium from German invasion in August 1914.

On 31 July Albert wrote to the Kaiser, in a letter carefully translated by his German-born wife, reminding him of the respect due to Belgian neutrality. Wilhelm replied with the ultimatum of 2 August and hostilities began when Germany's demand for free passage of her troops was refused.

At 0800 hours on 4 August the Germans invaded Belgium. The fortified city of Liège was reached on 5 August, its last fort surrendering on the 16th; Brussels surrendered on 20 August, Namur capitulated on 25 August. Nearly 2,000 civilians were killed, 3,000 houses destroyed. The historic city of Louvain, with its famous library and cathedral, was destroyed, 79 inhabitants were shot. The Provinces of Brabant, Hainault and Antwerp were occupied and many more civilians executed.

Tales of German atrocities, many of them exaggerated, abounded, fuelling the propaganda campaign for the Allies to come to the help of 'Poor Little Belgium'. The concept of German *Kultur* equating to barbarism was perpetuated by the Dutch artist, Louis Raemakers, in a series of harrowing cartoons that chart the Germans' bloody progress through Belgium. Elsie Knocker, one of the 'Two at Pervyse' (see below) reported in her memoirs,

> 'Atrocities were at their height in those first months of the war, when the Germans were in a hurry to terrorise their way to a quick finish. Every unexpected resistance of the Belgian Army brought immediate reprisals against the civilian population... I did see Belgian children with their hands and feet cut off, and I saw one baby nailed to a door. The Germans forced Belgian civilians to walk ahead of them as they advanced to form a living screen... By the beginning of October nearly 1,500,000 people, or 20 per cent of the population, had left Belgian territory: a million went to Holland, 250,000 to Britain and over 100,000 to France.'

A committee under Viscount Bryce, former Ambassador at Washington, was set up to investigate the conduct of German troops in Belgium. The conclusions of the committee were that there had indeed been systematic massacres of civilians; that looting, wanton destruction and incendiarism had occurred; that the rules and usages of war had frequently been broken, particularly in the use of women and children as shields; that the Red Cross and White Flags had frequently been abused; that 'murder, lust and pillage prevailed over many parts of Belgium on a scale unparalleled in any war between civilised nations during the last three centuries.' The report even contained details of gross individual atrocities of the type reported by Elsie Knocker. Yet when the Belgian Cardinal Mercier held an enquiry in 1922, no substantiation of these atrocities was found and any real supporting evidence for them had mysteriously disappeared. No matter: mere belief in them served to fuel the Allied fervour for the war.

WHAT HAPPENED

The Belgian Army fell back on Antwerp, from which it made sorties on 25 August and 9 September to divert the Germans from their main thrust, which was now into France. During the latter sortie the Belgians lost 6,000 men. On the 26th the Germans attacked Antwerp and again on 3 October. On the 9th the port surrendered. Winston Churchill's gallant attempt to relieve the Belgians in Antwerp (qv) with an expedition by the newly-formed **Royal Naval Division** (amongst them an excited Sub-Lieutenant Rupert Brooke) was too late, and a miserable failure. They left Dover on 4 October and were back in the port on the 9th.

Now the whole country, with the exception of what was left west of the Yser and the small area around Ypres, was under German occupation. King Albert had withdrawn his army (now comprising four divisions in line and two in reserve) along the Yser River, from Nieuport on the coast to Ypres. General Foch, having visited the King at Furnes, wrote in his memoirs of the Belgian Army that 'the nervous force of its soldiers was all that remained to replace the deficiencies of their equipment'.

On 14 October the King issued a last ditch command to his troops, comparable to Haig's 'Backs to the Wall' Order of the Day of 12 April 1918 (which in turn seemed to presage Churchill's stirring 'We shall fight them on the beaches' speech of 4 June 1940):

> 'You will now find yourselves alongside the gallant French and British Armies. Our national honour is at stake. Face to the front in the positions in which I shall place you, and let him be regarded as a traitor to his country who talks of retreat.'

His divisional commanders were then personally visited and given the following instructions:

1. Any General whose Division gives way will be relieved of his command on the spot.
2. Any officer whose men abandon their trenches will be relieved of his command.
3. Under no pretext whatsoever, even if the line is broken, is there to be any retirement.
4. Officers of the General Staff will be distributed among the troops of the front line.

They will remain there during the fighting encouraging others instead of grumbling themselves.

King Albert and Queen Elisabeth installed themselves in a modest villa at La Panne (de Panne) on the coast to the east of Dunkirk, refusing to move with their Government to Calais and then to le Havre. From La Panne the King continued to play an active role as the leader of his Army and Elisabeth, who had been medically trained, took a practical interest in the care of the wounded in hospitals close to the front line. She was the active patron of the hospital that bore her name near Poperinghe and visited Ypres under severe shellfire. The dedication of this family was further proved when on 8 April 1915 the King made an 'Easter Present' of his 13-year-old son to the 3rd Division of the Belgian Army. The delicate-looking Prince Leopold was to act as a Private, getting his hands blistered by digging (alternating with term-time spent in the rarefied atmosphere of Eton).

On 6/7 October the British 7th Division landed at Zeebrugge and Ostende, and '... moved off for its nine or ten mile trek to Bruges. With elastic step and cheery voice the men swung along to the inspiring strains of "Tipperary" (*With the Immortal Seventh Division*, A. J. Kennedy). The Seventh ended up in Ypres and took part in the **First Battle**. After Mons, le Cateau and the Marne, and with the Aisne Line stabilised, the BEF was moving northwards to cover the Flanders crisis. After two months of mobile warfare and the 'Race to the Sea', the front line was soon to settle down into the stalemate of trench warfare.

On 16 October the Battle of the Yser opened. Rear-Admiral Hood brought up a Royal Naval flotilla to Middelkerke and bombarded the German coastal batteries. Naval activity heightened and on 31 October a German submarine sank the British seaplane carrier *Hermes.*

Meanwhile repeated, inexorable, German attacks in the Nieuport and Diksmuide areas continued through to the 23rd. Supported until this time only by 6,000 French Marines, the small Belgian force, deploying its entire army, was expected to hold a 22-mile front, from the sea to Zuydschoote (8km north of Ypres). And hold they did, until by 24 October the Belgian resistance started to fail. The troops were exhausted and running out of ammunition. Reinforcements in the shape of the renowned French 42nd (Grossetti) Division arrived to relieve them but the line was too thin. The Allied defences were on the point of breaking and then, at the suggestion of General Foch who declared, 'Inundation formerly saved Holland, and may well save Belgium. The men will hold out as best they can until the country is under water', Belgian engineers saved the day by opening the floodgates at Nieuport thus letting in the sea and swamping the crisscrossed drainage system of canals and ditches (watergands). Behind the river the engineers dammed twenty-two culverts under the Nieuport-Diksmuide railway embankment forming a catchment area for the coming floods. The railway, Line 74, is now a cycle path, thus the battlefield can be defined by the lines of the River Yser and the railway embankment which became the Belgians' defensive line.

By 30/31 October the operation, assisted by the high tides caused by the full moon of 29 October, was successfully concluded. The Battles of the Yser were over, ending with a furious bayonet charge to the sound of bugles which repulsed the enemy at Ramskappelle. The Belgian Army, with 20,000 casualties in this battle alone, was reduced to 65,000 men. In one regiment only six officers remained.

According to the King's ADC, Commandant van Overstraeten, the French feared their Belgian brothers lacked 'both ability and energy' and urged the distribution of the weak Belgian remnant amongst French units. As General Pershing was to dig in his heels later in the war, about the dispersion of his American forces, Albert 'would neither agree to being deprived of his constitutional prerogatives, nor let his army be split up.' They continued to hold the line between Diksmuide and the sea. The conditions they had fought in were horrendous (see the section on Diksmuide and Vladslo below). The land itself was forbidding:

'Water is everywhere: in the air: on the ground, under the ground. It is the land of dampness, the kingdom of water. It rains three days out of four. The north-west winds which, breaking off the tops of the stunted trees, making them bend as if with age, carry heavy clouds of cold rain formed in the open sea. As soon as the rain ceases to fall, thick white mists rise from the ground giving a ghost-like appearance to men and things alike,' wrote the Belgian author, le Goffic, while in Dixmude. Add to these natural miseries the man-made horrors of modern warfare and it is little short of a miracle that they held on so long.

But now the Germans diverted their attention southwards towards Ypres.

THE BATTLEFIELD TOUR

• **The Route:** It is recommended that the tour begins from Ypres at the end of the Salient tour. It then visits the Gas Memorial at Steenstraat; Kippe - Belgian Memorials to the 3rd Regiment, 3rd Division, Armand Van Eecke and Albertina Marker ; Houthulst - Belgian Cemetery and Albertina Marker; Diksmuide - Statue of Gen Baron Jacques de Dixmude, Ijzer Tower, Trenches of Death, Demarcation Stone; Albertina Markers at the Old Railway Line and the Heron Stream; Memorial Chapel, O-L-Vrouwehoekje and Demarcation Stone, Oud-Stuivekenskerke; Viconia Château and Tervate Bridge Albertina Markers; Memorial to 1st Grenadiers; Pervijze OP Tower, Albertina Marker, sites of Billets of 'the Two'; Ramskapelle Franco-Belgian Memorial and Old Station; Ramscapelle Road Mil and Nieuwpoort Comm CWGC Cemeteries, Demarcation Stone and Albertina Marker; Nieuwpoort - Monuments to the Yser, Lt Calberg, Albertina Marker, Monuments to Hendrik Geeraert, Monument to King Albert I, Visitors' Centre, British Memorial to the Missing.
• **Extra Visits:** Memorial to Bros Raemdonck, Kippe; Vladslo German Cemetery; Halifax 1944 Crash Site Mem, Ramskapelle; Monuments at Uniebrug and St Joris; Coxyde Mil CWGC

Cemetery; Raversijde Atlantic Wall Open Air Museum; Oostende - New Comm CWGC Cemetery and Monument to HMS *Vindictive*.
• **[N.B.]** The following sites are indicated: 22nd Regiment Memorial, Houthulst; Pilot W. Coppens Memorial, Klerken; Käthe Kolwitz Tower, Lange Max Gun, Koekelaere; Calvary, Diksmuide; Mon to Belg 1st Grenadiers, Tervate; Plaque to Belg 3rd/23rd Regts of Line, Schoorbakkerbrug; Demarcation Stone, Fr 16 BCP Square, Ramskapelle; Memorial to French 81st Division, Nieuwpoort.
• **Total distance:** 39.0 miles
• **Total time:** 6 hours, 30 minutes
• **Distance from Calais:** see 1st, 2nd, 3rd Ypres Tour
• **Base towns:** Ieper, Dixsmuide, Ostende
• **Maps:** Belgian Survey 1:50,000 11/12 and 19/20

From the Grand' Place set your mileometer to zero and drive out round the Cloth Hall and turn left past St George's Church on Elverdingsestraat, passing the HQ of the CWGC on the right at No 82. Continue to the first roundabout and turn right signed A19, Veurne. Continue to the next roundabout and turn right on the N379 signed Centrum and turn left at the next main junction signed Diksmuide on the N369. Continue under the motorway bridge past Essex Farm CWGC Cemetery on the right. Continue on the N369 direction Diksmuide to the large cross on the left.

• Memorial to the 1st Victims of Gas, Steenstraat/6.1 miles/5 minutes/ Map 5a/1/Lat & Long: 50.91816 2.84107

This 15m high Cross of Reconciliation commemorates the victims of the 22 April 1915 gas attack. It replaces the original 1929 Memorial (designed by sculptor Real del Sartre which was blown up by the Germans in 1942 as they objected to the inscription which referred to them as 'Barbarians'). *Continue 200m to just before the large Steenstraete building on the right before the bridge over the Ieperlee Canal.*

• Memorial to Belgian 3rd Infantry Regiment, Merkem/6.2 miles/5 minutes/ Map 5a/2/Lat & Long: 50.91963 2.84370

Here is the large white cross surmounted by a Crusader's sword which is the Memorial to the 162 officers, NCOs and soldiers of the Regiment who fell at Steenstraat from 24 April to 10 May 1915, in the later stages of the German gas attacks.

Extra Visit to Memorial to the Brothers van Raemdonck. (Map 5a/3) Round trip: 1.00 mile. Approximate time: 45 mins.

Cross the Canal bridge and pull in on the slip road to the left. Here there is a sign 'Monument Gebruders Raemdonck'. Park. (**Lat & Long: 50.92075 2.84476**).
Walk to the Canal and turn right along the canal path which is a cycle path. Continue some half a mile to where a Flemish flag is flying by pylons some 200m after the pylons cross the canal.

A path leads to the impressive stone Memorial with large crosses on two of the sides. A Plaque commemorates the brothers Sergeant Edward (age 22) and Frans (age 20) van Raemdonck of 6 Komp 24 Linie and soldier Aimé Fievez of the same regiment. Many legends and myths have grown up about these three soldiers. In summary the company was ordered to cross the canal to take prisoners from the German position called the *Stampkopstelungen*. Frans was killed by a hail of bullets and against orders Edward insisted on trying to get his brother's body back. Some two weeks later their bodies were found (the story goes that they were locked in each others' arms) alongside the body of

Belgian 3rd Division memorial, Kippe.

A LA GLORIEUSE MEMOIRE
DES 152 OFFICIERS
SOUS-OFFICIERS ET SOLDATS
DU 3ᵉ REGIMENT DE LIGNE QUI, DU 24
AVRIL AU 10 MAI 1915, SONT TOMBES A
STEENSTRAAT, EN CONTRIBUANT A
BRISER L'OFFENSIVE ALLEMANDE
DECLENCHEE LE 22 AVRIL
AU MOYEN DE GAZ ASPHYXIANTS

Memorial to Belgian 3rd Inf Regt, Steenstraat, with detail of plaque.

Memorial to the Brothers van Raemdonck.

Memorial to the First Victims of Gas, Steenstraat.

Extra Visit continued

French-speaking soldier Fievez. The three were buried in Westvletern Belgian Cemetery under three marked headstones. In 1973 they were exhumed for burial in the crypt of the Ijzer Tower (qv). Only one coffin was discovered containing the mingled remains of the three soldiers. The headstones were left in situ and the remains moved to the crypt. Ironically this meant that a Walloon soldier was buried in this place sacred to Flemish Martyrs. Walloons maintain that Fievez was trying to assist the brothers and he has become a Walloon hero. Flemish nationalists revere the brothers as icons (Edward was a dedicated nationalist even before the war). Since the Ijzer Tower complex no longer welcomes extremist rallies, this area has become the focal point for their gatherings. The Monument was inaugurated on 19 August 1933 and is constructed from blocks from the *Stampkop* on a site that was in No Man's Land. There is a Plaque to their cousin, Clemens de Landtsheer, 1894-1984, who was a pioneer of the Ijzer Pilgimages and renowned film maker on nationalistic, military and folklore subjects.

Continue towards Kippe, crossing three 'beeks' (streams), the Lobeek, the St Jansbeek and the Langewadebeek.

• Memorial to Belgian 3rd Division, Kippe/8.2 miles/5 minutes/Map 5a/4/Lat & Long: 50.94545 2.86189

On the left is a large concrete Memorial, which looks like a chunk of a pill box, with the Division's battle honours and ORBAT.

Continue to the Kippe crossroads, signed to the right to Houthulst.

• Albertina Marker, Kippe/9.1 miles/5 minutes/Map 5a/2/Lat & Long: 50.95697 2.86572

This is one of the series of stone markers inaugurated on 17 February 1984 at Marche-les-Dames 50 years after the death of Albert 1 (and also 70 years after the start of the Great War) as a reminder of the events of that war. They bear the official monogram of the King and the shield of the Province of West Flanders. They were designed by Pieter-Hein Boudens.

The marker is to the left of the crossroads and commemorates the one-day battle of 17 April 1918 when the Belgian forces succeeded in halting the German offensive. There were heavy losses on both sides.

Continue straight on for some 0.3 miles to the statue on the left.

Albertina Marker, Kippe.

• Memorial to Armand Victor Van Eecke, Kippe/9.4 miles/5 minutes/ Map 5a/6/Lat & Long: 50.96195 2.86740

This fine statue of a young Belgian soldier age 22, killed on 9 September 1918, and erected by his parents, is surrounded on three sides by a tall hedge. On the base are his many honours and medals and a poem describing the loss of this young ex-student of Leuven High School who became an Adjutant (Officer Cadet) in the 5th Coy of the 3rd Inf Regt.

Turn round and return to the Albertina crossroads and turn left direction Houthulst. In the centre of Houthulst (13.7 miles) turn right on the N301 signed Militaire Begraafplaats and continue towards the forest.

The forest, which Napoleon called 'the key to the Low Countries', saw fierce action by the retreating Belgian army in 1914, when they suffered heavy losses. The occupying Germans strongly fortified the forest and from there directed their heavy artillery on the Allied lines. There was more fighting here in 1917 and finally in September 1918 when it was retaken by the Belgians. Large parts of the

Statue of Armand Victor Van
Eecke, Kippe.

Belgian Cemetery, Houthulst,
Italian headstone.

Renovated Belgian headstone in
Houthulst Belgian Cemetery.

forest are restricted military areas, some used by the Belgian Army Disposal Service which carries out controlled explosions of the Iron Harvest that is still being dug up by the ton.

Continue to the large cemetery on the left at the edge of the forest.

• Belgian Military Cemetery, Houthulst, Albertina Marker/14.3 miles/ 15 minutes/Map 5a/7/Lat & Long: 50.96654 2.94738

As well as containing 1,723 Belgian graves (the majority of whom fell in the 28/29 September 1918 liberation offensive), concentrated here in 1923-4 and of which 493 are unknown, the cemetery contains the graves of 81 Italian prisoners of war working in German labour camps. The other Belgian casualties in the area were repatriated to their home villages. The cemetery has an elaborate and imaginative lay-out which from the air would appear as a six-pointed star, within which are many circles, crescents and lines. Outside the wall at the end of the cemetery is an **Albertina Marker** to the Battle of Houthulst Forest of 28 September 1918.

The ruined wood, site of the as-yet un-landscaped Cemetery, was visited by Pres Wilson and his entourage from the Paris Peace Conference, accompanied by King Albert and Queen Elisabeth. It was part of their itinerary that started at Adinkerke, stopped along the Yser Canal near Nieuwpoort to examine the lock and visited some trench lines. The party had a congenial al fresco picnic, filmed by the Queen.

Turn round and return to Houthulst. Continue towards Diksmuide on the N301.

N.B. Just before leaving the village (15.4 miles) is a grey stone marker stone to the right to the **Belgian 22nd Inf Regt (Map 5a/8 Lat & Long: 50.97869 2.94457).**

Continue to the village of Klerken.

N.B. On the right in W. Coppens Plein (17.4 miles/**Map 5a/9/Lat & Long: 50.99587 2.91090**) is a small grey marker to **Heldhaftig Piloot W. Coppens** van de Belgische Luchtmachl 1914-1918, erected on 13.8.1967. Coppens started his career in 1912 with the 2nd Grenadiers who were to play such a large part in the defence of the Yser and then joined the Belgian Air Service, paying for his own training at a school in Hendon. On 14 October 1918 in a dog fight in which he was credited with his 37th victory he was shot down and suffered injuries which resulted in his losing his left leg. He later served as a military attaché. He died on 21 December 1986.

Plaque to Belgian WW2 Pilot W Coppens, Klerken.

Continue to the junction with the N35 (20.1 miles).

Extra Visit to the German Cemetery at Vladslo (Map 5/7/8: Lat & Long: 51.07071 2.93027). Round trip: 9 miles. Approximate time: 35 minutes.

Turn right to Esen and then left towards Vladslo. Continue through Vladslo and keep on the same winding road over the N363 following signs to Deutscher Soldaten Friedhof to the cemetery on the left.

By the forest known as the Praetbos, this cemetery contains 25,664 burials. Many soldiers were buried in the surroundings and in 61 small German Military Cemeteries in Belgium. In 1956 the *Deutsche Kriegsgräberfürsorge* undertook a huge programme of concentration and the original 3,233 remains buried in the cemetery beside a German First Aid Post in the woods were moved into the present cemetery of Vladslo. Because of the density of burials in such a small space, the cemetery is virtually one mass grave. Around the graves with their standard flat marker, each listing several names, are some of the original, non-standard headstones of the early days of the war.

The burial ground is enclosed by a beech hedge, the height of a man. Oak trees are planted amongst the ten plots. The visitor enters through a brick entrance hall where the roll of honour, in parchment books, is kept. At the back of the cemetery is the famous pair of statues, 'The Grieving Parents', created by the well-known artist and sculptress Käthe Kollwitz in memory of her son Peter, who is buried under the flat gravestone in front of the statues. For many years Kollwitz's original wooden cross was preserved in Roggeveld cemetery, Esen.

Plaque bearing Peter Kollwitz's name, ninth from top.

The Grieving Parents by Käthe Kollwitz, Vladslo German Cemetery

Born in Königsberg on 8 July 1867, Käthe, married to a doctor, was a graphic artist, specialising in etchings, woodcuts and lithographs. On 23 October 1914 her 18-year-old musketeer son, Peter, who had volunteered in Berlin, was killed near Esen, attacking the 11th Belgian Infantry Regiment holding the Yser at Diksmuide. It was a dreadful night. A Belgian officer described the seemingly suicidal attacks of the mainly young German forces in his diary:

"The enemy has concentrated many fresh troops opposite Diksmuide and given the order to take the town, cost what cost. Scarcely an assault has been beaten off, when they arrive again, with ever-increasing strength. What have they been promised to let themselves be killed in such large numbers? What strong drinks have been poured out to give them such a wild courage? Drunk from blood, with devilish faces and howling like beasts, they charge again and again, falling over the heaps of dead, trampling down the wounded with their heavy boots. They are mown down by the hundreds but are coming on again. Some of them are able to reach the breast-works where it comes to cruel hand-to-hand fighting, striking with rifle-butts, sticking with bayonets. Skulls are smashed, bodies are torn open apart; but all in vain, nowhere are they able to break through. Eleven times in the northerly and easterly sector, fifteen times in the southerly sector, the waves were smashed to death."

No wonder the Germans called these battles 'The Massacre of the Innocents'.

Käthe sought to express her personal grief in a tangible, artistic form, but anguished for years over the form it should take. Should it be a monument for her son alone, or for the entire grieving legion of mourning parents? Should it be one figure or two, should the figure of the dead child be included? Käthe became bitterly anti-war and her art expressed her strong pacifist feelings and her revulsion to bloodshed. Her style and beliefs were anathema to the rising National Socialist movement after the war in Germany and, when the group of figures was reaching completion in 1932, its final form was reviled by the Nazis. The father's tight-lipped expression, the way he clutches his body with his arms to comfort himself: the mother's attitude of total sorrow, her head bowed, her hand pressing her long gown to her cheek – all were perceived as expressions of weakness by the new

Extra Visit continued

regime. German parents should be proud to have sacrificed their son for the Fatherland. The statues were erected in nearby Esen, where Peter was originally buried, in July 1932, probably just in time to prevent their destruction by the Nazis. In 1956 the 1,539 Germans, among them Peter Kollwitz, were moved here from the small cemetery called Roggeveld near Esen. The statues moved with them.

There has been much dispute between the German and Belgian authorities over the statues, now highly regarded as a work of art. Their soft stone is deteriorating and the Germans wished to remove them back to the Fatherland. The Belgians refused and are deciding how best to preserve the grieving pair. In the meantime, the statues are encased in green wooden boxes during the potentially damaging winter months.

N.B. A little further on and to the right in the Praetbos is a house built in typical German style. Now a farmhouse, it served during the war as a rest house for German soldiers returning from the front line, much as did Talbot House in Poperinghe.

Some 4.8 kms further on is the Käthe Kollwitz Tower in Koekelare (**Map 5/8a, Lat & Long: 51.08956 2.97878**) which contains an exhibition of her life and work. **Open** Tues-Fri 0930-1200 and 1400-1700. Also Sat-Sun and holidays in July/Aug.

There are several charming cafés and restaurants in the main square where there is parking.

Also in Koekelaere, at Clevenstraat 6, is the small **German Marine Corps in Flanders Museum**, once the home of the famous **'Lange Max' gun. Open**: Sun, May-Sept 1400-1800, Tel: + (0) 497 33 58 35, (**Map 5/8b, Lat & Long: 51.11681 2.98234**).

Return to the junction with the N301.

Turn left at the T junction on the N35 to Diksmuide. Continue to the traffic lights in the town centre by the church on the left and turn right. Continue to the Grote Markt Square (20.6 miles).

Diksmuide. On 25 January 1920, Diksmuide was presented with the *Croix de Guerre* by President Poincaré, as it 'Won undying fame in the first days of the War by heroic, never-to-be-forgotten combats. Proved herself worthy of this glory by the fortitude with which she daily supported bombardments and fires, confident that her sacrifices were helping to save the Country and the Common Cause.' The award was well-deserved.

Dixsmuide was the scene of bitter fighting from 16 October to 10 November 1914. Here the 6,000 men of the French Naval Brigade *(Fusiliers Marins)* under the formidable Admiral Ronarc'h with the 5,000 strong Brigade of the Belgian 3rd Army under General Meiser held out for a month against a vastly superior enemy force. When they arrived in the pouring rain against the tide of retreating refugees the Yser was the only defence against the Germans. They immediately organised the construction of trenches around the town and fortified the bridges and dykes of the Yser Canal. They then sustained particularly violent attacks on 16-17 October and on 20 October heavy shellfire began to fall on the town and the civilians were forced to evacuate. Fires broke out and soon the town was in ruins. The Marines mounted heroic efforts to repel the attacks which culminated in the desperate battles of 24 October when the repeated German assaults resulted in hundreds of casualties on both sides. But still the heroic Marines stood firm until the advancing floods caused the Germans to turn their attention towards Nieuwpoort.

In November, however, the Germans renewed their attack on Dixsmuide. Some of the Belgian defences crumbled in the southern sector and the Germans entered the town through the breach when house-to-house fighting ensued. The Germans then placed unarmed prisoners at their head as they attacked the positions on the Yser. Among them was the Naval Lieutenant St Sérieyx who had fought with his men to the last cartridge. Asked by the Germans to point out a fordable place over the river and then to ask the remaining defending forces to surrender he defiantly jumped into the river, followed by his men, and swam to the other side.

That night the bridges and the Flour Mill (la Minoterie) on the banks of the river were blown up by the defenders who withdrew behind the embankment and Dixsmuide was then occupied by the Germans. For 4 years the French and Belgians in the opposing sector mounted continual attacks on the occupiers until on 29 September 1918 the ruins of Dixsmuide were finally retaken by the Belgians.

Continue to the Grote Market.

• Diksmuide Market Square/21.2 miles/15 minutes/Lat & Long: 51.03312 2.86450

In the square is the **Tourist Office** (at No 28, **open** 1000-1230 and 1300-1730, Tel: + (0) 51 51 91 46), the picturesque Town Hall and a statue to Gen Baron Jacques de Dixmude, who as Col J. Jacques commanded the 12th Belgian Inf Regt which defended the town at the end of October 1914. He went on to command the 3rd Division and was ennobled after the war. The statue was sculpted by Alfred Courtois and stands on a pedestal with statues at the four corners sculpted by his son, Antoine. There is a variety of attractive restaurants in the Square.

A square called Place d'Italie recalls that Diksmuide was the only town to receive the *Grande Croix d'Italie* from Mussolini in 1922. In the public park is a **Marker to the French Marines** and their Admiral, Ronarc'h, who defended the town from 16 October to 10 November 1914. It was erected in 1963.

Return to the traffic lights and turn right signed Veurne on the N35. Continue to the canal.

On the left is the **Hotel Sint Jan** (qv). This is on the site of the **Minoterie** (qv). Until the German occupation of World War II, there were preserved trenches here, which were destroyed when all metal was sent back to Germany to make munitions.

Cross the canal and turn left and follow signs to Ijzer Tower.

• Ijzer Tower/21.8 miles/40 minutes/Map 5/1/ Lat & Long: 51.03265 2.85410

Listed as an International Peace Centre, the tower is a symbol of Flemish nationalism, which came to a head during the First World War. Its history is long and complicated and goes back to the 18th Century when the rich vein of Flemish culture – art, music and literature, which had been influential for centuries throughout Europe – was suppressed by the French-speaking regime. After Waterloo, new links with the Dutch promised a 'window' of Flemish renaissance and King William 1 of Orange permitted a Dutch-speaking University in Ghent. But the 1830 Revolution, led by the French-speaking nobility, closed the window and set the clock back. During the 19th Century, Flemish intellectuals began working to build up a renewed Flemish identity, but when the First World War broke out in August 1914, all education was still being conducted in French and during the Yser campaign, 80 per cent of all officers in the Belgian army were French-speaking. The soldiers on the other hand were predominantly Flemish-speaking and resented their orders being given in French. Intellectuals, teachers, students and priests, disturbed by the situation, started a movement for Flemish identity that went far beyond the linguistic problem. To them it became a matter of human rights. At first the soldiers expressed their misery about the war in general through the medium of their desire for Flemish recognition, but soon the movement became more intensely nationalistic. In 1917 they addressed an open letter to the King expressing their unhappiness.

Although Albert was a fair and human man, he was above all a Belgian,

Stained glass window to the Brothers Raemdonck in the Chapel in the Ijzer Tower.

Aerial view of the Ijzer Tower complex. Just to the right and behind the top of tower the small Memorial Chapel to Comte Paul de Goussencourt (qv) may be seen in the fields.

'Rat-catcher' diorama - note the rat on the point of the bayonet and the dog) in the animals at War Exhibition, Ijzer Tower.

and a French-speaking one at that. His advisers warned him that he had to keep his country together at all costs – it was the period of general unrest and dissatisfaction: the Russian Revolution, mutinies in the French army. The Germans, occupying 90 per cent of Belgium, were deliberately attempting to inflame the two different linguistic elements. In 1916 they had allowed the re-opening of the Flemish University at Ghent.

The letter was ignored. Outspoken Flemish soldiers were penalised by their French-speaking officers with heavy oppression. 'Martyrs' were created, as explained in the crypt of the Tower. The Flemish artist Cpl Joe English, born in Bruges in 1882 of Irish antecedents, became the artist of the Yser Front and dedicated his art to the emancipation of the Flemish. There are many examples of his work in the Tower. English, who was an active member of the Association of Flemish Catholic Students, designed the provocative headstones in the shape of a Celtic cross with the inscription *Alles Voor Vlanderen: Vlanders Voor Kristus* ('All for Flanders: Flanders for Christ') that were erected on Flemish martyrs' graves to replace what was thought to be the inappropriate official cross with a French inscription. You will see them in and around the crypt and also above the crypt in Zonnebeke local cemetery. The military authorities

Headstone of the Brothers Raemdonck and Aimé Fievez in the Crypt of the Ijzer Tower.

defaced these 'Joe English' stones, which after the war could be seen in many local churchyards, by covering the inscription with concrete, or blowing them up and using the resultant rubble in road-building.

After the Armistice Flemish soldiers threatened to refuse to hand in their arms unless something was done about the language problem and a direct appeal was again addressed to the King. He promised palliatives but died in 1934 having done nothing radical to improve the situation. Flemish resentment ran high and what was to become an annual pilgrimage began in Diksmuide, the land around which was literally drenched with the blood of dead Flemish soldiers of the Yser campaign. What was originally a pilgrimage to commemorate the sacrifice of the Flemish soldiers of the Yser gradually took on a more political flavour.

On 16 March 1946 the opponents of Flemish nationalism blew up the 50 metre high tower that had been built in 1930 on the pilgrimage ground containing the graves of the most famous Flemish martyrs. The present 84 metre high tower – like a giant Joe English headstone – was soon built and a great Pax Gate erected using the rubble of the original tower. The new Crypt was inaugurated in 1958 and the Tower in 1965. It is still the focal point of an annual pilgrimage **on** the last Sunday in August which unfortunately has also occasionally been used by European right-wing extremists as a meeting point.

Today the country is still split between the more prosperous northern Flemish speaking area (about 60 per cent) and the southern French-speaking Walloons (about 40 per cent). In the middle is the uneasy capital Brussels, mostly French-speaking, but with bi-lingual street signs and duplicated ministries.

Extensive renovation has taken place over the past few years and the entire grounds are now enclosed and entry is through a turnstile. Further major restructuring will take place for the WW1 Centenary years from 2014. Telling the personal stories of soldiers, refugees and civilians on both sides, its aim is 'not the history of war itself but the perception of history' and its message is strongly 'No More War!' The Flemish emancipation struggle is widely examined.

Iron wreaths at the entrance are a reminder of the prison camps at Orne and Auvours where Flemish soldiers were incarcerated for their beliefs.

Open: Daily in Jan, Feb, March, Oct, Nov, Dec 1000-1700. April, May, June, July, Aug, Sept 1000-1800. **Closed** Dec 24-26, 31, Jan 1, 2 and for three weeks after the Christmas Holiday. Tel: +(0) 51 50 02 86. Fax: +(0) 51 50 22 58. e-mail: info@ysertoren.org, website: www.ysertoren.org.

Beyond the great Peace Gate you will approach the Crypt, at whose entrance is a Calvary, which has push-button talking machines in several languages which tell the story of the martyrs (Joe English, Renaat de Rudder, the brothers Van Raemdonck (qv), Frans Van der Linden, Frans Kusters, Bert Willems and Juui De Winde) buried there. Above the crypt are the words, 'Here are our bodies, like seed in the sand, hope for the harvest, oh Flanders.'

The Tower, which was declared 'A Memorial to Flemish Emancipation' on 23 December 1986, has a large entrance hall with an audio-visual presentation of *In Flanders Fields – WW1*, a Chapel with stained glass windows by Eugeen Yoors (mainly from Joe English drawings) and a shop. On the lower floor is a reconstructed dugout. A lift takes you up to the Panorama hall on the 22nd floor with its 144 windows with magnificent views over the battlefield of the Yser, extending as far as Mount Cassel on a clear day, and a 67 square metres painting. Each floor on the way up has a different exhibition. They deal with the fight for the Dutch language, the Student Movement, the conduct of what they call the 'Stupid War', the Armistice, the consequences of War and growing Flemish power.

Return to the crossroads and go straight over.

N.B. On the left is a large white **Calvary (Lat & Long: 51.03549 2.85467),** a religious monument that was dedicated to all the soldiers and civilians who died in the Great War. It was a National statement to counter the very Flemish statement made by the Ijzer Tower. On 23 September 1928 it was solemnly blessed by the Bishop of Bruges in the presence of the Duke and Duchess of Brabant, the future King Leopold III and Queen Astrid. The Calvary was once the object of large pilgrimages.

Continue and stop at the large red brick building on the right.

View of the trenches and the Ijzer River.

Belgian Memorial at the Trenches of Death.

• Trenches of Death, Demarcation Stone, Diksmuide/22.9 miles/20 minutes/Map 5/3/ Lat & Long: 51.04586 2.84297

The old entrance building erected by the Touring Club of Belgium, which bore a plaque proclaiming it was a listed building, underwent extensive rebuilding and modernising in 2002 when it changed from private to provincial ownership. It contains many fascinating original photographs which graphically show the horror of life in the trenches in this sector. Stairs lead to an upstairs room which gives good views over the battlefield.

Behind it is an imposing **Memorial** proclaiming 'Here our Army held the invader in check 1914-1918'.

Open: 1 April-15 November every day, 1000-1700. 16 November-31 March, 0930-1600, Tues & Fri. Tel: + (0)51 50 53 44.

The trenches themselves are marvellously preserved in concrete and one can walk through them to the Demarcation Stone at the end and then return along the parapet. Its galleries, shelters, firesteps and chicanes, concreted duckboards and sandbags give a realistic idea of a working trench.

This was the Belgian forward defence line throughout the whole of the Yser battles (see 'Battles of the Yser' above) separated from the enemy only by the River Yser itself. For fifty months the men in it were subjected to attack by shell and mine, grenade and bullet. Sometimes the Germans infiltrated the trench and there was hand-to-hand fighting. Death was never far away, hence the sinister name, *'Boyau de la Mort'*.

After the land between Diksmuide and Nieuport had been deliberately flooded at the end of October 1914 to halt the Germans, the trenchline was dug by soldiers totally exposed to German fire. Progress was then continued by saps. Sentry boxes and observation points were set up, the most famous being the Mousetrap, with loopholes on three sides of its concrete walls, which was erected in 1917. The trench line was exposed to the Germans on three sides. Lethal snipers from the trenches on the German bank were particularly effective. The Germans also built strong fortifications on their side of the river, one of the most notorious being the 'Flour Mill' (*Minoterie*) on the right bank opposite the present Ijzer Tower, with machine-gun and grenade launchers permanently targeted on the trench.

The King and Queen of the Belgians.

Our Lady's Memorial Chapel complex from the ruined tower.

Lekeux in his OP.

Lekeux with the famous unexploded shell.

St George.

Demarcation Stone with inscription 'Here the Invader was Brought to a Halt'.

After the war the first Belgian **Demarcation Stone** (qv) was unveiled here on Easter Sunday 1922 by King Albert of the Belgians. Their Touring Club had raised the necessary 250,000 Francs for the erection of the Belgian stones. It was a glorious occasion, with flags and garlands, a huge crowd including many veterans and war wounded, and, according to the magazine, *Le Courrier de l'Armée,* 'vibrant' speeches from the representatives of the French and Belgian Touring Clubs.

Communications to the Belgian rearlines were made by two footbridges, well known to the Germans. One led to Kaaskerke, the village whose spire can be seen to the left. Over this bridge under the cover of darkness soldiers brought sacks of earth to repair their parapets. The other led to Lettenburg on the Nieuport road and this was used to carry wounded to the rear and to bring up supplies and ammunition. A Decauville narrow gauge railway (like those built on the Somme) was constructed to bring up the heavy mortar shells.

The soldiers manning the trench spent three days in its hell to be followed by three days of rest in the rearline villages.

Continue past the trenches and keep left at the Y junction signed to O-L [Our Lady] Vrouwhoekje, with the Yser to the right. Continue to the right turn signed to O-L Vrouwhoekje. Do not turn right but continue to the left to an Albertina Marker on the left.

• *Albertina Marker, Old Railway Line/23.8 miles/5 minutes/Map 5/4/ Lat & Long: 51.04808 2.82471*

The old railway line, now a cycle path, runs left to right. An Information Board describes the importance of Line No 74, the 13.5km track from Diksmuide to Nieuport, which marked the Belgian front line after the flooding. The **Albertina Marker** commemorates the Battle of the Yser, 18-31 October 1914.

It is now possible during your tour to clearly identify the land that was flooded. The cycle track forms the left hand or western boundary and the Yser the right hand or eastern boundary.

Turn round and immediately turn left on Oud Stuivekens, following signs to O-L Vrouwekerke (Vrouwehoekje) finally making a sharp (easily missed) right hand turn along a narrow cobbled road to the Chapel and tower on the left.

• *O-L Vrouwehoekje (Our Lady of the Victory) Memorial Chapel, Memorials, Observation Tower, Demarcation Stone, Oud-Stuivekens- kerke/25.1 miles/20 minutes/Map 5/5/Lat & Long: 51.05877 2.83235*

This chapel, inaugurated on 6 September 1926, was built on the site of the old church. All but the tower was demolished and this was fortified and used by the Belgians as an OP and shelter. In the ruins of the tower stairs lead up to an Orientation Table and superb views over the battlefield. On the tower wall is a Plaque to Martial Lekeux, who commanded the shelter. Beside it is a Demarcation Stone inscribed 'Dixmuide' in remarkably pristine condition, the inscription 'Here the Invader was brought to a halt' still clearly readable. The inscription goes that it was not defaced by the Germans during WW2 as were most of the Markers because the local farmer hid it in a pile of sugar beet!

Between the tower and the Chapel is a **Monument to the Cyclist Carabiniers**, christened by the Germans 'The Black Devils' as their dark green uniforms appeared almost black, and beyond it a **Memorial to the 5th Lancers**. Around the Chapel are 41 stone markers with Belgian Regimental badges. Inside it are several memorial tablets and the most beautiful **stained glass windows** including remarkable portraits of the Belgian King and Queen, the Patron Saints of the Infantry (St Maurice), the Artillery (St Barbara), the French Army (St Ludovic), the French Airforce (N-D de Lorette) and St Martial etc. Two windows commemorate **Edouard Lekeux**, one showing him as an artillery officer, the other describing the incident when a shell entered the shelter but did not explode. This was ascribed to the presence of a statue of the Virgin Mary and Child, a large version of which stands in the centre of the windows. Lekeux was in a Seminary before the war, enlisted when it broke out and after the war became a Franciscan Monk with the name Martial.

The chapel is open during the summer months but if locked the key is held in the house opposite. A ceremony of remembrance is held here each year on the last Friday in August. Attached to the farm behind the Chapel is an original **Bunker**.

Return to the last junction and turn right. Continue some 20m to the Albertina Marker on the right.

• Albertina Marker, Heron Stream/25.4 miles/5 minutes/Map 5/6/Lat & Long: 51.06106 2.82710

This is to the Reigers Vliet (Heron Brook), The Great Watch 1914-1918. Herons are occasionally seen here today.

Continue.

You are now driving through the area that was flooded in 1914 with the Heron Brook (which is parallel to the Yser) on the right and the railway line to the left.

Continue following signs to the village of Viconia Kleiputten.

The village was destroyed during the war and rebuilt further along the road after the war.

After the Church on the left turn right and continue following signs to the Château.

• Albertina Marker, Viconia Château/26.7 miles/5 minutes/Map 5/9/Lat & Long: 51.07558 2.82718

After crossing the river (see below), the Germans' first action was to take the Château. The Albertina Marker records that this was a forward post (actually of course a German one) as it was on somewhat higher ground than its flat surroundings. The Château is now an hotel (**Gasthof Kasteelhoeve Viconia**. 23 rooms. Tel: + (0)51 55 52 30. E-mail: info@viconia.be website: www.viconia.be **Closed** during the winter.)

Continue.

The German advance was towards you as you drive, still in what was the flooded area. Ahead is the Yser Dyke (Ijzer Dijk). The Germans were on the other side of the Yser.

Turn left at the dyke and stop on the left at the Albertina Marker by the bus stop.

• Tervate Bridge Albertina Marker/27.4 miles/5 minutes/Map 5/10/Lat & Long: 51.08035 2.83971

On the opposite bank of the Yser the remains of the old bridge can be made out. This is where the Germans crossed having repaired the small bridge that was partially destroyed by the Belgians. The Albertina Marker to the left records the events of 21-23 October 1914 here. It was this crossing that threatened the whole of the Belgian defences and was only stopped by a combination of the flooding and the determination of the 2nd Battalion of the 1st Grenadiers (qv). The German attack, made at night, had been a surprise, and if it had succeeded it would have outflanked Dixmuide and Nieuport, the two keys to the defensive line. Oddly, in 1940 as the British prepared a defensive perimeter around Dunkirk, the Germans found a small unguarded sheep bridge over the Dunkirk-Veurne canal and crossed it, nullifying the British defences. It could have happened here.

Continue to a right turn to Nieuwpoort. Turn right and continue.

N.B. To the left is a **Monument to the 2nd Bn, Belgian 1st Grenadiers (Map 5/11/Lat & Long: 51.08140 2.84396)**, an elite regiment commanded by Major d'Oultremont which held the Germans here and at Tervate. Meanwhile its sister regiment the 2nd Grenadiers were fighting below Ramskapelle (qv). Both had been in the conflict from the beginning and their soldiers, a mixture of professionals and militiamen, were cold and tired. But they held on.

Remains of the old Tervate bridge across the Yser.

Albertina Marker at the Tervate Bridge.

Plaque to the 3rd/23rd Regiment of Line, Schoorbakkestraat, now disappeared.

Monument to 2nd Bn, Belgian 1st Grenadiers, Tervate.

The Old Station House, Pervyse.

Continue along the Yser Dyke to the junction with the N302 at the Schoorbakkerbrug.

> **N.B.** On the **Schoorbakkerbrug** ahead was a **Plaque to the 3rd/23rd Regiment of Line** who defended it in 1914. On our last picture-taking recce it had disappeared and none of the historians in the area could track it down.

Turn left on Schoorbakkestraat towards Pervijze. Continue to the outskirts and an easily-missed red brick house on the right.

• The Old Station House, Pervyse/32.0 miles/5 minutes/Map 5/13/Lat & Long: 51.07516 2.79859

Now a private house but still with the original 'PERVYSE' white sign clearly visible, this is on the line of the old railway (running left to right over the road) and there are Information Boards beside it. During the war there was an OP on top of the station and the houses on the edge of the village were made into machine gun shelters.

Continue to the village church.

There is a green CWGC sign on the entrance and buried in the churchyard **is Flying Officer A. Robertson**, R. Can Airforce, 29 November 1943 (**Map 5/14**).

Turn left on the Dixsmuide N35 road and some 400 yards later on the right is an Albertina Marker.

• Pervyse Albertina Marker and Observation Tower/Site of Billets of 'The Two'/32.4 miles/20 minutes/Map 5/15/16/Lat & Long: 51.07215 2.79257

Behind the **Albertina** is the ruin of the WW1 OP Tower. The upper brick-built section was constructed by the Germans in WW2. It is the ruined tower of St Nicholas Church, used as an OP in 1914 after it was dynamited by the Belgians in October.

Here in Pervyse a pair of extraordinary women known as 'The Two', Elsie Knocker – later Baroness T'Serclaes – and Mairie Chisholm, Chief of her clan – set up, against all odds and much opposition, their first-aid post to support the Belgian Army. They had met before the war through their shared passion for motorbikes and again when they joined in August 1914 Dr Hector Monro's Volunteer Ambulance Corps. The eccentric Scottish doctor gathered together a piece-meal force of two doctors, a Padre, three male stretcher bearers and a bevy of enthusiastic women with a mixture of nursing, driving and organisational skills. Rejected by the War Office the British, French and American Red Cross they were eventually accepted by the Belgian Red Cross and permitted to travel to the fluctuating Belgian front. From Ghent they were driven back to Dunkirk by the advancing German tide through streams of refugees and the wounded, all the time giving what assistance they could.

When the Allied defensive line was formed along the Yser they returned to Belgium and worked wherever they saw a need. They set up temporary bases in and around Dixsmuide and Furnes (Veurne). Eventually 'The Two' established themselves in a cellar in the shattered village of Pervyse. From there they sallied forth at night, often under fire, to bring in the wounded to tend.

Although disapproved of by many of the British 'top Brass' their bravery and fortitude soon became legendary. They were visited by a succession of VIPs including Marie Curie (who was running an X-ray unit at Furnes), Sir Bernard Dawson (Chief Medical Officer of the BEF), the King and Queen of the Belgians (who created them Knights of the Order of Leopold II), Prince Alexander of Teck and Bruce Bairnsfather (who drew a cartoon specially for Elsie).

Elsie (who was divorced after an unhappy first marriage and with a child who was to be killed as a pilot in WW2 – Wing Commander K. D. Knocker on 3 July 1942) managed to snatch the time

OP Tower and Albertina Marker, Pervyse.

Cartoon drawn for the Baroness de T'Serclaes by Bruce Bairnsfather.

Christmas Truce Figures, Old Station, Ramskapelle.

to marry a Belgian pilot, the Baron Harold de T'Serclaes, but he was killed soon after their brief honeymoon. The Two were eventually accepted by the Establishment and awarded the MM and the Order of St John of Jerusalem. When the British took over the Pervyse sector in July 1917, however, they were again under threat of ejection by Gen Sir Henry Rawlinson. Elsie stood her ground: 'The General had to admit defeat', she reported, and they were allowed to continue. The authors had several long-range UK to Canada conversations with her.

Their truly horrific and remarkable wartime experiences are graphically described in the Baroness's biographies, *The Cellar House at Pervyse* and *Flanders and Other Fields* and more recently, *Elsie & Mairi Go to War* by Diane Atkinson and *Op Naar de Grote Oorlog – Mairi, Elsie en de Anderen in Flanders Fields* by Patrick Vanleene. This Flemish language book contains some superb photographs and Patrick has identified for us the location of the principal posts used by The Two. **Please respect the fact that these are on private land**

1. The Cellar house - their first post: Schoorbakkerstraat 33. The modern house is built on top of the original cellar **(Lat & Long: 51.07496 2.79838).**

2. The 'sick and sorry' House - their second post: Veurnestraat 22, now the **Café Druivenhof.** The building was rebuilt in a completely different style to the original **(Lat & Long: 51.07346 2.79186)**

3. The House with Sandbags – their third post: Veurnestraat 7. It is now a small farmhouse but rebuilt in a similar style **(Lat & Long: 51.07346 2.79228).**

Turn round, return to the church and follow signs to Nieuwpoort on the N355. Turn right on the N356 signed to Ramskapelle.

To the right along the embankment of the old railway lines are the vestiges of many Belgian shelters or bunkers **(Map 5/7)**. Most of them were built in brick from the ruins of local houses destroyed during the combat but there are the occasional concrete ones which could be from WW2. They can really only be seen by taking the cycle path.

Continue into Ramskapelle.

'The Two' in their Wolseley Ambulance, presented by Sutton Coldfield and District St John Ambulance, Pervyse 1917.

Ramskapelle was strategically placed on the railway to Dixsmuide and on the edge of the flooded area. On 30 October it was captured by the Germans just as the flood waters reached it. Its loss was crucial as there were no lines of defences in its rear. A desperate counter-attack was mounted preceded by a fierce artillery bombardment followed by a bayonet charge to the sound of bugles by the remnants of the Belgian 6th, 7th and 14th Regiments and the 2nd Grenadiers, all supported by the French 42nd Infantry Division. The enemy was thrown into disorder, Ramskapelle was recaptured and as the flood waters crept slowly forward the line re-established.

Geoffrey Malins, the official war film maker, came out to Belgium at the end of 1914 and on his first visit to the battlefields arrived here at Ramskapelle. He commented,

'What a terrible sight it was. The skeletons of houses stood grim and gaunt and the sound of the wind rushing through the ruins was like the moaning of the spirits of the dead inhabitants crying aloud for vengeance. The sounds increased in volume as we neared this scene of awful desolation and the groans became a crescendo of shrieks which, combined with the crash of shellfire, made one's blood run cold.'

Continue to the main square and stop on the right by the churchyard wall.

• Franco-Belgian Plaque, Ramskapelle/35.5 miles/5 minutes/Map 5/18/Lat & Long: 51.10941 2.76219

The Plaque commemorates the bayonet charge of 31 October 1914 by the **French 16th Chasseurs à Pied** (Light Infantry) and the **Belgian 6th Regiment** (the 'Blue Devils'). It was erected on 30 October 1938.

Opposite the Church is the **Restaurant Taverne de Lanternfanter.** closed Mon. Tel: + (0) 58 23 56 80 email: maertenklaas@skynet.be which makes an excellent lunch stop.

Turn immediately right past the churchyard signed to the Station on Hemmestraat. Continue to the overhead lights marking the old railway line/cycle path and ruins on the right behind a modern house.

• The Old Station, Ramskapelle/14th Regiment Plaque/ Christmas Truce Sculptures/Albertina Marker /35.8 miles/10 minutes/Map 5/19/Lat & Long: 51.11079 2.76715

The station which played an important part in the battle has been left as it was when abandoned in 1918. It had served as an observation point for the first line. Beside it is a **Plaque to the 14th Regiment of Line**, October 1914. There are Information Boards here and an Albertina Marker to The Battle of the Yser 18-31 October 1914. By turning right after the Regimental Plaque, a striking sculpture showing the busts of a Belgian, a British and a German soldier is on the left beside the ruin. It was unveiled on 29 January 2009 and is by self-taught sculptor William Livermore of Durbuy. It commemorates the Christmas Truce and is entitled *Verbroedering 25-12-1914*. It is to be taken symbolically or allegorically as there was no Christmas Truce in this area. Beside it is a small Plaque to the 14th Line Regiment and remnants of railway buffers and a picnic table.

Extra Visit to Memorial to Halifax Crash (Map 5/19a/Lat & Long: 51.10839 2.78546) Round trip: Approx 2 miles. Approximate time: 10 minutes.

Continue over the old railway line to the Memorial on the left surrounded by a fence and hedge. The Memorial is near the site where at 1604 hours on 28 July 1944 **Halifax EY-XMZ340** of 78 Squadron crashed, killing its pilot, **Flying Officer Lt William Gladstone Hoffman**, age 21. Hoffman had been hit by flak after dropping 16 25kg bombs on St Joris and managed to fly on to avoid Nieuwpoort before crashing here. His crew managed to

*Franco-Belgian Bayonet Charge Plaque,
Ramskapelle Church.*

*Memorial to Halifax Crash, July 1944,
Ramskapelle.*

Belgian Cemetery, Ramskapelle.

*Demarcation Stone and Windmill 16
B.C.P French Memorial, Ramskapelle.*

Extra Visit continued

parachute out but the chute of **Flying Officer Russell Harty Winter,** age 29, failed to open and he was killed. Five other crew members landed safely but were taken prisoner. Two civilians, Desiré Verhaeverbeke age 33 and Marie Couvreur age 36 were also killed. Hoffman and Winter are buried in St Joris Communal Cemetery.

Every year a ceremony of remembrance is held here with family members and local people. In the **Lantern Taverne** (qv) is a picture commemorating the event.

Return to the church.

N.B. By turning left along Molenstraat and continuing to the end of the road, on a landscaped area to the right there is a **Demarcation Stone** (**Map 5/20a, Lat & Long: 51.10917 2.75905**) in good condition. Its caption 'Here the Invader was brought to standstill' in three languages and the fact that it was a gift of the *Société Générale de Belgique* Touring Club of Belgium is still clear. Behind it is a model windmill with the caption 'SQUARE 16 Franse Jagers', **French 16th Chasseurs à Pied**, 16 B.C.P. Français, 30-10-1914.

Turn right and continue to the cemetery on the right.

• Belgian Cemetery, Ramskapelle/36.3 miles/10 minutes/Map 5/20/Lat & Long: 51. 11387 2.76363

There are 632 graves, 400 of which are unknown, concentrated here after the war. Outside the wall is an **Albertina Marker.**

The old railway ran from behind the cemetery across the road ahead.

Continue under the E40 motorway.

We are now back in the flooded area.

Continue over the Noordvaart Bridge to the T junction with the N367.

It was at this point that the water flooded in from the sea.

Extra Visits to Unie Bridge Memorials, St Joris Memorials (Map 5/23/24/22) Round trip: 3.0 miles. Approximate time: 30 minutes.

Turn right at the T junction and continue through St Joris to Oud St Joris. On the right is the local cemetery with a green CWGC sign.

In it is a row of **9 CWGC WW2 graves**, including an RAF Crew of six, 13 March 1942.

Continue under the motorway to just before the bridge over the Ijser and stop just before the Mannekensver sign on the ramp to the right.

To the right is a grey stone semi-circular **Memorial to the 14th Regiment of Line** (Lat & Long: 51.12690 2.80077) who 'defended the last tattered remnants of their Fatherland on 22nd, 23rd, 24 October 1914 where 900 heroes spilled their blood.' In front of it is a polished black marble column.

Cross the road and walk down to the statue by the bank of the Ijzer.

The fine statue of a **Granite Soldier** mounts guard over the river. He represents the 7th Regiment of Line who lost heavily to artillery and machine-gun fire. They held the line here until the 22nd when they were relieved by the 14th

Granite Soldier guarding the Yser, Unie Bridge.

Extra Visit continued

Regiment. The bridge is called the 'Unie' or 'Union' Bridge and was taken by the Germans on 24 October. The Belgian artillery, often working without any cover, stubbornly resisted the German assaults, hauling guns up on the river bank into the infantry lines. They then scored some direct hits on the houses in which the Germans concealed their machine guns. However the Germans outflanked the bridge and the 14th had to withdraw beyond St Joris (St George) where you go next.

Turn round and continue to the church on the right in St Joris.

On the roadside just before the church is a **Memorial to the 3rd Belgian Carabiniers /Map 5/22(Lat & Long: 51.12986 2.77918)** who distinguished themselves here against Units of the German Navy on 22 April 1918.

By the church is the **Tomb of Lt-Gen Baron Dossin de Saint-Georges** (1854-1936) who on 20 October 1914 ordered the flooding of the Nieuwendamme Polder, a week before the flooding of the Yser Plain.

Memorial to 3rd Belgian Carabiniers, St Joris.

Tomb of Baron Dossin de Saint-Georges, St Joris Church.

Return to the T junction.

Turn left. Continue on the N367 past the T-junction direction De Panne. On the left is

• Ramscapelle Road Military CWGC Cemetery/Nieuport Communal CWGC Cemetery/37.4 miles/30 minutes/Map 5/21/Lat & Long: 51.12872 2.76787

Most of Plot I of the cemetery was made in July and August 1917 when the British XV Corps held the front line from St George's (now Sint Joris) near Ramskapelle to the sea. It was considerably enlarged after the Armistice from isolated graves and small cemeteries in the surrounding battlefields. Here are now 841 WW1 burials, 312 of whom are unknown. There are two Special Memorials to men originally buried at Nieuport whose graves were destroyed by shell fire and who are known to be buried here. The cemetery was designed by Sir Edwin Lutyens.

Continue to the local cemetery to the left.

Just past the petrol station is the vast **Nieuport Communal Cemetery (Lat & Long: 51.13016**

Ramscapelle Road Military Cemetery.   *CWGC Plot, Nieuwpoort Communal Cemetery.*

2.76456) which contains 70 WW1 burials in two plots, one of 19 and the other of 51 by a Cross of Sacrifice, mostly from June-August 1917, 3 of them unknown, and in a separate plot by the rear left hand hedge 31 WW2 graves from the withdrawal to Dunkirk in 1940.

To the right of the WW1 Plot is the imposing **Memorial to Hendrik Geeraert**, 'the hero of the flooding', the lock keeper who actually opened the flood gates in Nieuport, and **14-18 and 40-45 Plaques**.

Continue to the Demarcation Stone on the left.

• Demarcation Stone/37.8 miles/5 minutes/Map 5/25/Lat & Long: 51.13279 2.76076

This stone by the Witte Brug is in excellent condition and still bears its inscription.

Opposite is the **Hotel Martinique** 3-star with restaurant – excellent cuisine – 5 en-suite bedrooms, Tel: + (0) 58 04 08 e-mail: info@hotelmartinique.be

Continue on the N367 to the T junction with the N380 and turn left into Nieuwpoort.

Note that the spelling of the town is now variable between 'Nieuwpoort', the modern day spelling and 'Nieuport', the '14-'18 version!

Immediately park on the right in front of the bridge ahead. In the small park to the right is

• Plaque to Lt Calberg, Monument to the Yser/38.0 miles/10 minutes/ Map 5/26/27/Lat & Long: 51.13401 2.75810

On the small brick monument is a **Plaque** that commemorates the special engineer company ('*Sapeurs et Pontonniers*'– Engineers and Bridgebuilders) that was formed on 2 September 1915 to continue to control the flood plains of the Yser. Calberg was mortally wounded here at the lock on 16 October 1917 and died in hospital.

The remarkable **Yser Monument**, designed by Pieter Braecke, is in the form of a woman (*La Belgique*) who turns away from the enemy protecting the Belgian crown in her hands. Around her are a blind soldier, a wounded soldier, a sick soldier and a fit soldier, representing the resistance.

It was inaugurated on 26 October 1930 by the League of National Souvenir, whose President was Prince Mérode and whose bust is shown in *bas relief*. The monument overlooks the Albert I Memorial (visited later) and the complicated complex of sluices known as the 'Goose's Foot'.

The sluice gates at Nieuport control the amount of water that is allowed to remain in the polder (reclaimed land) that lies between the town and Dixmude. The arrangement is referred to locally as De Ganzepoot (the Goose's Foot). A simpler analogy might be to imagine that one's

Detail of the Yser Memorial.

Figure of La Belgique, Yser Memorial, Nieuwpoort.

body is the sea, the arm represents the channel from the sea to Nieuport, one's wrist the lock gates and one's spread fingers the waterways that reach across the land. Thus by opening the gates at the wrist the flood waters can spread over the polder from the body, down the arm and then through the fingers to the polder.

Cross the first of the 6 waterways.

This is the **Veurne Ambacht.**

Immediately after the bridge on the right is

• *Albertina Marker/38.1 miles/5 minutes/Map 5/28/ Lat & Long: 51.13354 2.75740*

This stone at the Sluizenbrug marks the flooding of 29 October 1914.

Cross the second waterway.

This is the **Veurnevaart Veurnesluis.**

Continue to the T junction. Turn right and stop.

• Bust to Hendrik Geeraert/38.1 miles/5 minutes/Map 5/31/30/Lat & Long: 51.13328 2.75615

This small head is on the wall of the Café De Sluiswachter to the left.

Beyond is the old Taverne De Gansepoot (Goose Foot) where there is a blind alcove on the facade. This is where Geeraert's bust should have been erected (and which still bears the inscription to 'H. Geeraert, Batelier *Chef Eclusier, Inondeur Yser'* – Chief Lock Keeper and Flooder of the Yser – 1914-1918), but in a splendid piece of lateral thinking it was decided to place it on the other café, one of his favourite drinking holes. Geeraert , who was a ship's captain, died in 1925 and was buried in Nieuport Communal Cemetery (qv) with great pomp. [Note that in March 2012 the building was for sale.]

Opposite it on the right is a 1942 **WW2 Memorial** (**Map 5/29**).

Continue to "where the road meets the roundabout".

Monument to the Hero of the Flooding, Hendrik Geeraert, Nieuport Cemetery.

The Bust of Hendrik Geeraert, Hero of the Flooding.

Where the Bust should have been.

Extra Visit to Coxyde Mil CWGC Cemetery (Lat & Long: 51.10363 2.64307). Round trip: 10 miles. Approximate time: 40 minutes.

From the roundabout take the second exit on the N34 leading towards the coast at Nieuwpoort Bad, with the tramline to the left, and beyond it a great selection of restaurants and on the right a line of recent residential buildings. Turn left at the first traffic lights onto Astridlaan. Some 500m later turn right on the N396, Canadalaan, to Oostduinkerke. Continue to Koksijde on the N396.

Coxyde, as it was known during the war, was some 10 kilometres behind the front line (although occasionally shelled) and the village was used for rest billets. Here the cartoonist **Bruce Bairnsfather**, who had just been created the first ever 'Officer Cartoonist', was attached to the French when he was requested by their Intelligence Department to come and draw the *Poilu* in the trenches. They had seen the extraordinary effect that his collection of cartoons, *Fragments From France*, had had on British morale. Based at the French HQ Bairnsfather was taken round their trenches day after day – an experience that he found depressing in the extreme, compounded by his inability to communicate in their language. Nevertheless he found the French Officer's Mess devoid of 'that frigid atmosphere which some of our headquarters can and do assume'.

Headstone of Lt T.E. Hulme, Coxyde Military Cemetery.

In Koksijde centre continue on the N396 towards de Panne and some 500m beyond the village on the right are the gates and the beautiful landscaped path leading to

Coxyde Military CWGC Cemetery

The cemetery was started by the French and was mostly free from the shelling. When the British took over from the French in this sector in June 1917 it became one of the most important Commonwealth cemeteries along the coast and was used at night for the burial of the dead brought back from the front line. The French took over again in December 1917 and continued to use the cemetery. During 1918 British Naval casualties from the Dunkirk naval base were buried here. It was again used in WW2 during the defence of the Dunkirk-Nieuport Perimeter in May 1940. It now contains 1,507 UK burials of WW1 and 154 from WW2, 22 of them unknown, most from the Defence of Dunkirk and Airmen throughout the war. The French graves have been removed. Here the critic, philosopher and poet **Lt T[homas] E[rnest] Hulme** (qv), killed on 28 September 1917 at Nieuport with the RM Artillery, is buried. There are also 3 unfortunate 'Shot at Dawns': **Pte W. Wycherley**, 12 Sept 1917; **Sapper A. Oynes**, 20 Oct 1917 and **Rfm Cheeseman**, 20 Oct 1917.

The path to Coxyde Military Cemetery.

The Cemetery Report contains interesting details of the manner of death of many of the men buried here. For instance **Lt A.J.L O'Beirne** of 57 Sqn RFC, Queens Own Oxford Hussars, age 29, died of wounds in aerial combat on 28 July 1917 while on long-distance reconnaissance from the Ypres area. He was the only son of Major O'Beirne of the R Warwicks.

The Cemetery was designed by Sir Edwin Lutyens.

Return to "where the road meets the roundabout" in Nieuwpoort.

Drive onto the roundabout.

N.B. By driving round it to the fourth exit and turning down it on Koningen Elisabethlaan two more Memorials may be visited. The street changes its name to Willem de Roolan at the junction with Langestraat. At this point on the wall on the left of house No 2 is a small bronze **Plaque to the site of shelter for 20 men of the Sapeurs and Pontonniers (Lat & Long: 51.13194 2.75674).**

Further down Willem de Roolaan on the right is the ruin of the St Laurent Tower, also known as the Dove Tower. This 13th Century tower was part of a church. It was destroyed in 1916 by enemy fire. On it is a large bronze **Plaque to the Sapeurs and Pontonniers (Lat & Long: 51.13082 2.75741)** and commemorates the flooding of the Yser at Nieuport, 1914-1918.

Plaque to Shelter for 20 Sapeurs & Pontonniers, Nieuwpoort.

From the roundabout take the fifth exit right past the Geeraert Bust and turn left on the N380. Cross the Veurnevaart and the next waterway, the Veurne Ambacht. Continue to the next bridge, the Ieper Brug, over the Ijzer River. Keep left and continue over the Kreek Nieuwen Damme and continue to the obelisk immediately on the left.

N.B. This **Memorial is to several French Regiments of the 81st Division** - Infantry, the Artillery, the Cuirassiers and the Engineers (**Map 5/32, Lat & Long: 51.13589 2.75787).**

Continue over two more waterways to the large parking area and stop.

• Memorial to King Albert 1/New De Ganzepoot Museum/British Memorial to the Missing, Nieuport/39.0 miles/50 minutes/Map 5/34/33 /Lat & Long: 51.13673 2.75535

In the car park is an Information Board describing how the bricks in the King Albert Memorial were made of mud from the Yser Plain.

The impressive King Albert I Memorial, erected on the initiative of Belgian veterans, is beside the lock gates at Nieuwpoort. The brick rotunda was designed by Julien De Ridder. It surrounds a mounted statue of the king sculpted by Karel Aubroek and was inaugurated on 24 July 1938 in the presence of the Royal Family. On the wall behind the equestrian statue of the King is a bronze plaque to the German-born Queen Elisabeth (which was damaged by a bomb at the end of WW2) and around the rotunda are panels representing the spiritual and industrial life of Belgium and within are inscribed two poems by August Van Cauwelaert. A lift (which is closed over the lunch-time period) takes one to the balcony at the top of the memorial from which there is a panoramic view over the Ijzer and Nieuwpoort. The monument was restored in 1974. At night it looks spectacular when floodlit.

Plaque to the Sapeurs and Pontonniers on the Dove Tower.

French 81st Division Memorial, Nieuwpoort.

King Albert Memorial, Nieuwpoort.

British Memorial to the Missing, with Jagger's superb lions, Nieuwpoort.

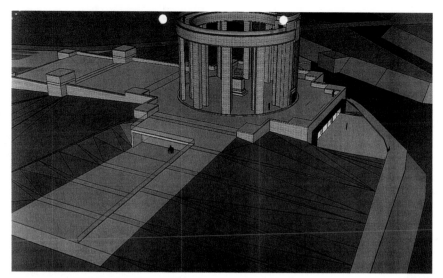

Artist's Impression of the new De Ganzepoot Visitor's Centre, Nieuwpoort.

In the summer of 2014 a **new Visitor's Centre/Museum** will open beneath the Memorial. Entitled 'De Ganzepoot' (qv) it will progressively host a series of exhibitions about WW1 in Nieuwpoort on the themes of the Inondations; Lady Dorothie [sometimes seen as 'Dorothy'] Feilding (member of Dr. Munro's Red Cross Flying Ambulance Corps, along with Elsie Knocker and Mairi Chisholm); Belgian war artists; the Battle of the Dunes; British and Australian Tunnellers and finally (in 2018) the reconstruction of the town.

Beside it is:

The fine British Memorial in the form of a pylon of Euville stone, 8 metres high, is guarded by three recumbent lions. Bronze bands around the pylon record the names of 566 officers and men (notably of the RND) who lost their lives in the Antwerp Raid of 9 October 1914 and who died in later actions along the Belgian coast from July-November 1917 and who have no known grave. The Memorial was designed by W.B. Binne with the sculptor C.S. Jagger (qv) and was inaugurated in 1927. Around it are the words by Laurence Binyon known as 'The Exhortation'.

Nieuwpoort (or Nieuport as it was then known) formed the extreme left of the Allied line on the North Sea. In an attempt to relieve Antwerp the 87th French Territorial Division and the French Brigade of Fusiliers Marins plus the British 3rd (Cavalry) and 7th (Royal Naval) Divisions arrived on the coast in early October 1914. Alone the RND reached Antwerp where they made their famous but abortive raid (qv). The French Marines and the two British Divisions covered the retreat of the Belgian forces from Ghent. On 9 October the British were placed under Sir John French's command and the whole British Army was withdrawn to Ypres and la Bassée.

The British 4th Army (1st and 32nd Divisions followed by the 66th (E Lancs) Division) took over the sector again in June 1917 and held it throughout the German attacks of July until November 1917. By then Nieuport was virtually razed to the ground. The remains were riddled with trenches made by the French. Australian and British Tunnelling Companies which had moved into the area in June but offensive tunnelling proved to be impracticable. The Companies, therefore, concentrated upon the construction of tunnelled dugouts, wells, subways and covered elephant shelters.

On 10 July 1917 the Germans mounted a fierce bombardment followed by a major offensive. Remnants of the 1st Division were cut off and annihilated when bridges were demolished, save for 70 men who managed to swim the river. The 32nd lost its advanced trenches but retained the bridgehead. Although bitter fighting continued until the 17th the thin new line held, although the 1st Division sustained over 2,000 casualties and the 32nd nearly 1,000. The 49th (W Riding) Division then took over the sector, followed by the 33rd. No large offensives then ensued although monthly casualties remained heavy as the Divisions were rotated. In mid-November the 41st Division left for the Italian Front and the remaining British forces were relieved by two French Divisions.

So ended the British occupation of Nieuport.

- ## *End of Yser Battlefield Tour*
OR

Extra Visit to WW1/WW2 Museum, Domein Raversijde (Map 5/35), Ostende New Comm CWGC Cemetery (Map 5/36), HMS Vindictive Memorial (Map 5/37). Round trip: 23 miles. Approximate time: 3 hours 15 minutes

From the King Albert 1 Monument, keeping to the right on to Westendlaan direction Oostende on the N318, continue to the large sign to the Domein and the Restaurant Walrave on the left, opposite Ostende Airport. Park by the modern reception building of the Domein.

The Domein Raversijde Visitor Centre (Lat & Long: 51.19818 2.84896) houses some temporary exhibitions and a book and souvenir stall. The Domein itself is a unique complex, a royal estate originally of King Leopold II and then after WW2 that of Prince Charles (Karel), King Albert 1 and Queen Elisabeth's second son. Charles was a Cadet at the British Naval Colleges at Osborne and Dartmouth and served on HMS *Renown* with the British Navy in the Far East. During the two World Wars the Domein was incorporated into the German coastal defences. Charles served as Regent from 1944-1950 whilst Leopold III was imprisoned in Germany and afterwards settled permanently in this charming, 50-hectare coastal hideaway. In 1981 he sold it to the Belgian State which has

---

Bunker and Range-finder, Aachen Battery Atlantic Wall Museum, Raversijde.

Bomb-proof shelter, Aachen Battery, Atlantic Wall Museum, Raversijde.

The Aachen Battery, 1919.

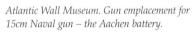

Atlantic Wall Museum. Gun emplacement for 15cm Naval gun – the Aachen battery.

Extra Visit continued

since developed and expanded it into an area of historic and touristic interest. Part of it, known as 'The Memorial', perpetuates the memory of Prince Charles, including his personal Pavilion, a simple fisherman's hut. There is also an Archaeological Site and a WW2 Enigma Machine – the only one in Belgium – a natural park and pond system, sporting facilities and a restaurant. During the summer months many interesting events and temporary exhibitions are staged.

A path leads from the Reception via the Prince's quarters (some of them German buildings dating from the WW2 period) to the Open Air Museum which consists of two exceptionally well-preserved series of German coastal defensive systems – one from WW1 and the other from WW2.

One may visit each one separately or make a long visit to cover them both. Visitors are equipped with audio machines (choice of 4 languages) for a self-guided tour. Expert guides can be hired by prior appointment at an extra fee. Allow 90 minutes for a thorough tour of each set of bunkers.

The WW1 bunkers are the only well-preserved '14-'18 coastal defences remaining today. The main site is the Aachen Battery, dating from 1915, containing a wonderfully original communication centre, a bomb-proof shelter, observation posts, and the remains of huge gun emplacements – all looking unbelievably modern in design and conception. The circular gun emplacements housed 15cm Naval guns with a 360° field of fire mainly targeted at the Yser Front towards Nieuport. The bunkers are inhabited by the most life-like figures dressed in authentic uniforms and surrounded by original equipment. The bunkers were manned by German Naval personnel who controlled the Naval guns but who, unusually, were dressed in field grey. Some of the uniforms, notably that of one of only 6 Generals of the Coastal Artillery, are quite unique and rare.

In the inter-war years the structures were the subject of many military lectures on successful coastal defences. Several of the young German officers who served here in WW1 came back to advise on the new construction of coastal defences in WW2. It is thanks to Prince Charles, who resisted any attempt to demolish them (as has systematically been done to the extraordinary series of bunkers in Calais) that this marvellous 2 kilometre stretch of WW1 and WW2 history has been preserved in its integrity in the dunes between Middelkerke and Oostende. This is a fantastic site which deserves a visit.

Contact: Atlantic Wall Open Air Museum, 636 Nieuwpoortsesteerweg, 8400 Ostende. Tel: + (0) 32 59 70 22 85. E-mail: domein.raversijde@west-vlaanderen.be, website: www.west-vlaanderen.be/raversijde

Open: Atlantic Wall Section 24 March-11 November 1030-1700. Prince Karel Memorial 1400-1700. Weekends, Public and School holidays 1030-1800. Groups by appointment.

From the Domein parking turn left and continue on the N318 and keep left at the junction with the N341 through Mariakerke. Continue to the traffic light junction with the R31 and turn right signed E40 Brussels. Continue to the church on the left and turn right at the traffic lights beside the church onto Stuiverstraat and continue to the cemetery on the right.

• Ostende New Communal CWGC Cemetery (Lat & Long: 51.21031 2.91532)

This is a vast and impressive local cemetery with an imposing entrance with tall obelisks at each side. On entering, straight ahead up the central aisle is the Oostende Memorial and behind it Belgian military graves with flat white headstones bearing a simple cross and the name of the man buried below. To the right is the CWGC Plot with its Cross of Sacrifice. The cemetery was used by the Germans from October 1914 to October 1918. It now contains 50 WW1 burials, 27 of them Navy, including men from *HMS Vindictive, Prince Eugene* and *Sir John Moore,* notably **Commander Godsal.** Some date from 1919,

Extra Visit continued

such as **Assistant Paymaster A.McQueen, RNR and Fireman J.E. Dobson**, MMR of RFA *Hughli*. The Royal Fleet Auxiliary ships were mainly manned by civilians. The RFA *Hughli* was a salvage ship, carrying explosives for clearing obstructions. She hit a mine on 26 April 1919 and sank off Nieuport with the loss of 19 crew members.

There are 366 WW2 burials, including Polish, French and Dutch, of which 75 are unknown. They include **Pilot Officer Donald Gordon Cobden**, who played rugby for the New Zealand All Blacks in 1937. In 1938 he came to England and joined the RAF (for whom he played rugby). On 11 August 1940 during the Battle of Britain Cobden was engaged in a dogfight with a large group of Messerschmidt BF 110s off the coast of Harwich during which he went missing – on his 26th birthday. His body was later washed ashore on the Belgian coast and buried here. There are also 8 non-war burials and 8 non-UK burials. The Cemetery Report and Visitor's Book are housed in the shelter at the end of the WW2 Plot.

Headstone of Commander A.E. Godsal, DSO, RN, Croix de Guerre, Ostende New Communal Cemetery.

IMPORTANT NOTE. Driving through the busy centre of Ostende with its many road and building works is extremely difficult. You may easily miss the turnings in the description below and we strongly advise that you rely instead on your satnav.

Continue to the roundabout and turn left on Zilverlaan. Continue to the second crossroads and turn left on Gistelsesteenweg. Continue over the dual carriageway and follow the road left and right to the ring road, Verenig de Naties Laan. Continue to the roundabout and take the first small exit to the right and turn left on Perronstraat. Continue to the next main crossroads, turn right and continue to the ornate bridge (with amazing sculptures, some Egyptian in style, some with bas relief train engines) over the railway. The memorial is just over the bridge beside the dock to the right. Park on the approaches to the bridge just before the barrier (Lat & Long: 51.22508 2.92830) and walk from here over the bridge, turning right towards the old Hangar No 1 building. Look over the railings to the left

HMS *Vindictive* Memorial (Lat & Long: 51.22523 2.93043)

For a few days in October 1914 Ostende was the seat of the Belgian Government but by 14 October the port was closed and the town was occupied by the Germans the following day. Thereafter Ostende was periodically bombarded by ships of the Royal Navy and bombed by Allied airmen. The town was finally entered by the British on 17 October 1918 without opposition.

In a small park is the bow section of HMS *Vindictive* sunk inside Ostende Harbour on 10 May 1918, with the inscription 'In Memoriam 23-IV-1918 10-V-1918'. The *Vindictive* had originally been part of the audacious raid on the German Submarine Base at Zeebrugge.

By 1917 German submarine warfare was having a serious impact on food and materiel supplies to the UK. Many of the submarines were based at Zeebrugge and supplied via Bruges. Zeebrugge is at the end of an 8 miles long stretch of canal from Bruges and Admiral Roger Keyes decided that if the canal could be blocked it would seriously disrupt

The bow section Memorial of HMS Vindictive, Ostende.

Extra Visit continued

the German campaign. Three old ships, the *Thetis, Iphigenia* and *Intrepid* were filled with concrete to be sunk across the canal beside the Mole while with them was HMS *Vindictive* carrying a raiding party aboard. The raiders were to land in darkness and with the added cover of smoke provide a diversionary attack to occupy the defenders. Additionally, the submarine C5, filled with explosives, was to be blown up under the approach to the Mole to prevent the arrival of reinforcements.

As planning progressed it was clear that more transports would be needed to carry the raiding party and by the time the assault force set sail, led by Roger Keyes, it numbered over 70 vessels.

The *Vindictive* arrived at the Mole just after midnight on St George's Day, 23 April, 1918 and the raiding party, while suffering heavy casualties, managed to create the needed diversion, C5 exploded as planned, the block ships were sunk and barely an hour after she had arrived HMS *Vindictive* pulled away en route to Dover. The results were patchy. Submarine activity was inconvenienced rather than hampered though some German vessels were trapped in the canal for the remainder of the war. Of the assault force some 180 men were killed and another 400 wounded or captured. Keyes was knighted and eight VCs were awarded.

Just two weeks later, on 9 May 1918, the somewhat battered *Vindictive* returned to Belgium, laden with concrete and explosives, commanded by Commander A.E. Godsal, RN. She was soon targeted by German guns and she was struck by a shell which killed Godsal. Lt Crutchley then gave the order to clear the engine room and abandon ship. Engineer Lt-Commander Bury, last man to leave the engine room, then blew the main charges. The old ship sank and lay at the bottom of the channel, her task achieved, virtually sealing the port and effectively preventing its use as a submarine base.

The Royal Marines Museum in Portsmouth has one of *Vindictive's* anchors and in St Ann's Church in the town is a memorial cross to an unknown stoker from the May attack. *Vindictive* remained a tourist attraction after the war but apart from the bow section which now remains, it was cut up and many pieces made into souvenirs. In 2003 the American auction house George Glazer had on offer a bronze golf club made from a *Vindictive* propeller and inscribed to Admiral E. G. Pallot DSO. Price $950.

Return to the King Albert Monument in Nieuwpoort.

FIRST YPRES

18 OCTOBER-11 NOVEMBER 1914

'Shall I ever forget this day?
It will be indelibly stamped on my memory.
How anyone survived to tell the story is a mystery to me.'
An infantry Captain at Gheluvelt.

'You see why you should walk lightly if you ever go to Ypres,
the very stones of which are memorials to men
who perished on the Field of Honour.'
Maj J.M. Halley, 62nd Field Coy, RE.

SUMMARY OF THE BATTLE

In an attempt to break through the rapidly stabilising allied line and to reach Calais, von Falkenhayn launched the 4th and 6th (Ger) Armies against the BEF at Ypres on 18 October 1914. The fighting, toe to toe, staggered on with no real advantage gained by either side until heavy rains brought the contest to an end on 11 November. The British lost 2,350 officers and 55,800 soldiers. German losses were more than 130,000.

OPENING MOVES

Following II Corps' brief encounter at le Cateau the BEF continued its retreat from Mons and crossed the River Marne on 3 September. Von Kluck, believing that the Allies were beaten, altered the main thrust of his attack to come east of Paris and crossed the river only a day after the BEF. This change of direction exposed his right flank (doubtless von Schlieffen turned in his grave) and on 6 September the French 6th Army struck at it with 150,000 men, while the remainder of the Allies, including the BEF, about faced and drove the Germans 40 miles back to the Aisne River. The Schlieffen Plan was finished. Its failure was probably due to Von Moltke's steady weakening of the German right wing, contrary to Schlieffen's death-bed plea to 'keep it strong'. On 14 September he was replaced by General Eric von Falkenhayn.

That same day, 14 September, General Joffre began an attack on the German positions beyond the Aisne with the BEF and the French 5th and 6th Armies. The gains against the well-entrenched Germans were small and after two days Joffre began moving forces to the north-west in an attempt to get around the end of the German line. Von Falkenhayn responded by moving reserves to outflank the outflankers who responded in similar measure. The line grew longer and longer towards the coast in a 'race to the sea', which ended when the Allies reached Nieuwpoort in Belgium in the first week of October 1914.

The BEF had moved north in the 'race' in two parts. II Corps went directly to la Bassée and immediately came into action on 11 October in the 25-mile gap south of Ypres, and I Corps went first to St Omer where the C-in-C, Sir John French, had to make a choice. Either I Corps should go further to the north where thinly stretched French forces together with the recently arrived

British 7th Division were maintaining their hold on Ypres and their contact with the Belgians on the coast, or he should reinforce II Corps at la Bassée. He sent I Corps to Ypres and the First Battle began.

WHAT HAPPENED

Le Cateau was the last of the old-style one-day battles. The fighting at Ypres was never so simple. The title 'First Ypres' seems to describe a clear-cut contest, over a set period, with an agreed victor, yet by the end of 1914 the measure of victory was changing. It was no longer 'he who held the ground' but 'he who had the will to fight' who prevailed, and the will depended upon many things, including national reserves of manpower. 'Kill the enemy' became not just a tactical requirement but a strategic necessity. Everywhere, all the time, each side was intent upon killing the other. 'All Quiet Along the Potomac Tonight', goes the haunting song from the American Civil War, which goes on to intone that the loss of 'a private or two now and again will not count in the news of the battle'. That daily loss, even when there was no official 'battle' in progress, became significant during the First World War.

It was never 'All Quiet on the Western Front'. The BEF would lose hundreds of men by 'natural wastage' every day from 1915 onwards, yet every so often the enemies lumbered dinosaur-like into battle against each other and engaged in periods of ferocious killing that were graced with distinctive names. So it was with 'First Ypres', where the blood of a quarter of a million soldiers began etching a line of trenches that would stretch from the North Sea to Switzerland. Yet when the battle began (and historians cannot agree on the exact date) the leaders were still hoping for a great victory, a decisive battle. It was not to be.

LEGEND: MAP 6: FIRST YPRES: 18 OCTOBER-11 NOVEMBER 1914

1a. Lijssenthoek CWGC Cem & Info Centre	26. Hooge Crater & Trenches
1b. Talbot House & Poperinge	27. Hooge Museum
1. The In Flanders Fields Museum	28. Hooge CWGC Cem
2. St George's Memorial Church	28a. Menin Road Museum
3. The Menin Gate Mem & Indian Mem	29. Sanctuary Wood Museum & Trenches
4. Essex Farm CWGC Cem	29a. Mount Sorrel Can Mon
5. John McCrae and 43 Div Mems	30. Hellfire Corner
6. John McCrae's Dressing Station	31. Hill 60 Museum
7. Yorkshire Trench	32. 14th Light Div, Queen Victoria's Rifles & 1st
8. Breton Mem	Australia Tunnelling Coy Mems
8a. Ledwidge Mem/Artillery Wood CWGC Cem	33. Tunnellers Mem St Eloi
9. Hedd Wyn Mem Plaques	34. Crater St Eloi
10. Cement House CWGC Cem	35. Museum Messines
11. Steenbeek Albertina Mem	36. New Zealand Kowhai tree, Ross Bastiaan Plaque
12. 20th Light Div Mem	and Mié Tabe Peace Post, Messines
12a. Harry Patch Mem	37. Island of Ireland Peace Tower
13. German Cemetery Langemarck & Info Centre & 34th	38. Hyde Park Corner CWGC Cem
Div Mem	39. Ploegsteert Memorial & Berkshire CWGC Extension
13a. Pte Dancox VC Memorial Namur Crossing	Cem/Interpretation Centre
14. Canadian Brooding Soldier Mem/Bellew VC Plaque	40. Hollandseschuur Craters
15. New Zealand Mem	41. Croonaert Chapel CWGC Cem
15a. 48th Highlanders of Canada, Gas Attack Mem	42. 1st CAP Mem
16. Tyne Cot CWGC, Visitor Centre & Mems	43. Bayernwald Trenches etc
17. Passchendaele Memorial Museum, Zonnebeke	44. Wytschaete Mil CWGC Cem
17a. Scottish Mem, Frezenberg	45. 16th Irish Div Mem
18. Polygon Wood CWGC Cem	46. Spanbroekmolen Crater
19. Buttes New British CWGC Cem	47. Lone Tree CWGC Cem
20. Australian 5th Div Mem & New Zealand Mem to	48. Kruisstraat Craters
the Missing	49. Messines Ridge Brit CWGC Cem
21. Black Watch Corner	50. NZ Mem
21a. Sgt Nichols VC Mem	51. London Scottish Mem
22. South Wales Borderers & 2nd Bn Worcesters Mems	52. NZ Mem Park
23. 18th Eastern Div Mem	53. Prowse Point CWGC Cem
24. Gloucester Regt Mem	54. Christmas Truce Cross
25. Kings Royal Rifle Corps Mem	55. Bainsfather Plaque

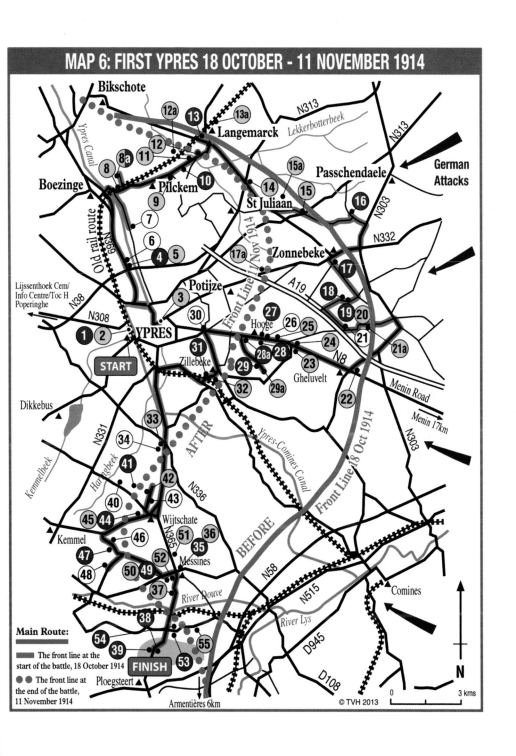

MAP 6: FIRST YPRES 18 OCTOBER - 11 NOVEMBER 1914

The armchair analyst can divide First Ypres into neat and separate parts:

Battle of Armentières	13 Oct-2 Nov
Battle of Messines	12 Oct-2 Nov
Battle of Langemarck	21 Oct-24 Oct
Battle of Gheluvelt	29 Oct-31 Oct
Battle of Nonne Boschen	11 Nov

These classifications are geographical and the actions associated with them are best described during the battlefield tour below which, to simplify touring, covers First, Second and Third Ypres simultaneously. Running together the October and November actions, the 'First' Battle of Ypres is generally accepted to have opened on 18 October 1914 when the Germans began a three-week period of repeated mass attacks against the British positions. The British occupied a salient which bulged forward with a 16 mile-long perimeter into the German line (see **Map 6**). The heart of the Salient was Ypres, its defence now the responsibility of I Corps, and German attacks were concentrated along the axis of the Menin Road which enters Ypres from the east, passing as it does so the hamlet of Gheluvelt, barely 8 miles from Ypres Cathedral.

On 31 October Gheluvelt was lost and the Germans were on the brink of breaking through the line, outflanking the BEF and making a run for the Channel Ports. In one of the most remarkable actions of the War the 2nd Worcesters charged the enemy at Gheluvelt and saved the day. The Germans made one more major effort along the same axis when on 11 November 12½ divisions attacked across a 9-mile front with almost 18,000 men against 8,000. It wasn't enough. On that day, weighted down with mud and casualties, the First Battle of Ypres ended. The Salient perimeter had shrunk to 11 miles, but Ypres had not fallen. It never would.

THE BATTLEFIELD TOUR

• This is done in conjunction with Second and Third Ypres. See Map 6 page 103, and page 240.

NEUVE CHAPELLE

10-13 MARCH 1915

'The attack which we are about to undertake is of the first importance to the Allied
Cause. The Army and the Nation are watching the results, and Sir John French is
confident that every individual in the IVth Corps will do his duty and inflict a
crushing defeat on the German VIIth Corps which is opposed to us'.
Written note from General Rawlinson, Commanding IV Corps,
given to every soldier before Neuve Chapelle.

'The G.O.C. the Division desires me to convey to you and all ranks under
your command his deep appreciation of the splendid work performed by
your battalion during the last few days' hard fighting. For my own part I
find it difficult to express adequately my admiration for the way in which
you have fought. I mourn with you for our gallant comrades who have
fallen, but the splendid cause for which they have fought, and the brave
way in which they have died, must always be the greatest comfort to
those whom they have left behind, and stimulate them to fresh efforts'.
Message passed after Neuve Chapelle to the 13th Bn London Regiment
('*The Kensingtons*') by Brigadier Lowry-Cole commanding 25th Brigade.

We licked 'em on the Marne
And whacked 'em on the Aisne
We gave 'em hell at Neuve Chapelle
And we'll bloody well do it again
Anon.

SUMMARY OF THE BATTLE

This was the first British-initiated offensive of the war and was prompted by French doubts
about British commitment to the conflict. On 10 March 1915 following a massive but short
bombardment, General Haig's 1st Army attacked the village of Neuve Chapelle which was
taken on the first day. However, von Falkenhayn's rapid movement of reserves and a British
shortage of ammunition prevented a breakthrough. British casualties were about 13,000, the
German 14,000.

OPENING MOVES

On 15 February 1900 General French had led a dashing cavalry charge to complete the relief of
Kimberley after a 5-month siege by the Boers. Fifteen years later, now commanding the British
Expeditionary Force on the continent of Europe, he once again seemed to have in mind a cavalry
charge through enemy lines, something which, like the Kimberley affair, he hoped would have
great publicity and morale benefits.

By the end of 1914 the trench system behind which each opposing army sheltered was well defined along the Western Front and the prospect of huge casualties from frontal attacks had been signalled by First Ypres. Fertile minds like Winston Churchill were seeking alternatives to mutual mass bludgeoning in Europe as a way of settling the war and by 1915 the Gallipoli alternative was taking shape. The French, however, unlike the British, had the enemy on their soil which concentrated their minds to a much shorter focal length and in January and February they engaged in aggressive and successful operations in Champagne, retaking important ground from the Germans.

The Champagne offensives generated benefits in that large bodies of German troops were diverted from the Eastern Front, but they also had a tactical lesson that was to colour the next four years of warfare. The French had won back territory by a new and sophisticated use of artillery. First they chose a sector to attack where surprise was possible. Then, by massing their artillery, they pounded the enemy front line into oblivion. At a pre-determined hour, the barrage lifted and moved behind the front line to drop between it and the German reserves. Thus reinforcements were prevented, by a curtain of steel, from moving to the front. Meanwhile the French infantry advanced and captured the German front line positions.

At the beginning of March 1915, the Belgians held the line from the North Sea to Dixmuide and the French from Dixmuide to the top of the Ypres Salient. West of Neuve Chapelle were IV Corps under General Rawlinson and the Indian Corps under General Willcocks, both part of the 1st Army. The BEF had expanded to some 18 divisions, three times its original strength of August 1914 and was now divided into two armies. Sensitive to French innuendo that the British were not pulling their weight, the C-in-C decided to mount the first British offensive of the war, an attack with General Haig's 1st Army. He gave as his reasons for offering 'a vigorous offensive movement', 'the apparent weakness of the enemy in my front... holding as many hostile troops as possible in the western theatre (and)... the need of fostering the offensive spirit in the troops under my command'.

It was decided to attack the German salient at Neuve Chapelle with a view to taking the high ground around Aubers Ridge to the east of the village and of effecting a breakthrough. There were to be two phases: (1) take the village and the line known as 'Smith-Dorrien trench' to the east of the village (see **Map 7**); and (2) enlarge the gap in the enemy line and make towards the Aubers Ridge. On 9 March General Haig finished his Special Order for the Day with these words -

'To ensure success each one of us must play his part and fight like men for the honour of old England.' At least half of the fighting, however, was to fall to the Indian Division and not the men of old England.

WHAT HAPPENED

At 0730 on 10 March almost 500 guns opened fire on the German lines over a length of 2 miles. Thirty-five minutes later the guns lifted and the iron curtain fell across the village of Neuve Chapelle itself. Simultaneously the Garhwal Brigade, the assault formation of the Indian Corps, 'swarmed over the parapet and doubling over the intervening space of from 100 to 200 yards reached (except one battalion) its first objective without a check'. Interestingly amongst the heavy artillery available to the 1st Army was an armoured train named 'Churchill' and a battery of 9.2 inch howitzers with Holt caterpillar tractors in battle for the first time.

On the northern flank of the salient the assault by 8th Division met with similar success, only the Middlesex being held up just south of the Moated Grange. Complete surprise had been achieved and the village and Smith Dorrien trench were taken. Now was the time for urgency, to move on quickly to Phase 2, but communication between the two Corps commanders was confused, each waiting for the other to act, and it was five hours before General Haig ordered the attack to continue. The Germans had reacted quickly, bringing up reinforcements through thin British artillery fire. It was thin because the front had been widened but mainly because the British did not have enough ammunition to continue the bombardment at an effective rate. The shortage developed into a public outcry known as 'The Shell Scandal', which led to the appointment of

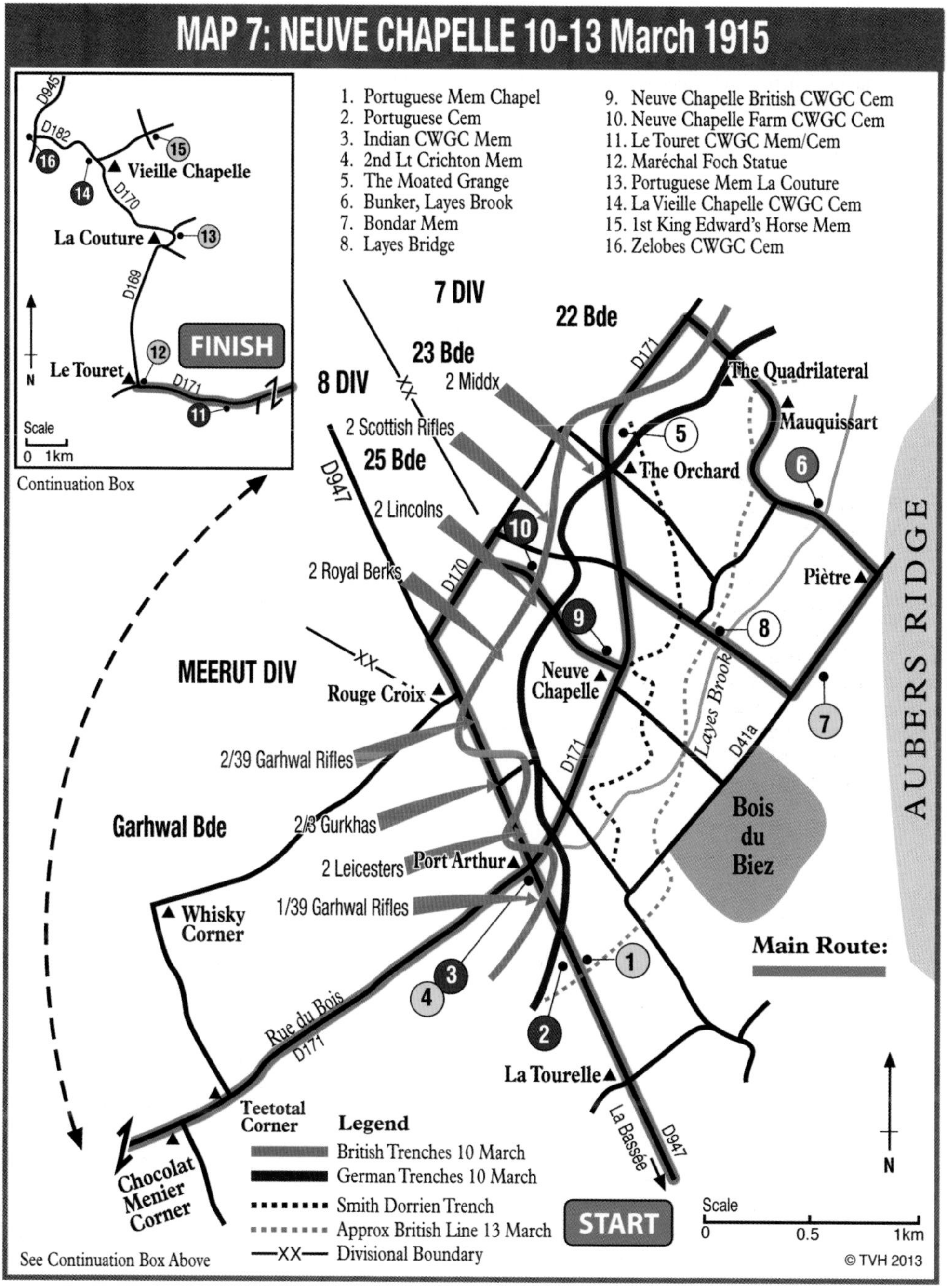

MAP 7: NEUVE CHAPELLE 10-13 March 1915

1. Portuguese Mem Chapel
2. Portuguese Cem
3. Indian CWGC Mem
4. 2nd Lt Crichton Mem
5. The Moated Grange
6. Bunker, Layes Brook
7. Bondar Mem
8. Layes Bridge
9. Neuve Chapelle British CWGC Cem
10. Neuve Chapelle Farm CWGC Cem
11. Le Touret CWGC Mem/Cem
12. Maréchal Foch Statue
13. Portuguese Mem La Couture
14. La Vieille Chapelle CWGC Cem
15. 1st King Edward's Horse Mem
16. Zelobes CWGC Cem

Continuation Box

D945
D182
16
14
15
Vieille Chapelle
D170
La Couture ▲ 13
D169
12 FINISH
N
Le Touret ▲ D171
Scale
0 1km
11

7 DIV
22 Bde
23 Bde
2 Middx
D171
The Quadrilateral ▲
8 DIV
2 Scottish Rifles
Mauquissart ▲
5
25 Bde
The Orchard ▲
6
2 Lincolns
10
2 Royal Berks
D170
9
8
Piètre ▲
MEERUT DIV
Neuve Chapelle ▲
Rouge Croix ▲
7
2/39 Garhwal Rifles
Layes Brook
D41a
Garhwal Bde
2/3 Gurkhas
D171
2 Leicesters Port Arthur ▲
Bois du Biez
1/39 Garhwal Rifles
1
Main Route:
▲ Whisky Corner
3
4
▲ La Tourelle
2
Rue du Bois D171
La Bassée D947
Teetotal Corner
N
Legend
Chocolat Menier Corner
British Trenches 10 March
German Trenches 10 March
······· Smith Dorrien Trench
······· Approx British Line 13 March
—XX— Divisional Boundary
START
Scale
0 0.5 1km
See Continuation Box Above
© TVH 2013

AUBERS RIDGE

Lloyd George as Minister of Munitions with the task of sorting things out. One of his actions was to introduce liquor licensing laws in an attempt to reduce absenteeism due to alcohol Even today, therefore, some effects of the battle of Neuve Chapelle remain – and not until 2005 were pubs allowed to stay open 24 hours a day.

The results at the end of 10 March were, however, considerable. A front of 4,100 yards from Port Arthur to just beyond the Moated Grange had been taken and to a depth in places of 1,200 yards. The whole of Neuve Chapelle village had been captured. Little more was thereafter gained. The Germans mounted a counter-attack at dawn on 12 March with 16,000 men against the Indian Brigade and the front of 8th Division, but this failed to make any advance. It did, however, pre-empt any further offensive action of substance by 1st Army so that on 13 March both sides settled down to consolidate the positions that they held.

The battle was over, but now the British felt themselves to be more substantial than just an adjunct to the French forces, the French had proof that the British were willing to fight, the Germans began to strengthen their lines opposite the British and everyone adopted the destructive artillery barrage as being standard practice for the battles to come.

THE BATTLEFIELD TOUR

• **The Route**: The tour begins in La Bassée, visits the Portuguese Cemetery and Memorial, Port Arthur (La Bombe) and The Indian Memorial, Private Memorial to 2nd Lt Crichton; the Moated Grange; Layes Brook; Layes Bridge; Neuve Chapelle British and Farm CWGC Cemeteries; the le Touret CWGC Cemetery and Memorial to the Missing and ends at the house with WW1 Statues
• **Extra Visits** to La Couture Portuguese Memorial, La Vieille Chapelle Communal (with Memorial to 1st King Edward's Horse) and New and Zelobes CWGC Cemeteries.
• **[N.B.]** The following sites are indicated: The Quadrilateral; Bondar WW2 Memorial, Chocolat Menier Corner.
• **Total distance:** 13.5 miles
• **Total time:** 2 hours 30 minutes
• **Distance from Calais to start point** via Béthune: 59 miles. Motorway Tolls.
• **Base towns:** La Bassée, Béthune
• **Maps:** IGN 2404 Est 1:25,000 plus IGN 2405 Est 1:25,000

From Calais take the A16/A26 direction Paris/Reims then the A26/E15 direction St Omer. Take Exit 6 to Béthune and the N41 to La Bassée and drive into the centre.
Set your mileometer to zero.

• *La Bassée/0 miles/RWC*
La Bassée has no hotels but makes a handy lunch break. There is a variety of restaurants, pizzerias and brasseries in and near the main square, Place du Géneral de Gaulle. Le Macpherson Pub/Brasserie is particularly good value. Closed Sun. Tel: + (0)3 20 29 00 67.

In 1914 la Bassée was a thriving town of small industry and agriculture when on 11 October 1914 their peace and prosperity was shattered by the occupation of the Germans when their front line was established two kilometres away. There followed four years of shattering fire and the town gradually disintegrated, the church being hit in the first days of the bombardment and the surrounding roads engulfed in flames. On Easter Sunday 1915 the German High Command ordered the evacuation of the civilian population – other than those who could be of practical use to them, like bakers, nursing sisters, but they too were finally evacuated on Saturday, 3 July 1915.

On 10 October 1918 the British took what remained of the devastated town. Between 1919 and 1933 the Mayor Alexandre Crespel oversaw the rebuilding of his town and the magnificent Town Hall was rebuilt, albeit some distance from the original, electricity and running water and wider streets were installed.

Once again, on 27 May 1940, the Basséens knew German occupation and damage to their buildings – until they were liberated in September 1944.

Drive north from la Bassée on the D947 signed to Estaires for 3 miles until you reach the clearly signed Portuguese Cemetery on the left. There is a chapel opposite. Stop and beware of the traffic.

• *The Portuguese Cemetery, Memorial & Fatima Chapel, La Bombe/3.3 miles/15 minutes/Map 7/2/1/Lat & Long: 50.57369 2.77645*

This has no connection with the battle of 1915 but relates to the Kaiser's Offensive of 1918 when the Portuguese came into action here on 9 April 1918.

The two-division Portuguese Army was dispirited by 1918. A change of government had meant that they no longer had political support at home and their morale was low. Anticipating a German offensive, the British area commander withdrew one of the Portuguese Divisions and before it could be replaced by a British force, the enemy struck directly at the one remaining Portuguese Division, now holding a double frontage. Unlike their forebears at Busaco in 1810, they broke, some taking the machines of a British cyclist battalion and pedalling their way to safety, others purportedly shooting a British driver and commandeering his vehicle to make their escape. Many others, however, fought hard against overwhelming odds when placed in a situation for which they were not trained to exploit. Brigadier F.P. Crozier in his 1930 memoirs, *A Brass Hat in No Man's Land*, was somewhat brutal in his descriptions of the Portuguese whom he found to his right on the line on the night of 7-8 April. To start with their equipment was 'all rusty and useless', while 'practically all the front line sleeps heavily and bootless in cubby holes covered with waterproof sheets, while their equipment hangs carelessly about'. Crozier's concerns about their lack of training and preparedness were justified. The attack was a disaster for the Portuguese. 'It has been a ghastly let down', he commented, 'If the Portuguese had never entered the line it would not have been so.' One of the problems was that 'the uniforms of the Germans and Portuguese are not dis-similar. Hundreds of Portuguese were mown down by our machine guns and rifle fire.' Crozier hinted that the 'political considerations' were behind the decision to use what GHQ perfectly knew to be ill-prepared Portuguese troops.

Their losses were indeed heavy – some 7,000 were killed in the action known as the Battle of the Lys during which Neuve Chapelle was lost – and they are commemorated with pride by their countrymen. A ceremony of remembrance is held at the cemetery, usually on the Saturday nearest the anniversary. It ends not with the customary *'vin d'honneur'*, but a *'porto de honor'!*

Contact: Union Franco-Portuguaise, 61 rue des Haies, 62136 Richebourg. Tel: + (0)3 21 26 23 69/21 26 05 38.

The cemetery, which is now in pristine condition, contains 1,831 burials, of whom 239 are unidentified. It was constructed between 1924 and 1938 with bodies brought in from cemeteries in Ambleteuse, Brest and Tournai in Belgium as well as from Le Touret. The superb ornamental wrought iron entrance gates, inspired by Leal de Camara, open on to the ranks of grey headstones inscribed *'Morto de la Patria'*. Many are *'Desconehcido'* (Unknown). At the rear is a fine stone monument with battle honours and many Plaques recording visits by various delegations.

Over the road is a small, beautifully maintained Chapel to Notre Dame de Fatima, surrounded by white-painted walls. It was built in the 1970s by the local Portuguese Immigrants' Association to honour their compatriots killed during the First World War.

During the Battle of the Lys the Portuguese, for divine protection, carried into their trenches a damaged statue of Christ, with legs broken off at the knees, the right arm broken and the chest wounded. When they were forced to leave the trenches they abandoned the statue and it was later retrieved by the Bocquet family who had originally erected it in 1877.

Portuguese Headstone.

Entrance to the Portuguese Cemetery, with Memorial in the background, la Bombe.

Chapel to Notre Dame de Fatima, la Bombe.

Cross to Lt William Bruce, VC, Cemetery Visitor's Book.

Indian Memorial, la Bombe.

When the village of Neuve Chapelle was rebuilt, the old statue was propped up beside a new calvary, and remained in situ throughout the Second World War. In 1958, on the 40th anniversary of the Lys battle, the French Government awarded Portugal's Unknown Soldier with the *Croix de Guerre* and the *Légion d'Honneur* and the Bocquets agreed to allow the statue to travel to the commemorative monastery of Bataliha (founded in 1385). Great ceremony and pomp attended the delegation (which included Portuguese veterans who had settled in France) which flew to Lisbon on a military plane bearing a message from President René Coty to President Salazar. On 9 April 1958 the 'Christ of the Trenches' was erected in Bataliha above the tomb of the Portuguese Unknown Soldiers (one from the First World War, one from Africa) where it remains to this day.

The cemetery lies roughly halfway between both front lines which crossed this road some 250 yards apart after the 1915 battle, and where they remained until the last year of the war.

Continue north to the next crossroads. The Indian memorial is on the left. Stop.

• *Neuve Chapelle Indian Memorial/Private Memorial to 2nd Lt Crichton, La Bombe(Port Arthur)/3.4 miles/20 minutes/Map 7/3, 7/4/ Lat & Long: 50.57508 2.77536*

This is Port Arthur crossroads, Richebourg, the southern end of the Indian Corps' front on 10 March 1915. The intended main thrust of the attack here (by the 1/39th Garhwalis) was west to east, enveloping the entire crossroads. The 1/39th was the one Indian battalion which didn't make its objective. Immediately on leaving the trenches the attack veered right towards what is now the Portuguese memorial area and entered part of the German line which had not come under the preparatory bombardment. The 1/39th suffered heavy casualties, all six British officers who were in the assault were killed. The Indian Corps consisted of two divisions, the Lahore and the Meerut, both of three brigades. Each brigade contained one British and three Indian battalions, a total Corps strength of some 24,000. The Corps had seen action at Neuve Chapelle in October 1914 and by the end of the year had suffered 9,500 casualties, 7,100 from Indian units. In the 1915 battle the Corps lost one-fifth of its strength and this is therefore an appropriate site for their memorial.

Detail, Indian Memorial.

Panel with names of those who died in captivity.

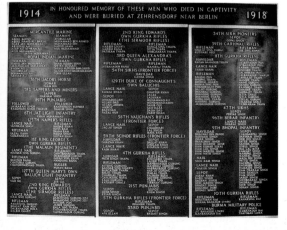

The Neuve Chapelle 'Christ of the Trenches'.

Private Memorial to 2nd Lt Crichton, la Bombe.

Designed by Sir Herbert Baker with Charles Wheeler, it is circular, with a lotus-capped 50ft high column flanked by two tigers, the whole complex acknowledging the connection with India, from the screen wall to the two domed chattris (loggias). It adds an exotic note to the somewhat featureless surrounding northern French landscape. The names of over 5,000 dead with no known grave are carved on the semi-circular wall, arranged in unit order. There is a special bronze panel adding 210 servicemen of Undivided India who died 1914-1918, whose graves at Zehrensdorf in E. Germany were unmaintainable, and a 1939-45 Cremation Memorial.

Here is commemorated **Lt William Bruce**, 59th Scinde Rifles, who was awarded the **VC** for his action on 19 December near Givenchy, who, though himself wounded, walked up and down his trench encouraging his men under heavy attacks until he was killed.

The Cemetery Report should be read for the evocative and colourful names of the Regiments, many raised by Nizams and Maharajahs, and the ranks, e.g: risaldar = major, jemadar = lieutenant, kot daffadar = quartermaster-sergeant, havildar = sergeant, naik = corporal, sepoy = infantry private, sowar = cavalry sergeant.

Walk round the outside of the memorial on the D171 Le Touret road.
On the grassy bank is the **Stone Memorial to 2nd Lt Cyril Alfred William Crichton,** 3rd Bn London Regiment, RF who died here on 10 March 1915. The eulogistic inscription is summarised in French. Crichton joined the HAC while studying law at the Inner Temple and went to Malta with his battalion before coming to France in January 1915. He was killed leading an heroic 'old school' charge on 'an obdurate trench that made a gap in the line'. His parents made strenuous efforts to find his grave as they wished to purchase the land on which it was sited. The story of their quest, the erection of the memorial and the subsequent discovery of Crichton's body in a different location in 1925 when it was removed to Le Touret CWGC Cemetery, visited later, is told in Barrie Thorpe's *Private Memorials of the Great War.* This rare private memorial was moved from the Estaires Road opposite the café to this safer spot in 1965. It was carefully repaired after the damage it sustained by bullets in 1940 and from being struck by a car. The CWGC has maintained the memorial since 1923 at the request (and subsequent bequest) of the family.

Turn right at the crossroads towards Neuve Chapelle, passing the Café Restaurant la Bonne Table on the left, which may – or may not – still be in existence by the time that you read this.

• La Bombe (Port Arthur)/3.4 miles/RWC

The name of the crossroads appears to have nothing to do with the war. Studious research at the bar of the old Auberge (and with the local history society) by the authors established only that the name originated in the Middle Ages and has some connection with the smuggling that went on at that time. However, over the door of the café for many years was the name 'Port Arthur' and the date '10 mars 1915', the opening day of the battle. On one outside wall the sign for La Bombe still exists.

There has long been an Auberge or Restaurant here, including for a time a gourmet restaurant run by Lille Chef, Charly Lahmeri. Sadly on our last visit this too seemed to have closed.

Edmund Blunden spent some time in this area, both in 1916 and 1917. In 1917 he described the building here as 'encircled with sandbag ramparts, a map of the whole building looking like a diagram of the intestines'. In the cellars there was enough room for 40 men and a tunnel led from them some 250 yards up the D171 towards Neuve Chapelle to the junction with 'Hun Trench', the whole construction being German.

Continue through the village, direction Laventie, and just after a sharp bend right at the junction of the D171 with the D170 there is a small courtyard farmhouse on the right with iron gates. On current maps it may be called 'Ferme de Lestre'. Stop.

• The Moated Grange/5.0 miles/10 minutes/Map 7/5/Lat & Long: 50.59590 2.78113

This is not the original building (known as Ferme Vanbesien in 1914), though it is on the original site and broadly to the same design and of the same size. It is the northern (left hand) end of the attack frontage for 10 March 1915. At the time of the battle it had been a strongpoint in the German line. The trenches in front of the Middlesex, just below the Grange, held by the 11th Jäger Battalion were not bombarded effectively, owing to the late arrival of the artillery. The leading waves of the Middlesex were cut down and the battalion had to be reinforced with two companies of the West Yorks for a later attack.

The orchard (see **Map 7**) immediately south of the Moated Grange (the orchard is no longer there) was, however, finally taken by the Middlesex and the West Yorks just after noon on 10 March. During the morning, 24th Brigade Trench Mortar Battery had dropped over 230 mortar bombs on to the Grange and when the West Yorks worked north from the orchard the German survivors surrendered. Two days later the 13th and 15th (Ger) Infantry Regiments counter-

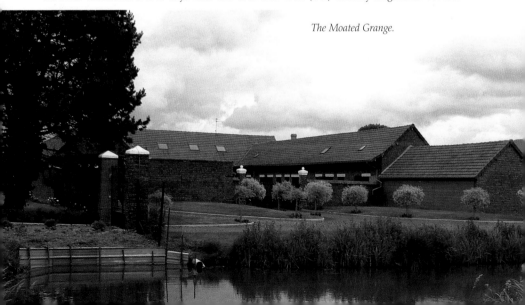

The Moated Grange.

attacked the Grange but were held off, in great measure due to the activities of the newly trained 'bombing' (grenade-throwing) detachments. One bomber, **Corporal W. Anderson** of the 2nd Green Howards, won the **VC** for his part in the action for leading three men in a bombing raid against a large group of the enemy.

Lt (later Lt-Gen, KBE, CB, DSO, *Légion d'Honneur, Croix de Guerre,* and other decorations) **Philip** (later Sir Philip) **Neame, RE**, also won his **VC** south of this area (approx location: **Lat & Long: 50.595146 2.780340,** which is also the approximate site of Anderson's VC action) for his action on 19 December 1914 in engaging the enemy single-handed, killing and wounding a number of them and rescuing all the wounded. After an extraordinary career in both World Wars (including being the only VC Olympic Gold Medallist – for shooting in Paris 1924) this member of the Faversham Shepherd-Neame brewing dynasty died in 1978. His son, Lt-Col Philip Neame, served with the Paras in the Falklands.

Another **VC** was awarded on 12 March 'at Neuve Chapelle' to **L/Cpl Wilfred Dolby Fuller** of the 1st Grenadier Guards who saw a party of the enemy trying to escape along a communication trench. Running towards them he killed the leading man with a bomb when the remainder (some 50 men) all surrendered to him. He was quite alone at the time. Fuller, was later treated for his wounds at No 3 Base Hospital, Sheffield, where King George V awarded him with the Cross of the Order of St George (3rd Class) conferred upon him by the Tsar.

Continue to the next crossroads and turn right [along what was known as Winchester Road] towards Mauquissart and Piètre on the Rue des Lurons, D168.

N.B. Some two hundred yards along the road and some one hundred yards to your right was the German defensive area known as **The Quadrilateral** (approx **Lat & Long: 50.59933 2.78822** - from nearest point on the road) which was taken by the 2nd Scots Guards on 12 March together with 400 prisoners. It was sadly one of the few places where the pressures of war and harsh military discipline led a soldier to desert. Private Isaac Reid left the forward areas the day before the Quadrilateral action, he was caught, court-martialled and executed in front of the Regiment on 9 April 1915. Reid is buried in Longuenesse (St Omer) Souvenir Cemetery.

One hundred yards further on was a line of a dozen or more craters, stretched across the road, created in later fighting.

Continue to the junction with a small 3.5 ton limit straight ahead, take it and continue to a

• *Bunker/Layes Brook/6.3 miles/5 minutes/Map7/6/Lat & Long 50.59119 2.79653*

This is on the left and immediately ahead is a small stream.

This is **Layes Brook**. In 1915 it was known as the Rivière des Layes, a tributary of the Lys or an old artifical drainage channel which, the Official History complains, was 'said to have been dug by the farmers without expert assistance. As a result it has not a proper flow, the water sometimes going north, sometimes south'. The drainage was 'got under control' by the British during the winter of 1915-16. Then it was a considerable obstacle, 'about ten feet broad with nearly vertical banks and three or four feet of water in it'. It was crossed on 8 light bridges brought forward by the leading battalions to enable the advance on the Bois de Biez to continue. The Germans had constructed a second line of defence along the eastern side of the stream with strong bridgeheads, such as the Bunker here.

In the attack which began at 0530 hours on 10 March over the stream to the Bois de Biez, Maj D.M. Watts of the 2/2nd Gurkhas was awarded the DSO and Capt A. Dallas Smith and Lt (and Adjutant) E.J. Corse-Smith were awarded the MC. Four Germans were captured here by No. 4 Coy and another 'who had lost his way, walked into the middle of No. 2 Company and was made prisoner'!

Also taking part in the attack was 1908 Olympic 400m Gold Medal Winner, Captain Wyndham

Layes Brook looking towards the site of the Moulin de Piètre.

Bunker beside the brook.

Memorial to Pilot Officer J Bondar, Bois de Biez.

Neuve Chapelle British CWGC Cemetery.

Halswell - the only Olympian to have won his medal in a walk-over. The race had to be run again because Halswell was obstructed by his competitors, but they refused to take part in the repeat and so he was awarded the medal. He led his men across the Brook despite being wounded by shrapnel, and was killed on 31 March as he attempted to rescue a fellow officer. He is buried in Royal Irish Rifles Graveyard, Laventie.

By about 0800 hours the Germans had rushed up reinforcements. The attack had been brought to a standstill and a withdrawal was ordered by Gen Jacob, commanding the Dehra Dun Brigade, to the western bank of the stream where the wounded were collected and retired. Gallantry awards were won by Riflemen Manjit Gurung, Partiman Gurung, Ujir Sing Gurung and Jagtea Pun of the 2/2nd Gurkhas for attending the wounded under fire and bringing them back.

Continue.

To the left the farm complex which is on the site of the **Moulin de Piètre** can be seen. The German defences were strong here and held up the 10 March attack by the Ghurkas.

At the Piètre crossroads turn right.

Many more bunkers can now be seen in the fields to the right as one drives along, crops permitting.

N.B. A WW2 Memorial **to the crash site of Polish Pilot, J. Bondar** is passed on the left (**Map 7/7**, 7.1 miles, **Lat & Long: 50.58360 2.79442**).

Take the next right just before the Bois du Biez.

In 1915 the wood consisted mainly of young trees with a thick undergrowth. After the fighting of October 1914 around Givenchy and la Bassée the Germans gained a foothold in the wood here and then established a stronghold. It was one of the objectives of the Dehra Dun Brigade 10 March 1915 attack. On 11 March their advance was stopped by thick fog and heavy fire from the wood. On 12 March it was the second objective of a further attack by the Sirhind and Jullundur Brigades. The artillery kept up a fierce bombardment on the wood, with it is thought, great success as 'for days afterwards the enemy was observed to be removing bodies from the wood for burial in the fields behind it.'

After 200 yards there is a small bridge over a stream.

• Layes Bridge/7.3 miles/5 minutes/Map 7/8/Lat & Long: 50.58489 2.79082

This is the centre of the battlefield, the British attacks coming from directly ahead of you, and the line of the stream, Layes Brook, which features strongly in detailed accounts of the fighting, can be seen clearly to north and south. The Germans had turned this area into a redoubt with barbed wire and 15 machine guns. On 12 March, under the impression that the German line had been broken, General Haig brought up cavalry units and ordered that the infantry attack be pressed forward 'regardless of loss'. It was pressed, but the soldiers were tired, ammunition was short and the German defenders were fresh reinforcements. The Layes Bridge redoubt was never taken and the attack petered out overnight and during the following morning.

Continue to the next crossroads with the D171 (Lat & Long: 50.58915 2.78117). Turn left and just before the church in Neuve Chapelle turn right down the Rue du Moulin to the British cemetery sign to the right and turn up the track to the grass track leading to the cemetery on the left.

• Neuve Chapelle British CWGC Cemetery/8.4 miles/15 minutes/Map 7/9/Lat & Long: 50.58580 2.77899

The cemetery was begun during the battle (when it was known as Moggs Hole Cemetery) and used until the following November. It now contains some 50 burials. There is a special memorial to five men of the Rifle Brigade, killed on 10-14 March 1915, (with headstones behind) who were originally buried in Neuve Chapelle Churchyard and whose graves were destroyed by shell-fire and buried here is 17 year old Pte M. Walsh of the Manchester Regiment, 25 July 1915. The Cemetery area lies between trench lines named Highland Street and Bomb Row.

Return to the main road and continue to the next CWGC sign to the right. Park on the left and walk up the grassy path to the cemetery.

• Neuve Chapelle Farm CWGC Cemetery/8.7 miles/15 minutes/Map 7/10/Lat & Long: 50.58746 2.7783

There are 35 identified British soldiers buried here and 21 of them are from the 13th Battalion the London Regiment, known as 'the Kensingtons'. The Regiment was typical of the proud Territorial forces that came to the Colours, its origins deriving from the Volunteer forces of 1859. Like most, its gestation was complex. However, the Haldane reforms of 1908 created the Battalion via the amalgamation of the Kensington Rifles (4th Middlesex) and the 2nd (South) Middlesex and in 1913 it became 'Princess Louise's Kensington Regiment'. On 2 August 1914 the Kensingtons arrived at Salisbury Plain for their annual training. That night they were woken up and ordered to return to their drill hall immediately. There they were told to be ready for mobilisation, which came two days later. Over the next fortnight the battalion was equipped and brought up to strength and on 16 August it left with other Territorial units for war training in Hertfordshire. Early on the morning of 3 November 1914, led by the band, they marched to Watford station and at 1100 entrained for Southampton. After a long wait they sailed on the SS *Matheran* at 0100 hours on 4

Neuve Chapelle Farm CWGC Cemetery.

Headstones of Capt. A. Prismall and 17-year-old Pte A. G. Gordon, Neuve Chapelle Farm CWGC Cemetery.

November, reaching le Havre that same afternoon and marching to St Martin's rest camp on the hill. By foot and train they moved to the area of Laventie and spent the winter manning trenches in what was known as a quiet sector, even exchanging souvenirs with the enemy during an unofficial truce on Christmas day. Nevertheless, by the beginning of March the battalion had 96 casualties, 27 of whom were killed. Then came Neuve Chapelle.

The Kensingtons were in reserve with 25th Brigade. Their task was to follow up the assault battalions. They had a hot meal with the rest of the brigade at Rouge Croix, filled their water bottles with tea, and with two extra bandoliers of ammunition each and their rations in a sandbag, marched forward in great anticipation 'of making a decisive step towards the winning of the war'. They never came into contact with the enemy because after the first day the attack made no progress, though they began to suffer casualties from enemy artillery fire. On 11 March they were reinforced with a draft of 133 men, including **Lt M. A. Prismall**, son of **Captain A. Prismall** commanding B Company. For three more days they suffered under continuous bombardment and then came the order to move out. As the battalion was about to leave Captain Prismall was killed by a shell on 14 March. He lies in this cemetery with the other volunteers. He was 53. A **17 year old, Pte A.G. Gordon,** R Berks, 10 March 1915, is also buried here, among the 60 graves (nearly half unidentified) in this small cemetery surrounded by a beautiful stone wall.

Another battalion which suffered severely and with bravery in the Battle of Neuve Chapelle was the 2nd Scottish Rifles, who went into the battle on 10 March some 900 strong of whom 700 went 'over the top'. Six days later, only 143 were fit enough to parade for roll-call after the battle. The story is well-documented in John Baynes' book *Morale: A Study of Men and Courage.*

Continue to the T junction. Turn left and left again at the next junction and return to Port Arthur. There turn right on the D171 (the Rue du Bois). Continue, passing a small turning to the right (which was known as **'Factory Corner'**) *to the next turning to the right up the D166, rue des Berceaux.* This was **'Teetotal Corner'**.

It was in this area that another spontaneous manifestation of that curious phenomenon the **Christmas Truce** took place on 25 December 1914. The sector was held by the 39th Garhwal Rifles and at dawn the Adjutant of the 2nd Bn, Capt E.R.P. Berryman, noticed that no shots were being fired and then heard the Germans (of the 16th Westphalian Regiment) singing and shouting in their trenches. Before long German and Indian were shaking hands and gifts of biscuits, cigarettes and cigars were exchanged for brandy, plum pudding and whisky. The

Germans allowed the Indians to bury some of their dead. The jolly scene was stopped by Maj Keith Henderson of the 1st Bn who blew his whistle 'and signalled and shouted for all to come back' [*Christmas Truce*, Malcolm Brown & Shirley Seaton]. When the affair was reported to the Commanding Officer leave for all officers taking part in the truce was stopped. Two of them, Capt William George Stanhope Kenny (age 33) and Lt John Charles St George Welchman (age 26), were killed on 10 March in the Battle of Neuve Chapelle, the only officers to reach the German trench they were attacking. Kenny was killed in the trench which he held for some time 'with superb courage', despite being twice wounded. They are both buried in Laventie Mil Cemetery.

Continue, shortly passing another turning, this time to the left.

N.B. This was known as **Chocolat Menier Corner (Lat & Long: 50.56434 2.75132)** and is at the junction with the Rue du Bois and the Rue du Pont Moreau (whose wartime name was Prince's Road). It was so called because of a large advert for the chocolate which was on the side of a ruined café on this site, known as the Café du Ciseau d'Or. (At 53 Southwark Street, London SE1 1RU is the Chocolate Menier Factory Theatre/Restaurant/Bar in the old factory built in 1870: office@menierchocolatefactory.com).

Near here, too, at Richebourg l'Avoué, in the Battle of Festubert, an interesting **VC** was won. On 18 May 1915 **Lt John George Smyth** of the 15th Ludhiana Sikhs, Indian Army, took a volunteer bombing party of 10 men who transported 96 bombs to within 20 yards of the enemy line over exceptionally dangerous ground after two other parties had failed in the attempt. Eight of the party were killed but with the remaining two (Lance-Naik Mangal Singh and a Sepoy) Smyth delivered the bombs, having swum a stream all the while under howitzer, machine-gun and rifle fire. Singh was awarded the 2nd Class Indian Order of Merit and all the Sepoys received the Indian DSM. Smyth went on to become Brigadier the Rt Hon Sir John Smyth, Bt, was awarded the Russian Order of St George, raised the 19th London Division in India in 1941, commanded the 17th Division in Burma in 1942, was the MP for Norwood 1950-66, founder and Chairman of the VC and GC Association and author of books about the VC and the George Cross.

Continue, passing a turning to the left (which was **Rum Corner** and by 1918 a light railway known as the 'Kings Road' ran across here), *to the large Memorial on the left.*

• Le Touret Memorial and CWGC Cemetery/12.7 miles/20 minutes/ Map 7/11/Lat & Long: 50.56049 2.72264

This is probably the most elegant and elaborately designed Memorial and Cemetery complex on the Western Front. It comprises a loggia surrounding an open rectangular court encased by three solid walls and a colonnade on the east. Small pavilions mark the end of the gallery and there is a fascinating round tower at the back. It commemorates those missing with no known grave in this area over the period from the arrival of the BEF to the eve of the Battle of Loos (25 September 1915). Their names are inscribed inside the colonnade in Regimental order. It does not include any Canadian names (they are commemorated at Vimy) or, in theory, Indian (commemorated at Neuve Chapelle) although there is one Indian name. On Panels 26/27 – the Sherwood Foresters panels – is the name of **Private Jacob Rivers, VC,** 12 March 1915, age 34. His VC was awarded for two acts of bravery on 12 March, when on his own initiative he advanced on the enemy and hurled bombs, causing them to retire. Also commemorated is **Pte William Francis Elmes** of the 2nd R Sussex, 9 May 1915 age 34, who had served in the S African Campaign. His two brothers also fell in the war. Commemorated on the memorial are the 25 men from Wadhurst (qv) killed in the Battle of Aubers Ridge whose loss inspired the twinning between Aubers and Wadhurst. On Panels2/3 is **Capt the Hon John Beresford Campbell,** DSO, Coldstream Guards, age 48, 25 January 1915. His son, Lt Donald Campbell of the same Regiment, age 20, was killed on 19 July 1916 and is buried at Essex Farm (qv).

Graves and War Stone, Le Touret Memorial and CWGC Cemetery.

Decorative Tower, Le Touret Memorial and CWGC Cemetery.

Decorative Column, Le Touret Memorial and CWGC Cemetery.

The Memorial, designed by J.R. Truelove, was, according to Philip Longworth's *The Unending Vigil*, the story of the IWGC and the CWGC, unveiled at the same hour and the same day in August 1930 as the Memorials at Vis-en-Artois (also designed by Truelove), Pozières and Cambrai. CWGC records now show that it was unveiled by Lord Tyrrell on 22 March 1930.

At the entrance are some of the new-type CWGC **Information Panels** describing the Memorial and the B.E.F. in French Flanders. They bear a QR Code.

The Cemetery, begun in November 1914 by the Indian Corps, was used continually by field ambulances and fighting units until taken by the Germans in April 1918. In its spacious lawns there are over 900 burials, including that of **Lt Cyril Alfred William Crichton** (qv) who, until 1925, was buried under a special Private Memorial (visited earlier) near where he fell opposite the old Auberge de la Bombe. He was a Territorial.

Continue to the village of Le Touret to the junction with the D169. On the right hand corner is

• House With Statues of WW1 Personalities/ 13.3 miles/5 minutes/ Map 7/12/Lat & Long: 50.56224 2.70775

Surmounting this extraordinary house (sometimes screened by trees and shrubs), known as the Villa des Verdures, is a concrete equestrian statue of Marshal Foch, built by the sculptor Alphonse Wallaert after the war. Wallaert who was known as 'The Poet of Concrete', died in La Couture in 1958 at the age of 87. Other personalities commemorated around the tower are President Poincaré and the King and Queen of the Belgians.

*Statue of Marshal Foch,
Roof of House in Le Touret.*

Extra Visit to Portuguese Memorial, la Couture (Map 7/13, Lat & Long: 50.58128 2.71479), Vieille-Chapelle Communal (and 1st King Edward's Horse Memorial, Lat & Long: 50.59375 2.70950), Vieille Chapelle New (Map 7/14/15, Lat & Long: 50.59206 2.69682) and Zelobes Indian (Map 7/16, Lat & Long: 50.59297 2.68622) CWGC Cemeteries. Round trip: 7.4 miles. Approximate time: 40 minutes

Turn right direction la Couture on the D169 and continue to the church in la Couture on the right. In front of it is

The Portuguese Memorial. This impressive Memorial (beautifully renovated in 2010) shows a Portuguese soldier (note the distinctive ribbed tin helmet) attacking 'Death' overlooked by the female figure representing Portugal. It was sculpted by Teixeira Lopes and inaugurated on 10 November 1928. The first stone was laid on 11 November 1923 by Marshal Joffre when the village was awarded the *Lacet de la Croix de Guerre*, Portugal's highest honour. So began a lasting warm relationship between this region of France and Portugal. As the war progressed the village, with the church roughly at its centre, was turned into a defended area protected all round by trenches and barbed wire.

Continue on the D170 to La Vieille-Chapelle and turn right on the D182. Continue past the church to the cemetery on the right with the green CWGC Tombes de Guerre sign on the wall.

La Vieille Chapelle Communal CWGC Cemetery. There are two CWGC graves in the cemetery, both from May 1940 – **Pte A. Leitch,** R Scots and **Sgt J. Fox,** RA. To the right of the impressive local War Memorial is a stone **Memorial to the 1st King Edward's Horse, the King's Oversea Dominions Regiment** unveiled in 1921. It lists the officers and men who were killed or died on service in France 1915-1919, 'many of whom were killed in a very gallant defence of this locality, April 1918'. Over the 9/10/11 April 1918, during the Kaiser's Offensive, strong German attacks came from your right towards Vieille

Portuguese Memorial, la Couture.

Headstone of T/2nd Lt Schofield, VC, La Vieille-Chapelle New CWGC Cemetery.

Memorial to 1st King Edward's Horse, La Vieille Chapelle Communal Cemetery.

Extra Visit continued

Chapelle. The King Edwards Horse established defensive positions around the D170/D182 junction where you last turned, here and at Fosse (about a mile up the D172 opposite). By around 2200 hours on 10 April those at Fosse were isolated and Lt Addison of the Horse organised and inspired a stubborn resistance by a mixed force despite being hampered by retreating Portuguese. Such was Addison's spirit that a German breakthrough was averted but he was killed by a shell splinter on 11 April and buried by the Germans. Lt Noel Goodricke Addison, MC, age 25, is commemorated on the Dud Corner Memorial at Loos and the CWGC lists his date of death as 9 April, which according to the Regimental records would seem to be incorrect.

Turn round and return to the junction with the D170 signed to Vieille Chapelle. Continue to the cemetery on the left.

La Vieille-Chapelle New CWGC Cemetery. Burials started in the village in the Old Military Cemetery near the school which was closed in November 1915. Burials were then made in this cemetery. It was used by fighting units and Field Ambulances until March 1918 when the village and cemetery fell into German hands. When the Germans withdrew in September 1918 further burials took place here. After the Armistice British, Indian and Portuguese graves were concentrated here from the surrounding battlefields. The Portuguese graves were later removed to the Portuguese Cemetery (qv). It now contains nearly 1,000 British and Indian soldiers, approximately one-third of which are

Extra Visit continued

unidentified. The original graves are in Plots I and IV, Rows A and B. Here are buried two **VCs** from April 1918. **T/2nd Lt John Schofield,** 2/5th Lancashire Fusiliers, led a party of 9 men against a strong-point at Givenchy and was attacked by about 100 of the enemy. His skilful use of men and weapons resulted in the taking of 20 prisoners. He then proceeded with a party of 10 towards the front line where he met large numbers of the enemy and opened fire on them. Under point-blank fire he climbed on the parapet and by his fearless demeanour forced the enemy to surrender. As a result 123 of them, including several officers, were captured. Schofield was himself killed a few minutes later. **2nd Lt Joseph Henry Collin,** 1/4th King's Own (R Lancaster) Regt, after offering a gallant resistance against German attacks on his platoon position, 2nd Lt Collin, with only 5 of his men remaining, slowly withdrew, contesting every inch of ground. They then attacked a machine gun. After firing his revolver into the enemy he seized a Mills grenade and threw it into the hostile gun team, putting the gun out of action, killing 4 of the team and wounding two others. He then took a Lewis gun and engaged a second hostile machine gun, keeping the enemy at bay until he was mortally wounded.

The village of Vieille-Chapelle was 'adopted' by Paddington after the war.

Continue on the D182 to the T junction with the D945. Ahead is Zelobes Indian Cemetery. Turn left and park in parking area across the road. Walk up to the path to the cemetery.

Zelobes Indian Cemetery. 1914-1915. Zelobes remained in British hands from the early days of the war until 11 April 1918 when it was captured by the Germans and held by them until 30 August. The cemetery, which is approached

Headstone of Rifleman Birshamsher Rai, Assam Military Police, Zelobes Indian Cemetery, La Couture.

by a long grassed path and enclosed by a beautiful dark stone wall, was used by Field Ambulances from November 1914 to October 1915 and then after the Armistice isolated graves were concentrated into it. It now contains 105 Indian and British soldiers, 73 of whom are identified. It is worth visiting to read the wonderful Indian Regimental names inscribed on the headstones. The include the Assam Military Police who were part of the Ghurka Forces and fought so well that as a commendation in 1979 they were given the name 'Assam Rifles'.

Return to the house with the Foch statue.

• End of Neuve Chapelle Battlefield Tour

OR continue into Béthune on the D945 for RWC (see Loos tour).
OR go on to take the Aubers or Fromelles Tours (see pages 128 and 179).
OR the Festubert-Givenchy Tour (see page 139).

SECOND YPRES

22 APRIL-25 MAY 1915

'There was a curious smell, which was quite noticeable – we all remarked on it –
and then after a time the casualties started coming in.
It was most dramatic: long, long lines of Canadian soldiers, single file,
each man with his hand on the shoulder of the man in front.
There would be a man in front who could see – all these other chaps couldn't;
hundreds and hundreds of these chaps stumbling along, single file.'
A First World War Doctor.

'Of one's feelings all this night – of the asphyxiated French soldiers –
of the women and children – of the cheery steady British
reinforcements that moved up quietly past us
going up, not back – I could write, but you can imagine.'
Col John McCrea.

SUMMARY OF THE BATTLE

At around 1700 hours on 22 April 1915 the Germans attacked the north-eastern edge of the Ypres Salient using poison gas in what is generally accepted as the first major use of gas in warfare. Subsequent defensive fighting against repeated gas attacks resulted in a shortened Salient, but no breakthrough. Allied casualties were about 60,000, German 35,000.

OPENING MOVES

At the end of 1914, the German General Staff decided that, having failed to defeat France quickly and now being faced by enemies in both the east and the west, they would concentrate upon the Russian front. General Erich von Falkenhayn considered that Russia, struggling with internal political discontent, was the weaker of his two immediate protagonists and would succumb to concentrated German might. As far as the Western Front was concerned he instructed his commanders only to do enough 'lively activity' to keep the enemy occupied. One of the things that seemed likely to 'occupy' the French and British was to try out poison gas on them.

Article 23 of the 1907 Hague Convention, which Germany had signed, forbade the use of 'poisons or poisonous weapons', but before April 1915 the Germans had already tried out gas. Shrapnel shells containing a form of chemical irritant were tried out near Neuve Chapelle in October 1914 and tear gas shells had been used at Bolimow in Poland in January 1915, but neither trial produced any significant result. Von Falkenhayn was, however, supportive of the idea of developing a gas weapon and extensive testing was carried out at the Kummersdorf artillery ranges near Berlin. In the Second World War another secret weapon was tested there – von Braun's V2 rocket.

Germany possessed the most powerful chemical industry in the world and it was not difficult to consider other ways than shelling in which an enemy might be enveloped in a gas cloud. What was more difficult was to decide where to use the gas and several German commanders considered the use of such a weapon to be unethical. However, Falkenhayn persisted and keeping in mind his need to draw attention away from his intended effort in the east, he looked for a sensitive spot on the Western Front. Ypres was such a place.

The 4th (Ger) Army had been on the edge of breaking through during First Ypres (cf. Gheluvelt page 93) and the Salient was the only significant piece of Belgian soil not yet occupied. Added benefits were that the BEF had been decimated in defending Ypres and any activity there would demand wholehearted British attention as well as the fact that the French knew full well that holding Ypres was the key to keeping the Germans out of the Pas de Calais. Therefore Duke Albrecht of Wurtemberg and his 4th (Ger) Army facing Ypres were chosen to try out the new weapon. Preparations began in February 1915.

The simplest method of delivery of the gas was by cylinder, since that was the standard commercial container. Train loads of the heavy 3.5ft long objects were brought into the lines. It is estimated that some 30,000 cylinders were brought up into the forward areas and inevitably some were damaged – by accident or enemy action – so that the presence of the gas weapon was fairly common knowledge among German soldiers as time went on. Now and again German prisoners were taken who spoke about the presence of gas. However neither the French nor the British authorities took the reports seriously enough to take any precautions, though early in April Canadian troops were warned about the possibility of a gas attack following the mention of gas in the French 10th Army's 30 March intelligence bulletin.

The cylinders were dug into their firing positions in groups of 20, each group covering 40 yards of front and, 24 hours ahead of the intended assault time, the German soldiers were given their final briefings. At 0500 hours on 22 April 1915 everything was ready – except the wind. It was blowing the wrong way.

WHAT HAPPENED

As the German infantry waited, hoping for the wind to change direction, their field artillery pounded the front line defences and heavy 17-inch guns bombarded the rear areas. When the day matured it became warm and sunny, perhaps lulling the defenders into a degree of laxity and certainly making the Germans hot and uncomfortable in their heavy equipment. By late afternoon the attack was in the balance. Soon it would be dark. The offensive could not be made at night. Then, soon after 1600 hours a breeze began to develop from the north-east and one hour later the Germans opened the nozzles of thousands of gas cylinders and a fog of death rolled slowly across No Man's Land.

Below the Pilckem Ridge was the Canadian 3rd Brigade and alongside them, north of the ridge, the French Algerian 45th Colonial Division and it was upon these two formations that the fog descended. **Sir Arthur Conan Doyle** described what happened:

'The French troops, staring over the top of their parapet at this curious screen which ensured them a temporary relief from fire, were observed suddenly to throw up their hands, to clutch at their throats, and to fall to the ground in agonies of asphixiation. Many lay where they had fallen, while their comrades, absolutely helpless against this diabolical agency, rushed madly out of the mephitic mist and made for the rear, over-running the lines of the trenches behind them. Many of them never halted until they had reached Ypres, while others rushed westwards and put the canal between themselves and the enemy.'

By 1900 hours there was no organised body of French troops east of the Yser Canal. Between the Belgians (who held the ground north of the 45th Division's area) and the Canadian 3rd Brigade there was now a gap of 8,000 yards. The way to Ypres was open. The German advance (four reserve divisions – the 45th, 46th, 51st and 52nd) was cautious and limited. Their objective had been to take the Pilckem Ridge and no more and by the time they reached it darkness was falling. Thus it was not until the following morning that they realised how successful their attack had been and just how close they were to Ypres, which they could now see quite clearly ahead of

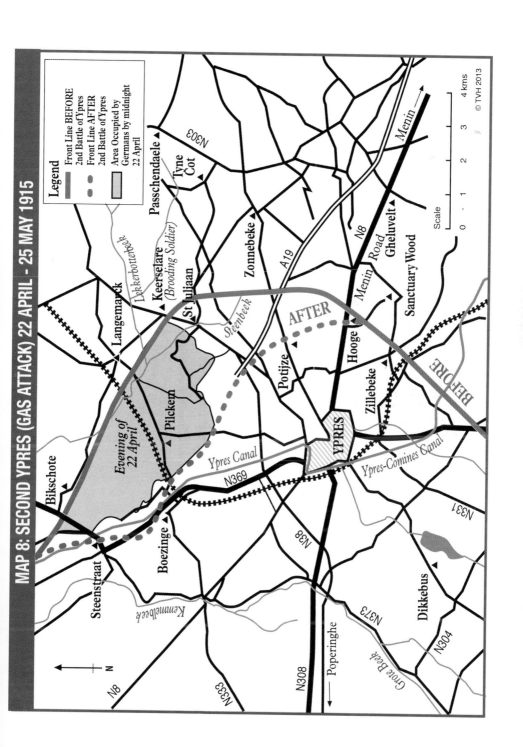

MAP 8: SECOND YPRES (GAS ATTACK) 22 APRIL – 25 MAY 1915

them (see **Map 8**). The Canadians around St Julien, meanwhile, had reacted to the gas with determination despite the fact that the French panic had left their northern flank unprotected. Brigadier General R.E.W. Turner commanding the Canadian 3rd Brigade ordered his reserve battalion, the 14th, into line beside the already positioned 13th and 15th battalions and held strong German attacks north of Keerselare (cf 'The Brooding Soldier' page ??) until they finally stopped at about 1830 hours. Two platoons of the 13th fought to their last man and **L/Cpl Frederick Fisher** of the battalion won a posthumous **VC** for his actions that day. His citation as published in the *London Gazette* gives the date of his action as the 23rd, but Canadian authorities say that this is incorrect. Sir Max Aitken, the Canadian Record Officer, later (as Lord Beaverbrook) wrote *Canada in Flanders*, the story of Canadian actions to 1916, including an entire chapter, with maps, covering the gas attacks.

Curiously, the fact that the Canadians stood and fought through the gas attack meant that they suffered less from it than they might have done had they followed the example of the French colonial troops and streamed back to the rear. The *Official History* explains: 'It early became evident that the men who stayed in their places suffered less than those who ran away, any movement making worse the effects of the gas, and those who stood up on the fire step suffered less – indeed they often escaped any serious effects – than those who lay down or sat at the bottom of a trench. Men who stood on the parapet suffered least, as the gas was denser near the ground. The worst sufferers were the wounded lying on the ground, or on stretchers, and the men who moved back with the cloud.'

General Smith-Dorrien commanding the 2nd Army first heard news of the attack at about 1845 hours on the 22nd and immediate moves were made to bring up reinforcements to plug the line. General Foch heard at midnight what had happened and reacted typically with three steps that should be taken: (1) hold; (2) organise for a counter-attack; (3) counter-attack. In fact counter-attacks did begin that night and following Foch's proposals it was agreed that 'vigorous action' east of the canal would be the best way to check any German attempts to advance. The enemy, however, struck first and on 24 April following a one-hour heavy bombardment the Germans released a gas cloud at 0400 hours immediately to the north-east of Keerselare and on a front of 1,000 yards against the Canadian Division. Throughout the day pressure on the Canadians forced them to withdraw to second-line positions, Keerselare being captured early in the afternoon. The following day, Sunday, 25 April 1915, the day of the Gallipoli landings, the Germans made a fierce effort to break the British lines. They made gains, but they did not break through.

The struggle continued in a series of engagements classified as the Battle of s-Gravenstafel, 22-23 April; Battle of St Julien, 24 April-5 May; Battle of Frezenberg, 8-13 May and Battle of Bellewaerde, 24-25 May. Overall the Germans made net gains. On 4 May the British made tactical withdrawals in order to shorten their lines, reducing their frontage from 21,000 yards to 16,000 yards and shortening the greatest depth of the Salient from 9,000 to 5,000 yards.

At le Cateau (qv) in 1914, General Smith Dorrien, Commanding II Corps, had made a stand despite the orders of Sir John French the Army Commander not to do so. Most authorities believe his action may well have saved the BEF. Sir John, however, while initially praising his Corps Commander, later began to cold shoulder him in a way that affected his Command. Smith Dorrien in his memoirs (*Memories of Forty-Eight Years Service*) speaks of the Field Marshal ignoring the letters he wrote asking for an interview to discuss the situation. In one he wrote '*I have had more to fear from the rear than from the front*'. This friction between the senior commanders of the BEF was going on over the first 5 months of 1915 i.e. including the Second Battle of Ypres, and Smith Dorrien does not even mention the battle in his memoirs. It would appear that his mind might not have been wholly occupied with the fighting. On the 7th of May he was replaced by Lt General Sir H. Plumer, the probable excuse used by Sir John French being the withdrawals made on 4 May. Ironically, barely six months later Sir John was forced to resign because Haig, his subordinate, believed that '*none of my officers commanding corps had a high opinion of Sir John's military ability*.' Obviously a happy crew.

In the World of 'If', the Germans might have taken Ypres and then the Channel Ports: if they had not used the gas just as a tactical distraction, but part of a major attack; if they had had reserves ready to follow up the initial success; if the wind had been in the right direction early on 22 April they would have seen how successful the gas had been and could have called up forces to exploit the break in the French lines. If they had used their secret weapon properly, say many, they could have won the war with it. The 'after-the-event' experts say the same thing about the British use of the tank on the Somme. Perhaps the most relevant 'If' belongs to the Canadians, courtesy of Rudyard Kipling, because they kept their heads when all about were losing theirs.

THE BATTLEFIELD TOUR

This is done in conjunction with First and Third Ypres – see page 237.

AUBERS RIDGE

9–10 MAY 1915

'The Gallipoli attack 6th to 8th May could only use 18,500 shells.
Haig was expending 80,000 on Aubers Ridge for less result,
a far less object – and twice the loss of life.'
Liddell Hart, *The Real War.*

'After Aubers Ridge surprise was abandoned.'
Alan Clark. *The Donkeys.*

'When we put memorial crosses for those who had fallen in the action
of May 9 there was a sergeant-major who put a white cross on the
grave of his son, and a private who put a cross on the grave of his father.'
W. Linton Edwards, 4th Bn Black Watch,
later Editor *Leeds Mercury.*

SUMMARY OF THE BATTLE

On 9 May 1915 the First British Army made a two-pronged attack on the German line that ran from just south of Neuve Chapelle to Bois Grenier some three miles north of Fromelles. At 0500 hours six hundred artillery weapons opened fire followed forty minutes later by an infantry advance. The southern prong consisting of the Indian and I Corps aimed towards Aubers Ridge while that of IV Corps, 6,000 yards to the north, headed for Fromelles.

The barrage had been inaccurate and short of shells, the German wire had not been cut and no small-arms supporting fire had been arranged for the advance. Little or no progress was made and by 0300 hours the following morning all the British troops were back where they had started and nearly 12,000 officers and men were casualties.

OPENING MOVES

By the spring of 1915 it was apparent that the Germans were concentrating their efforts on the Eastern Front and, following the battle of Neuve Chapelle in March, General Joffre, seeing an opportunity to take advantage of the situation, asked Sir John French if he would co-operate in a combined attack towards the ridges at Vimy and Aubers. The French were to take Vimy and the British, Aubers.

The British agreed. Sir John, convinced that the short artillery preparation at Neuve Chapelle had been a success, insisted that it be repeated and set his 1st Army's objective as, 'to break through the enemy's line on its front and gain the la Bassée to Lille road between la Bassée and Fournes-en-Weppes.'

The plan was to attack both north and south of **Neuve Chapelle.** The Indian and I Corps were south, essentially astride the D947 at **la Bombe** crossroads heading for the ridge and **la Cliqueterie Farm**. Some 6,000 yards to the north IV Corps, centred on the D175, was to head towards **Rouges Bancs** and **Fromelles** and then swing south with 7th Division to la Cliqueterie to join up with the southern force. Thus, in theory, having broken through the German lines, the 1st Army, now in possession of Aubers Ridge, would catch the Germans in a pincer trap.

WHAT HAPPENED

The attack was planned for the early morning of 8 May. Since the success of the operation depended initially on the attacking troops breaching the German wire, trench mortar batteries were attached to the infantry brigades for close support but in the event did not materially affect the outcome. The 1st Wing of the Royal Flying Corps was given the task of aerial reconnaissance, supposedly reporting back when successive target lines were reached by the infantry, the lines to be marked with strips of white linen 7 feet by 2 feet carried for that purpose. The effectiveness of the system was not tested as none of the designated lines were reached.

Owing to bad weather the French decided to postpone the operation for 24 hours, the decision reaching General Haig at 1700 hours on the 7th, just 60 minutes before the troops were due to move into their forward positions for the attack. Inevitably forward movements had already taken place and some troops were thus stuck uncomfortably in the open for 24 hours before going into battle, but by midnight of 8 May all units were ready for the next morning's assault.

The sun rose at 0406 hours and at 0500 hours a 40-minute barrage opened, with a furious final 10 minutes. But the shells were not of sufficient calibre, the 4.7″ guns had worn barrels causing faulty aim and range and the bombardment failed in its objective of destroying the German wire and prepared defences. The operation was virtually doomed from the start.

The Southern Attack

Below la Bombe crossroads no covering small arms fire was given as the leading companies of the 2nd and 3rd Brigades of the 1st Division moved into No Man's Land intending to form a line some 80 yards short of the German positions. They were met with heavy machine-gun fire. Many fell dead on the ladders and parapets. Nevertheless some men doubled forward and formed a line not far short of the intended objective.

The Indian Corps to their left across and above the crossroads fared little better – they too lacked supporting small arms fire. The leading troops were only able to advance a few yards from their own parapets and though some following troops tried to press on they were soon driven back until the trenches were blocked with casualties, though some brave men reached the enemy. A German diarist recalled a handful of Gurkhas 'running like cats' reaching the wire and attacking with knives. All were killed and buried later that day in a communal grave.

When the barrage lifted at 0540 all three brigades attempted to storm the German lines. The lifts were too quick, being made before the attacking troops were within fifty yards of the enemy, and the wire had not been cut. Small parties from the leading battalions crossed the German trenches here and there (one from the Munsters was seen waving a green flag) and then disappeared. The Munsters suffered a double tragedy. Their CO, Lt Colonel Rickard, was killed and all but three of the survivors of the green flag party were later killed by friendly fire. Within two hours 2nd and 3rd Brigades lost some 60% of their strength. The 2nd Royal Sussex and the 1st Northants were 'virtually annihilated', with 551 and 560 casualties respectively, the shallow jumping-off trenches clogged with the dead and wounded.

Inadequate efforts were made to organise further attacks, the British artillery merely prompting the Germans to rain shells down upon the men lying out in No Man's Land. General Haig, hearing that the French were making good progress on their part of the front, decided to renew the attack later in the day. He ordered the reinforcement of 2nd and 3rd Brigades and the replacement of the Dehra Dun Brigade with the Bareilly, these actions being carried out in broad daylight. The *Official History* dryly observes 'These reliefs ... were attended by much confusion and heavy losses'. Brigadier General Thesiger, commanding the 2nd Brigade, reported that his brigade was not fit to renew the offensive and it was replaced by the 1st (Guards) Brigade.

There was a succession of postponements until, eventually, the attack began at 1557 hours. The 1st Black Watch (1st Division, 1st Brigade) was the only battalion to be in position to go over the top at zero hour, some battalions arriving after it was clear that the assault had failed. The Scots moved forward with their pipes and some 50 men reached the German front line trenches to find the occupants in flight. They turned the Germans' own machine guns round to fire upon them but

MAP 9: AUBERS RIDGE-FROMELLES, 9/10 MAY 1915 (See also Map 13)

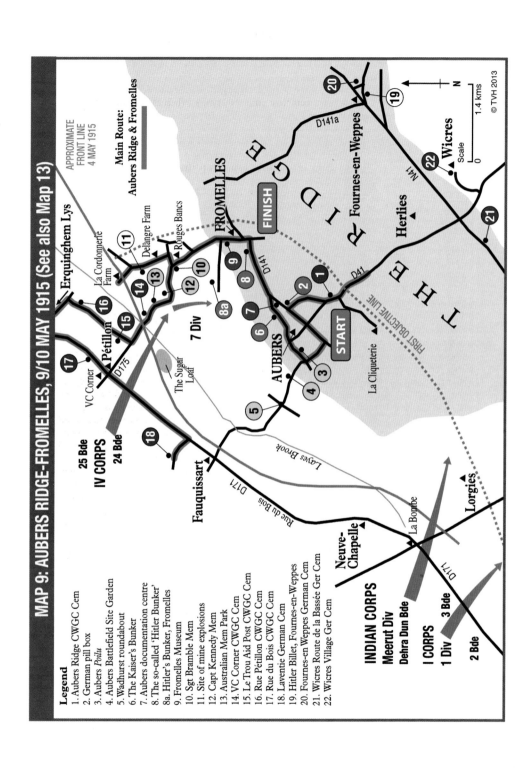

© TVH 2013

Legend

1. Aubers Ridge CWGC Cem
2. German pill box
3. Aubers *Poilu*
4. Aubers Battlefield Site Garden
5. Wadhurst roundabout
6. The Kaiser's Bunker
7. Aubers documentation centre
8. The so-called 'Hitler Bunker'
8a. Hitler's Bunker, Fromelles
9. Fromelles Museum
10. Sgt Bramble Mem
11. Site of mine explosions
12. Capt Kennedy Mem
13. Australian Mem Park
14. VC Corner CWGC Cem
15. Le Trou Aid Post CWGC Cem
16. Rue Pétillon CWGC Cem
17. Rue du Bois CWGC Cem
18. Laventie German Cem
19. Hitler Billet, Fournes-en-Weppes
20. Fournes-en Weppes German Cem
21. Wicres Route de la Bassée Ger Cem
22. Wicres Village Ger Cem

APPROXIMATE
FRONT LINE
4 MAY 1915

Main Route:
Aubers Ridge & Fromelles

Scale
0 _____ 1.4 kms

N

INDIAN CORPS
Meerut Div
Dehra Dun Bde

I CORPS
1 Div   3 Bde

2 Bde

Neuve-Chapelle

La Bombe

Lorgies

D171

Rue du Bois

D171

Fauquissart

Layes Brook

25 Bde
IV CORPS
24 Bde

VC Corner

D175

Pétillon

The Sugar Loaf

7 Div

La Cordonnerie Farm

Erquinghem Lys

Delangre Farm

Rouges Bancs

FROMELLES

FINISH

D141

AUBERS

START

FIRST OBJECTIVE LINE

La Cliqueterie

THE

RIDGE

D41

D141a

Fournes-en-Weppes

Herlies

Wicres

N41

were subsequently surrounded and almost all killed. **Cpl John Ripley** of the 1st Battalion, who was the first man to climb the enemy's parapet, was awarded the **VC**.

In the Meerut Division the relief of the Dehra Dun Brigade by the Bareilly cost two hundred men through artillery fire and was not complete until 1600 hours. When the brigade did go over the top it came under intense direct machine-gun fire, the enemy standing on his parapets and taking aim. Finally, when all the companies in the leading battalions had been sent forward and shot down, the attack was called off. The brigade had lost over 1,000 men in a few minutes. In this action another **VC** was won, this time by **L/Cpl David Finlay (qv)** of the 2nd Battalion Black Watch (Meerut Division, Bareilly Brigade) who led a bombing party of twelve, ten of whom fell. Finlay then went to the assistance of a wounded man and carried him to safety over the fire-swept ground. Somewhat confusingly, Finlay's action was on 9 May, therefore technically speaking it was in the Battle of Aubers Ridge. However it physically took place in the area of the Battle of Festubert (which some authorities describe as lasting from 9-27 May 1915).

The Northern Attack

The IV Corps plan was to attack with 24th and 25th Brigades of 8th Division astride the D175 road towards Rouges Bancs and Fromelles. The brigades were moved up into the forward trenches on the night of 8 May and were in position by 0230 hours. Each was allocated a small force of cyclists and mounted troops 'to assist the advance beyond the German front line'. What might appear to be a more sensible allocation were sections of mountain artillery and trench mortars intended to take on the German machine guns. The preliminary bombardment was simultaneous with that in the south.

The attack began at 0540 hours. In 24th Brigade the 2nd East Lancs were stopped before they got half way across No Man's Land though a party of one officer and thirty men of the 2nd Northants got through the German wire thanks to a field gun that had been brought up in support. At 0610 the 1st Sherwoods were sent in to help the East Lancs but were cut down like the others. Here, as in the south, the barrage had been ineffective and the Germans were choosing their targets over open sights. Despite being under direct fire **Cpl J. Upton** of the Sherwoods rescued and tended many wounded men, actions for which he received the **VC**. Meanwhile, under pressure to push on, the supporting battalions were moving into the forward trenches crowding those still there and the casualties coming back, all falling prey to the accurate enemy artillery fire.

The 25th Brigade had split its assault into two columns four hundred yards apart. The right hand column of the 2nd Rifle Brigade and the 1st Royal Irish Rifles found the wire in front of them had been cut and covered the 100 yards of No Man's Land at speed, taking over 250 yards of German front including prisoners of the 16th Bavarian Reserve Regiment. Interestingly this was Adolf Hitler's regiment. What might have been the outcome had he been there and been one of the prisoners!

The left-hand column formed by the 1/13th London (Kensington) Regiment was also initially successful. The battalion formed up at **la Cordonnière Farm** (various spellings, e.g. Cordonnerie) and was in its assault positions by 0200 hours. The preparatory bombardment failed either to cut the wire or to destroy the enemy defences. A planned 4.7" howitzer barrage on **Delangre Farm** failed to land a single shot on target. Nevertheless, at 0540 two mines of 2,000lbs of gunpowder 70 yards apart, which had been prepared by 173rd Tunnelling Company, were exploded under the German front line trenches. The Kensingtons rushed the craters. They had trained carefully for the operation and were proud to be the first TA unit to have been used as an assaulting force in a major operation. Despite the withering opposition the Kensingtons took the craters and the track leading to Delangre, but the farm possessed a number of machine guns and the Kensingtons were unable to advance further or to receive substantial reinforcements. At 0610 hours **Brigadier Lowry-Cole,** commanding the 25th Brigade, reached the German trenches to find many men streaming back towards their own lines, bringing with them German prisoners whose presence led to a bombardment by our own guns. He leapt onto the parapet intending to rally his men, but was shot and killed. He is buried in Le Trou Aid Post CWGC at Fleurbaix (qv). Elements of the 2nd Lincolns did reach the Kensingtons including **Acting Corporal Richard Sharpe** who was the first to reach the enemy line and who, using grenades, cleared 50 yards of trench, efforts for which he received the **VC**. He later became a Company Sergeant Major and served in WW2.

When Haig heard of the stalemate he issued orders for the attack to be resumed but it became clear that, due to the severe losses already incurred and the difficulty of bringing up fresh troops, apart from the inadequacy of the artillery support, this was not practicable and during the night of 9 May the order was given to retire. Thus the remnants of the Kensingtons made their way back pursued by a strong German counter-attack around 0230 hours on the 10th. One Kensington remembered,

'We crawled about 120 to 150 yards through German barbed wire and across ground raked by a withering cross fire. It was a hailstorm of lead bullets splitting up the ground and filling the air with the buzz as of angry bees and bursting shells.'

The Kensingtons had lost 13 officers and 423 other ranks. They had ceased to exist as a fighting unit.

The battle of Aubers Ridge had been a failure.

THE BATTLEFIELD TOUR

• **The Route:** The tour continues on from the end of the Neuve Chapelle Tour via 'The Bunker Route' and starts at Aubers Ridge CWGC Cemetery, visits the Rue du Plouich Bunker, continues through Aubers village to 'The so-called 'Kaiser's Bunker' and the Aubers Historical Centre and then finally looks at the so-called 'Hitler's Bunker' (see also Fromelles Tour).
• **[N.B.]:** The following sites are indicated: Bois du Biez Bunker and Bunkers en route to Aubers; Aubers *Mairie*, The Battlefield Site Garden, Wadhurst Roundabout.
• **Total Distance:** 3.0 miles
• **Total time:** 1 hour
• **Distance from Calais to start point:** See Neuve Chapelle Tour
• **Base town:** Béthune
• **Maps:** IGN 1:25,000 2404 Est plus 2405 Est

We have called the following Approach Route the **'The Bunker Route'** as it takes in several considerable German bunkers, some of which may become difficult to find without the GPS references here included.

From the 'Foch House' (qv) return to the la Bombe crossroads on the D171. Turn right on the D947direction La Bassée. Continue to the first crossroads and turn left on the D72 signed Lorgies. Continue to the T junction and turn right on the D72 signed Lorgies Centre. At the junction keep left past the Mairie on the D72 signed to Herlies/Illies.

N.B. **Bois du Biez.** Before leaving the village there is a small calvary on the left. By turning left here on the rue du Bois du Biez, and continuing along the small road for approx .6 mile to a sharp left turn, taking this left turn (still called Bois du Biez), and stopping after about 100 yards, about 100 yards into the cleared area of the wood on the right a significant **German Bunker (Lat & Long: 50.57733 2.79484) can be seen.**

You are effectively travelling north along a German reserve line. At this point the main German line is about 2 miles to your left (west) and pretty well remained there from 1915 to 1918.

Continue and if in doubt at any STOP sign or junction go straight over on the D72. Continue as the road becomes very narrow to the Bunker on the left.

Bunker No 1, Hameau de L'Halpegarbe, Illies. Lat & Long : 50.57337 2.81573
Continue to the T Junction with the D141. Straight ahead is

'Bois du Biez Bunker'.

Bunker No 2. Lat & Long: 50.57778 2.82158.
This bunker may well have been placed here to cover a junction between a local narrow gauge railway and a mainline which ran adjacent to each other about 100 yards behind the bunker.
Turn right on the D141 and take the first turning left on the CV401 signed to Herlies.
Continue to the Exit sign for l'Aventure (Commune d'Illies) short of a large water tower. On the left is

Bunker No 3. Lat & Long: 50.57822 2.82956.
Trench maps of early 1917 show a buried pipe line or communication cable running back from the bunker to a building at the last turning.
Continue and take the first left signed Herlies on the D141. Continue into the Centre of Herlies on the rue du Stade. At the roundabout turn left direction Aubers (signed to Fromelles) on the D41. Continue to the cemetery on the right.

Set your mileometer to zero.

• Aubers Ridge British CWGC Cemetery/0 miles/15 minutes/Map 9/1/ Lat & Long: 50.58923 2.83654

The cemetery, which is situated right on the objective line of the first day of the battle, contains concentrations from several wartime cemeteries. It has 593 UK, 124 Australian, 1 Indian burial and 1 Special Memorial. There are also some '39-'45 graves. The burials start in 1914 and range through the dates of all the battles in the region. Many are Unknown Australians from the July 1916 Fromelles Battle in Plot I, and Plot II is almost entirely of men of the 61st (S Midland) Division from the same action. The single Indian is **Sepoy Abdullah** of 58th Vaughan Rifles, 25 September 1915 (Neuve Chapelle). **Captain W. I. Maunsell**, 2nd Cameronians, 8 February 1915, age 31, was the 'Beloved son of Surgeon General T. & Mrs Maunsell.'

'Bunker No 1'.

'Bunker No 2'.

'Bunker No 3'.

In the WW2 Plot is buried **Pilot Officer Jozef Bondar** (qv) of 303 Sqn RAF, 28 June 1941, to whom a **Memorial** was erected (see **Map 7/7**) in June 2003. This Polish pilot fought for his country in Poland in 1939, escaped to Rumania and thence to France where he flew a Potez 25 with the French Airforce in North Africa until the fall of France. He then joined the RAF in July/August 1940. The Sikorski Institute in London has a file on Bondar. He was shot down in a classic attack from the rear when returning from escorting a raid on the Comines electrical supply. The instigator of the Memorial is Jocelyn Leclercq, who founded the research group Antiq'Air Flandre-Artois (qv).

Continue towards Aubers on the D41 and after barely 100 yards turn right on the narrow Chemin de Valmonchy and at the fork keep to the left on Rue du Plouich. Continue to the crossroads where, on the right, is

Aubers Ridge British CWGC Cemetery in its June glory.

• *Rue du Plouich Bunker/.6 miles/5 minutes/Map 9/2/Lat & Long: 50.59738 2.83323*

The bunker looks remarkably like the ruins of an Irish famine cottage. The concrete structure with mesh reinforcement was in fact constructed within an existing house. It overlooked the British lines and was connected to the artillery command centre. It incorporated a telephone room and was well camouflaged. The road ahead, the D141, runs along what was a railway line running west into German lines.

Turn left and continue to the roundabout and turn right signed Centre Village. At the T junction turn left. In front of the Church on the left is

Rue du Plouich Bunker.

• *Aubers Village Centre & Poilu/1.2 miles/10 minutes/Map 9/3/Lat & Long: 50.59552 2.825528*

Records exist in the town of the original meeting on 4 April 1925 during which it was decided to employ the Parisian sculptor, Descatoires, to make the monument in the form of a 2.25m high Poilu on a Belgian granite base. The inscription was to be in letters of 'great character'. The monument cost 32,000 Francs.

When mobilisation was declared between 2 and 18 August 1914, men of the village left to fight. The following month refugees started to arrive from the Lille area and on 10 October a large German contingent entered the village, searching the church and many houses. On 17 October Smith-Dorrien's 9th Brigade occupied the Ridge and British soldiers were seen in the village for the first time. On 20 October the Germans launched their offensive and on 23 October the British troops were forced to withdraw. All but 200 or so inhabitants were then evacuated and the village remained in German hands until October 1918 when it was liberated by the 47th (London) Division.

N.B. By continuing past the church you will pass the fine *Mairie* (**Lat & Long: 50.59514 2.82394**) on the left with its floral displays, elegant first floor meeting room and balcony.

At the roundabout, (later in the war the junction, then a crossroads, was known as 'Tramway Corner'), turn right and on the right, just before the first right turn, is **The Battlefield Site Garden** (**Map 9/4, 50.59521 2.81899**). This has been established in memory of the Aubers Ridge Battle and the 'Men of Wadhurst'. Aubers has a very active Twinning Association with Wadhurst in Sussex. This arose because 25 men of Wadhurst, named on a Memorial in their church, were all killed in the Battle of Aubers Ridge on 9 May 1915. They are commemorated on the Le Touret Memorial (qv). In this small, peaceful park is a seat bearing a Plaque. A German light railway – a 'tramway' - ran from the village northwards from Tramway Corner along this road to the front line a mile ahead.

The next roundabout (approximately 1 mile from Aubers Church) is called the **Rond Point Wadhurst** (**Map 9/5**).

The Aubers Poilu.

Aubers-Wadhurst Twinning Plaque, Battlefield Site Garden.

Turn round and take the first left signed Centre Village. Return past the Poilu. Bear right and continue over the stop sign, direction Fromelles on the Rue Houdringue to the dentist's surgery on the left. Just behind its modern extension (therefore difficult to spot and behind a gate) is

• 'Kaiser's Bunker'/1.4 mile/5 minutes/Map 9/6/Lat & Long: 50.59692 2.82952

This ivy-covered pill-box is so called because it is said that Wilhelm II (or maybe the Kronprinz) visited the bunker during the German Occupation. It is a German third-line pill box, the top floor of which was used as a watch tower and the ground floor for stabling the horses and donkeys that the Germans used for carrying ammunition and supplies. It was also a place of rest for German soldiers coming out of the line.

Once the Germans were entrenched on the ridge they began a massive programme of defensive building in reinforced concrete. According to local historians there were between 7 and 8,000 pill-boxes and bunkers by the end of the German occupation in the 'Département du Nord', some 700 in the Aubers-Fromelles sector. Today the area still seems littered with their remains and probably some 200 exist in one form or other.

Continue to the school on the right (marked by a magnificent flowering cherry in the springtime). Beside it is

• Aubers Historical Circle Archives/1.5 miles/Map 9/7/Lat & Long: 50.59737 2.83087

Kaiser's Bunker, Aubers.

Aubers has an extremely active Historical Circle, of which the President is the Mayor, M Pierre Descamps. His distinguished and gallant father, Henri-Clotaire Descamps (qv), a senior officer in the Gendarmerie, founded the Resistance Cell, *Verité Française*, was betrayed, arrested by the Gestapo and beheaded in Brandenbourg-sur-Havel on 5 December 1942. He was awarded the *Légion d'Honneur*, the *Croix de Guerre* and several Resistance decorations.

The Circle's impressive archives are available to serious students on request. **Contact** the *Mairie*, Tel: + (0)3 20 50 20 38.

Continue to the T junction and turn left, direction Fromelles on the D141. Continue to the bunker on the left just before the Fromelles village sign.

• So-Called 'Hitler's Bunker'/2.3 miles/10 minutes/Map 9/8/Lat & Long: 50.60236 2.84801

This was so called because during his famous 1940 tour of his WW1 haunts, Adolf Hitler was said to have visited this pill-box. He fought in the Aubers-Fromelles sector as a Corporal from 10 March 1915 to 25 September 1916 with the 16th Bavarian Regiment. It is now believed that the true 'Hitler's Bunker', one in which he briefly sheltered during the war, is in Fromelles (qv).

The Bunker is becoming somewhat overgrown but the letters 'ERBAUT von der 4FPK' (BUILT by the 4th FIELD PIONEERS) are still visible above the entrance. It was on the German 5th line

So-called 'Hitler's Bunker' with detail of inscription (inset), Aubers.

of 19-20 July, the Battle of Fromelles, and a single gauge railway ran immediately behind it from Aubers to Fromelles. At this point also, and perhaps the reason for the bunker, by 1917 a light railway led from the rear of the bunker north westward to the front line at Fauquissart, and to hide the inevitable activity here screens had been erected along the lines.

Continue to the T junction. Turn left and stop in the car park opposite the Mairie of Fromelles (2.6 miles, **Lat & Long: 50.60596 2.85405***).*

• End of Aubers Ridge Battlefield Tour

OR Continue with Fromelles Tour

FESTUBERT-GIVENCHY

15-27 MAY 1915

'Well lads, you may have been boys yesterday;
you're men now – yes, men.'
Col Harry Walker, Black Watch, after the Battle of Festubert.

SUMMARY OF THE BATTLE

At 2330 hours on 15 May between Neuve Chapelle and Festubert the 2nd and Meerut Divisions of 1 Corps began the first British night attack of the war followed, three and a half hours later in daylight, by 7th Division to their south. Early local success was marred by lack of materiel which had been 'loaned' to Gallipoli and inadequate artillery support. After ten days, during which time the Canadian Division became involved, the battle stalled with limited gains. British casualties were 16,648 officers and men, German about 5,000.

OPENING MOVES

As far as the French were concerned the fighting at Aubers and at Festubert was part of the same Joffre-inspired overall plan whose main objective was the taking of Vimy Ridge. General Foch, who commanded the French forces during the offensive, believed that the British short artillery bombardment at Neuve Chapelle was fundamentally ineffective and planned long systematic barrages before any French attacks. The British C-in-C, Sir John French, plagued by a shortage of shells and a proliferation of duds as well as being concerned by the situation in Ypres following the German gas attacks of 22 April and later, needed some convincing to undertake what he saw as another offensive. The battles of Neuve Chapelle in March 1915 and Aubers Ridge earlier in May had indeed suffered from too short an artillery bombardment and poorly defined daily infantry objectives, although at Neuve Chapelle the brief preliminary barrage had introduced the element of surprise into the attack.

This time, however, learning from the French successes, it was decided that a longer, two-day continuous night and day bombardment would precede the attack and that the attacking troops would be given specific objectives to be achieved on the first day. Surprise was to be gained by attacking at night.

The plan was imaginative. The night attack was to be double-pronged (see **Map 10**). One prong immediately below Port Arthur (la Bombe) was to be carried out by the Garhwal Brigade of the Meerut Division and the other, on their right, by 5th and 6th Brigades of 2nd Division. Their immediate objective was to take the first two lines of German trenches before dawn and then, at that moment, a fresh attack by 7th Division 600 yards to the south, just above Festubert, would hopefully allow some of the German defences to be taken from the rear. Once this movement was underway further limited objectives were to be attempted.

WHAT HAPPENED

The British bombardment began on 13 May between Port Arthur (la Bombe) and Festubert with a view to making the night attack on 14 May. However the assault was delayed for 24 hours

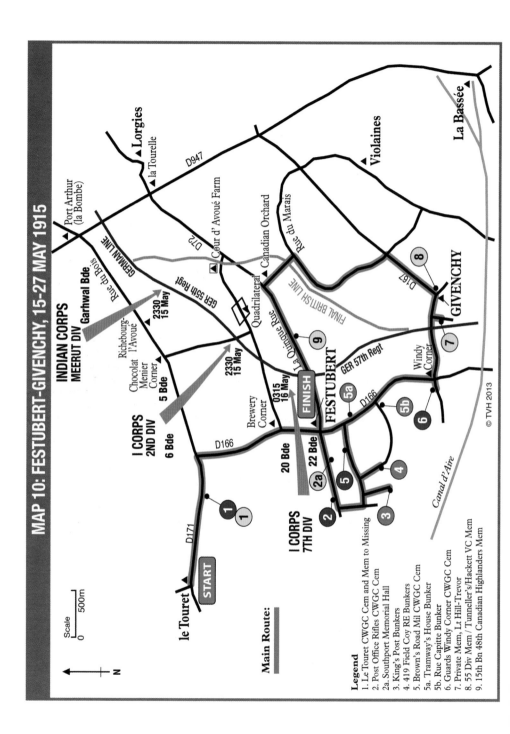

MAP 10: FESTUBERT-GIVENCHY, 15-27 MAY 1915

Legend
1. Le Touret CWGC Cem and Mem to Missing
2. Post Office Rifles CWGC Cem
2a. Southport Memorial Hall
3. King's Post Bunkers
4. 419 Field Coy RE Bunkers
5. Brown's Road Mil CWGC Cem
5a. Tramway's House Bunker
5b. Rue Capitte Bunker
6. Guards Windy Corner CWGC Cem
7. Private Mem, Lt Hill-Trevor
8. 55 Div Mem / Tunneller's/Hackett VC Mem
9. 15th Bn 48th Canadian Highlanders Mem

© TVH 2013

because it was felt that the enemy wire had not been thoroughly cut in front of the Meerut Division. To increase the element of surprise as to the hour of the attack the bombardment programme included a number of stops and starts and cheers from front-line infantry as if they were about to go over the top.

At 2330 hours on 15 May the attack began. On the right 6th Brigade almost reached the German line before they were fired upon and quickly took and consolidated the enemy trenches, shining a pair of car headlights back towards their own lines to signal success. The 5th and Garhwal Brigades, however, were spotted and came under heavy machine gun and rifle fire, the enemy using flares or 'light balls' to illuminate the area and no progress was made. It was decided that another attempt would be made and that it should coincide with the 7th Division attack, but with the enemy artillery active upon the forward trenches this proved to be impossible and the idea was dropped.

At 0315 the 7th Division attack began, the 20th and 22nd Brigades having moved up to their jump-off positions overnight, the enemy positions being generally only around 100 yards away. The opposition was fierce and the Commanding Officers of the leading regiments of 22nd Brigade were both killed while urging their men on – Lt Col R. E. P. Gabbett, 1st Royal Welch Fusiliers (buried in the Guards Cemetery at Windy Corner) and Lt Col H. R. Bottomley, 2nd Queens (who died of wounds two days later and is buried in Béthune Town cemetery). Nevertheless the German defences were taken and the advance pushed on as far as the **Orchard** where it stopped.

In the 20th Brigade leading elements of the forward regiments, the 2nd Scots Guards and the 2nd Border Regiment, moved out into No Man's Land too early and came under 'friendly fire'. However they carried the first lines of trenches, and by-passed the **Quadrilateral,** a major German defensive position in the unassaulted area between the divisions which was firing upon their flank. The ground was difficult, including a deep dyke that had to be crossed, but finally with help from a party of 1st Royal Welch, which had drifted over from their sector, the Scots reached the area above the **Orchard**, an advance during which **CSM Frederick Barter (qv)** won the **VC**. Barter called for volunteers to help him extend the line when they reached the German first line trenches and eight 'bombers' responded. They then attacked the German position, capturing three German officers, 102 men and 500 yards of trenches. Barter then found and cut eleven of the enemy's mine leads. He was commissioned as a 2nd Lt on 26 August 1915, went on to become a Captain and to win the MC and survived the war to serve as a Major in the Home Guard in WW2. In an odd twist of fate, while Barter was in Palestine in April 1918, his life was saved during an action by **Rifleman Karanbahadur Rana**, for which Rana was awarded the **VC**. Barter died on 15 May 1952. Following another shelling by British guns, however, heavy machine gun fire from the flanks and a German counter-attack, the troops fell back to the captured enemy breastworks.

Thus, by 0900 hours on 16 May, looking from bottom to top (see **Map 10**), 22nd Brigade of 7th Division had advanced some 600 yards to the Orchard, 20th Brigade was only at the German front trenches, 2nd Division were in and beyond the trenches but the Garhwal Brigade attack had failed. Thus the central area where the Quadrilateral posed a major threat had not been taken and during the day unsuccessful attempts were made to pinch it out by attacks from above and below.

General Haig now decided to concentrate his effort in the 7th and 2nd Divisions' areas so a bombardment of the Quadrilateral and the centre was begun at 0245 hours on 17 May. But during the night the Germans had begun a withdrawal of some 900 yards to a new defensive line towards which they were hurrying reserves, a fact that was not discovered for several days. Opposition was therefore patchy and both 2nd and 7th Divisions were able to make early advances, the Quadrilateral falling by 1015 hours. This relative success in the south led Sir John French to change the ultimate objective of the 1st Army from that of taking Aubers Ridge to that of gaining access to the canal below la Bassée, thus swinging the axis of the battle towards the south-east. However bad weather, more friendly fire, water-filled ditches, delays in getting orders to the front line, growing casualty numbers and stiffening German resistance from their new defensive line stopped all forward activity. It was decided that the Canadian Division should replace the 7th

Division and the 51st (Highland) Division the 2nd Division. The 51st had been named as the 'Highland' Division on 11 May. These changes were complete by 0900 on 20 May, the two new divisions being combined as Alderson's Force after Lt Gen Sir E.A. Alderson, Commander of the Canadian Division. Immediately south of them towards the canal was 47th Division.

Over the next five days local actions were carried out to secure the positions already gained in preparation for the assault towards la Bassée, the 3rd Canadian Brigade occupying the Orchard, named thereafter the **'Canadian Orchard'.** Coincidentally it was in this area in December 1914 that the first serious British attempt to use mines had been made when the Dehra Dun Brigade attempted to drive a shallow tunnel towards the German lines, hoping to place a charge of 45 pounds of gun cotton under them, but before the mine could be fired it was detonated by enemy fire.

During 25 May the Army's only kite balloon, owned and staffed by the Admiralty, was used to direct the preparatory bombardment for the next attack and during the night the 47th and Canadian Divisions launched their assault. The 47th gained an average of 400 yards over a 1,000 yard frontage broadly parallel to the canal in the direction of la Bassée. The Canadians made little progress, due not just to the stubborn resistance of the Germans now firmly established in their new main position, but also to the shortage of artillery ammunition that prevented a substantial initial bombardment and to being armed with their Ross rifle which overheated and readily jammed with mud. It was finally withdrawn in June after over 3,000 Canadians had thrown away their Ross weapons and taken the SMLEs of British casualties.

It was now clear that further progress was unlikely. Sir John French, concerned about the ammunition situation at Ypres, moved much of his munitions there and in response to a French request sent the 2nd Division to relieve their 58th Division in the Vermelles area. The Battle of Festubert was over and it would be 1918 before any serious change in the positions of the front lines would take place.

THE BATTLEFIELD TOUR

• **The Route:** The tour starts at the Le Touret Memorial (so could practically be done after the Neuve Chapelle Tour), visits the Post Office Rifles and Brown's Road Mil CWGC Cemeteries and two groups of 1918 British Bunkers in Festubert; Guards, Windy Corner CWGC Cemetery; the Private Memorial to Lt Hill-Trevor and the 55th Divisional & Tunnellers/Hackett VC Memorials in Givenchy-les-Bassée, Memorial to 15th Bn (48th Can Highlanders), Festubert and finishes on the N41.

• **[N.B.]** The following sites are indicated: Bunker, No. 100 Rue Capitte and Tramways House Bunker, Festubert .

• **Total Distance:** 10.00 miles

• **Total time: 1** hour 45 minutes

• **Distance from Calais to start point:** See Neuve Chapelle Tour

• **Base towns:** La Bassée, Béthune, Lille

• **Map:** IGN 1:25,000 2405 Est

At the Le Touret Memorial set your mileometer to zero, return along the Rue du Bois towards la Bombe.

The **VC of L/Cpl Joseph Harcourt Tombs** of the 1st King's (Liverpool) Regt was won on 16 June 1915 near Rue du Bois for crawling out repeatedly under fire to bring in wounded men, one of whom he dragged in using a rifle sling placed round his own neck and the man's body. Tombs survived until 1966.

Continue and turn right to Festubert on the D166.

EDMUND BLUNDEN

This is virtually the centre of the author, poet and scholar Edmund Blunden's wartime experiences in this part of Northern France. Blunden, who went on to succeed Rudyard Kipling as 'literary adviser' to the Imperial War Graves Commission in 1936, wrote what is probably the most brilliant, sensitive and vivid of Great War autobiographies – *Undertones of War,* published in 1928.

The scholarly, slightly frail-looking Blunden enlisted in August 1915 in the Royal Sussex Regt. and was commissioned in the 11th Bn. After training at the Bull Ring at Etaples ('Eatapples' or 'Heeltaps') he soon moved to Le Touret and then moved rapidly between Béthune, La Bassée, Festubert, Hinges, Cuinchy, Richebourg St Vaast, Cambrin and Givenchy – many of which will be visited on this tour or in the tours of Neuve Chapelle and Loos.

One of his first wartime poems was *A House in Festubert:*

> With blind eyes meeting the mist and moon
> And yet with blossoming trees robed round,
> With gashes black, nay, one great wound,
> Surprising still it stands its ground;
> Sad soul, here stay you.
>
> It held, one time, such happy hours;
> The tables shone with smiles and filled
> The hungry – Home! Their home is ours;
> We house it here and laugh unkilled.
> Hoarse gun, now, pray you -....

Continue into Festubert to the crossroads by the church.
The church, as was practically the entire village, was razed during the war and rebuilt in 1924. It bears some traces of damage from WW2.
Turn right on the D7 signed to Beuvry.
On the left is passed the village *Salle des Fêtes,* known as **The Southport Memorial** Hall **(Map 10/2a. Lat & Long: 50.54347 2.73210)** as Southport 'adopted' the village after the war during the Reconstruction and paid for the building of the Hall in which a commemorative Plaque was erected. The present building is modern and when it was built the Plaque was moved to the right of the entrance. For many years veterans from Southport returned to Festubert and when they were no longer able to travel, members of the Sefton Dunkirk Veterans' Association continued the links on their behalf. In 2000 a new Plaque to commemorate their visit was unveiled on the left of the entrance.
Continue to the cemetery on the right.

• Post Office Rifles CWGC Cemetery/2.2 miles/10 minutes/Map 10/2/ Lat & Long: 50.54270 2.72553

Designed by Capt W.C. von Berg, this cemetery does not contain a War Stone. It is little-visited as lack of signatures in the Visitor's Book shows and the fading inscriptions on the headstones are difficult to read. It was used in April-June 1915 before and during the Battles of Aubers Ridge and Festubert and originally contained 40 graves, 38 of them belonging to the London Regt (mainly the 8th Bn).

After the Armistice it was increased by concentration from surrounding battlefields, particularly from the part of the line defended by the 55th Division in April 1918. There are now 400 burials in the cemetery.
Continue to the next left turn (very quickly reached and easily missed) and turn down Rue de la Veine.

Post Office Rifles CWGC Cemetery, Festubert.

King's Post Bunker with detail of Lancashire Rose on Bunker, Festubert.

419th Field Coy, RE Bunkers, Festubert.

You are now entering the wooded and marshy area behind Festubert.

Keep straight on as the road narrows, follow the sharp left bend and turn first right on Rue des Malvaux. Continue to house No 315 on the right.

• King's Post Bunker/2.9 miles/10 minutes/Map 10/3/Approx Lat & Long: 50.53536 2.72467

On **private ground** to the left of the house is the impressive bunker known as the King's Post after the King's (Liverpool) Regiment who fought in this area in April 1918. It clearly bears the insignia of the Lancashire Rose, the divisional sign of the East Lancashires, and the imprint of the Royal Engineers. It was designed as a brigade headquarters.

Turn round, return to the T junction and turn right and then next right on Rue du Plantin. Continue on the very narrow road to house No 337 on the right.

• Group of 1918 British Shelters/3.5 miles/5 minutes/Map 10/4/Lat & Long: 50.53671 2.73106

On **private ground** behind the house (and almost impossible to see) is a complex group of shelters, many of which bear the Red Rose crest of Lancashire and 55th Division. They were built by 419th Field Company, Royal Engineers in June 1918 following the battle which halted the German advance here in April 1918.

Turn round, return to the T junction (once known as Estaminet Corner) and turn right. Continue to the cemetery on the left.

• Brown's Road Military CWGC Cemetery/3.9 miles/15 minutes/Map 10/5/Lat & Long: 50.54042 2.73309

The Cemetery (which has a lovely holly bush in the corner) was begun in October 1914 and used by fighting units and Field Ambulances until November 1917. It then contained 299 graves. After the Armistice it was enlarged by concentration from small cemeteries and isolated graves from the '14-'15 and '18 battles. It now contains 1,071 burials of which 407 are Unidentified. There is a Special Memorial to 3 soldiers. There are 21 Canadian and 6 S African burials here. In a row containing 9 Cameronian Officers all killed on 10 March 1915 lies **Lt-Col Wilfrid Marryat Bliss,** age 49, OC 2nd Cameronians. The brother of **Pte J.C.C. Milne,** Black Watch, age 22, 23 November 1914, Pte A.J. Milne, 2nd Black Watch, age 32 was killed in Mesopotamia on 21 April 1917 and is commemorated on the Basra Memorial (qv).

Also buried here are some of the unfortunate 'Shot at Dawn' victims: **Rfm W. Bellamy,** 1st Border Regt, 16 July 1915 age 34 (IV.9.19), **Pte G.H. Lawton** (V.G.13), and **Pte 'Bertie' McCubbin,** (V.B.16) both of the 17th Sherwood Foresters, 30 July 1916.

In this Cemetery there is an unusually high proportion of senior NCOs and Officers. It was designed by Charles Holden.

Continue to the main road and turn right on the D166.

The turning here was known as Ration Corner, no doubt because of the light railway that ran across the road between it and beside the bunker some 50 yards further on. The railway brought up supplies and the bunker was known as **Tramways House (Map 10/5a. Lat & Long: 50.54050 2.73706)**. It is on the left hand side and almost impossible to spot behind a small dense Leylandia rectangular enclosure at the edge of a private garden. From January 1919 until the early seventies it was occupied by a Frenchwoman who said it made an ideal home.' It was probably constructed by 427th Field Coy, RE. and played a major role in the 155th Bde defeat of a German attack in April 1918.

Continue to the first turning right, Rue Capitte.

Brown's Road CWGC Cemetery, Festubert.

Headstone of Rfm W. Bellamy, Brown's Road CWGC, Festubert.

Windy Corner, Guards CWGC Cemetery.

Bunker, 100 Rue Capitte, Festubert.

Row of HLI headstones, Guards Cemetery, Windy Corner.

Placing a flower ..., Guards Cemetery, Windy Corner.

Tramways House' Bunker, Festubert.

N.B. By turning right here, a **Bunker**, incorporated into a shed, may be seen 100 yards along by the first house on the left, No. 100 Rue Capitte. **Lat & Long: 50.53456 2.74181.**

Continue.

After the battle both sides set about constructing strong points and defence lines. By 1918 this road was known as the 'Village Line' (British). The old 'Festubert' British line ran erratically parallel about 1,000 yards to the left while to the right were various reserve lines.

Continue to the crossroads.

This was **Windy Corner**, so called because German guns were ranged on the crossing and to venture over it would certainly make one 'windy'.

Further down the D166, just across the canal in Cuinchy, was Blunden's Battalion HQ in 'one of the best of the tottering anomalies of houses here, which no specialist could have cured.... "Kingsclere", a tall villa with mattresses stuffed into the upper windows.' It had a cellar, 'a delicate retreat from the glaring heat-wave outside, and a piano in it, and marguerites and roses in jars on the table'. The site is at **Lat & Long: 50.52075 2.75651.**

Turn sharp right signed to the Guards Cemetery and follow the road, Rue Berthelot, to the cemetery on the right.

• Guards CWGC Cemetery, Windy Corner/5.2 miles/10 minutes/ Map 10/6/Lat & Long: 50.52880 2.74177

The Cemetery was begun by 2nd Division in January 1915 beside a house used as battalion HQ and dressing station. It was used by 4th (Guards) Brigade from February 1915 and was closed at the end of May 1916 when it contained 681 graves. It was enlarged after the Armistice when 2,700 bodies were brought in from the surrounding battlefields and small cemeteries. It now contains 3,442 burials (including 31 Canadians and 9 Indians) of which 2,196 are unidentified. There are Special Memorials to 6 men buried in Indian Village North Cemetery and to 5 Indians originally buried here but afterwards cremated 'in accordance with the requirements of their faith'. The Cemetery was designed by Charles Holden. In it are some groups of touching headstones, several of the HLI of 9 July and 25 September 1915 and of the Queens of 25/26 September 1915. Here is buried **Major John Mackenzie**, 1st Beds, age 44, 17 May 1915, who won the **VC** in Ashanti in 1900, and **Guardsman G.E. Kelsall,** Coldstream Guards, age 22, 11 August 1915 whose headstone bears the moving message, 'In a grave that we may never see May someone place a flower for me.'

Return to the crossroads, go straight over into Givenchy-les-la-Bassée and turn right past the modern church on Rue du Moulin. Continue to the white stone statue on the right.

• Private Memorial to Lt H. G. E. Hill-Trevor/6.2 miles/10 minutes/ Map 10/7/Lat & Long: 50.52499 2.75470

This impressive statue, surrounded by a well-tended area of granite chippings enclosed by a low stone wall, is to **Lt Hillyar George Edwin Hill-Trevor**, 1st Scots Guards, age 18, died on 21 December 1914. He was the only son of the Hon George Hill-Trevor and a direct descendant of the Duke of Wellington. He was educated at Wellington and the RMC Sandhurst. He was commissioned in the Scots Guards in August 1914 and promoted to Lieutenant in November.

On 21 December the Scots Guards were given the objective of capturing some trenches along the Rue d'Ouvert (to the east of Givenchy). The attack started in darkness at 0415 and at first met no opposition. When they reached Givenchy, however, the right flank of the Cameron Highlanders lost direction and nearly engaged the Scots Guards. In the few casualties that were incurred that day, the young Hill-Trevor was killed in his first action. He is commemorated on the Le Touret Memorial (qv).

The Memorial, incorporating a mourning female figure on an ornate base with an inscription describing Hill-Trevor's death, was erected after the war near where he died. In 1927 General du Cane, whose wife was Hill-Trevor's aunt, funded minor repairs and arranged for the IWGC to care for it. In 1998 the Battlefield Memorials Project Fund of the WFA (qv) paid for major work to the Memorial and its foundations and it is now in perfect condition. The figure has echoes of the beautiful memorial erected to Lt George Cecil north of Villers Cotteret. He was killed during the First Battle of the Marne.

Hill-Trevor's statue stands exactly where the Orchard Trench system led forward from the southern end of the Village Line and across the road to the front lines.

Return to the main road and turn right.

Givenchy was 'adopted' by Liverpool after the war and the village *Salle des Fêtes* is known as 'The Liverpool Memorial Village Hall'.

Continue to the large memorial facing you at the junction.

• 55th W Lancs Div Memorial/Tunnellers' & Hackett VC & Collins Memorial/6.7 miles/20 minutes/Map 10/8/Lat & Long: 50.52792 2.76176

The inscription below this large cross with the Divisional badge describes how around this site from 9-16 April 1918 the Division was continuously attacked along the line of the Canal by three German Divisions. With its left flank turned, the Division held its ground and inflicted severe loss upon the enemy. 'This most gallant defence, the importance of which it would be hard to over estimate', wrote Sir Douglas Haig in his Despatch of 20 July 1918. The Division's Battle Honours (Somme 1916, Ypres 1916-17, Cambrai 1917, Givenchy-Festubert 1918 and the Advance in Flanders 1918) are inscribed on the memorial and it also describes how units of the W Lancs Division Territorial Force were formed in 1918 and fought in France and Belgium from November 1914 onwards. On 3 January 1916 it was reassembled as the 55th (W Lancs) Division and served under that title throughout the remainder of the campaign. At each corner is a post with the attractive Divisional badge of a red rose and the words, 'They win or die who wear the rose of Lancaster'.

To the left of the Memorial is the new **Memorial to the Tunnelling Companies of the First World and to Spr William Hackett, VC of 254 Tunnelling Coy & Pte Thomas Collins**.

On 21 June 1916 the 2nd Bn RWF took over the section of the line in front of the 'The Duck's Bill' a small German salient about 300 yards north east of this corner. At approx 0200 the following

AROUND THIS SITE FROM THE 9TH TO THE 16TH APRIL 1918 THE DIVISION CONTINUOUSLY ATTACKED FROM THE CANAL TO FESTUBERT BY THREE GERMAN DIVISIONS AND WITH ITS LEFT FLANK TURNED, HELD ITS GROUND AND INFLICTED SEVERE LOSS UPON THE ENEMY.

.."THIS MOST GALLANT DEFENCE, THE IMPORTANCE OF WHICH IT WOULD BE HARD TO OVERESTIMATE".....

SIR DOUGLAS HAIG'S DESPATCH DATED 20-7-18

Details of inscription on the 55th W Lancs Div Memorial, Givenchy.

THEY WIN OR DIE — WHO WEAR THE ROSE OF LANCASTER

55th W Lancs Div Memorial, Givenchy, with detail of Red Rose insignia.

Private Memorial to Lt Hill-Trevor, Givenchy.

morning a German mine exploded under the battalion's 'B' Coy, killing some two-thirds of their strength, including two Officers and the CSM. They remain entombed in the area. The explosion left a huge crater, some 120 yards long, 70 yards wide and 30 feet deep. Capt Stanway (who was later to take over command of the 6th Bn Cheshire Regt) led an attack which pushed back the 150-strong German raid which followed the explosion. For this gallant action the Crater was named 'Red Dragon' in honour of the RWF's Regimental Cap Badge.

As the mine exploded No 254 Tunnelling Coy RE was working on a shaft (called Shaftesbury Shaft) towards the German lines and the gallery where the men were digging was blocked, burying several men alive. Some Tunnellers were rescued through an escape hole that was frantically dug. Sapper William Hackett helped three men to safety but refused to abandon his wounded comrades until the last man, seriously injured Thomas Collins of the 14th Welsh Regt (Swansea Pals), was rescued. Sadly, however, the gallery collapsed again and both men were entombed. For this act of gallantry Hackett, a simple miner who could neither read nor write, was awarded a Posthumous VC.

This family man with a wife and two children, tried to enlist in August 1914 but was refused several times on medical grounds. Despite being diagnosed with a heart condition he was eventually accepted by the REs in October 1915. In May 1916 he arrived in France with 172nd Tunnelling Coy and was transferred to 254 Coy here at Givenchy.

Strangely, 43 year old Hackett is commemorated on the Ploegsteert Memorial (qv) and 22 years old Collins on the Thiepval Memorial.

The Tunnellers' Memorial, principally the brain child of Peter Barton (qv), was unveiled on 19 June 2010. It commemorates all the men who worked underground during the War, as well as Hackett VC and Collins. It is a black, understated slab of durable Lakeland slate, 'Brathay' blue-black for the outer frame which represents the timber sett of a typical tunnel, 'Kirktone' green for the engraved interior. It exactly reproduces the standard dimensions for Tunnelling Companies galleries, 4 feet high, 2.6 feet wide, with a circular base with the same dimensions as Shaftsbury Shaft plus the trench map reference for the shaft: 36 C Ad 55.23, enabling the visitor to imagine the cramped conditions in which they worked.

The transparent 'T' represents the Tunnellers' shoulder title and leads the visitor's view to the site of the original shaft head near the water tower, the site where Hackett and Collins still lie.

Beside it is a detailed **Information Panel** with an imaginative impression of Shaftesbury Shaft, a map showing the site of Red Dragon Crater and information and photos and extracts from the diaries of Sapper John French.

In October 2009 the long-lost diaries of this Cornish tin miner who joined 254th Tunnelling Coy and arrived in France on New Year's Eve 1915 were discovered, when his 99 year old sister, Emily, died. They cover French's experiences in vivid, and sometimes humorous,

Memorial to Tunnellers & Spr Hackett VC & Pte Collins, Givenchy.

detail for the following two years. He was an eye witness of the blowing of the Red Dragon Crater and describes the furious attempts to rescue the five entombed men in the Shaftesbury gallery and the tragic further fall which killed Hackett and Collins. French, who was eventually commissioned, was awarded the MM in December 1917 and the MC in April 1918.

On 7 August Edmund Blunden (qv) was given the task of leading some 100 men in restoring a sap near the lip of the crater. Blunden threw himself energetically into the demanding task but was disappointed that, rather than being complimented for his work, he was reprimanded by his General for 'the irregularity of an officer's publicly transferring a duckboard from trench to trench'...

It was whilst in this sector that the battalion heard the rumour that they were moving down to the Somme. It gave rise to one of Blunden's most evocative wartime poems, *Two Voices*.

> ..."There's something in the air" I hear,
> ..."We're going South, man", deadly near.

Continue on the D167 and at the first crossroads turn left by the water tower signed to Violaines on Rue d'Ouvert, the D167e. Continue on the winding road through Violaines and turn left signed Lorgies-Chef-Lieu.

You are now approximately at the limit of the British advance (it came towards you **see Map 10**). After some 1.9 miles from the last stop and some 100m short of the T junction ahead is the site of **Canadian Orchard** (qv), now a caravan park (Camping de l'Etang) and lake surrounded by trees. At this point the Lantern Tower of Notre-Dame de Lorette on the ridge can clearly be seen to the left.

Continue to the T junction and turn left on the D72 Rue de Lille towards Festubert.

You are now driving along what was the **Quinque Road**. Here Blunden recalled, 'two German machine guns were famous, "almost legendary monsters" here. 'Blighty Albert' and 'Quinque Jimmy' fired across a road called Kinky-Roo which our ration parties and others used.'

Here on 29-30 October 1914 the 2/8th Gurkhas, shivered in the unaccustomed cold, in trenches half full of mud and water and which were too deep for the tiny men to be able to fire over the parapet. Nevertheless they held on despite repeated enemy artillery and howitzer fire, driving back several enemy attacks. It was, however, a costly affair for the battalion who lost 5 British and 2 Gurkha officers and 37 ORs killed, 3 British and 1 Ghurka officer and 61 ORs wounded with 1 British and 2 Ghurka officers and 109 ORs missing – 'buried by shell fire'. Again on 19 December the Ghurkas (the 2/2nd) came under severe trench-mortar fire and were forced to withdraw to a new line slightly further back.

Continue a half a mile to where a small path crosses the road. Stop at the memorial on the left.

Memorial to 15th Bn (48th Can Highlanders) & Battle of Festubert/9.3 miles/5 minutes/Map 10/9/Lat & Long: 50.54799 2.75429

On 23 October 2011 this fine bronze Plaque on a brick wall was unveiled in an impressive ceremony with regimental representatives and dignitaries from Canada and the locality. It commemorates the participation of the Regiment in the battle of Festubert, 20 May 1915. On 18 May the Canadian 3rd Brigade was called up from Reserve and moved into combat round the area of the Orchard (qv). The 14th and 16th Bns captured a German strong-point called the North Breastworks and on 20 May the 15th advanced from this area along the Quinque Road, encountering heavy German artillery and machine-gun fire. Nevertheless they continued their advance despite the loss of their own machine guns but eventually were forced to fall back on the North Breastworks. By the end of the Battle on 25 May their casualties were 150 men from the total 2,468 Canadian 1st Division casualties. They are buried in Aire Communal, Arras Road, Béthune, Cabaret Rouge, Etaples, Guards Cuinchy, Hinges, Le Touquet and Pont-de-Hem cemeteries and their Missing are on the Vimy Memorial.

This was a militia unit from Toronto. The Regiment has raised several such Plaques along the Western Front.

Memorial to 15th Bn (48th Can Highlanders) & Battle of Festubert.

Continue.

This stretch of road lies between the German front line (about where you are) and the British line at Festubert village and much attacking and counter attacking went on here in 1918. After spying out the German line the Colonel of the 1st Bn The Liverpool Scottish was walking back along this road towards Festubert with another officer and two runners when they ran into a party of ten Germans. So surprised were each group that the Colonel just had time to hit one of the Germans on the head with his swagger stick before making off to safety.

Return to Festubert Church (10.00 miles).

• *End of Festubert-Givenchy Battlefield Tour*

LOOS

25 SEPTEMBER 1915-8 OCTOBER 1915

'Our new armies entered into action for the first time and
fought with conspicuous valour, and tens of thousands of
them fell in the futile carnage of the Loos offensive.'
Lloyd George, *War Memoirs.*

'I had come to the conclusion that it was not fair to the Empire to
retain French in command. Moreover, none of my officers
commanding corps had a high opinion of Sir John's military ability.'
General Haig in his Diary.

'My Darling Darling we've had such terrible losses
which made me very depressed and sad. . .'
General French in a letter to his mistress during the battle.

'What's happened?" I asked. "Bloody balls-up,"
was the most detailed answer I could get.'
Robert Graves, *Goodbye to All That.*

SUMMARY OF THE BATTLE

On 25 September 1915 as part of the French Artois offensive, Douglas Haig's 1st Army attacked German positions at Loos. The British used gas for the first time causing many casualties to their own side. There were no significant positive results and the affair provoked the forced resignation of Sir John French. British casualties were 43,000, German 20,000.

OPENING MOVES

Even halfway through 1915 it had not been a good year for the Allies. There had been the heavy British casualties at Neuve Chapelle, the disaster at Gallipoli and the steady reverses on the Russian front. General Joffre had prompted his forces into a number of attacks along the Western Front in what he called the 'war of stabilization'. This could perhaps be likened to a boxer moving around the ring, feeling out his opponent's strengths, before attempting a knock-out blow.

In June 1915 Joffre proposed his knock-out blow: a two-pronged offensive. One attack, the main one, was to be in Champagne and entirely French. The other was a joint Franco-British affair in Artois. Each prong was to break through the German lines. A general offensive would follow along the entire Franco-British front that Joffre believed could 'possibly end the war'. The Artois offensive was also to be a two-pronged affair with the British 1st Army attacking just north of Lens at Loos and the French 10th Army just south of Lens.

General Haig toured the area allocated for the 1st Army's attack and declared it to be unfavourable because the flat open ground would be swept by machine gun fire from the enemy's front trenches. Joffre refused to change the plan and Kitchener, visiting Sir John French in August, told him that co-operation was essential and that 'we may suffer heavy losses'. Haig, conscious of what had happened at Neuve Chapelle because of the shortage of artillery, decided that the only way in which he could get enough concentration of fire to neutralize the German machine guns was by adopting a very narrow frontage for the attack.

Accordingly he planned to attack with two divisions only, the 15th and the 9th. While the two division assault was being planned a new weapon became available – British poison gas. Haig immediately saw gas as a means of neutralizing those enemy defences that he did not have enough artillery to take on and extended the attack frontage to six divisions in line, their flanks to be protected by smoke screens. On 16 September he wrote to Sir William Robertson, General French's Chief of Staff, 'In my opinion under no circumstances should our forthcoming attack be launched without the aid of gas.' He was over-ruled and told that because of the need to co-ordinate the offensive with the French 10th Army the attack had to be made and that it would go in on 25 September. Haig therefore produced a plan with two options: one for a wide front, one for a narrow front.

1. Wide Front. If the weather conditions were favourable on 25 September the attack, with gas on the whole front, would take place on that day with 6 divisions.

2. Narrow Front. If the wind did not permit the use of gas a two division assault would be made, the wider attack with gas to be postponed until favourable conditions on the 26th or 27th or not at all.

All that remained was for the Allies to agree the time that their infantry would assault. The British wanted to go over the top as early as possible in the morning so that positions gained could be consolidated by nightfall. The French didn't want to leave their trenches before 1000 hours, so that they could visibly control the last phase of their bombardment. In the event the French attack went in 5½ hours after the British. Something similar would happen again on 1 July 1916 on the Somme.

WHAT HAPPENED

The preliminary bombardment which covered the 18-mile frontage of the 1st Army (i.e. covered the main assault and diversionary actions north and south of it) was carried out by 110 heavy guns plus 84 guns and howitzers and began at first light on 21 September. It continued day and night until the moment of the assault on 25 September. As a precaution against the enemy finding out about the gas it was given a codename – 'the accessory'.

In England and along the front line observers anxiously monitored the wind direction. Four times a day the Met Office in London sent reports and 40 specially trained gas officers stationed along the assault trenches sent in hourly reports during the night of 24 September. The required wind direction for a gas attack was from somewhere between north-west and south-west and at 2145 hours on 24 September, having received a favourable forecast, Haig ordered that the gas attack should take place on the morrow. The exact time would be 'notified later during the night'.

Early on the 25th, although the general forecast remained favourable, things looked changeable and the meteorologist, Captain E. Gold, attached to Haig's staff, advised that the sooner the gas was released the better. At 0500 hours Haig went on to the battlefield rear area and asked his ADC Major Alan Fletcher to light a cigarette. The smoke drifted north-east, a borderline but acceptable direction. Fifteen minutes later the General ordered the attack to go ahead. Robert Graves, who was in the battle (see below) wrote that one front-line report at 0530 said, 'Dead calm. Impossible discharge accessory', to which the reply was, 'Accessory to be discharged at all costs.' At 0550 hours the gas was released, emissions continuing on and off for 40 minutes. As there wasn't enough gas available to allow a continuous gas cloud, the gas cylinders were turned on and off and smoke candles burned in between to fool the enemy.

At 0630 hours the infantry scrambled out of their trenches and headed across No Man's Land in a haze of smoke and gas. There were six divisions in line, the 2nd, 9th (Scottish), 7th, 1st, 15th

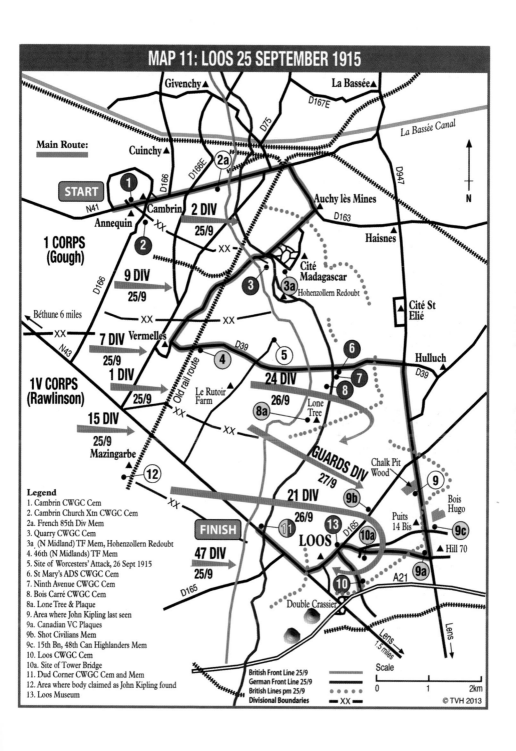

MAP 11: LOOS 25 SEPTEMBER 1915

Givenchy▲

La Bassée▲

D167E

La Bassée Canal

Main Route:

Cuinchy▲

2a

D75

START 1

N41

Cambrin

Annequin

2 DIV
25/9

Auchy lès Mines

D163

Haisnes

N

1 CORPS
(Gough)

2

9 DIV
25/9

Cité
Madagascar

3a

Hohenzollern Redoubt

Cité St
Elié▲

Béthune 6 miles

7 DIV
25/9

N43

Vermelles

1 DIV

1V CORPS
(Rawlinson)

25/9

15 DIV
25/9
Mazingarbe

D166

3

D39

4

5

6

7

8

Hulluch

D39

24 DIV
26/9

8a

Lone
Tree

Le Rutoir
Farm

GUARDS DIV
27/9

Chalk Pit
Wood

9

Bois
Hugo

12

FINISH

47 DIV
25/9

D165

21 DIV
26/9

11

13

LOOS

9b

9c

Puits
14 Bis

9a

Hill 70▲

10a

10

A21

Double Crassier

Lens
1.5 miles

Lens

Legend
1. Cambrin CWGC Cem
2. Cambrin Church Xtn CWGC Cem
2a. French 85th Div Mem
3. Quarry CWGC Cem
3a. (N Midland) TF Mem, Hohenzollern Redoubt
4. 46th (N Midlands) TF Mem
5. Site of Worcesters' Attack, 26 Sept 1915
6. St Mary's ADS CWGC Cem
7. Ninth Avenue CWGC Cem
8. Bois Carré CWGC Cem
8a. Lone Tree & Plaque
9. Area where John Kipling last seen
9a. Canadian VC Plaques
9b. Shot Civilians Mem
9c. 15th Bn, 48th Can Highlanders Mem
10. Loos CWGC Cem
10a. Site of Tower Bridge
11. Dud Corner CWGC Cem and Mem
12. Area where body claimed as John Kipling found
13. Loos Museum

British Front Line 25/9
German Front Line 25/9
British Lines pm 25/9
Divisional Boundaries

Scale

0   1   2km

© TVH 2013

MAP 12: LOOS – ATTACK OF THE 2ND WORCESTERS 26 SEPTEMBER 1915

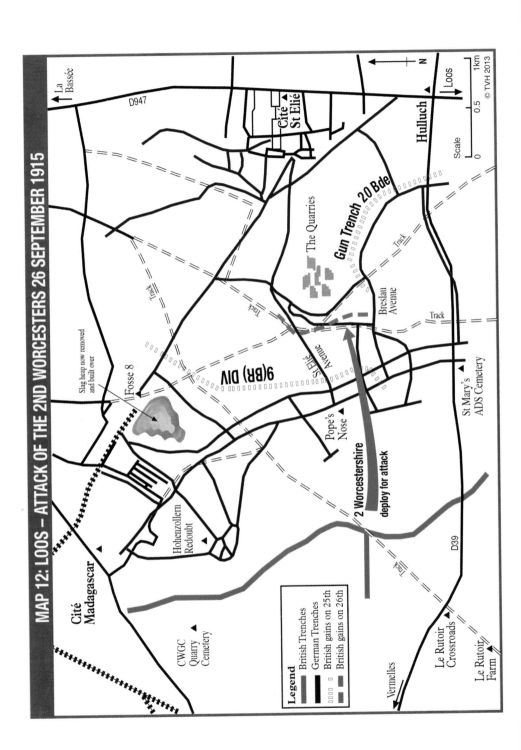

Cité Madagascar

La Bassée

D947

Cité St Elié

The Quarries

Gun Trench 20 Bde

Hulluch

Loos

© TVH 2013

N

Scale

0   0.5   1km

Slag heap now removed and built over

Fosse 8

Track

Track

Track

9(BR) DIV

St Elié Avenue

Breslau Avenue

Track

Hohenzollern Redoubt

Pope's Nose

St Mary's ADS Cemetery

2 Worcestershire deploy for attack

CWGC Quarry Cemetery

D39

Vermelles

Le Rutoir Crossroads

Le Rutoir Farm

Legend
British Trenches
German Trenches
British gains on 25th
British gains on 26th

(Scottish) and 47th (London Territorial). Two separate divisions, the 21st and 24th, were kept back in reserve, but they were not under command of General Haig. General French kept them under his control. On the extreme right 47th Division rapidly reached the area of the Double Crassier (slag heaps) while on its left the 15th Division made spectacular progress, advancing completely around Loos to the north of, then later taking, the town after all-night street fighting. The remaining division of Rawlinson's IV Corps, the 1st, had mixed fortunes. Some units reached as far as the village of Hulluch and others retreated under enemy shell fire. South of the corps boundary, the Vermelles to Hulluch road, the gas had proven its worth, but further north in Gough's 1 Corps area alongside the la Bassée Canal the officer in charge of gas on 6th Brigade's front decided not to turn on the gas because the wind wasn't right. General Horne ordered it turned on and many men were poisoned by their own gas. Eventually Horne listened to his brigade commanders and stopped the attack.

Overall, particularly at Loos itself, the first day had gone well. There was a potential break in the German line to be exploited. Now was the time to punch through the weakened enemy defences with our fresh reserves. Where were they? They were too far away, too tired and too new to mount a successful follow-up assault. Why? Whose fault was it? The generals blamed each other.

The broad sweep of the British plan had been agreed at least one month before between Joffre and General French at a conference at Chantilly – including the formation of a two divisional infantry reserve. Yet instead of forming the reserve from seasoned divisions already in France, General French nominated two raw, untried 'K' (Kitchener volunteers) Divisions, the 21st and 24th, which had arrived in France in September. They had never been in the trenches or under fire and they were held many miles to the rear under Sir John's control as part of XI Corps, which also included the newly formed Guards Division. On the night of 24 September, the two K Divisions marched 10 miles through rain to within five miles of the front line. It took over six hours. The previous night they had rested, but on each of the two nights preceding that they had marched more than 20 miles.

Sir Douglas Haig had assumed that the two reserve divisions would move forward at 0630 hours together with the main assault and come under his control ready to follow up a breakthrough. They did not. Sir John French said that he put the divisions under Haig's command at 0930 hours. Haig didn't agree that that had been done. On 29 September he wrote to Lord Kitchener, 'No reserve was placed under me. My attack, as has been reported, was a complete success... The two reserve Divisions (under C-in-C's orders) were directed to join me as soon as the success of the 1st Army was known at GHQ. They came on as quick as they could, poor fellows, but only crossed our old trenchline with their heads at 1800 hours. We had captured Loos 12 hours previously and reserves should have been at hand THEN'.

At first, despite their tiredness, when they did eventually arrive the reserve divisions had some success but German counter-attacks forced them back, only the arrival of the Guards Division on 27 September preventing what might have been a headlong retreat of the novice soldiers. The battle ventured on without concentrated central effort or achievement until the first week in October. It had been, wrote Lloyd George in his memoirs, 'a futile carnage'. Two months later Prime Minister Herbert Asquith wrote a secret letter to Haig saying that Sir John French had resigned and 'I have the pleasure of proposing to you that you should be his successor.'

The Loos Trenches in Blackpool

After the Loos battle, the 'Divisional Military Authorities' in Blackpool built a replica of the trenches at Loos at Squire's Gate, presumably for training purposes. It was then decided to make the system open to the general public as an educational and tourist attraction and also to raise funds for the nearby King's Lancashire Military Convalescent Home. Convalescent soldiers acted as guides and pointed out features such as the defensive structure known as 'the Redoubt', the 'Telephone Dug-out', the 'Traversing System' to avoid enfilading, the 'Sentry Post', the machine gun posts, the snipers' loopholes, the sandbagged parapets, the drainage system, the Battalion HQ, the medical facilities, the cookhouse and the stores and the communication trenches. Money was also raised by selling postcards and a guide leaflet, which cost 1d, to these 'couple of miles of admirably planned and cleverly constructed Trenches, a perfect reproduction of this astonishing aid to modern warfare'.

The Other Battles of Loos.
While the British offensive of September 1915 is the focus of the above tour, it must not be forgotten that that there was a **French Offensive in May 1915**, resulting in heavy casualties and a **Canadian Offensive on Hill 70 in August/Sept 1917**.

THE BATTLEFIELD TOUR

• **The Route:** The tour begins at Annequin, visits Cambrin Military CWGC Cemetery and the Churchyard Extension CWGC Cemetery; Auchy les Mines and Quarry CWGC Cemetery and the 46th (N Midland) TF Memorial, Hohenzollern Redoubt and then follows the centre of the line of the British attack from Vermelles: a further 46th (N Midland) TF Division Memorial; the Rutoir Crossroads; St Mary's Advanced Dressing Station CWGC Cemetery; 9th Avenue and Bois Carré CWGC Cemeteries; Hulluch – passing Puit 14 Bis and the Chalk Pit, Canadian VC Plaques, the Museum and the British CWGC Cemetery, ending at Dud Corner north-west of Loos.
    The battlefield has changed very little in the intervening years and particularly rewards the use of a good map and binoculars.
• **[N.B.]:** The following sites are indicated: Memorial to the French 58th Division, Auchy; Replanted Lone Tree, Memorial to 15th Bn, 48th Can Highlanders at Hill 70, Memorial to Executed Civilians, Site of 'Tower Bridge', Double Crassier, Loos; Memorial to Cpl Filip Konowal, VC, Lens.
• **Total distance:** 15.0 miles`
• **Total time:** 3 hours 50 minutes
• **Distance from Calais to start point:** 56 miles. Motorway Tolls.
• **Base town:** Béthune
• **Map:** IGN 2405 Est. Lens 1:25,000

From Calais take the A16/A26 direction Paris/Reims then the A26/E15 direction St Omer and take Exit 6 to Béthune. Follow signs to Centre Ville and the Grand' Place.

Béthune. Early in 1918 Béthune was described by Major A. M. McGilchrist in his Liverpool Scottish history as 'the hub of the sector, a busy town in which places of refreshment and amusement ranging from a first-class restaurant, an excellent officer's club, a well stocked Expeditionary Force Canteen and several cinemas to others of a more dubious character, catered for every taste and every pocket.' But in April of that year most of the town centre was destroyed during the bombardments accompanying the 'Kaiser's Offensive', see below. The Town Hall (like many other buildings around the centre) was rebuilt in 1920 by J. Alleman, its stonework depicting events of the town in WW1 when it won the *Croix de Guerre* and the *Légion d'Honneur* (the town lost 557 of its sons in battle and 97 civilian casualties in the war). It is listed as an historic monument and houses the municipal archives. There is parking around the famous belfry (qv) which also houses the **Tourist Office** (qv) and a variety of **Restaurants and Brasseries**.
    In the 14th Century Church of St Vaast (rebuilt by the architect Cordonnier) is one of the **Commemorative Tablets**, designed by Lt Col M.P.L. Cart de Lafontaine (qv), executed by Reginald Hallward and with an inscription by Rudyard Kipling, commemorating the sacrifice of

the British and Dominion troops in the diocese. Like Arras, Béthune has underground chambers known as *boves* which were used as shelters during the war.

Perhaps the most vivid account of WW1 life in Bethune is that of **Robert Graves** in *Goodbye to All That*. His 1915 memories include the queues of up to 150 men at the Army brothel, 'The Red Lamp', (fee 8 francs or 8s.) [In an article in 2011 the Daily Mail claimed that at one time there were over 130 'official' brothels in 35 towns and that the 1915 traffic in one of them was 171,000.] Graves also met the Prince of Wales (who was billeted in the Hotel de France and whose favourite restaurant was The Globe) in the public baths. *'Dressed in nothing at all, he graciously remarked how bloody cold the water was.'* When not in reserve Graves had 'a beautiful Louis XVI bedroom at the *Château* Montmorency.'

The Indian GHQ was housed in the *Château* in October 1914 and the town remained in Allied hands throughout the war. It was continually shelled and bombed by Gothas and Taubes and then on 9 April 1918 in the German Offensive the town was again under imminent threat. On the 18th the population was evacuated and the bombardment redoubled. Fifty thousand incendiary shells and gas shells rained down on the town. Nine hundred houses were destroyed, the Church of St Vaast and the Town Hall in ruins. Finally, on 28 August 1918 the Allies began to drive the Germans from the Lys Salient. By 2 October the remains of Béthune were no longer under threat.

Take the N41 direction Beuvry/Annequin.

Just before entering Annequin there is a convenient **Courte Paille Restaurant** (part of the great Accor chain) on the right. Varied menu, will do speedy service on request.

Enter Annequin and set your mileometer to zero when passing the Mairie on the right.

• Annequin/0 miles/RWC/Lat & Long: 50.50953 2.72703

Here in September 1915 was the principal British and French artillery observation station on the dump of Fosse 9 de Béthune, then, at 135 feet high, the most prominent feature of the whole area. It was, however, some 2 miles from the front line trenches and its vision was restricted by the Cité spur and Hill 70.

Continue to Cambrin and stop on the left by the Café Beaulieu.

• Cambrin Military CWGC Cemetery/.6 miles/15 minutes/Map 11/1/ Lat & Long: 50.51151 2.73971

Walk up the path following the CWGC sign to the left.

This cemetery was once called Cambrin Château and described as being 'behind the Mayor's House'. It was begun in February 1915 and used as a front line cemetery until December 1918. It contains many graves from the Battle of Loos and in Row D there are 57 officers and men of the 1st King's (Liverpool) Regt, who died on 25 September 1915. Designed by Charles Holden it contains 816 burials, including **Lt H.C. Soden**, King's Liverpool Regt, age 19, 3 May 1916 whose headstone bears the words, 'This memorial is substituted for one erected by officers, NCOs and men of his company RIP' and **L/Cpl W.W. Boak**, RE, 29 May 1916, 'Salvation Army Bandsman.'

In 1918 an 'economy campaign' to salvage materials from the front line for use on defensive works was launched, and search parties went out at night to the front line and beyond to collect anything useable. Cambrin was an area where such materials were collected and as a result one battalion reported that over its period of 10 days in the trenches it never needed to requisition any barbed wire or pickets even though they had not only carried out the usual repairs, but had also constructed a new belt of double-apron fencing.

Return to your car and continue to the Mairie on the right.

Headstone of Lt H.C. Soden, Cambrin Mil CWGC Cemetery.

Outside the *Mairie* is the striking town War Memorial ('chosen from a catalogue'). It is an exact copy of Bartholdi's New York Statue of Liberty by sculptor Julien Flament. It was erected in 1926 and cost 35,000 francs, raised by a tombola! There are four other replicas of the statue in France (on the Pont de Grenelle at Paris, at Roybon (Isère), Saint Etienne (Loire) and at Saint Cyr sur Mer (Var).

Between the village and Givenchy, about a mile and a half to the north, the ground was high enough above the water table (other than immediately beside the canal) to allow mine warfare and much of it took place along that line, being topped off just beyond the canal with the 'Red Dragon' Crater (qv). The fighting therefore generally consisted of contesting the lips of craters with saps leading out from the lines or from isolated posts. Tunnels led forward from Cambrin on the Support Line to the front line, both sides keeping the positions that they had occupied following the activities of 1915 until 1918.

Turn right after the Mairie, following CWGC sign, to the church on the left and stop on the right.

• Cambrin Churchyard Extension CWGC Cemetery/.8 miles/15 minutes/ Map 11/2/Lat & Long: 50.50972 2.74043

The large CWGC plot is behind the local graves. The Cemetery was taken over from French troops in May 1915 and used for front line burials until February 1917 when it was closed (except for 3 graves from 1918 in the back row). Designed by Charles Holden it contains 1,211 Commonwealth burials and 98 French graves. The graves are grouped by battalion, with striking groups of 79 graves of the 2nd Argyll & Sutherland Highlanders, 15 of the 1st Cameronians, 35 of the 2nd RWF and 115 of the 1st Middx, all dating from 25 September 1915, the first day of the Battle of Loos, and buried shoulder to shoulder, many 2 and 3 to a headstone. Where there is a row of such 'Unknown' soldiers with no religious insignia there is a plain headstone with a Latin Cross in the middle. Many of the named headstones bear extremely moving personal messages, such as that of Pte J. Gore, which makes a reference to McCrae's poem, *In Flanders Fields*.

Headstone of Capt A. L. Samson, Cambrin Churchyard Extension CWGC Cemetery.

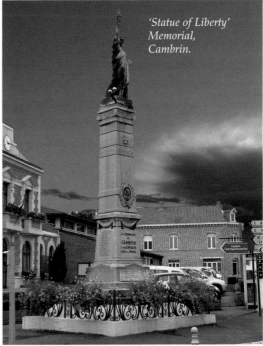

'Statue of Liberty' Memorial, Cambrin.

Middlesex Men shoulder to shoulder, Cambrin Churchyard Extension CWGC Cemetery.

Headstone of three Middlesex Men, 25 September 1915, Cambrin Churchyard Extension CWGC Cemetery.

Here is buried Captain A.L. Samson of 'C' Coy, 2nd Bn RWF, a friend of Robert Graves, killed near Cuinchy, 25 September 1915. He describes in *Goodbye to All That* how he found Samson's body 'hit in seventeen places. I found that he had forced his knuckles into his mouth to stop himself crying out and attracting more men to their death.' Graves wrote the poem *The Dead Fox Hunter* in his honour....

> We found the little captain at the head,
> His men lay, well aligned.
> We touched his hand – stone cold – and he was dead,
> And they, all dead, behind
> Had never reached their goal, but they died well.
> They charged in line, and, in the same line, fell.

Also buried here is **L/Cpl W. Pardoe,** 25 September 1915, a friend of the writer Frank Richards, also of the 2nd RWF who was killed while sniping in the Fromelles battle when officers carried their swords and **Captain the Hon Ernest William M.M. Brabazon, DSO,** age 31, Coldstream Guards, 17 June 1915, the son of the Earl and Countess of Meath.

Return to the main road and turn right.

Just after the petrol station on the right there is a group of CWGC signs to the left to Woburn Abbey, Cuinchy Communal and the Guards Cemetery, Windy Corner (qv). It was along the tow-path of the La Bassée Canal at Cuinchy, 1,100 yards north of here that on 25 September 1915 **Capt Arthur Gordon Kilby,** 2nd S Staffs, led his company in an attack on 'a strong German redoubt' in which he was wounded. He nevertheless continued to lead his men to the enemy wire under heavy machine gun fire where his foot was blown off. He then continued to cheer on his men and use his rifle. For this action Kilby, who already had the MC, was awarded a posthumous **VC**. Kilby's body was eventually found on 19 February 1929 and he is buried in Arras road CWGC Cemetery, Roclincourt. His entire group of WW1 medals (including his MC) was sold by Spinks on 19 July 2012 for £240,000 to an anonymous buyer.

Another **VC** won at Cuinchy, near the railway, but on 1 February 1915, was by **L/Cpl Michael O'Leary** of the 2nd Irish Guards. When storming the German barricades he rushed ahead, killed five Germans, rushed another barricade and killed another three, taking two prisoners, although he had run out of ammunition, and marched them back to the start line 'as cool as if he had been for a walk in the park'.

Continue towards Auchy (this route was called 'Spotted Dog'.)

N.B. On the right you will pass a **Memorial to the French 58th Division (Map 11/2a. Lat & Long: 50.51495 2.76259),** behind which the Double Crassier is visible in the distance. The Division defended this front sector, running from Cuinchy in the north to Grenay in the south until on 15 May British troops took over. The Memorial is about 200 yards from the front line ahead and one of the forward-leading saps in the area was appropriately named 'Lunatic'.

Memorial to French 58th Div, Cambrin.

Continue into Auchy Centre (you are now behind the German front line) *and turn right on to the D163 towards Cité du 8.*

It was in this area of 28th Brigade, that the gas blew back over the British lines and caused many casualties. The failure of the brigade to advance negated the success of 26th Brigade towards whose area you are travelling. It was also in this area that the poet-author-raconteur Robert Graves, serving with the RWF, observed the muddled and tragically ineffective gas attack. His memories of the loosing of the 'accessory' are graphically and often amusingly described in his gossipy, and sometimes imaginative, autobiography, *Goodbye to All That.* It should be compulsory reading for anyone studying the Loos battle.

Follow the one-way circuit to the first small roundabout and turn left. Continue to the next small roundabout and turn right. Go straight on, ignoring the first turn left and all other alternatives on the Rue de Vermelles. At the very edge of the village turn left signed Omnisport and follow that sign to a T-junction. At that junction turn right signed to the 46th Div Memorial.

• 46th (N Midland) TF Division Memorial, Hohenzollern Redoubt, Auchy/4.4 miles/10 minutes/Map 11/3a/Lat & Long: 50.50034 2.77852

Great concern was raised during 2005/6 about the dumping of waste on the historic remnants of the redoubt. The matter was taken up by, among others, the All-Parliamentary War Graves & Battlefields Heritage Group (qv) and the British Consul-General in Lille. This finally resulted in a permanent embargo against further dumping.

On 13 October 2006 a Memorial was inaugurated commemorating the 46th (N Midland) TF Division. The instigators were Kevin Martin, Don Jenkins and Michael Credland the architectural designer (The Lincolnshire Friends of the Hozenhollern Redoubt) with local historian Jean Luc Gloriant. Aided by Regimental and private donations the Lincoln Co-op provided the bulk of the £7,000 required and their stone masons constructed the octagonal Portland stone Memorial in the form of a traditional 'Broken column'. It is on a 46sqm plot donated by the local farmer, Michel Dedourge, the bottom step is 46" across, the height of the shaft is 46", the top of the column is tilted at an angle of 46° (and bears a Plaque with a short description of the battle and a poem by Kevin Martin). Gun metal Plaques cast by Taylors of Loughborough on each facet commemorate the Lincs, Leics, Notts & Derby (Sherwood

Memorial to 46th (N Midland) TF Div, Hohenzollern Redoubt.

Foresters), N Staffs, S Staffs, 1st Monmouths, RFA and RE. The inscription on the front was chosen by Martin Middlebrook. It is a quotation from Ivor Novello's *Keep the Home Fires Burning*, written in 1915 after the battle: "Their country found them ready." The ceremony was officiated by Chaplain Ray Jones (qv) and members of the Khaki Chums (qv) represented the Midlands soldiers of 1915.

The Memorial commemorates the Division's first, and one of its bloodiest, battles on 13 October 1915 (the day after the Germans shot Edith Cavell). Where you now are was just behind German lines on the edge of a feature known as the Hohenzollern Redoubt, a map of which is on the Memorial. The redoubt can be seen just ahead of the Memorial on the slightly higher ground of the feature which is known locally as le Mont d'Auchy and the forward British trenches were some 300 yards beyond that. An ineffective bombardment was carried out at noon and an hour later gas and smoke were released towards the German trenches – also ineffective. At 1400 the 137th and 138th Brigades of the Division went into the attack coming, to a first approximation, directly towards you from the south west and the first two lines crossed No Man's Land unharmed. Some of the Midlanders reached the redoubt, but it was not taken. The Division's casualties were 180 officers and 3,583 men.

Return to the Vermelles road and turn left. Continue yards (after 150 yards you cross back into British territory) *some 300 yards to a sign to Quarry Cemetery to the left. If dry drive up the pot-holed track to the cemetery.*

As you drive up the track you are going in the direction of the attack of 26th Brigade of 9th Division on the 25th of September 1915.

• Quarry CWGC Cemetery, Auchy/5.3 miles/20 minutes/Map 11/3/ OP/Lat & Long: 50.5009 2.76880

This unusual and beautiful cemetery contains burials from the fighting in the area of the Hohenzollern Redoubt and was used mostly between July 1915 and June 1916, and (for two

Quarry CWGC Cemetery, Loos.

burials) in August 1917. Its existence is due chiefly to the fighting at Fosse 8 and at the Hohenzollern Redoubt. It was badly damaged by shell fire and not all of the 140 burials are individually marked because the original graves were lost. Therefore some headstones say, 'Buried near this spot', and the Report lists only 129 war graves. Many of the graves are those of cavalrymen who were used in the dismounted role and there is one German soldier. The 'Quarry' referred to is the one in which the burials have been made, which is an old chalk pit about 10 ft deep and reached by steps. It is not connected with the 'Quarries' which featured in the fighting near Hulluch.

In August 2012 a headstone marked 'Buried near this spot' was inscribed with the name '**Captain the Hon F. Bowes-Lyon,** The Black Watch, 27th September 1915 Age 26.' This was at the instigation of Bowes-Lyons' grandson who visited the cemetery in November 2011 and then wrote to the CWGC with documentation that showed that the body had been buried in this Cemetery, confirmed by the Graves Registration 1920 records. Indeed the grave marker with his name was still in place at the end of the War. The 1925 records omit the name. Bowes-Lyon was killed in the opening stages of the Battle of Loos. As he led an attack on the German lines, his leg was blown off by a barrage of German artillery and he fell back into his sergeant's arms. Bullets struck him in the chest and shoulder and he died on the field.

Headstone of Captain the Hon F. Bowes-Lyon, Quarry CWGC Cemetery, Auchy.

Fergus, who was the brother of the late Queen Mother, hence uncle of Queen Elizabeth, is commemorated on the Loos Memorial at Dud Corner and in due course this name will be removed.

For a fuller story of the Bowes-Lyon family and the Great War see http://www.westernfront association.com/great-war-people/brothers-arms/2604-captain-fergus-bowes-lyon-8th-black-watch.html

Stand with your back to the main entrance to the cemetery.
You are looking across what was No Man's Land on 25 September. The front line of 26 Brigade was behind you. Some 330 yards straight ahead below the power lines you should be able to define a slightly higher feature of ground with some trees and bushes on it. That is the Mont d'Auchy on which was the Hohenzollern Redoubt, a major German defensive position. The

memorial you visited earlier is about 1500 yards away from here and beyond the feature. It was taken by 9th Division that day and they pushed on beyond, towards the village of Haisnes. This remarkable achievement was the result of careful planning and the digging forward of Russian saps (tunnels barely below ground that can rapidly be converted into open trenches) so that when these were opened, and their heads joined by a trench, the assault line was only 150 yards from the redoubt. The attack was led by the 7th Seaforths and the 5th Cameron Highlanders, all wearing glengarries. Sadly, at mid-morning, Lt Col Gaisford commanding the Seaforths was killed. The Germans recaptured the Hohenzollern on 3 October.

Beyond the Hohenzollern was the slag heap of Fosse 8 (now removed and built over). It was to this area that **Maj-Gen Thesiger**, commanding 9th Division (formed on 21 August 1914 and almost entirely composed of Scottish Battalions), went, on 27 September, to investigate the situation, having heard that '73rd Brigade was unsteady'. On reaching the eastern face of the Hohenzollern he was killed by a shell, together with two of his staff. Haig heard of this 'irreparable' loss whilst visiting 1 Corps HQ and ordered Maj-Gen Bulfin, then commanding 28th Division, to assume command of 9th Division. Maj-Gen Thesiger is commemorated on the Loos Memorial at Dud Corner (qv) as is Lt Col Walter Gaisford.

To your right on the skyline are the twin peaks of the Double Crassier (slag heaps) and to their left a mineshaft (*Puits*). In front of them is a road running left to right and using binoculars on a clear day it is possible to see Dud Corner Cemetery and Memorial at the bottom right hand side of the peaks. To a first approximation the peaks mark the bottom (southern) end of the Loos battlefield and the N41 road that you travelled on from Annequin to Auchy marks the top from which description you can get a good idea of the frontage of the attack. The distance as the crow flies from here to the Double Crassier is about 1.4 miles.

Return to the metalled road and turn left on the C6.

To the left is a straight tree-lined track on the line of the old railway.

Continue into Vermelles.

• Vermelles

Take the first left as you enter the village which is the D39 to Hulluch.

The village sits like a lollipop head at the western end of its stick the D39 Hulluch road, the Corps boundary which stretches ahead in your direction of travel. IV Corps were south, i.e. to the right exclusive of the road, I Corps north. It was in areas like Vermelles that final arrangements were made before battalions moved forward through communication trenches to the front line. Tea would be brewed, hot meals served (on rare occasions), orders issued, heavy kit left behind, routes signed and 'farewell' notes written. As you drive now you are following exactly the route taken by 7th Division as it moved into its forward trenches in preparation for its attack. How would you be feeling? Rupert Brooke's brother, Arthur, a 2nd Lt in the Post Office Rifles, was killed here on 14 June 1915 and is buried in Fosse No 7 Mil Cem, Mazingarbe.

Continue and as you leave the built-up area there is a memorial on the right. Stop.

• 46th (N Midland) TF Division Memorial/7.0 miles/5 minutes/Map 11/4/Lat & Long: 50.48908 2.75457

This, like the more modern Memorial visited earlier, commemorates the attack on the Hohenzollern of 13 October 1915, the week following the 'official' end of the Loos offensive. During our last visit this Memorial appeared in somewhat poor condition. It stands where the old railway running from Auchy past the western edge of Loos to Bully-Grenay crossed the road and its route is clearly defined. On the 14th, **Captain Charles Geoffery Vickers** of the Sherwood Foresters (139 Brigade of the Division) won the **VC** for actions on the Hohenzollern.

Continue to the next small crossroads. Stop. The farm to your right down the small road is le Rutoir or Rutoire.

46th (N Midland) TF Division Memorial, Vermelles.   *The replanted 'Lone Tree', le Rutoir.*

N.B. Lone Tree. By going down the narrow road and then turning first left up a narrow cart track (once metalled but now very pot-holed and which finally deteriorates to a dirt track (**Map 11/8a. Lat & Long: 50.47945 2.77956)**, which becomes a quagmire when wet), a cherry tree will be reached after some 0.8 mile. To the left the Crosses of the St Mary ADS Group of cemeteries may be seen and to the right, across the fields, the Double Crassier.

The tree was planted by WFA members, the farmer M Fouquenelle and British, German and local dignitaries on Monday 25 September 1995, the 80th Anniversary of the opening of the Loos Battle. It is on the site of the famous 'Lone Tree' which features on contemporary trench maps. Beside it is a tri-lingual bronze Plaque (based on the form of a Gallipoli grave marker) on a granite base, 'Lone Tree replanted in memory of all those who lost their lives at the Battle of Loos 1915'. A small ceremony is held at the Tree annually on the Anniversary.

• Le Rutoir(e) Crossroads/2nd Worcesters' Attack/7.8 miles/20 minutes/ Map 11/5/Lat & Long: 50.48638 2.77084

It is very rare to be able to identify precisely where a battalion action took place and even rarer also to have a clear account of what happened there. The situation becomes almost unique when the ground remains much the same as it was in 1915-18. Using Maps 11 and 12 you can be in just such a unique position.

> *Walk (it may be possible to drive) 700 yards north-east up the partly surfaced small road from the crossroads. You are now where the 2nd Worcesters deployed for their attack on 26 September 1915.*

By 26 September 7th Division was stuck in front of the Quarries. 2nd Worcesters, part of a temporary brigade under Colonel Carter of the King's Regiment, was ordered to attack the Quarries. (From where you are now they are about 800 yards away immediately in front of a large coal heap due east – the heap was very much smaller in 1915.) This is how the Regimental History tells the story:

'At 1 p.m. the Battalion filed into a big communication trench at Vermelles. This trench was a very long one and progress along it was difficult. The troops were carrying heavy loads and were hampered by wearing gas-masks, for several leaking gas-cylinders were lying in the trench. Crowds of wounded men were sheltering in the trench or making their way back, and other parties of all kinds impeded the advance. One by one the Worcestershire companies reached the forward lines, but not until 4.45 p.m. did the rearmost platoon get clear of the communication trench. Then the Battalion deployed for attack behind the original British front line. In front of them was a wide stretch of open ground – the former "No Man's Land"– on the far side of which was the old German front line (about 500 yards away), occupied by troops of the 7th Division. Still further forward on slightly rising ground a tangle of broken ground marked the near edge of the Quarries, the objective of the attack.

The Battalion deployed in four 'waves' – 'C' and 'D' Companies leading, 'A' and 'B' following, each company being formed in two lines. Colonel Lambton gave the signal, and the advance began.

With bayonets fixed, the companies of the 2nd Worcesters swept forward across the open, wave after wave, in splendid order. The platoons came under a heavy fire as they reached the old German front line. That trench was found to be wide and deep, crowded with disorganised or wounded men of the 7th Division ... **Colonel Lambton** ... coolly walked up and down the parapet under a heavy fire, directing the reorganisation of the attack. **Major-General T. Capper**, commanding the 7th Division, appeared in the trench and assisted in the direction of the fight ... Colonel Lambton again signalled the advance ... The German rifles and machine-guns opened a devastating fire. Officers and men went down in rapid succession under a hail of bullets. On the left flank **Major P. S. G. Wainman** led his men forward, waving his stick till he fell riddled with bullets. Further to the right, General Capper himself rushed forward with one of the Worcestershire platoons, cheering them on until he was hit and fell mortally wounded.

The leading groups reached a line of broken chalk, a half-dug trench within two hundred yards of the enemy's position. There they flung themselves down ... and held their ground opposite the enemy's line during the remaining hours of daylight ... Night fell amid pouring rain, and it became possible to collect the wounded and count the loss. Of the 2nd Worcestershire nearly half had fallen – 13 officers and more than 300 N.C.O's and men. The 2nd-in-Command, all four Company Commanders, the Machine-Gun Officer, the Medical Officer and three out of the four Company-Sergeant-Majors were casualties ... All through the night the stretcher-bearers worked across the field of battle, searching for the wounded ... The Chaplain, the Rev. J.R. Stewart, earned general admiration by arriving in the front-line, leading a small party carrying cans of hot tea and jars of rum, which he personally distributed all along the line.'

Maj-Gen Sir Thomson Capper is buried in Lillers Communal CWGC Cemetery. His grave stands alone near the gardener's shed. Maj Philip Stafford Gordon Wainman is buried in Vermelles British Cemetery. He is listed as Captain.

The Loos Battle was exceptional in that three Major-Generals were killed during it, within a week: **Capper, Thesiger** (qv) and **Maj-Gen F.D.V. Wing**, commanding 12th Division, killed on 2 October and buried in Noeux-les-Mines Comm Cemetery. Conan Doyle in his *British Campaigns in Europe 1914-1918* conveniently, for the sake of poetic licence, has them all dying on the same day, which he then described as the worst day for the British Army, as far as generals were concerned, since Waterloo!

Return to your car, continue along the Hulluch road.

To the left a water tower marks the top, and to the right the Double Crassier marks the bottom end, of this well-defined battlefield.

Continue to the first British cemetery on the right. Park.

Ninth Avenue CWGC Cemetery.

The immaculate grass path leading to the Ninth Avenue CWGC Cemetery, Loos.

My Boy Jack? St Mary's ADS CWGC Cemetery, Loos.

Bois Carré CWGC Cemetery with the Double Crassier behind across the Battlefield.

• St Mary's ADS CWGC Cemetery/8.7 miles/20 minutes/Map 11/6/ OP/Lat & Long: 50.48573 2.78909

The attack eastwards along, inclusive and immediately north of this road up to the southern edge of The Hohenzollern Redoubt was made by the 20th and 22nd Brigades of 7th Division. 20th Brigade had the area from the road to inclusive the German position known as Breslau Avenue (see Map 12). The leading battalions, the 2nd Gordon Highlanders and the 8th Devons, set off at 0630 in a cloud of their own gas. They were wearing smoke helmets, but these made it very difficult to breathe, and when they took them off to draw breath, many men were overcome by the gas. Despite heavy casualties from enemy artillery Gun Trench was taken and elements of both battalions reached the Lens-la Bassée road.

The Advanced Dressing Station was set up during the battle and after the Armistice the cemetery was established on the same spot. Of the more than 1,760 burials in the cemetery (the majority from the battle of Loos) 90 per cent are unknown, evidence of the chaos that existed on the battlefield. One of them, reburied here in September 1919, was a lieutenant of the Irish Guards. In July 1992 the headstone marking his grave was changed to read **'Lieutenant John Kipling'** when the CWGC believed that it had identified the body – on the grounds that Kipling was the only full lieutenant of the Irish Guards killed or missing in the Loos battle. This late identification was particularly ironic as his father, Rudyard Kipling, who sat on the committee of the Imperial War Graves Commission, spared no efforts to find his son's body, but in vain. Following extensive research the validity of the identification is strenuously disputed by the authors and described in their book *My Boy Jack?: the Search for Kipling's Only Son.*

Stand by the wall in the back left hand corner of the cemetery.
Look over the loggia in the cemetery beyond (Bois Carré) to the tall tower in the distance. That is the area of the Chalk Pit, some 1.7 miles away, where John Kipling was reported to have been killed. Looking to the right past the Double Crassier (the double slag heaps) is a large flat-topped slag heap which appears to have a wireless mast coming out of it. The body buried under the Kipling headstone was found beyond that slag heap which is 2.5 miles from here and 3.5 miles from where he was last seen alive. On a clear day, half way between the Double Crassier and the flat-topped slag heap, the Lantern Tower of Notre-Dame de Lorette is visible on the skyline some 6 miles away and between it and the cemetery is Dud Corner Memorial.
Continue to the next small turning to the right with CWGC signs. Drive up if dry to the immaculately maintained narrow grassed path to the right. Walk up it to

• Ninth Avenue CWGC Cemetery/10 minutes/Map 11/7

This tiny cemetery contains only 46 headstones, 41 of which are of the 1st Cameron Highlanders killed in action 25-29 September 1915. They are actually buried under 'Grave No 5' (a small flat stone marker in the centre). It is surrounded by a beautiful flint wall.
Continue to the next grassy path to the right. At the end of it is

• Bois Carré CWGC Cemetery/10 minutes/Map 11/8

This cemetery contains 174 known UK and 53 Unknown burials. The name means 'Square Wood'and the cemetery actually is square. The gardener's hut is beautifully faced with flint – perhaps in reaction to Rudyard Kipling's comment when visiting St Mary's ADS Cemetery in 1924, 'Spoilt by the gardener's hut'!

These three cemeteries cluster pretty well along what was the old German front line.
Return to the track.
NOTE. This track continues to the town of Loos, passing Lone Tree CWGC Cemetery and the Chalk Pit – an interesting walk.

When the Loos battle opened at 0630 on 25 September the Irish Guards, part of the Guards Division, were 16 miles as the crow flies behind Vermelles. The Division had been formed in September and had three brigades, the old 4th (Guards) Brigade becoming the 1st Guards

Brigade. The 2nd Brigade had the 1st Scots Guards, the 1st Coldstreams, the 3rd Grenadiers and the 2nd Irish.

During the day the Irish marched towards the front along roads crowded with refugees, cavalry and wounded. The *Official History* described the journey thus –'The confusion and congestion of the traffic on the roads had been appalling.' It was a journey that took 15 hours and they finally reached billets in the area of Noeux les Mines, some 4 miles west of Vermelles, at around 0100 hours on 26 September. They were wet and exhausted. At 1330 they marched out towards the battle but when they got beyond Vermelles there was no one to tell them what to do or where to go. After discussing things with the Scots Guards on their right it was decided to occupy a line of old German trenches between le Rutoir and Lone Tree (see **Map 11**) but it was midnight before everyone was settled in, some men having had less than four hours sleep the previous night and none having had any rest during the day.

Two and a half hours later they were on the move again and occupied a line of trenches some 500 yards further on, broadly along the track where you are now and facing towards Puits 14bis. No 3 Company of the 2nd Battalion was on the extreme right and next to it was No 2 Company with 2nd Lt John Kipling.

At 1600 hours on 27 September the Irish left their positions and set off for Puits 14bis and Chalk Pit Wood (just to the left of Puits 14Bis), their objectives. These were virgin soldiers. This was not only their first time into battle but as they went forward they had to cope with the returning stream of remnants of the 21st and 24th Divisions whose earlier efforts had failed. At first things went well and the Irish got into Chalk Pit Wood and even across the Loos-Lens road into Bois Hugo as well as around Puits 14Bis with the Scots, but a storm of German machine gun fire fell on them and drove them back in a confusion which only stopped at the Loos-Hulluch road where the Coldstreams, called up to help, held firm. Rowland Feilding of the Coldstreams described the scene (*War Letters to a Wife*) as he moved up past the Lone Tree:–

'The ground was strewn with our dead, and in all directions were wounded men crawling on their hands and knees. It was piteous, and it is a dreadful thing that there are occasions when one must resist the entreaties of men in such condition, and leave them to get in as best as they can, or lie out in the cold and wet, without food and under fire and they often have to do for days and nights together.'

Fielding also described the efforts of the Coldstreamers to

'stop the returning stream of battle stragglers' from the chaos at the front and how 'young Dermot Browne....began to deal with them very thoroughly, as they deserved, with a heavy hunting crop which he carried.'

Rudyard Kipling summarised what had happened to John's Regiment in *The Irish Guards in the Great War*: 'Evidently, one and a half hours' bombardment against a countryside packed with machine guns, was not enough to placate it. The Battalion had been swept from all quarters, and shelled at the same time, at the end of two hard days and sleepless nights, as a first experience of war, and had lost seven of their officers in forty minutes.' One of those officers was John Kipling, last seen alive in the area of Puits 14Bis and the Chalk Pit.

Return to the metalled road and continue along the D39 to the small crossroads just before the Hulluch sign.

To the left is the area of the Quarry and Gun Trench. With the Devons in Gun Trench was the war poet **William Noel Hodgson**, who was to be killed on the Somme on 1 July 1916 after writing the prophetic poem, *Before Action*. For his action at Loos Lt Hodgson was awarded the **MC**. The Devons' action here is acknowledged in the naming in trench maps of many of the features between here and the Quarries.

Continue to the roundabout with the replica pit head and turn right on the main la Bassée-Lens road (D947). In due course the road begins to rise towards Loos-en-Gohelle and on the right are some deserted factory buildings.

Behind them is the Chalk Pit where John Kipling was last seen on 27 September 1915 yet the body that is claimed to be his was found some 3.5 miles away to your right. It seems unlikely to us that they are one and the same.

The full story is told in our biography of John Kipling, *My Boy Jack?*
Continue to the junction with the D165 to the right signed Loos en Gohelle.

N.B. Memorial to Executed Civilians. By turning along this road, the Rue Hoche, and continuing some .5 mile, the Memorial will be reached on the right hand side **(Map 11/9. Lat & Long 50.46664 2.80533).** Inaugurated on 23 May 1937 it is to 6 Civilians, aged between 49 and 82, and a wounded French soldier. According to the *Journal de Lens* of that day they were shot by the Germans whose cavalry had entered the town on 4 October 1914 followed by four 'Regiments de la Garde' the following day. There then ensued a fierce 3 day battle between the invaders and the French Chasseurs. The Germans finally occupied the area of Fosse 15 ['Tower Bridge'] whilst the French continued to hold the lower part of the town. The rapidity of the attack meant that civilians were unable to evacuate the area. Sixty nine years old Télésphore Petit was keeping 76-years old Placide Doby company when a German patrol burst in. (By coincidence the officer was an engineer who had worked on the installation of the buildings above Fosse 15 before the war). They were looking for a French soldier in hiding. Hearing the noise, neighbours 80-years old Alexis Meurdesoif and 50-years old Auguste Lenfant emerged, only to be arrested by the Germans, who then found Gustave Dejeux of the 109th RI hiding in a barn belonging to Etienne Crespel. On 14 October M. Crespel discovered the bodies of his four friends and that of the little soldier. He too was then taken by the Germans who bound him to a tree for 24 hours. He was then led to Fosse 15 where lay the bodies of 68-years old

Memorial to Executed Civilians, Loos.

Jean-Baptiste Marquette and 49-years old Paul Delaby. He was ordered to bury them. On 15 October he was led in the direction of Hulluch to the bodies of Meurdesoif, Petit, Doby and the soldier Dejeux, their bodies mutilated and tied together by wire. Once more he was ordered to dig a trench and bury the men. For some reason he was then released and returned home to find his poor mother dead, killed 'by the emotions that she had just endured'. He buried her too. Crespel told no-one of his ordeal for a year. He then told Mme Meurdesoif of the fate of her husband, but she too kept the dreadful secret. When the British attack of 25 September 1915 liberated Loos, a few joyful inhabitants, including M Crespel, returned to their homes. When the remaining citizens returned to the ruins of their homes after the Armistice M Crespel revealed his ordeal to his incredulous neighbours. The bodies were exhumed and indeed identified.

Twenty three years later, funds were raised in the town and M. Saint Georges, 'a talented painter and decorator', designed the marble Memorial which is on the precise spot where the men were shot. Originally it was framed by two trees 'offered by the British government'.

Continue to the large mine buildings of Fosse Ernest Cuvelette on the right, just short of the roundabout.

Note that to the left of the road the large new Loos Penitentiary will be built virtually beside the Aerodrome Bénifontaines (seems a rather risky conjunction) and beyond the airfield is Bois Hugo.

• *Puits 14Bis/11.2 miles/Map 11/9/Lat & Long: 50.46283 2.81447*

A puit (literally a well, here meaning shaft) is a minehead and the area was once dotted with them. Most had winding gear and this, now dismantled, was a typical example. On the opposite side of the road is Bois Hugo and the local airfield. The hill immediately ahead is Hill 70. The area between here and Hill 70 was the secondary objective for the 44th and 46th Brigades of 15th Division who were attacking from the right starting beyond the built-up areas. As with 7th Division, the 15th Division was affected by our own gas remaining about our jumping-off trenches. To encourage the men to go forward **Piper Laidlaw**, of 7th KOSB, a leading battalion of the 46th Brigade, marched up and down the parapet as men waited to open the attack on Hill 70, playing his pipes (notably Blue Bonnets over the Border) until he was wounded, an action for which he was awarded a **VC**. Laidlaw later featured in the film of the Great War, *Forgotten Men*. It was also in this area that the Guards Division filled the gap left by the retreating 21st and 24th 'K' Divisions, one of the company commanders of the Irish Guards being Captain H.R.L.G. Alexander, later to become Lord Alexander of Tunis.

Continue to the roundabout on the D947.

N.B. By taking the third exit from the roundabout signed to Centre Commercial and then the first turning left and following the signs, the **Memorial** to the **15th Bn**, **48th Highlanders of Canada, Hill 70** is reached. It commemorates the Battalion's role in capturing Bois Hugo on the extreme left flank of the Canadian Corp's offensive against Hill 70 on 15 August 1917 **(Map 11/10b, Lat & Long: 50.46174 2.81646).** It is at the corner of the Parc des Cytistes and was unveiled on 22 September 2012.

Go straight over to the next roundabout. Turn right and stop after 100 yards under the sign Chemin des Croisettes.

• Canadian VC Plaques, Loos/11.8 miles/5 minutes/Map 11/9a/Lat & Long: 50.45529 2.81493

The roundabout you have just gone over is on the site of the formidable German Redoubt, Hill 70. The two Plaques (both in English and French) on a brick wall under the sign were inaugurated on 7 September 2008 by the British Columbia (Duke of Connaught's Own) Regiment Association. They commemorate two **VC**s won here.

One is to **Pte Michael James O'Rourke, MM,** 7th Bn, 1st British Columbia Regt, on 15-17 August 1917. O'Rourke, born in Limerick in 1878, was a stretcher-bearer who 'worked unceasingly for three days and nights bringing in the wounded, dressing their wounds and getting them food and water. During the whole of this period the area in which he worked was swept by heavy machine-gun fire and rifle fire and on several occasions he was knocked down and partially buried by enemy shells. His courage and devotion in carrying out his rescue work in spite of exhaustion and incessant heavy fire inspired all ranks and undoubtedly saved many lives.'

The other is to **Coy Sgt-Maj Robert Hill Hanna**, 29th Bn British Columbia Regt, who was born in Kilkeel, Co Down in 1887. On 21 Sept 1917 Hanna's company met with heavy resistance here. They 'beat off three assaults and all the officers of the company had become casualties. This warrant officer, under heavy machine-gun and rifle fire, coolly collected and led a party against the strong point, rushed through the wire and personally killed four of the enemy, capturing the position and silencing the machine-gun. This courageous action was responsible for the capture of a most important tactical point.' Hanna was later promoted to Lieutenant.

Continue to the T junction and turn left, following signs to Centre Ville to the next junction.

N.B: By turning left here and immediately right on rue René Cassin, the site of the famous 'Tower Bridge' (previously erroneously reported to be on the site of the Loos British Cemetery) may be reached **(Map 11/10a. Lat & Long: 50.45660 2.79658)** on the left after 100 yards. It is in a park near the Cassin College and two big circles that mark the spot of the two towers are still visible.

Tower Bridge was actually the pithead of Fosse 15 (qv), with double winding gear towers that seemed to Tommy to resemble the famous London landmark (another nickname for it was 'The Crystal Palace').

Memorial to 15th Bn, 48th Highlanders of Canada, 15-25 Aug 1917, Hill 70.

Plaques to Canadian VCs – O'Rourke & Hanna - Hill 70, Loos.

'Tower Bridge', Loos, before the battle.

> **N.B: continued**
>
> The giant steel structure dominated the area for miles around – it served as a guiding point for the British infantrymen as they attacked in the cold light of dawn of 25 September – and, despite the hurricane of shells that fell around it, Tower Bridge, albeit it in a somewhat mangled state, still stood after the battle.

Continue to the crossroads with the D165. Turn left and continue to the roundabout in Place de la République with the Mairie to the left. Park.

• *Museum Alexandre Villedieu, Loos/12.9 miles/30 minutes/Map 11/13/ Lat & Long: 50.45686 2.79237*

The Museum is in the top floor modern annexe to the rear of the *Mairie*. Organised by the indefatigable volunteers of the Association '*Sur les Traces de La Grande Guerre*', it contains many artefacts found on the surrounding battlefield – Allied and German. It is named after a French soldier found locally, on whose body was a Waterman fountain pen in perfect condition (on display in the Museum). The Museum concentrates on human interest stories (British, Canadian, French and German), illustrated with photographs, letters and other artefacts and there are close links with many of the families of soldiers who were killed on the battlefields.

There are some fascinating anecdotes - for example the story of the heroine of Loos, Emilienne Moreau, who at the age of 17 tended the wounded of 25 September 1915, killing several German snipers. Her deeds were recognised with the Military Medal, and the *Croix de Guerre* and other awards. During WW2 she became an active member of the resistance and was awarded the *Legion d'Honneur* and other decorations. She died in 1971.

The story of the search for **John Kipling**'s body (qv) is well described and another interesting story is the indefatigable quest by researcher Peter Last to identify one of the two soldiers of the Cameron Highlanders found near the Cora Shopping Centre in July 2001. He was eventually successful in identifying one of the bodies as that of **L/Cpl John Young Brown** who was finally laid to rest with full Military Honours and in the presence of some family members, in the Loos British CWGC Cemetery on 20 October 2004.

The Museum describes the three main Battles of Loos: the costly French attack of 9 May 1915, the disastrous British attack of 25 September 1915 and the Canadian engagement of 15-23 August 1917.

There are photographs of the extraordinary graffiti carved by Canadian soldiers in the tunnels which ran across the Lens-Loos road between Loos and Dud Corner as they passed through en route to their assault on Vimy Ridge (excavated by the Durand Group and others) not visitable by the public at the moment).

Among recent acquisitions is a folder of beautiful watercolours by German War Artist, Max Gehlesen. Born 1881 and a graduate of the Hamburg Beaux-Arts Academy, Gehlesen was appointed Official War Artist to the German Army. During the war years he produced a portfolio of 207 watercolours, 69 from the Pas de Calais area and 137 from the Somme (the latter have been acquired by the Historial at Péronne). The paintings from the area of Lens include two charming portraits of local girls (who have not been able to be identified). After the war the Germans had no appetite for pictures of the war that they had lost and Gehlesen packed the paintings away in a leather folder. He went on to paint in more *avant-garde* styles and died, almost in obscurity, in 1930.

Many exhibitions and events are planned for the WW1 Centenaries, when the large hall on the ground floor will be used. The Association produces an excellent newsletter, *Echo des Tranchées* http://asso.sltdlgg. pagesperso-orange.fr/

Small entrance fee payable. Guided visits of Double Crassier, Loos, Dud Corner and 'The Kipling Trail' available for small groups. Ring or e-mail for an appointment.

Contact: Enthusiastic curator, M Alfred Duparcq, c/o *Mairie de Loos*, Tel: + (0)3 21 78 31 29.
E-mail: a.villedieu@wanadoo.fr or Gilles Payen at the same address or Jean-Louis Delattre, Tél: +(0)3 21 70 59 75 Website: http://perso.wanadoo.fr/asso.sltdlgg/index.htm

Self-portrait of Max Gehlesen, Museum A. Villedieu, Loos.

Advert for Waterman Pen, Loos Museum.

Marker for Loos Battlefield Walks, Loos Mairie.

Loos British CWGC Cemetery.

Turn left following the sign to Loos British Cemetery. Continue uphill to just short of the road bridge. The cemetery is on the left.

• Loos British CWGC Cemetery/13.4 miles/20 minutes/Map 11/10/ Lat & Long: 50.45140 2.79739

This vast (11,364 square metres) cemetery contains nearly 3,000 WW1 burials, of which two-thirds are unknown, and a small number of WW2 graves. It is beautifully landscaped with spacious lawns and an ornamental wall behind the Cross of Sacrifice approached by steps. The cemetery was begun by the Canadian Corps in July 1917 and the original graves are in Plot I, Rows A and B and Plot II Row A. The other graves were concentrated here after the Armistice from battlefield graves and other small cemeteries in the vicinity. Special Memorials commemorate British and Canadian soldiers believed to be buried among them. The great majority fell in the Battle of Loos and it is sobering to read the Kipling message 'Known unto God' over and over again along the long rows of graves.

Turn round and return to the Mairie. Turn left on the D165. Continue to the junction with the N43.

N.B. 1: By turning left here on the N43 Route de Béthune and continuing some 1.5 miles a Memorial **Plaque to Cpl Filip Konowal, VC** may be seen on the left (**Map 11/10a, Lat & Long: 50.43873 2.811223**). It is beside a **Demarcation Stone** and flanked by recreated sandbags in a small recess. Konowal, a Russian of Ukrainian origin, served with the 47th (British Columbia Regt) Bn, Can EF.

He was awarded the Empire's highest medal (the only Ukrainian in the War to win a VC) by King George V personally, who commended him for his audacity and bravery. It was awarded for his action on 22/23 August 1917 at Hill 70 when, under heavy fire, in a fight to clear up cellars, craters and machine-gun emplacements, he single-handedly bayonetted 3 enemy and killed 7 more in a crater. When a machine-gun held up the attack he personally killed 3 of the crew and destroyed the position with explosives, continuing his advance until he was severely wounded. Konowal was then promoted to Sgt. He was later appointed Military Attaché at the Russian Embassy in London, and then served with the Canadian Siberian Expeditionary Force. In July 1919 Konowal intervened in a brawl between a friend and an assailant, killing the latter. He was held in gaol. Veterans raised enough money for his bail and in 1921 he was eventually tried but was found Not Guilty 'by reason of insanity' brought on by his serious war wound. He was institutionalised for 7 years and emerged having greatly improved. Sadly he discovered that his wife had died in the 1932-33 Famine in the Ukraine and his daughter was missing. The medals, including the VC, of this extraordinary soldier were acquired by the Canadian War Museum in Ottawa in 1969. They then went missing in the '70s, only to emerge again in an antique shop in London, Ontario in 2004 and thence finally to return to the War Museum. Konowal died in Ottawa in 1959.

Dud Corner CWG Cemetery with part of the Double Crassier behind, Loos.

N.B. 2: By going straight over here, **The Double Crassier** is reached on the left **(Lat & Long: 50.45140 2.77911).** The attack here came from right to left, heading due east as you drive, and was by the 140th and 141st Brigades of 47th Division. The gas worked well and on the extreme right of the attack German fire was attracted off target by the use of dummy figures – heads and shoulders pulled up and down by strings. In the 141st Brigade, the lst/l8th London (London Irish Rifles) Regiment which led the assault came on behind the gas and smoke cloud dribbling a football and by 0730 the trench line between the Double Crassier and the N43 had been taken. The Division advanced so well that elements penetrating into Loos village became mixed up with 15th Division north of the N43 and went on to the area of Hill 70 from where you have just come. On the first day of the battle, and mostly before 1000 hours, the 47th Division lost more than 1,200 officers and men.

A tour of this area is conducted from the Loos Museum (qv).

Turn right on the N43. Continue up the hill to the British cemetery on the crest on the right. Stop, and be careful of the fast-moving traffic.

• *Dud Corner CWGC Cemetery & Loos Memorial/15.1 miles/20 minutes/Map 11/11/OP/Lat & Long: 50.46011 2.77147*

During the battle of Loos many British shells that were fired were duds and on finding much unexploded shot lying around here the troops nicknamed it 'Dud Corner'. The memorial is virtually on the site of a German strongpoint (*stutzpunkte*) called the 'Lens Road Redoubt' captured by the 15th (Scottish) Division on the first day. The walls surrounding the cemetery which form the memorial record the names of almost 21,000 men with no known grave who fell in the battle of Loos 1915 and the later battles of the Lys, Estaires and Béthune. One of the names, still not removed on our last visit, was that of **John Kipling** (see above). The body claimed to be that of

John Kipling was found some 1.6 miles west of here, yet he was last seen, badly injured, 1.6 miles north-east of here, i.e. the two locations are over 3 miles apart   Also commemorated on the wall is the 20-year-old, highly regarded war poet, **Charles Hamilton Sorley**, of the 7th Bn. the Suffolk Regiment. Three **VC** winners are commemorated, two from the Loos battle – **Temporary Lt Col A.F. Douglas-Hamilton** commanding 6th Cameronians for actions at Hill 70 on 25 and 26 September 1915 and **Pte G. Peachment** of the 2nd KRRC for bravery near Hulluch on 25 September 1915 – and **2nd Lt F.B. Wearne** of the Essex Regiment for actions in 1917. Also commemorated here is **Maj-Gen George Handcock Thesiger** (qv), Commanding 9th Division, age 47, 26 September 1915.

2nd Lt John Kipling, 1915.

The name of **Capt the Hon Fergus Bowes-Lyon** will be removed from the wall in due course as a headstone bearing his name in Quarry Cemetery was inscribed in August 2012 (qv).

A viewing platform on the north-west pier of the memorial offers a remarkable panorama over the battlefield, as does a position near the Cross of Sacrifice at the far end of the cemetery. On a clear day all the places visited on the tour can be identified. The architect was Sir Herbert Baker and the memorial was unveiled on 4 August 1930 by Sir Nevil Macready, Adjutant-General to the BEF in 1914.

There are some 1,800 burials in the cemetery (666 UK Army and 1116 Unknown, 2 UK Airmen, 16 Canadian and 12 Canadian Unknown), including **two VCs** – **Capt A.M. Read** of the 1st Northants for conspicuous bravery during the attack of 25 September 1915 near Hulluch, and **Sgt Harry Wells** of the 2nd Royal Sussex for actions on the same day near le Rutoir. Shortly before he died Rudyard Kipling left an endowment to fund the nightly sounding of the Last Post here, but no such ceremony now takes place.

Climb to the top of the left hand loggia.

With binoculars there are some extraordinary views of the battlefield from this vantage point. Looking across to the Double Crassier, from left to right the twin pylons of the Vimy Memorial and the Lantern tower and Basilique of Notre-Dame de Lorette may be seen.

• *End of Loos Battlefield Tour* (but see STOP PRESS on page 333)

"The Loos Football", with Double Crassier behind, by Michael St Maur Shiel (See STOP PRESS page 336, Item 10).

FROMELLES

19-20 JULY 1916

'Boys you won't find a German when you get there.'
Australian Brigadier-General Elliot.

'They strolled on through the grass like sportsmen after quail,
occasionally shooting at Germans who had settled in
shell holes and who now started up to run farther'.
C.E.W. Bean about the Australian 14th Brigade at Fromelles.

SUMMARY OF THE BATTLE

At 1800 hours on 19 July 1916 the Australian 5th Division which had arrived from Egypt less than two weeks earlier, accompanied by the British 61st Division, attacked German positions at Fromelles. Despite briefly entering and holding part of the German line the Australians were driven out by enemy counter-attacks and were back in their own lines the following day. The 5th Division lost some 5,500 men, the 61st about 1,500 and the Germans almost 2,000.

OPENING MOVES

On 1 July 1916 the great Battle of the Somme began and by the end of the first day the British had lost around 60,000 casualties. The Germans had suffered too and within days each side was bringing in fresh troops to replace those lost or exhausted. The British staff looked around for some way to discourage the Germans from bringing troops from other parts of the front and came up with the idea of making a massive three-day artillery assault in the area of Fromelles as if in prelude to an attack on Aubers Ridge.

Following a conference with General Haig, General Haking, the XI Corps Commander, persuaded G.H.Q. that an infantry assault should actually be made with a view to taking out the small German salient at Fromelles known as the **Sugar Loaf**.

Many staff officers expressed doubts about the idea, particularly whether there was sufficient artillery to support an attack. Haking thought otherwise and planned to use a mix of over 250 field guns and more than 60 medium and heavy weapons which would give one gun to every 15 yards of the 4,000 yards frontage of the attack. In addition it was intended that early on the day of the attack, 17 July, the barrage would lift from the German front trenches to the rear areas leading the Germans to think that the infantry assault was imminent and to come out of their dugouts to man the front line. At that point the artillery was to rapidly return its fire to the front trenches, a process that was to be repeated a number of times so that when the actual attack finally came the enemy would be slow to come out, thus enabling the attackers to cross No Man's Land unopposed.

The infantry plan was to attack the right hand (western) side of the salient using the British 61st Division and the left hand side with the Australian 5th Division, the dividing line between the divisions being roughly north to south through **VC Corner.**

WHAT HAPPENED

The bombardment began on 16 July but without the heavy guns, because rain and mist had prevented them identifying (registering) their targets. On the morning of 17 July the mist still lay over the battlefield and Haking asked for a 24-hours postponement while the 1st Army Commander, Sir Charles Monro (qv), felt that the operation should be cancelled. Haig opted for an attack at 1800 hours on 19 July with the final bombardment to begin at 1100 hours on that day.

The delay at least gave the Australians some rest. They had marched for two days and nights to get to the front line and many had gone without sleep leaving them tired and exhausted. The day dawned bright and sunny and as the troops moved into their attack positions they were closely watched by the Germans in Observation Posts on Aubers Ridge (e.g. the **Kaiser's Bunker** (qv). Early in the afternoon enemy artillery fire fell heavily upon the assembly areas, destroying communication trenches and causing many casualties. Nevertheless, at 1800 hours the infantry moved forward, some through friendly artillery fire, and the attack began. They had been told to head for the third and last line of the German front trench system.

Advancing with three brigades side by side the 61st Division came under intense artillery and machine-gun fire, both in the assembly trenches and in No Man's Land, and only on their extreme right did they reach the enemy trenches – but even there they were driven back and no permanent gains were made. German defence works were formidable. The 16th Bavarian Res Regt had 75 shelters built into its parapet, 60 of which were undamaged by our artillery. Australian after-action reports estimated some parapets to be 8ft high.

The Australians too advanced with three brigades 'up' (i.e. side by side). Right to left they were the 15th (alongside the 61st Division), the 14th and the 8th. At 1830 Brigadier-General Elliott reported that the German fire had died away and that the attack had succeeded. It was not so. The 15th had been badly cut up by the ferocious German fire and dead and wounded lay in and around **Layes Brook** and the **Sugar Loaf**. The 61st Division asked the 15th Brigade to support them in another attack at 2100 hours but this was cancelled – though not before the 15th had gone in, suffering more casualties. The 14th had crossed No Man's Land readily and went on through the German positions, moving across open fields looking for the third line, which they could not find, and then scattering into small groups of isolated posts in ditches and shell holes. It was the same story with the 8th who even took part of a communication trench that led back to **Delangre Farm**, but as night fell the Germans brought up reinforcements, gradually surrounding the separated 'Diggers' (a name given to the Australians in Gallipoli when having landed at ANZAC they were told that all they had to do was to 'dig, dig, dig'.)

Around 0330 hours the order was given to return to their old lines and for the next six hours the Australians fought their way back. At the end of the fighting the Bavarians (the opposing Germans were part of the 6th Bavarian Reserve Division) agreed to a truce that allowed many lives to be saved but the Australians had lost 5,533 men in little over one night. No substantial effect on the movement of Germans to the Somme had resulted and the relatively poor performance of the under-strength 61st Division, which in England had been a second-line force used as a source of reinforcements, added to the Australian feeling that the British were lacking in fighting resolve.

The whole affair had been a costly failure.

THE BATTLEFIELD TOUR

• The Route: The tour presumes continuing on from the Aubers Tour and starts at the Fromelles *Mairie*. It then visits the new Museum and CWGC Cemetery at Pheasant Wood, the 'original Hitler Bunker', WW2 private Memorial to Sgt Bramble, the sites of Delangre and Cordonnerie Farms, WW1 Private Memorial to Capt Kennedy and friends; the Australian Memorial Park; the CWGC Cemeteries of VC Corner, Le Trou Aid Post, Rue Pétillon Military and Rue du Bois Military; Laventie German Cemetery. It returns to the *Mairie*. (**See Map 9 page 130 and Map 13 page 181**).

MAP 13: FROMELLES 19-20 JULY 1916 (See also Map 9)

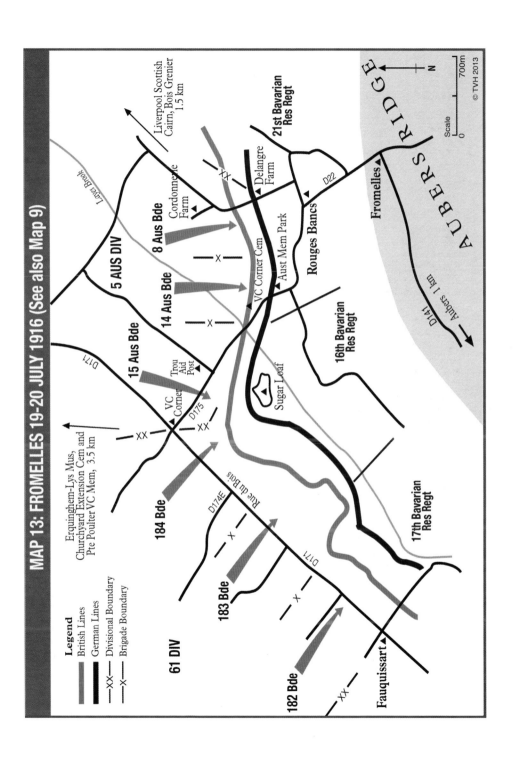

Legend
British Lines
German Lines
XX— Divisional Boundary
X— Brigade Boundary

Liverpool Scottish
Cairn, Bois Grenier
1.5 km

Layes Bk

Cordonnerie
Farm

8 Aus Bde

5 AUS DIV

14 Aus Bde

VC Corner Cem

15 Aus Bde

Aust Mem Park

Trou
Aid
Post

VC
Corner

D175

D171

Sugar Loaf

Rue du Bois

184 Bde

D174E

61 DIV

183 Bde

182 Bde

D171

Fauquissart

Erquinghem-Lys Mus,
Churchyard Extension Cem and
Pte Poulter VC Mem, 3.5 km

21st Bavarian
Res Regt

Delangre
Farm

D22

Rouges Bancs

16th Bavarian
Res Regt

Fromelles

17th Bavarian
Res Regt

AUBERS RIDGE

Aubers 1 km

D141

N

Scale

0   700m

© TVH 2013

• **Extra Visits** to 'Hitler's Bunker', Fromelles; Liverpool Scottish Cairn, Bois Grenier; Erquinghem-Lys Museum, Cemetery Extension, Rev Railton Mem, Duke of Wellington Regt Roundabout & Pte Poulter, VC, Memorial, ; the site of Hitler's Billet and German Cemeteries at Fournes-en-Weppes and Wicres.

• **[N.B.]:** The following sites are indicated: White City CWGC Cemetery, Bois Grenier; Suffolk CWGC Cemetery, Erquinghem-Lys

• **Total Distance:** 7.5 miles

• **Total time:** 2 hours 50 minutes

• **Base towns:** Béthune, Lille

• **Distance from Calais to start point:** 70 miles

• **Map:** IGN 1:25,000 2404 Est

• *Fromelles Mairie/0 miles/Map 9/9/Lat & Long: 50.60596 2.85406*

The Museum of the *Association Souvenir de la Bataille de Fromelles,* housed for many years in the attic of the *Mairie,* was a well-loved Museum, mainly the work of ex-Mayor, Francis and his son, Benoit Delattre, Martial Delebarre, Henri Delepierre and Carol Laignel. Many hours of loving care were put into the cleaning, preserving, presenting and careful labelling (in three languages) of the extraordinary variety of exhibits, many of which had been found on the surrounding battlefield and a number of which are quite unique. It had a wonderful atmosphere and retained the personal feeling so lacking in some new, expensive and technology-led museums.

It featured many soldiers who fought in the Battle of Fromelles of July 1916 and local men too, with photos and documents, such as local Resistance hero Henri-Clotaire Descamps (qv). There were collections of pickelhaube, grenades, maces, gas masks, binoculars, rifles, pumps, entrenching tools and other items found in the gallery beneath the bunker in the Australian Park and, rarest of all, the plaque that was on the wall of the house in Fournes where Hitler was billeted in 1916 (qv). There was a special headstone made by the CWGC to commemorate the Australians of 5th Division killed in the 19-21 July 1916 attack.

Possibly doomed to closure in the next couple of years for health and safety reasons it was in any case closed in December 2012 and be replaced in July 2013 by the new Museum described below. Hopefully many of these treasures will be displayed in the new Museum while others will be stored 'in reserve'.

The Association of knowledgeable, dedicated and enthusiastic volunteers still thrives, providing guides to the battlefield and offering support to the new project.

Contacts are: M. Hubert Huchette, *Maire de Fromelles* (*Mairie* Tel: + 03 20 50 20 43) ; Bernard Lebleu, *1er Maire Adjoint,* (ber-lebleu@orange.fr Tel: +03 20 50 20 15/0668948840); Jean-Marie Doual (English-speaking guide, Tel: +03 20 07 27 17); Martial Delbarre (French and English speaking, martial.delebarre@wanadoo.fr) Jean-Marie Bailleul (Tel: +03 20 58 58 65) and probably the main contact, Gervais Heuvenaghel (Tresoriers with his wife Régine, regine.houvenaghel@ wanadoo.fr Tel: +(0)3 20 50 30 02.

With the Mairie on the left continue on the D22 and take the first turning left on the D22C signed Mémorial Australien. Pass the Café **Au Gallodrome** *(the social hub of the village and where the Anciens Combattants Association meets), and the Church and continue to the new Cemetery and site of the new Museum on the left.*

• *Fromelles (Pheasant Wood) Military Cemetery and Fromelles Museum /.4 miles/60 minutes/Map 9a/Lat & Long: 50.60804 2.85082*

The Cemetery.

Dedicated on 19 July 2010 by HRH the Duke of Kent in the presence of HRH Price Charles and the Duchess of Cornwall, HE Ms Quentin Bryce, Governor-General of Australia, Lt-Gen Ken Gillespie, chief of the Australian Army, Sir David Richards, Chief of the General Staff of the British Army and other dignitaries, this unique cemetery was the first to be built in over half a century

Interior of Museum, Fromelles.

CWGC Stone to Australian 5th Division 19-21 July 1916.

since the last cemetery of WW2 was completed. It was an extremely moving ceremony, in large part due to the presence of many families with their own personal stories of the men, Australian and British, buried here, and to the burial, with full military honours, of the final Unknown Soldier. His body was brought to the Cemetery on a Catafalque on a brown military wagon pulled by four matching horses, followed by Prince Charles and the other dignitaries.

Its Architect, Barry Edwards together with the Project Manager David Richardson and the Director of Works and Technical Service (also a horticultural expert), worked to a tight schedule to complete this beautiful and calm cemetery. It is built in the traditional format and style inspired by Fabian Ware and is reminiscent of other cemeteries in the area designed by Sir Herbert Baker, with headstones of Portland stone. The Cross, terrace, ornamentation of the wall copings and entrance building are of durable, creamy French limestone. A warm red brick (known as 'Boom') wall with limestone trimmings surrounds the site. There is no War Stone because Lutyens originally intended that it should grace only cemeteries containing more than 1,000 burials.

The graceful hexagonal-shaped cemetery, sited below the rebuilt church of Fromelles, was created to be the final resting place of the more than 250 soldiers of the 5th Australian Division and the British 61st (South Midland) Division who had been killed in the attack of 19 July 1916 on well-defended German strongholds to the west of the ruined village of Fromelles – a diversion to deflect German resources from the continuing Somme battle. The Australians lost some 5,533 killed, wounded or missing, the British 1,457.

The Germans buried the Allied dead in mass graves whose location was unknown until in 2007.

In 2003 Australian school teacher from Victoria, Australia, Lambis Englezos, who had long researched the battle of Fromelles, was convinced that the large number of missing Australians had to be buried somewhere in the vicinity and diligently scoured German and Red Cross archives and histories, discovering some aerial photographs which showed several pits dug for mass graves. In conjunction with British battlefield archaeologist, Peter Barton of the War Graves and Battlefield Heritage Group, he worked with the Australia History Unit and many other experts and enthusiasts to contact the Bavarian regimental archives. Eventually their curator provided the team with documents that showed plans for the burials near Pheasant Wood. After consultation with the CWGC, exploratory excavations were undertaken in May 2008 and soon remains were found, unusually somehow missed by the impeccable Imperial War Graves Commission's Graves Registration Unit.

Soon an impressive group of internationally renowned archaeologists under the Oxford Archaeology team led by Dr Louise Loe and the Glasgow University archaeological Research Division (GUARD) moved into the area. They included specialists in forensics, radiographers, photographers, osteo-archaeologists, pathologists, mortuary managers, and anthropologists. Offices, laboratories and a mortuary, x-ray facility and a survey data-processing suite were soon erected on the site where some 250 bodies were eventually meticulously examined for all clues of identification and all the fascinating artefacts were examined and collated, analysed and matched with information about individual missing soldiers against army records, lists of the fallen etc. Advanced DNA matching techniques were employed in the largest undertaking of its type. The remains could often be identified as coming from a specific geographic area. Then came the quest for relatives whose DNA could be compared for a match, by appeals in local newspapers, using the media and 'road shows'. The result was the identification of 119 Australian soldiers in the first years of researches, but work is on-going and on 19 July 2012 the graves of 9 further identified men were dedicated.

The story of Pheasant Cemetery is told in full in the CWGC's publication *Remembering Fromelles* compiled by Julie Summers. See also www.cwgc.org/fromelles/ and www.defence.gov.au/ fromelles/

Standing with one's back to the cross and looking over the wall of the Cemetery, the French and Autralian flags at 'The Cobber' site and the British flag at the Kennedy Memorial, visited later, on a clear day can be seen straight ahead on a clear day on the horizon, over the red roofed buildings.

The Museum. The new Museum, part of the Australians' Western Front Remembrance Trail project which is planned to be completed for the Centenary of WW1 in 2014 and which has a budget of 10 million Australian dollars.

Fromelles (Pheasant Wood) CWGC Cemetery, awaiting the Dedication, 19 July 2011.

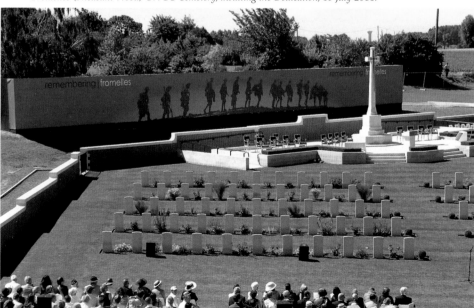

Prince Charles following the Catafalque of the final Unknown Soldier to be buried in Fromelles (Pheasant Wood) Cemetery on 19 July 2011.

The objective of the Australian Remembrance Trail is "to improve visitors' understanding and appreciation of the achievements and sacrifices of Australians in the main theatre of conflict during the First World War ... This approach recognises the significant efforts of many locals over decades and will ensure the Australian funds are spent carefully and in the best locations to appropriately commemorate and honour the service of our First World War heroes". In Fromelles more than 5,500 men of the 5th Australian Div became casualties in 24 hours.

The Museum is being built on the lawn in front of the Cemetery with the full co-operation of the *Mairie* of Fromelles and the Association who with the Région de Pas de Calais are matching the Australians' contribution to the anticipated Euros 1,300,000 budget. Building to the design of Serrero Architects commenced in August 2012, with an opening date of early 2014. Many of the wonderful exhibits in the original Museum will be on show here in a low profile, octagonal, one-story building, half sunk in the slope. The progress of the Battle of Fromelles will be explained from Australian, British and German points of view, focussing on a large central map. The personal stories of 7 soldiers who took part in the Battle will be followed using letters, photographs and other artefacts and there will be audio-guides in English, French and German. The Church is visible from the lobby area, the Cemetery visible from another opening.

There is a Museum Boutique, Cafeteria and disabled, and toilet, facilities. An entrance fee will be payable.

Continue following signs to Mémorial Australien and VC Corner 'Australien' Cem. Continue to the first turning left, rue de la Biette.

Artist's impression of the new Fromelles Museum.

Extra Visit to 'Hitler's Bunker', Fromelles. Round (driveable) trip 1.0 miles. Approx time: 30 mins (Map 9/8a, Lat & Long: 50.60979 2.84032)

Turn left and continue past two small turnings to a sign to the left to Circuit des Etangs (Route of the Pools). Park. Enter the gate and continue along the picturesque pathway to a sign to the left.

The path is named in honour of **Henri-Clothaire Descamps** (qv Aubers tour) after the hero of both wars, eventually beheaded by the Germans in 1942.

Continue along the path past the pool until the end of the gravelled section (**Lat & Long: 50.60979   2.84032**).

Access to the bunker, which can be seen in the field to the left, now becomes virtually impossible if wet. The land is naturally very marshy and it can be quite dangerous. However the bunker is clearly visible and within good photographic range from here.

The Bunker has recently been bought by the Commune of Fromelles and when funds are available it will be made more accessible and visitable. Its importance (apart from the fact that it is remarkably well preserved) lies in the fact that local research seems to point to the fact that this was the actual Bunker called on by Adolf Hitler in his capacity as Company Runner en route to his billet in Fournes-en-Weppes [not the so-called 'Hitler Bunker' in Aubers!].

The story goes that Hitler returned to this bunker on 26th June 1940 after the fall of France when he is recorded as having visited two bunkers at Fromelles, including this one at N.16.c.1.1. (the Germans meticulously located each of their bunkers).

Return to the D22 and pick up the main Itinerary.

Pathway sign in honour of Henri-Clotaire Descamps, Fromelles.

'Hitler's Bunker', Fromelles.

Continue to a sharp bend to the left and stop.

• *Private Memorial to Sgt Bramble/1.00 mile/5 minutes/Map 9/10/Lat & Long: 50.62082 2.84468*

This grey polished granite Memorial commemorates Sgt Kenneth Walter Bramble, pilot of 609 Sqn, RAF, whose Spitfire was shot down in aerial combat by Obfw Maerz of 5/JG26 near this spot at 0830 in the morning of 21 July 1941 as he returned from a bombing raid on Lille. It was erected by Antiq'Air Flandre-Artois (qv) in 1999 after research by Joss Leclercq (qv). Sgt Bramble was actually found near the row of trees that can be seen on the horizon to the left (over the fences held up by WW1 pickets) near Fauquissart. Sgt Bramble is buried in Merville Comm Cemetery Extension, 15 kms north of Béthune.

Turn right and then first left on Rue de la Cardonnerie and continue on the narrow road to the copse surrounding a modern house on the right.

You have driven through the German trench system to what was effectively their front line.

Monument to Sgt Bramble, 21 July 1941, Fromelles.

• *Delangre Farm/1.5 miles/5 minutes/Lat & Long: 50.62082 2.84468*

This was the site of the heavily armed **Delangre Farm** and to the left were craters which had been blown by 173rd Tunnelling Coy on 9 May 1915 during the unsuccessful British IV Corps attack on Aubers Ridge. Oddly the German defenders in 1915 were the same ones as in 1916 – the 6th Bavarian Reserve Division. Delangre Farm was the final objective of the attack and there was a long German communication trench beside it which was the objective of the 8th and 14th Australian Inf Bde into which some men of the 8th penetrated briefly.

Continue round the bend and immediately up the track to the left is a farm.

• *Cardonnerie Farm/1.6 miles/5 minutes/Lat & Long: 50.62271 2.84450*

This is **Cardonnerie** (sometimes marked as 'Cordonnerie') **Farm**. In driving from one farm to the next you have crossed first the German front line and then the Australian front line.

Return to the Bramble Memorial and continue round the bend on the D22C to a Calvary on the right.

The area to the left is Rouges Bancs.

• *Private Memorial to Capt P.A. Kennedy & Others/2.6 miles/5 minutes /Map 9/12/Lat & Long: 50.61638 2.83796*

This perfectly maintained (by the Association Souvenir de la Bataille de Fromelles) Memorial is to Capt Paul Adrian Kennedy, Rifle Brigade, kia 9 May 1915, also to Lt Talbot Fitzroy Eden Stanhope, 2nd Lt Henry Ralph Hardinge and Lt Edward Henry Leigh, also of the regiment. All these officers are commemorated on the Ploegsteert Memorial (qv).

Capt Paul Kennedy was the third-born of the four sons of Sir John (who died in 1913) and Lady Kennedy. By the time he arrived in France in September 1914 his oldest brother, Archibald, had already been killed in the Retreat from Mons on 26 August 1914. Paul Kennedy was wounded on the Aisne but was back on active service in March 1915. He was shot by a sniper while leading 'B' Coy of the 2nd Rifle Brigade on 9 May 1915 and though brought in by his men, died of his wounds. His youngest brother Patrick was killed near Villers Bretonneux on 24 April 1918.

After the war Lady Kennedy and her one surviving son, Leo (T/Capt A.L Kennedy, MC) began the search for news of the three missing Kennedy brothers. Patrick was discovered to be buried in Crucifix Corner Cemetery, Villers Bretonneux and Archibald was buried in Le Cateau Mil (International) Cemetery.

As Paul's body was never found, Lady Kennedy purchased the small plot of land where his men told her they had laid him to his final rest. On it she placed a fine wooden crucifix carved in Austria with a marble plaque on the plinth, surrounded by a garden and iron railings. She made local arrangements for the site to be cared for and visited it regularly until her death in 1939. After WW2 the monument fell into disrepair and in 1954 the CWGC contacted both Leo Kennedy and the local Commune. They both reacted to restore the memorial. The original wooden crucifix was moved to the church for safe keeping and a new, more durable crucifix, carved in Austria, was erected in its place. A beech hedge replaced the old iron railings. Leo died in 1965 but since then the Commune of Fromelles has continued to maintain the memorial to a very high standard. In 2003, to redress a certain amount of vandalism, it was refurbished and a new copper beech hedge planted.

The 'Cobber' Statue and VC corner are visible behind the Memorial to the left.

As you round the right hand bend you are moving from within the German trenches to their front line.

Continue to the memorial park on the right.

• *Australian Memorial Park/2.8 miles/15 minutes/Map 9/13/Lat & Long: 50.61797 2.83536*

The park is situated around the remains of German fortifications on the part of their front line that was captured by the 14th Australian Brigade and held overnight on 19-20 July 1916. Under the

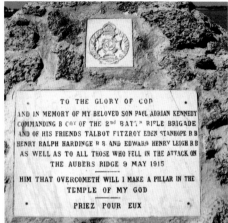

TO THE GLORY OF GOD
AND IN MEMORY OF MY BELOVED SON PAUL ADRIAN KENNEDY
COMMANDING B COY OF THE 2ⁿᵈ BATᵗ ᴺ RIᶠˡE BRIGADE
AND OF HIS FRIENDS TALBOT FITZROY EDEN STANHOPE R B
HENRY RALPH HARDINGE R B AND EDWARD HENRY LEIGH R B
AS WELL AS TO ALL THOSE WHO FELL IN THE ATTACK ON
THE AUBERS RIDGE 9 MAY 1915

HIM THAT OVERCOMETH WILL I MAKE A PILLAR IN THE
TEMPLE OF MY GOD

PRIEZ POUR EUX

Detail of Inscription.

*Private memorial to
Capt P.A. Kennedy
and others, Fromelles*

further bunker is a 25m gallery in which several of the items in the Fromelles Museum (qv) were found. The park contains a fine bronze statue entitled 'Cobbers' depicting the rescue of a wounded soldier. It also contains a battle exploit explanatory plaque. At the entrance is a Ross Bastiaan (qv) bronze plaque with a fine bas relief map of the battle and shows its context in relation to Ypres and other battles. This was unveiled by the Australian Chief of the General Staff on 1 September 1993. Also at the entrance are explanatory boards describing the action here and at the infamous 'Sugar Loaf' (qv), with photos. The statue is of Sgt Simon Fraser, 57th Bn AIF, whose company brought in 250 wounded men during the battle as, to quote him, 'the Germans treated us very fairly'. This fine statue recalls two episodes from the Gallipoli Campaign of 1915: the story of Pte Simpson ('The Man with the Donkey') who brought many wounded men down Shrapnel Gully until he himself was killed, and the Turkish statue of a Turk bringing in a wounded soldier on 25 April 1915. The figure here was sculpted by Peter Corlett and unveiled on 11 November 1998. Fraser, who was a farmer from Victoria, went on to be commissioned but was killed at Bullecourt on 12 May 1917. He is commemorated on the Villers Bretonneux Memorial. The statue is known as 'Cobbers' because Fraser described in a letter to his family at home how he and his fellow stretcher bearers brought in the wounded and recalled a wounded man crying out, 'Don't forget me, Cobber'.

Continue to the cemetery to the right.

Detail of Plaque.

Ross Bastiaan Plaque, Australian Memorial Park, Fromelles.

VC Corner CWGC Cemetery, Fromelles.

'Cobbers' Statue, Australian Memorial Park, Fromelles.

• *VC Corner CWGC Cemetery/3.00 miles/15 minutes/Map 9/14/Lat & Long: 50.61934 2.83343*

This unusual cemetery has no headstones and is the only completely Australian cemetery in France. On a screen wall are recorded the names of 1,299 Australians who died in the 19-20 July 1916 Battle of Fromelles, the Australian 5th Division's first attack in France. The unidentified bodies of 410 of the men are buried under the two lawns, each marked with a white stone Cross set into the grass. It is situated in what was No Man's Land between the Australian and German front lines and was designed by Sir Herbert Baker. It is said that after the war, when the local people returned from their evacuation, the women who lived nearby were simply able to scoop up the thousands of bones in their capacious apron pockets and bring them to the newly made cemetery. The stonework in the cemetery was refurbished in 2003 and gleams a brilliant white in the sun.

According to the book *Don't Forget Me, Cobber*, by Robin S. Corfield, the cemetery got its name from 4 VCs won in the fighting in Rue du Bois (which runs from south of here to la Bombe) and Rue Delvas on 9 May 1915. The Black Watch **VCs of L/Cpl Finlay** (qv) and **Cpl Ripley** (qv) were won there on 9 May 1915. Ripley survived until 1933 but Finlay was killed in Persia on 21 January 1916 and is commemorated on the Basra Memorial, Iraq. This Memorial bears the names of more than 40,500 Commonwealth soldiers who died in what was then Mesopotamia from Autumn 1914 to August 1921. It was originally situated within the Basra War Cemetery but in 1997 was removed, stone by stone, by 'presidential decree' – an incredible, and extremely costly, engineering feat. It is now located 32 kilometres along the road to Nasiriyah in what was a major battleground of the First Gulf War of 1990. At the time of writing this entry it was again the site of conflict and the current state of Iraqi cemeteries and memorials is the subject of a report on the CWGC website (qv). Also on 9 May the **VC** of **Cpl James Upton** (qv) of the 1st Sherwood Foresters was won at nearby Rouges Bancs so was that of **Cpl Charles Richard Sharpe** (qv), 2nd Lincolnshires. However, in *Goodbye to the Battlefields*, H.A. Taylor maintains VC Corner takes its name from the episode of 16 May 1915 when **CSM Barter** (qv), of the Welsh Fusiliers, won the highest award for valour.

Note that this spot is not actually the original 'VC Corner'. This will be passed later in the tour.
Continue until the road bends to the right and then the left, crossing Layes Brook (a wide ditch).
You are now effectively on the Australian front line.

To the left is the site of the infamous **Sugar Loaf**. The object of the whole 19 July offensive was to attack what was known as the Sugar Loaf Salient in a feint to threaten Aubers Ridge and so to persuade the Germans to leave troops to defend it rather than transfer them to the continuing battle on the Somme, see Map 13. The feature lay opposite the boundary of two British Armies – the 1st and 2nd, so each of them could be expected to contribute artillery. Behind the Sugar Loaf and then crossing the two front lines ran the Layes Brook and this became a death trap for the Australians as fire rained down on it from the German defences. On the morning of 20 July the scene in No Man's Land in front of the Sugar Loaf was horrendous. During the previous day and night 5th Australian Division had lost 5,533 men and many of the wounded lay here. An Australian batman searching for his officer near the German wire was challenged by a Bavarian officer who then initiated an informal truce thereby saving many Australian lives.

The northern face of the Sugar Loaf was in the 184th Brigade sector and the 2/4th Berkshires and 2/1st Bucks were chosen as assault formations. The Bucks decided to make use of pipe-pushers (Barratt hydraulic jacks set about 5 feet underground which pushed forward a pipe full of ammonal) against the Sugar Loaf fortifications but to no avail.
Continue to the next turning to the right.
The track leading left here leads tortuously to the northern face of the Sugar Loaf some 500 yards away.
Turn right and follow the CWGC signs on the D175. Stop at the cemetery on the left.

Le Trou Aid Post CWGC Cemetery, Fromelles.

Entrance to Rue Pétillon Mil CWGC Cemetery, Fromelles.

Liverpool Scottish Cairn, Bois Grenier.

• Le Trou Aid Post CWGC Cemetery/3.4 miles/10 minutes/Map 9/15/ Lat & Long: 50.62364 2.82670

Surrounded by weeping willows, this is an extraordinarily beautiful cemetery. The Aid Post was established early in the war and the cemetery begun in October 1914, used until July 1915 and in 1916 it was described as being 'a short distance behind the present support line'. There was an actual hole (trou) here, surrounded by water, at the time, clearly marked on trench maps. The cemetery was enlarged after the Armistice (when it contained 123 burials) and now contains 356 UK, Australian and Canadian burials, 207 of them unknown, 1 French burial and 5 Special Memorials. Many are officers and men from the fighting at Le Maisnil (21 October 1914), Aubers Ridge (9 May 1915), Loos (25 September 1915) and Fromelles (19-20 July 1916). It was designed by Sir Herbert Baker.

Here is buried **Brigadier-General Arthur Willoughby George Lowry-Cole, CB, DSO (qv)**, age 54, of 25th Brigade who was killed on 9 May 1915 as he stood on the parapet a few hundred from this point trying to reorganise his men as the situation around him became chaotic. He had served in the Burmah, W African and S African campaigns and was Commandant Northern Nigeria 1899-1901. Also buried here is **2nd Lt George Mortimer Langdon Goodall**, 2nd E Lancs, age 21, 9 May 1915. He was a member of the Goodall family who produced playing cards, notably sets with backs of Bruce Bairnsfather's cartoons.

Continue to the next cemetery on the right.

• Rue Pétillon Mil CWGC Cemetery/4.2 miles/10 minutes/Map 9/16/ Lat & Long: 50.63132 2.83553

The cemetery was begun in December 1914 and used by fighting units until March 1918. It then fell into enemy hands. At the Armistice it contained 12 battalion burial grounds made by units which had occupied HQ and Dressing Stations at 'Eaton Hall' adjoining the cemetery. It was then enlarged by concentrations and now contains over 1,500 burials, nearly 50% unidentified. There are Special Memorials to 2 Indian soldiers, 15 Canadians, 5 UK and 1 Australian. There are 4 named German graves and 8 Unknown. It was designed by Sir Herbert Baker.

Here serried rows of Unknown Australian soldiers lie shoulder to shoulder and also buried here are **Lt A.C.G. Lonsdale**, KRRC, age 23, killed on 10 March 1915 who was a 'Scholar of Eton and Radley and Undergraduate of Trinity College, Cambridge', and **Lt Col G.C. Shakerley, DSO**, KRRC, age 46, 15 May 1915. Listed as 'Major' in the *Official History*. Shakerley was mortally wounded leading the 1st KRRC in a night attack which started at 1130 on 15 May during the Festubert battle when each man wore a white patch on his back. The frontage of the attack was from Chocolat Menier (qv) to la Bombe. Half of the leading companies almost reached the enemy breastworks before a shot was fired and secured it with little loss, but the initial success was not sustained.

> ## Extra Visit to Liverpool Scottish 'Dicky's Dash' Cairn, Bois Grenier; Erquinghem-Lys Cemetery Extension & Museum, Rev Railton Memorial, Pte Poulter, VC Memorial (Map 13)
> ## Round trip: 17 miles. Approximate time: 1 hour 30 minutes
>
> *Continue to the T junction and turn right and continue along the small winding road to the junction of the D175/176. Turn left signed to Bois Grenier. Continue to the junction with the D62 (in 1917 an area known as 'The Birdcage') and turn right along the D62 signed to Radinghem. After some 200m take the first right at Chemin du Vieux-Bridoux and park.*
>
> Here, in a landscaped 'Garden of Peace, is the **Memorial Cairn and Plaque to the 2nd Bn, Liverpool Scottish (Lat & Long: 50.63972 2.88147)**, unveiled in June 2005 in the presence of members of the Liverpool Scottish Association, the Lord-Lieutenant for Merseyside, members of the Dickinson family and local dignitaries, including Mr Jack

Extra Visit continued

Thorpe, local historian and son of a Normandy veteran, who had supported the project. The Cairn, made from Lancashire stone, is close by the site of a famous exploit in the Battalion's history, known as 'Dicky's Dash', after Capt Alan Dickinson MC's trench raid on 29 June 1917 along the 'Old Bridoux Road'. Preparations for the raid had begun earlier in the month. Captain Dickinson's 'C' Company, having won a competition for the best company, was chosen for the raid which was to be in daylight, but the other company commanders complained and so they all tossed for it. 'C' Company won.

Over the next three weeks the Company practised the raid in trenches especially constructed at Erquingham (qv), about three miles to your rear. The object of the raid was to break into the Bridoux Salient (this Salient was some 300 yards straight ahead of the memorial, its width about 400 yards, spread equally across the road projecting into the enemy lines. Bridoux is the name of a village up the road that was in the enemy area. Once inside, the task was to kill as many Germans as possible, identify the units there and to bring back prisoners.

Before midnight on 28 June, C Company's raiding party about 150 strong, marched out of Erquingham and spent the night just west of Bois Grenier, 1,500 yards back up the road, where they had dinner and a tot of rum. At 0100 hours they set off for the Salient which on their side was practically unoccupied. The whole operation was planned in detail with three phases running to a rigid time schedule. The break-in to the Salient was made at the edges at 1505 hours and went well as did the approach across No-Mans Land but at the enemy's parapet a fierce struggle began. Artillery fire from both sides caused many casualties and the fighting was intense. At around 1530 hours the raiders began to withdraw and though they did not capture any prisoners, they were praised by the Corps and Divisional Commanders for their courage. The raiding party suffered almost 70% casualties. Two DCMs were awarded, seven MMs and Captain Dickinson was awarded the MC for his training and planning. Ironically he had not been allowed to go on the raid and had to stay at raid HQ.

Captain Dickinson was one of three brothers who served with the Regiment.
Return along the D22 and continue towards Bois Grenier.

N.B. On the left will be passed **White City Cemetery (Lat & Long: 50.64188 2.88011)** which was used by fighting units from October 1914 to December 1915 when it was closed. The cemetery contains 92 Commonwealth WW1 burials, nine of them unidentified, and three German graves. It was designed by Sir Herbert Baker.

Continue through Bois Grenier following signs to Armentières over the railway on the D22 to the junction with the D22B. Turn left and left again at the next junction signed to Fleurbaix. Turn right before the railway signed to Erquinghem-Lys Centre. Continue to a row of poplars on the left, at right angle to the road.

N.B. Here **Suffolk Cemetery, La Rolanderie Farm** is signed **(Lat & Long: 50.66983 2.85554).** The Farm was used by the 34th Division as a Brigade Headquarters in February and August 1916 and in March 1918. The Cemetery was made between 8 and 19 April 1918. Later the farm became HQ 121st Brigade, and was severely shelled and bombed. The cemetery contains the graves of 43 soldiers from the United Kingdom, of whom 36 belonged to the 11th and 12th Suffolk Regiment, and of whom eight are unidentified. The name, originally La Rolanderie Farm Military Cemetery, was changed in May 1925 at the request of the late O.C. 11th Battalion, Suffolk Regiment.

White City CWGC Cemetery, Bois Grenier.

Extra Visit continued

N.B. continued

In the farm in 1917 Capt Basil Rathbone (later to find fame playing Sherlock Holmes) served as an intelligence officer with the 2nd Liverpool Scottish. In an interview with Edward R. Murrow in 1957, Rathbone related the story of how he disguised himself as a tree to get near the enemy camp to obtain information.

"I went to my commanding officer and I said that I thought we'd get a great deal more information from the enemy if we didn't fool around in the dark so much . . . and I asked him whether I could go out in daylight. I think he thought we were a little crazy. . . I said we'd go out camouflaged - made up as trees – with branches sticking out of our heads and arms . . . We brought back an awful lot of information, and a few prisoners, too."

In 1918 Rathbone received the MC for conspicuous bravery. Bairnsfather drew such a 'tree' idea in his cartoon 'Frustrated Ingenuity'.

Continue over the railway to the T junction and turn left signed Centre Ville on rue d'Armentières and first right before the Mairie signed to Erquinghem-Lys Churchyard Extension. Park by the Church.

Bairnsfather's Camouflage Tree Cartoon.

Extra Visit continued

Memorial to Rev David Railton (Lat & Long: 50.67895 2.84641)

This was unveiled in June 2011 by Railton's Barrister grandson (also David) in a moving ceremony. The Memorial was at the instigation of the indefatigable Jack Thorpe who had researched the Rev Railton, who served as Padre with the 19th Western Division in Erquinghem in July 1916, having won the MC for his bravery in rescuing wounded soldiers on the Somme under heavy fire.

At that time British casualties were buried in the village churchyard and Railton was billeted in the Curé's house next to the Church. After attending to the burial of a comrade, David Railton noticed a rough wooden cross inscribed 'An Unknown Soldier of the Black Watch'. This caused the Padre to muse on the fate and future remembrance of all these 'Unknown' men and gradually he formulated the concept of a permanent memorial to the symbolic 'Unknown Warrior' in Westminster Abbey. He felt that he should wait until the war was over to submit his idea to the relevant authorities and it was not until August 1920 that he approached the Dean of Westminster with his proposal.

The plans moved quickly from that date and in November 1920 instructions were issued by the War Office to the GOC British Troops in France to exhume four bodies from unidentified graves – one from each of the four greatest battles of the war: The Aisne, the Somme, Arras and Ypres. The bodies were transported to St Pol sur Ternois, (where there is now a commemorative Plaque) placed on stretchers in front of the altar, covered with the Union flag. Brig-Gen L.J. Wyatt was blind-folded and indicated one of the four. The other three were then buried in a local military cemetery.

The chosen Unknown Soldier was then transported to Boulogne (where there is another commemorative Plaque) and the next day, 10 November, was taken to the port on a French military wagon where he was met by Marshal Foch. The coffin was then taken on board HMS *Verdun* (chosen for its emotive name) to Dover and thence by train to Victoria station (where there is another commemorative Plaque) in the carriage which transported the body of Edith Cavell in 1915. The next day the Unknown Warrior was met at the Cenotaph by King George V and then moved on a gun carriage to Westminster where he was interred, covered by soil from the battlefields of the Western Front, with full pomp and circumstance at the same time as a the French Unknown Soldier was laid to

Unveiling of Memorial to Rev David Railton, with Piper Rob Whyte, June 2011, Erquinghem-Lys.

Headstone of Josef Suwelack, Flugzengführer, Erquinghem-Lys Churchyard Extension CWGC Cemetery.

German headstones face British headstones, Erquinghem-Lys Churchyard Extension CWGC Cemetery.

Extra Visit continued

rest in Paris under the Arc de Triomphe. Beside the tomb hangs Railton's tattered Union Jack and his words, 'They buried him among Kings because he had done good towards God and towards His house.

Every bereaved mother, and the rest of the family, was comforted to believe that this was 'their lad'. The full story is told in the book *They Came This Way in The Great War* by Jack Thorpe and Delphine Isaaman (qv), on sale in the Museum (see below) where the Rev Railton's exceptional story is also recounted.

The Memorial is in the shape of a flame (of remembrance) and beside it is an Information Panel.

Erquinghem-Lys Churchyard Extension Cemetery. The village was occupied by the Germans early in October 1914 and taken by the 1st SLI on 16 October. It remained in Allied hands until 10 April 1918 when it fell during the Kaiser's Offensive and was retaken in September 1918. The Churchyard was first used by the Allies between October 1914-January 1915 when 27 graves were made. The Extension was begun in April 1915 and used by units and field ambulances until April 1918. It now contains 558 WW1 burials 8 unidentified, 130 German burials and one unidentified Russian (a German POW). Burials include **L/Cpl Henry George Phillips** of the Fijian Labour Corps, incorporated into the KRRC, Footballer for Raith Rovers, **James Todd**, 16th Royal Scots (McCrae's Battalion) and Australian League Rugby Player, **Frank Cheadle**.

Many of the graves are of the Liverpool Scottish from 'Dicky's Dash' trench raid (qv). The cemetery, designed by Sir Herbert Baker, has an unusual feature in that the bulk of the German graves face the British graves with a wide gap between them – a sort of No-Man's Land. Two other German burial are of the Pilot Josef Suwelack (see Museum entry) and his Photographer/Observer Oskar Teichmann

To the left of the Cemetery parking area is the **Musée de la Cité d'Ercan**. Inaugurated on 5 June 2005, the Museum, run by the *Association Erquinghem-Lys et son Histoire*, charts the history of the town including exhibitions on WW1 and WW2. It tells the story of German Flyer, **Josef Suwelack**, a pre-war aviation enthusiast who had been awarded the *Ritterkreuz* on 8 December 1914. As he flew in his Albatross over the British lines towards Armentieres on 13 September 1915 he was shot down by 2nd Lt Shield and his observer, Cpl Bennett, as they patrolled the Bois de Biez area in their B.E.2c. Suwelack and his

Extra Visit continued

observer, Lt Oskar Teuchmann. The Albatross was brought down intact but Suwelack and Teuchmann were then shot. A book, *Josef Suwelack 1888-1915*, is available in the Museum of which members of the Suwelack family are generous patrons. The story of Rev David Railton is also told and his connection with the 'Unknown Warrior'.

The Museum is open on Sundays from 1430-1800 hours March-mid Nov or by appointment. Tel: + (0)3 20 48 05 22. Entrance is free of charge (but donations will be accepted) **Contact:** Jack Thorpe, Place de l'Eglise, 59193 Erquinghem-Lys E-mail: jack.thorpe@orange.fr

Jack, who has done some remarkable research about the village during the War and has been instrumental in the erection of Memorials and the close relationship with the Duke of Wellington's Regt, is pleased to help visitors to specific graves in the area to research their relatives' war history. If possible visitors are asked to leave their e-mail addresses so that Jack can send them information, as he has done for many families.

Jack's British father, a UK soldier who married a French girl and settled in the village, worked in the Cemetery for the CWGC and the young Jack came to know every headstone and its history.

Follow the one-way circuit back to the Mairie.

Beside it is a bench with a **Plaque in memory of Paul Barbier**, 1873-1947, Professor of French at the University of Leeds, who enlisted with his three other brothers and sister (who served as a nurse) in the French Army and served as an Interpreter with the British and Australians for 5 months in Erquinghem-Lys in 1914. His story was revealed to the village by his grand-daughter Delphine Isaaman.

Drive straight over onto the Rue Delpierre and continue to just before the railway line.

Park, walk over the crossing and turn immediately right to the brick memorial.

On the plinth is the Regimental badge of the Duke of Wellington's (West Riding) Regt and a **Plaque to Pte Arthur Poulter VC (Lat & Long: 50.67258 2.84564)** of the 1/4th Bn, erected by the Historical Society of Erquinghem-Lys, at the instigation of Jack Thorpe, on the site where Poulter performed the acts of bravery that won him the award. It was unveiled on 14 November 1998 by Pte Poulter's great granddaughter in the presence of a contingent from the Regiment. Beside it is an Information Panel.

Memorial to Pte Poulter, VC, Erquinghem- Lys.

Detail of Plaque.

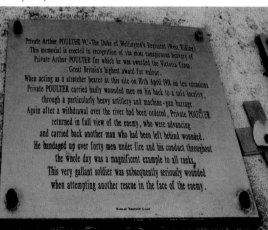

Extra Visit continued

On 9 April 1918 the 1/4th was hastily moved up to support the line at Erquinghem against the German breakthrough. After crossing the Lys they assembled at this point under heavy fire to hold the railway line from Armentières.

Detail of Memorial Marker to Duke of Wellington's Roundabout, Erquinghem-Lys.

Only one officer and nine men returned from the five officers and 139 ORs who had gone into action. For hour after hour and under fire, Pte Poulter carried the wounded on his back to a first aid post (the small chapel that can be seen further down rue Delpierre). He was himself eventually hit and badly wounded near Kemmel on 27 April when he was temporarily blinded. His eight brothers all survived the war.

Pte Poulter, who was born in East Witton, Middleham, in 1894, was the youngest of twelve children. He worked for the brewers, Timothy Taylor & Co (who provided the beer at the unveiling ceremony), married in August 1916 and after the war went on to have two daughters and eight sons. He died on 29 August 1956, age 62.

In November 2005 The Duke of Wellington's Regiment was presented with the Freedom of the Town and its keys in a special and colourful ceremony, establishing strong links with the inhabitants.

Return to the junction with rue d'Armentiéres and turn right direction Armentiéres. Continue under the motorway to the roundabout.

Here on Saturday 15 May 2010, Alma Company of the Duke of Wellington's Regiment exercised the Freedom of Erquingham Lys, parading the colours through the town, which ended in the naming of **The Duke of Wellington's Regiment Roundabout (Lat & Long: 50.68121 2.86023)**. The town is also strongly connected with Yorkshire, home of the Regiment, being twinned with Skipton.

Return to Rue Pétillon Mil Cemetery and pick up the main itinerary.

Continue to the T junction and turn left. Continue to the crossroads and turn left direction Béthune on the D171. Continue to the cemetery on the right.

• Rue Du Bois Military CWGC Cemetery/5.6 miles/10 minutes/Map 9/17/Lat & Long: 50.62901 2.82272

The village of Fleurbaix in which the cemetery is situated remained in Allied hands during most of the war until it was captured by the Germans on 9 April 1918 after a gallant defence by the 2nd Suffolks. It then remained in German hands until September 1918. The original cemetery, begun in November 1914 and used until December 1916, was then reopened in January 1918. It comprised what is now Plot I and Rows A and B of Plot II and included 27 Australians from the Fromelles Battle of 19-20 July 1916. After the Armistice the cemetery, which was designed by Sir Herbert Baker, was enlarged and now contains 844 burials, 395 of them Unknown. There is a Special Memorial to 13 men.

Buried here is **Pte Albert Drew Hughes**, age 22 of the 2nd Wilts, 25 (listed as 26 in the Debt of Honour Register) May 1915, one of 4 brothers. His brother, Rfmn Enos George James Hughes, London Regt, age 31, was killed on 1 September 1918 and is buried in Assevillers New Brit Cemetery on the Somme.

Australian headstones with flag, Rue du Bois Military CWGC Cemetery.

In 1918 a light railway from the Trou Aid Post area joined the road here and continued north along the D171.

Continue to the crossroads with the D175.

This is the Pétillon Crossroads. During the war this was actually known as **VC Corner** – not the area of today's VC Corner Cemetery. The D171 road ahead, which was the main road from Armentières to Béthune, was just behind the British front line and essential to their supply system. A continuous stream of soldiers, ammunition and supplies was moved along this busy road. This section of the Rue du Bois was known as Rue Tilleloy during the war. It was here, quite unusually for the second Christmas of the War, that a brief truce took place on 25 December 1915. It was described by Lt Wyn Griffith of the 15th RWF in his book *Up to Mametz*. On Christmas Eve a message forbidding fraternisation of the kind that had taken place the previous year had been read out, but towards midnight snatches of song wafted over from the German trenches and a few drunken soldiers clambered out of their trenches. A few minutes later 'there was a rush of men from both sides, carrying tins of meat, biscuits and other odd commodities for barter'. After 'a feverish exchange of "souvenirs"... an irate Brigadier came spluttering up to the line, thundering hard, throwing a "court martial" into every other sentence' and the fun was stopped dead. Blunden described some fraternisation that took place in 1915 in the Givenchy area at Christmas after which two young officers were arrested. He does not say what happened to them but only, 'Under arrest they marched towards the Somme battle of 1916.'

Continue straight over on the D171 towards Fauquissart.

The attack by 61st Division came from your right as you drive and occupied the entire length of this road from VC Corner to Fauquissart.

Turn right signed Cim Mil All Laventie on a very narrow road to the cemetery on the right.

German Cemetery, Laventie.

• German Cemetery, Laventie/7.4 miles/15 minutes/Map 9/18/Lat & Long: 50.61560 2.79470

This bare cemetery surrounded by savagely pollarded trees is punctuated by stark black crosses with a larger cross in the centre. It contains 1978 German soldiers, three of them bearing Jewish headstones. The burials are mostly of June/July 1918.

Turn round and return to VC Corner. Turn right to Fromelles. Return to the Mairie (11.2 miles).

• End of Fromelles 1916 Battlefield Tour

OR Extra Visit to Fournes-en-Weppes below.

Extra Visit to Site of Hitler's Billet & German Cemeteries, Fournes-en-Weppes & (Map 9/19,20) Wicres Route de la Bassée & Wicres Village German Cemeteries. Round trip: 16.5 miles. Approximate time: 1 hour 15 minutes.

From the Mairie take the D141 direction Le Maisnil and then next right on the D141a to the T junction in Fournes-en-Weppes.

To the right at the junction is the **l'Art des Mets**, a restaurant with pleasing ambience and décor, attentive service and good 'home cooking'. Kitchen closes at 1400 prompt. It is now listed in local restaurant guides as 'gastronomic'. Closed Mon, Sat lunchtime and Tues, Wed & Sun evening. www.restaurantlartdesmets.fr Tel +(0)3 20 50 23 02.

At the T junction turn left on the D141 direction 'Mairie/PTT' and continue 100m to a house on the right.

Plaque from Hitler's Billet, formerly on show in the Fromelles Museum.

Site of Hitler's 1916 Billet, Fournes-en-Weppes.

Extra Visit continued

Hitler's Billet (Lat & Long: 50.58406 2.88582). House No 966, s the house in which Hitler was billetted in 1916 (then Cordon's the Butcher) and on which the Plaque, which was exhibited in the old Fromelles Museum (qv), was erected in 1942. Hitler was a Company Runner and each morning he would bicycle to Wavrin to get orders from Capt Wiedemann, then proceed to Fromelles (qv) and return at noon. The procedure would be repeated in the afternoon. His rest periods were spent in Haubourdin.

Turn round and turn sharp right on the D97 signed to Cimetière Militaire Allemand Fournes-en-Weppes and then first right, still following signs. Continue to a huge UNEAL Co-operative warehouse at a dead end and stop. The path to the cemetery (not signed) is to the left beyond the warehouse.

Fournes-en-Weppes German Cemetery (Lat & Long: 50.58601 2.89022). Happily the signs of graffiti visible on a previous visit were absent on our last visit. The cemetery is planted with some beautiful trees, including a magnificent copper beech in the centre round which the grey stone crosses, which date from 1914-1918, are ranged. There is a

---

German Cemetery, Fournes-en-Weppes.

Extra Visit continued

large stone cross to the left. The cemetery contains 1,739 named soldiers with 177 Unknown.

Turn round and turn left and then left again at the main street. Continue to the impressive Poilu War Memorial on the right.

Beyond it is the excellent **Auberge les Vieilles Poutres** with a variety of menus, fresh local products. Tel: + (0)3 20 50 23 13. Closed Mon/Wed/Thurs/Sun evenings.

Continue to the roundabout on the N41 and turn right onto the N41 direction Béthune. Continue over the 1st roundabout and at the 2nd roundabout take the 3rd exit on the D22 signed to Wicres Route de la Bassée German Cemetery and immediately turn right and continue along the small road to the rear of the cemetery.

Wicres Route de la Bassée German Cemetery (Lat & Long: 50.56468 2.84996).

From the rear of the Cemetery the Double Crassier at Loos is visible on the horizon. The Cemetery is unusual in that the flat headstones are laid in flower beds. It contains 584 burials from 1914, 1915 and 1916. In the centre is a dramatic grey Monument by sculptor Richter supported by two mourning figures of Angels, which is a Memorial to the Prinz Friedrich der Niederlande and the 2nd Westfaelisches No 15 Regiment. In a circle around the Monument are pillars bearing the names of the Missing. By 1916 the Germans had constructed a light railway that ran from Wicres village to the N41 and then past the cemetery en-route to la Bassee.

Return to the D22 and turn right signed to German Cemetery Wicres Village. Take the small first turning left and continue to Wicres following signs to the German Cemetery. Continue to the Church. Stop.

Wicres Village German Cemetery (Lat & Long: 50.57010 2.86806).

The Cemetery contains 2,824 '14-'18 graves, including one French headstone at the rear to **Belischow Ivan**, a Russian POW, 11-8-1916. It was started in September 1915 by the 13th Westphalian Infantry Regiment to bury their dead of the Battles between La Bassée and Neuve Chapelle. Later other Regiments (representing nearly every district of Germany) were buried here and the cemetery was extended.

Wicres Route de la Bassée German Cemetery.

Extra Visit continued

To the right is a large, crumbling stone Monument to '*Den Getrefeuen vom 25-9-1915* (the 210 soldiers killed on the mine attack of 25 September 1915). They lie in 21 mass graves near the memorial.

The inscription roughly translates,

'Passer-by remove your hat, you are standing in a holy place, crosses surrounded by laurel indicate powerful words: Heroes, killed in battle for the glory and existence of Germany. Their names will never be forgotten. Let them remain sacred to us.'

On the other side is a quotation from Revelation 2-10:

'Only be faithful unto death and I will give you the crown of life.'

Another Memorial to *Den Opfern vom 20-03-1916* (the Victims of the Explosion of 20-03-1916) bears plaques with 5 individual names and the word *Glück* (Luck) with crossed hammers, the insignia of the Pioneers. There are several rounded Jewish headstones with the Star of David and there are clear white inscriptions on the grey stone crosses.

N.B. Wicres Churchyard Cemetery
In the nearby local cemetery is a CWGC Plot containing 4 graves - of 3 RWF, of April and June 1916 (**Capt H.P. Williams, Pte A. Hayward and Pte J. Cottrell** - and 1 Unknown).

There are two other German Cemeteries in the vicinity: **Illies** (to the west of the N41 with 2,619 named burials and 255 Unknown) and **Salomé** (on the D145 with 2,548 burials).

Return to the Mairie of Fromelles, OR continue to la Bassée to the left or the Commercial Centre at Englos to the right on the D7 for RWC.

Memorial to 210 soldiers killed in a mine attack, 25 Sept 1915, Wicres Village German Cemetery.

CWGC Plot, Wicres Churchyard.

VIMY RIDGE, ARRAS

9-12 APRIL 1917

'Suddenly every gun opened and the sky became one run of fire and
the hill rose up red and white and brown and gray, blown up bodily
in heaps by our shells: it was the worst shell fire ever seen ...
I believe the Somme was child's play to Vimy.'
John Masefield. Letters from France 1917.

'In the morning, tired and back from night duty, we lay down with the words,
"Now let us put the blankets over our heads and sleep."
Suddenly there was heavy drumfire. We jumped up,
all tiredness gone, for our country and our lives were at stake.'
A German Fusilier's memory of 9 April 1917 on Vimy Ridge

'Within forty minutes of the opening of the battle, practically the whole of the
German front line system on the front attacked had been stormed and taken.'
Sir Douglas Haig's Despatches.

SUMMARY OF THE BATTLE

On 9 April 1917, Easter Monday, the Canadian Corps, commanded by Lt Gen J.H.G. Byng, attacked what was probably the strongest of German defensive positions in northern France. They rehearsed their assault and used miles of tunnels to approach the enemy lines. By midday only the highest point of the ridge, Hill 145, remained in German hands and that fell the following day. German casualties were about 20,000, the Canadian losses were half that. Four VCs were won.

OPENING MOVES

Vimy Ridge forms part of the front that was known as the 'Arras Sector'. This ran from Lens in the north to Beaurains in the south. Arras itself was never occupied permanently by the Germans (though they spent two days in the town in September 1914), and a salient bulged east from the city into enemy territory throughout the war.

The front formed in September/October 1914, at which time the Germans took the heights of Notre Dame de Lorette and Vimy Ridge during struggles known as the first battle of Artois. In May 1915 in the second battle of Artois, the French mounted an attack towards Vimy with their seasoned 10th Army and gained the crest of the ridge, but were unable to consolidate their positions. In September 1915 as part of the third Artois Offensive, of which the British attack at Loos was the northern prong, the 10th Army again set their faces towards the ridge, but German counter-attacks drove them back.

Trench warfare, which had begun late in 1914, now became the order of the day and the French and Germans adopted a 'live and let live' policy. The Arras front became what was known as a 'quiet sector'. In March 1916 the British took over the Arras front from the French 10th Army which had lost a reported 135,000 men in trying to take the ridge. The British immediately set about trying to take the initiative with many patrols into German lines and J.B. Priestley who was in the Souchez area recalled in his memoirs (*Margin Released*):

"It had been quiet recently around there until we British arrived, but of course we had to hot it up for the sake of our morale, to keep our fellas on their toes ... So very soon, having asked for it, God knows why, we caught a packet. It was not long before our own B Company with a nominal fighting strength of 270 had been reduced to a grim and weary seventy."

In late autumn the Canadians came north from the Somme to relieve the British and settled for a cold winter of strengthening defences. At the end of the year, at Chantilly, the British and French agreed to continue their policy of joint offensives, a decision unaffected by the replacement of Joffre by Nivelle on 31 December. Nivelle, the new broom, proclaimed the need for an offensive of 'violence, brutality and rapidity', and told all and sundry that his plan would end the war by breaking through the German lines. As a preliminary to his assault, planned to begin on the Aisne in mid-April 1917, the British were tasked to attack on the Arras sector with their First and Third Armies, drawing German forces away from the Aisne.

The British preparation was very thorough and included the use of tunnels to bring troops forward to the front line without being observed or shot at. Arras itself has two major cave systems dating back to the seventeenth century and in the eastern suburbs these were enlarged and connected to a series of tunnels by special Tunnelling Companies – particularly by the New Zealanders. Twenty-five large caves were excavated with room for 11,000 troops and electric light, running water and ventilation systems were installed. In order to bring forward the vast amount of supplies of ammunition and stores needed, standard and narrow gauge railways were built and plank roads laid. A very deliberate policy of achieving air superiority was maintained by offensive flying, particularly in the days immediately prior to the attack. 'Boom' Trenchard mustered some 750 aircraft against the Germans' 260 and in the four days before the battle the RFC lost 131 machines, though contemporary reports put the figure as 28 (shades of the reports of RAF losses in the Battle of Britain in 1940). However mastery of the skies gave artillery observers the freedom to register their guns effectively. Three weeks before the assault the artillery began to bombard the German wire. Heavy artillery concentrated on the rear areas, on headquarters and on communications. As the day of the attack approached, the intensity of shelling increased by night and day and at intervals along the front gas discharges were made. The total frontage of the attack was just on 15 miles from Vimy Ridge to Croisilles southeast of Arras. The southern half was entrusted to the 3rd Army under Allenby and the northern half to the 1st Army under General Horne. The assault on what General Haig called 'an important tactical feature, possession of which I considered necessary', was delegated to General Julian Byng's Canadian Corps, part of 1st Army. The feature was Vimy Ridge.

LEGEND: MAP 14: VIMY RIDGE: 9-12 APRIL1917 (Notre Dame de Lorette Oct 1914-Oct 1915)

1. 158th Regt & Sous-Lt Léon Mem
2. 174th Regt & Sous-Lt Defrasse Mem
3. Gen Maistre Mem
4. N-D de Lorette French Nat Cem
4a. International Circle of Death Mem
5. N-D de Lorette Museum
6. Gen Barbot & Others Mem
7. Cabaret Rouge CWGC Cem
7a. Cabaret Rouge Mem
8. Czech Cem & Mem
9. Polish Mem
10. La Targette Museum
11. La Targette Hand & Other Mems
12. La Targette CWGC & French Nat Cems
13. Neuville-St-Vaast German Cem (Maison Blanche)
13a Browarski Museum & Church SGWs, Neuville St Vaast
13b. Augustin Leuregans & Fr 53rd Div Mem

14. Lichfield Crater CWGC Cem
15. Grange Tunnel & Preserved Trenches
16. Canadian No 2, Givenchy Road & Givenchy-en-Gohelle CWGC Cems
17. Vimy Ridge Canadian Nat Mem
18. Vimy Ridge Welcome Centre
19. 3rd Canadian Div Mem
20. Canadian Artillery Mem
20a. Bois Carré CWGC Cem
20b. Canadian 1st Div Mem
21. Zivy Crater CWGC Cem
22. Faubourg d'Amiens CWGC Cem
23. Arras Boves (Tunnels)
23a. 56th (1st London) Div Plaque
24. New Zealand Mem/Wellington Quarry, Arras Tunnels ═══

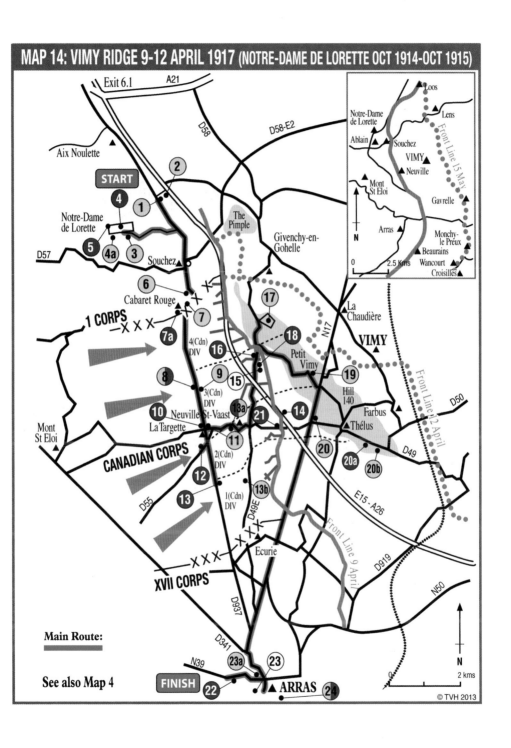

MAP 14: VIMY RIDGE 9-12 APRIL 1917 (NOTRE-DAME DE LORETTE OCT 1914-OCT 1915)

Exit 6.1
A21
D58
D58-E2

Aix Noulette

START

Notre-Dame
de Lorette

D57

D55

Mont
St Eloi

1 CORPS

CANADIAN CORPS

XVII CORPS

Souchez

Cabaret Rouge

4(Cdn)
DIV

3(Cdn)
DIV

Neuville St-Vaast
La Targette

2(Cdn)
DIV

1(Cdn)
DIV

Ecurie

The
Pimple

Givenchy-en-
Gohelle

La
Chaudière

Petit
Vimy

VIMY

Hill
140

Farbus

Thélus

D49

D50

E15 - A26

D919

D937

Front Line 9 April

Front Line 12 April

N17

N50

D341

N39

FINISH

See also Map 4

ARRAS

Main Route:

Inset map:
Loos
Lens
Notre-Dame
de Lorette
Ablain
Souchez
VIMY
Neuville
Mont
St Eloi
Arras
Gavrelle
Monchy-
le Préux
Beaurains
Wancourt
Croisilles
Front Line 15 May

N
0   2.5 kms

N
0   2 kms

© TVH 2013

WHAT HAPPENED

At 0530 on 9 April 1917 in driving sleet the British armies emerged from their tunnels and trenches and advanced behind a rolling barrage. It was Ludendorff's 52nd birthday. What a present! He was not in the best of spirits anyway, having heard that three days earlier America had declared war on Germany. He had observed all the careful preparations and had expected the British attack, indeed he had anticipated it with confidence, but the force of the assault broke through the German positions, in places to their third lines, and Vimy Ridge was effectively lost to the Canadians soon after midday. It took two days of counter-attacks and movement of reserves to stem the possibility of a British breakthrough, but in the week before Nivelle's offensive on the Aisne, the 1st Army (in effect the Canadians) took 4,000 prisoners and 54 guns while in the south the 3rd Army took 7,000 prisoners and 112 guns. The penetration made and held was estimated by Ludendorff to have been '12 to 15 kilometres wide and 6 or more kilometres deep'. Ten days after the attack began there were almost twice as many infantry opposite the British as there had been at the start. Haig's men had done what had been asked of them – 'take some German forces away from the Aisne'.

The Canadian achievement here was the result of a formidable artillery preparation, intensive training, particularly in rehearsing infantry movement to keep time with a creeping barrage, and very careful overall planning combined with Canadian dash and verve. One innovation which did not last long, however, was the idea that officers should 'steer' their men from the rear rather than lead them from the front and this was practiced during the training but it did not survive contact with the enemy.

The aerial combat over Vimy during this month of April 1917 was so costly to the British that they dubbed it 'Bloody April'. During those 30 days **Rittmeister Baron Manfred von Richthofen** increased his 'score' from 31 to 50, despite the numerical superiority of the RFC. But the Germans were flying over their own territory and their Albatross D111 triplanes were superior to the allied Spads and FEs – both in speed and manoeuvrability. One of the Red Baron's opponents that month was **Captain William Avery Bishop, DSO, DFC**, who won his **MC** on 7 April 1917 for shooting down a German balloon, and who, later in 1917, was awarded the **VC** 'for most conspicuous bravery, determination and skill'.

THE BATTLEFIELD TOUR

This incorporates the Notre-Dame de Lorette, Artois Battlefield Tour (see pages 50-53)
• **The Route:** The tour starts at the 158th RI Memorial, Tomb of S/Lt Léon, Memorial to S/Lt Defrasse then visits the Memorial to Gen Maistre, French National Memorial, Museum and International Circle of Death Memorial Wall at Notre-Dame de Lorette; Statue & Memorials to Gen Barbot/77th Division/Gen Stirn/Gen Plessner/ Departmental Memorial to the War in Algeria, Tunisia and Morocco, Souchez; Cabaret Rouge CWGC Cemetery, Czech Memorial & Cemetery and Polish Memorial; la Targette-Neuville St Vaast WW1 Museum, Flame in Hand Memorial and British, French and German ('Maison Blanche') Cemeteries; Canadian Memorial Park at Vimy Ridge; Arras – War Memorial, Wellington Quarry & Tunnellers' Memorial, *Boves*, Faubourg d'Amiens CWGC Cemetery and Arras Memorial; *Mur des Fusillés*.
• **Extra Visits:** Ablain-St Nazaire - Ruined Church; Neuville St Vaast - M Browarski Museum, SGWs St Laurent Church, Lichfield Crater CWGC Cemetery; Vimy Nat Park - 3rd Can 'Imperial' Div Memorial.
• **[N.B.]** The following sites are indicated: Auz Riez *Souterrain* entrance; Nr Neuville-St-Vaast - Memorial to Augustin Leuregons & French 53rd Div; Thélus – Can Arty Mem, Zivy Crater Cem, Bois Carré Brit Cem, 1st (Canadian) Div Memorial; Arras – 56th 1st (London) Div Plaque.
• **Total distance:** approx 22 miles
• **Total time:** 7 hours 45 minutes

- **Base town:** Arras
- **Distance from Calais to start point via A26/E15:** 61 miles. Motorway Tolls
- **Maps:** IGN 1:25,000 2406 Est Arras plus 2405 Est Lens

From the A26/E15 take Exit 6.1 signed Liévin, Lens, Douai, direction A21. Immediately after the péage fork right from the A21 onto the D301 signed to Bruay la B, Aix Noulette. Take the first exit signed Aix Noulette, Béthune on the D937. Continue through Aix Noulette, (where in October 1916 the Canadian 29th (Vancouver) Battalion, the Irish Fusiliers of Canada, relieved the 4th Middlesex – one wonders how many of the 'Out since Mons' men were left) *past the junction with the D51 to the* **Auberge de Lorette** (5 bedrooms – none en-suite, no restaurant, uncategorised hotel. Tel: + (0)3 21 72 25 25) on the right. *Park. There are two memorials on the left.*

Set your mileometer to zero.

• 158th Regt d'Infanterie Memorial/Tomb of Sous-Lt Jean R. Léon/ Memorial to Sous-Lt Jacques Defrasse/0 miles/15 minutes/Map 14/1 and 14/2/Lat & Long: 50.40896 2.73159

The Regimental Memorial was erected by survivors of the Lorette sector battle. Before it is the tomb of **Sous-Lieutenant Jean R. Léon**, *Légion d'Honneur, Croix de Guerre*, killed 26 May 1915.

Up the track marked *privé* to the left is the large **Memorial to Sous-Lieutenant Jacques Defrasse**, age 23, killed on 16 June 1915 during the second battle of Artois, like Léon, and to the 174th Regiment. On the side is a message attesting to his courage by the General commanding his division. He was killed in the assault on La Tranchée des Saules (approximately on the line of the track). Defrasse had just put up his rank stripes on his tunic which may be seen, with other personal belongings, at the Museum at Notre-Dame de Lorette, gifts from his family. He had been commissioned on 3 May 1915 at La Tranchée de Calonne.

Continue to the junction with the old 'European Centre for Peace' to the left.

Memorial to 158th Regt d'Inf, Aix Noulette.

Tomb of Sous-Lt J.R. Léon, Aix Noulette.

Memorial to Sous-Lt J. Defrasse, Aix Noulette.

Now only used for functions and conferences, its splendid mural on the façade of this interesting 1920s building now sadly peeling, it has an Information Board in the car park detailing the '*Sentier du Poilu*' (The Poilu's Path) with a timed, distanced walking route of battlefields in the area. Beyond it the Loos Double Crassier can clearly be seen.

Beside it will be built the new 600 sqm **WW1 Intrepretative Centre** to be opened in October 2014, the 100th Anniversary of the German Occupation of the area. It will use the latest modern technology - video, audio etc. some of which can be used via smart phones. There will be access to the personal stories of the men commemorated on the **International Circle of Death Memorial** at N-D de Lorette (see below), an Exhibition space and boutique.

Opposite over the road was the old Artisan Museum (another '20s building), now completely demolished, some of its contents salvaged by M. David Bardiaux for the 'Living Museum' at N-D de Lorette (qv).

Turn right signed to N-D de Lorette on the D58E3.

This road to N-D de Lorette will be improved and have interesting **Information Stations** en route for pedestrians as one ascends. At the top of the hill is

• *French National Cemetery, Basilique, Memorials and 'Living' Museum, International Circle of Death Memorial Wall, Notre-Dame de Lorette/1.6 miles/60 minutes/Map 14/3, 14/4, 14/4a, 14/5/OP/RWC/Lat & Long: 50.40012 2.71941*

This hill and Vimy Ridge, which is to the south-east and separated from it by the motorway, are adjacent features. On a clear day Vimy Ridge, Arras to the south and the battlefield of Loos to the north-east are all visible.

During the 'Race to the Sea' in 1914 the Germans took the hill and Ablain St Nazaire (see **Map 4 page 58**), pushing the French lines to the west of the present Basilique which has been built on the site of an old chapel.

In 1915 there were two major actions around Notre-Dame de Lorette. On 9 May the 21st Division and the 33rd Division under General Pétain attacked to the south of the hill as part of a 10th Army offensive and gains were made everywhere, but the feature was not cleared. Ablain St Nazaire was inside the German lines before the 9 May 1915 offensive while Mont St Eloi was just within the French and between them they indicate the maximum extent of the German salient towards the west. To a first approximation the May offensive came straight towards you from Mont St Eloi and it was over that distance that General Maistre's troops toiled for six months to reach the area of the Basilique where you are now. Before the Cemetery entrance, on the left at the top of the hill, is **a Memorial to General Maistre and the 21st Army Corps (Map 14/3)**, erected in 1925.

On 16 June as part of the same offensive the same formations attacked again, but any gains they had made were wiped out by German counter-attacks on 13 July, although in both actions the Moroccan Division had distinguished itself by its bravery and élan. The attack of 25 September 1915 was more successful. The village of Souchez was taken by the French 13th and 70th Divisions and Cabaret Rouge was cleared by the 77th Division, now sadly without their charismatic General Barbot. (See the account of the battle of Notre-Dame de Lorette, Artois page 57).

Once the hill was taken the French defences that ran from the far side of the orientation table, across the road and beyond the present Basilique were called the 'Maistre Line' and formed the third line of defence. In May 1916 the Prince of Wales's Own Civil Service Rifles were in the Brigade rest area at Camblain l'Abbé some five miles west of here as the crow flies – clearly much further on the march. It was a quiet Sunday in a quiet sector and everyone was relaxed. At no notice, in the early afternoon, the Battalion was told to get ready to move and to dress in Full Service Marching Order. Their task, they were told, was to occupy the Maistre Line. It was the last clear information they were to receive and what happened to them vividly illustrates the reality of warfare, so often neglected in preference to *Boy's Own* accounts. The story continues at the Cabaret Rouge which you travel to after this visit.

On the left opposite the Cemetery entrance, is an **Orientation Table** detailing the Artois fighting from October 1914 to September 1915, erected in 1975. Standing with your back to the cemetery, and looking out over the plain below, over the *Table d'Orientation*, the ruined tower of the Abbey at **Mont St Eloi** can be seen, left damaged as a reminder of the First World War, as was the ruined steeple of the church at nearby **Ablain-St-Nazaire** just 1 ½ miles away.

This part of the feature where you are now was also taken but the plateau of Vimy Ridge remained in German hands and stayed with them until the Canadian assault of 9 April 1917, almost two years later.

The hill, which is 165m above sea level, had its first Chapel in 1727 which was enlarged to a church in 1870. On 12 September 1920 the Association of Notre-Dame de Lorette was founded, with the aim of building a **Cemetery, an Ossuary, a symbolic lighthouse and a Basilique (Map 14/4)** in order to commemorate those who died. The foundation stone was laid by Marshal Pétain on 19 June 1921 and it was inaugurated on 2 August 1925 by President Painlevé.. The Association now has almost 3,000 members and the Memorial area was officially recognized as a National Monument in 1963. Members of the *Garde d'Honneur de Lorette* man the area from 0900-1630 in March, until 1730 in April and May and until 1830 in June-Aug, then again until 1630 up to 11 Nov. The cemetery contains 19,000 identified burials and six mass graves

Statue to Gen Maistre and 21st Army Corps with Notre-Dame de Lorette lantern tower in background.

The Basilique and cemetery, Notre-Dame de Lorette.

containing more than 16,000 soldiers, all arranged around a clear central area in which is the tower and the Basilique.

The first grave on the left as you enter the cemetery is that of **General Barbot** (qv) of the 77th Division who was killed on 10 May 1915, just after his division had attacked Souchez – you pass the divisional memorial later. Barbot is credited with saving Arras from occupation in 1914 not just once but twice. The tower, designed by Maître L. Cordonnier, is 150 ft high and has 200 stairs and 5 floors. At the top is a 3,000 candlepower light that rotates at 5 times per minute and when shining can be seen for more than 40 miles. In the crypt of the tower are an Unknown Soldier from the Second World War; the ashes of people deported to concentration camps; an Unknown Soldier from Indo-China and an Unknown Soldier from North Africa. To enter the tower there is a nominal charge which goes towards the upkeep of the memorial. On the first floor is a small museum which was opened in 1964 and (if it is not under repair) it is possible to climb to the top and to look out over the battlefield. The Basilique, or Chapel, was consecrated on 26 May 1927 in the presence of Marshal Pétain and has inside, on the left, a statue of Monseigneur Julien, the founder of the Association and on the right a statue of Notre-Dame de Lorette. The stained-glass windows commemorate famous historical events.

The Cemetry, Lantern Tower and the Basilique will be extensively restored for the Centennial.

On the esplanade between the tower and the Basilique is a bronze *Croix de Guerre* which supports the *Souvenir Français* eternal flame which is rekindled each Sunday morning from Palm Sunday-11 November after the 1100 Mass.

An ambitious and important **International Monument** will be completed in 2014 near the Cemetery in time for the Centennial commemorations which will start on 28 June 2014. A circular wall (thought to be the largest ever constructed), designed by Parisian architect Philippe Prost, will carry the names, in alphabetical order, of some **600,000 soldiers** killed in French Flanders and Artois – Allies and Enemies together. It is seen as a symbol of fraternity and an expression of peace. The monumental task of assembling the names was straightforward using the meticulous CWGC records for the British & Commonwealth names, but the German names were more difficult to discover as many of their records were destroyed in WW2. Amongst the French names are the North African Colonial Forces. Also included are Belgian, Czech, Polish, Portuguese, Russian...names.

The Circle will be permanently illuminated at night using solar panels. The circular horizontal form of the wall contrasts and balances with the perpendicular of the lantern tower and the circular shape creates a space between heaven and earth, a technical work of art in durable, weather resistant fibre-reinforced concrete. The budget for the project is Euros 6.5million. HM Queen Elizabeth and the German Chancellor will be invited to the opening ceremony.

Architect's impressions of the International 'Circle of Death' Memorial, Notre-Dame de Lorette.

The 'Living' Museum, Notre Dame de Lorette.

On the far side of the cemetery from where you are parked (you can drive round to it if you wish) is the excellent **Museum,** now known as *Le Musée Vivant* **[Living Museum]** (Map 14/5, **Lat & Long: 50.40159 2.71581**). The Museum is constantly being improved, both with its growing number of fascinating exhibits and its appearance. The owner, M. David Bardiaux (who also owns the Museum at La Targette, visited later) acquired many of the artefacts from the old demolished Artisan Museum and has placed the original stone *bas relief* frieze on a wall leading to the entrance. On the ground below it is a carpet of red poppies in season and a concrete ramp for wheel chair access leads to the entrance. The building beyond which houses the old Museum's Diorama and stereoscopic pictures has a room where students may take their picnics.

The Museum recreates the daily life of the soldier on the Artois front, with many interesting and realistic dioramas with sound effects in French, English and German, and collections of artefacts retrieved from the original battlefields or donated by families of veterans. They include the tunic of Jacques Defrasse (qv), which should not be missed. A later addition is a German 420 calibre 'Big Bertha' shell.

Behind the museum is an extensive recreated battlefield area with trenches, shell holes, barbed wire and many items of artillery.

Open every day (except 12 Dec - 2 Jan): 0900-2000. Tel: + (0)3 21 45 15 80. Entrance fee payable.

Beside it is the now smart **Bar/Restaurant/Salon de Thé, L'Estaminet de Lorette,** Tel: (0)3 21 45 29 07. It sells regional products and home-made patisseries. **Open** every day 0930-1830. Closed Dec/Jan/Feb.

When all other eating options are shut this pleasant restaurant can usually be relied upon. It serves hot food until well after 1400 hours and then snacks and pastries.

In front of the Museum is a **Memorial to Sous-Lieutenant Henri Merlin,** age 24, of the 10th Chasseurs á Pied, 3 March 1915. His citation by the General Commanding the 10th Army records that he fought to the last and when his last comrade died he killed himself rather than retreat.

Return to the small road leading down the hill before the Table d'Orientation, signed to Ablain-St Nazaire.

Memorial to Sous-Lt Henri Merlin, N-D de Lorette.

L'Estaminet de Lorette.

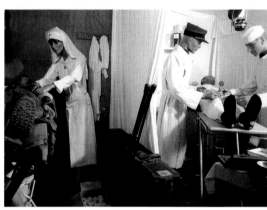

'Operating theatre' Diorama, 'Living Museum', N-D de Lorette.

Memorial to Gen Barbot and others, 77th Division, Souchez.

Ruined Church, Ablain St-Nazaire.

Extra Visit to Ruined Church, Ablain-St Nazaire. Round trip: 1.5 miles. Approx time: 10 minutes.

Drive down the steep narrow road to the ruined Church at the bottom on the right. There is parking on the left.

In front of the Church (**Lat & Long: 50.39277 2.720967**), which is a *Monument Historique*, is an **Information Board** (opposite the splendid *Art Deco* facade of the old Hotel de N-D de Lorette.) The Church has been kept in its wartime ruined state as a reminder of the destruction of war.

Return to the Table d'Orientation and pick up the main Itinerary.
Drive back to the bottom of the hill, with amazing views over the Douai Plain, the Loos Battlefield and Vimy Ridge, and turn right signed to Souchez.

As you drive down the D937 from here towards Cabaret Rouge and the German cemetery beyond you are driving essentially parallel to the German front line trenches of April 1917 which would have been erratically about 1,000 yards to your left. The Canadians' northern boundary included the village of Souchez ahead, the responsibility of the 4th Division and that line ran 4 miles south to beyond the German cemetery. Thus the Canadian build up and assault of 9 April 1917 might be imagined as 4 miles of the D936 picking itself up and hurling itself to the left!

On leaving the village of Souchez to the right are

• *Statue & Memorials to Gen Barbot/77th Division/Gen Stirn/Gen Plessner/Departmental Memorial to the War in Algeria, Tunisia and Morocco, Souchez/4.4 miles/10 minutes/Map 14/6/Lat & Long: 50.38628 2.74438*

On the large Memorial which depicts General Barbot leading his Chasseurs into battle are plaques to Generals Stirn and Plessner. It commemorates the period from October 1914 to February 1915 when the division was in the Souchez sector. The General was mortally wounded near Cabaret Rouge on 10 May 1915. Colonel Stirn, promoted to replace him, was killed two days later by a shell. The sculptor was Jules Déchin.

The nearby imposing **1952-64 N. African Campaign Memorial** was raised in 2002 by the survivors to their fallen comrades. It consists of large white archways joined by a pathway in which there is an eternal flame, flagpoles and a sunken pool. The names of the dead are inscribed in white on a black memorial wall reminiscent of the Vietnam Memorial in Washington DC.

Here around Souchez, particularly in the area of the local cemetery, was some of the fiercest fighting during the 1914/15 Artois battles. The Germans had fortified all the houses and built a number of strong points – the cemetery, the Cabaret Rouge – and armed them with machine guns. The heights of Notre-Dame de Lorette (visible on a good day behind the General's statue) seemed to dominate the French positions at the end of 1914, much as Monte Cassino seemed to dominate the way to Rome in 1944. During the second Artois battle from May 1915 the intensity of the struggle to clear 'the bloody hill' of Lorette, the village of Souchez and to gain Vimy Ridge, reached depths of horror and destruction only paralleled at Verdun. Even with Lorette under control Souchez stood in the way of a secure assault upon Vimy and it was not until 26 September 1915 that the village was finally re-taken. It had been in German hands for a whole year. On 23 September 1920 the village was awarded the *Croix de Guerre*.

Continue.

N.B. Some 100m beyond the sign for Cabaret Rouge CWGC Cemetery is a small **Plaque** (**Map 14/7, Lat & Long: 50.38267 2.74302**) erected in 2002 by the Arras *Souvenir Français*, on the left marking the exact site of the famous Cabaret Rouge, a small estaminet, named from the red bricks from which it was constructed.

We now pick up the story of the Civil Service Rifles who, having reached the Maistre Line, were then told to move forward towards Cabaret Rouge. Slowly, through crowded communication trenches, and enduring 'some hours of tear gas', the Battalion moved forward while the Germans were shelling the Ridge ahead. 'The air was just one solid mass of bursting shells'. The Regimental History continues – 'We had little or no information as to what was happening and as darkness had now gathered and we were in entirely strange trenches, there did not seem much chance of finding out'

Eventually at 2215 hours the leading Company (B) reached Brigade HQ in the cellars of the Cabaret Rouge and was told to report to the Commanding Officer of the battalion holding the front to the left ahead. There each man was issued with a further 100 rounds of ammunition and a number of bombs (grenades) and then told that the Support Line and Resistance Lines had been lost so that they were to make an immediate counter attack. The Company Commander was told that the formations on his left and right would co-operate and that a party of bombers from the Post Office Rifles would join him, but where these units were he didn't know nor did anyone else. One of his flanks, he was told, would rest on Ersatz Trench but where it was to be found was a mystery – 'he might just as well been told to rest his flanks on the Unter den Linden.' Whether there were British troops between him and the enemy and how much of the line he was supposed to capture also remained unknown. B Company had arrived exhausted at 0130 hours on Monday morning to be told that the counter-attack must go in at 0200 so it was impossible for the Company Commander to do a recce even if he knew where to go.

Despite the utter confusion the attack went in and B Company advanced up the slope of Vimy Ridge without fire support of any kind in almost total darkness, and exactly what happened is uncertain. Most of the Company were killed or wounded with survivors taking shelter in shell holes and awaiting rescue. Captain Farquhar, B Company Commander, was amongst the killed and is commemorated on the Arras Memorial (qv), as is his CSM, Frank Howett, both of whom were members of the Civil Service Rugby Football Club.

Today we know that Ersatz trench ran across this road exactly where the Cabaret Rouge Cemetery is, just 250 yards ahead, and that it ran for half a mile due east of there to Ersatz crater which lies under what is now a motorway – the Autoroute des Anglais.

Continue to the cemetery on the right.

• Cabaret Rouge CWGC Cemetery/4.9 miles/10 minutes/Map 14/7a/ Lat & Long: 50.38069 2.74158

This was started by the British 47th Division in March 1916 and used by fighting units including the Canadian Corps until September 1918. It was enlarged after the Armistice. There are over 7,000 burials and 60 special memorials. In Plot 8, Row E, Grave 7 is a headstone recording the fact that the Canadian Unknown Soldier was taken from here on 25 May 2000 to the tomb of **The Unknown Warrior** at the National War Memorial in Ottawa. Buried in Plot XXVII, Row A, Grave 14 is **Lt Col Victor George Howard Rickard**, 2nd Royal Munster Fusiliers, age 40, 9 May 1915, who was killed leading his battalion in the Battle of Aubers Ridge (qv). In Plot XXX, Row F, is buried **Lt Col A.L. Wrenford**, 4th E Lancs, 21 March 1918, who has a Private Memorial near Villerets (qv).

Under the entrance arch is a **Plaque to the cemetery designer, Sir Frank Higginson**, secretary to the IWGC 1947-1956, who died in 1958 and whose ashes were scattered in the cemetery.

Outside the Cemetery are **Information Boards** describing the work of the CWGC ('Who mows the Lawns') and Cabaret Rouge.

Between the wars pilgrims to the cemetery were able to refresh themselves at a nearby café (probably Cabaret Rouge itself) called 'The Better 'Ole' after Bairnsfather's famous cartoon. The French writer, Henri Barbusse, author of *Le Feu* (Under Fire) served in this area in 1915. In his diary he recorded his impressions of Cabaret Rouge. 'Never have I seen such total devastation of a

Plaque on the site of Cabaret Rouge.

Former grave of the Canadian Unknown Soldier, Cabaret Rouge CWGC Cemetery.

Entrance to Cabaret Rouge CWGC Cemetery.

village. Here, nothing with any shape left, not even a stretch of wall, a railing, a doorway left standing. It might have been a dirty, boggy wasteland near a town whose inhabitants had, through the years, been tipping on it their debris, rubbish, rubble from demolished buildings and scrap iron. In the foreground, the fog, the unearthly scene of massacred trees.'

Continue towards Neuville St Vaast. On the right is

• *Czech Memorial & Cemetery/Polish Memorial/5.9 miles/10 minutes/ Map 14/8 and 14.9/Lat & Long: 50.36589 2.74474*

The Czechs joined the French Foreign Legion in Paris in 1914, forming part of the 2nd Regiment of Infantry. Together with the Moroccans they fought in the May 1915 second Artois offensive as part of the French 10th Army taking this area but with heavy casualties. The memorial particularly refers to the 9 May 1915 attack towards the German strongpoint at Hill 140 (Thélus Mill) just north of Thélus village. They went over the top from this area and had 80 per cent casualties.

Thélus was not taken until the Canadian attack of 9 April 1917. The Memorial, sculpted by J. Hrvska, was erected in 1925 and behind it are graves from the First and Second World Wars, plus a memorial shelter put up in May 1968. Looking across the road, to the left of the Polish memorial (which was destroyed by the Germans in 1940 and rebuilt identically after the war) the tops of the pylons of the Vimy Canadian memorial on Point 145 the highest part of Vimy Ridge, can be seen on the skyline about a mile and a quarter away.

On the opposite side of the road is the Polish Memorial which commemorates the part played by the Poles in the Artois campaign, probably as members of the Foreign Legion. They too attacked Hill 145 on 9 May 1915. The memorial was inaugurated on 9 May 1935, twenty years after the attack.

La Targette is twinned with Sezemice in Poland.

Continue to the crossroads in the centre of La Targette village and park behind the Museum on the right on the D49.

• La Targette Memorials/Museum/6.7 miles/20 minutes/Map 14/10/11/ Lat & Long: 50.35474 2.74827

This striking village Memorial on the left of a huge hand and wrist (which bears an identification tag with the name of the village upon it) emerges from broken soil to hold aloft the flame of life – a concept explored in John McCrae's poem, *In Flanders Fields*, and in the sculpture on the Vimy Memorial. It was completed on 20 October 1932. In front of it are smaller Memorials to the original tomb (for 5 years) of **Lt Henri Millevoye** of 74th Rd'I, 25 Sept 1915; and to **Sous-Lt Henry Mouette d'Andrezel** of 36th Rd'I, same date and **Ernest Petit,** 1889-1964, the initiator of the reconstruction.

The village, within German lines after 1914, was entered on the morning of 9 May 1915 by troops of XX Corps and after five days of fighting the Germans were pushed to its far edge but the village was decimated, the destruction being completed by later French mining activities in May 1916.

Over the road is the well-maintained private **Museum** owned by David Bardiaux (who also owns the Notre-Dame de Lorette Museum). It contains a superb collection of uniforms, Allied and German gas masks, weapons and artefacts and has several well-presented scenes of trench, aid post and dugout life. 'Laser animation' in English and French. **Open** every day 0900-2000 (except Xmas and New Year). Tel: + (0)3 21 59 17 76. Entrance fee payable.

Return to the D937, turn right and continue to the junction with the D55.

N.B. At the junction with the D55 and the D937 is the **Relais St Vaast**. Tel: + (0)3 21 58 58 58. **Open:** Mon-Fri lunch time and Fri & Sat evenings. Annual Holiday mid-Aug. Specialities Pizza and Grills.

In the bank of the house opposite it on the Route de Béthune (D937) is the overgrown entrance to the **Aux Rietz Souterrain.** This has an interesting history, as told by Phillip Robinson (qv) in *The Underground War, Vimy Ridge to Arras.* It was taken over from the French by the British in February 1916 and used by 175 Tunnelling Coy from May, to be replaced by 185 Tunnelling Coy in November and in April 1917 was used by the Canadian 5th (British) Division. It became the HQ of the 2nd Canadian Division, the 5th Division Artillery and the Heavy Artillery and was said to have held up to 5,000 men. In the 1970's part of the *souterrain* was bought by a retired miner (M. Sergent) who constructed a nuclear shelter in it and later attempted to convert it to a visitable attraction complete with artefacts. The project, however, failed health and safety requirements. M. Sergent died in the 1990s and the *souterrain* **is no longer visitable**.

Turn right on the D55 (Chemin de Maroeuil) and continue to La Targette CWGC Cemetery a few metres off the road to the right.

Czech Memorial and Cemetery, Neuville St Vaast.

Polish Memorial, Neuville St Vaast.

Memorial to Sous-Lt Henry Mouette d'Andrezel, La Targette.

Torch in hand Memorial, La Targette.

German dressing station, diorama, La Targette WW1 Museum.

Overgrown entrance to Aux Rietz Souterrain.

Original resting place of Lt Henri Millevoye, la Targette.

La Targette CWGC and French Cemeteries.

• La Targette CWGC/French National Cemeteries/7.0 miles/20 minutes/ Map 14/12/Lat & Long: 50.35056 2.74881

The CWGC Cemetery, originally known as Aux Rietz Mil Cemetery, was begun at the end of April 1917 and used by Field Ambulances and fighting units until September 1918. One-third of the burials are of Artillery Units and there are 295 Canadian burials, 3 S. Africans and 1 WW2. Adjoining it is the French Cemetery built in 1919 from concentrations from the surrounding battlefields and other small cemeteries. It contains 11,443 burials (including 3,882 Unknown) from WW1 and 593 French, 170 Belgians and 4 Poles from WW2, all laid out in a perfectly symmetrical pattern which stretches up the slope to the three ossuaries.

Return to the D937 and turn right. Continue to the sign to the German Cemetery on the left.

• Neuville St Vaast (Maison Blanche) German Cemetery/7.6 miles/20 minutes/Map 14/13/WC/Lat & Long: 50.34334 2.75216

This is on the site of the heavily defended German position known as 'the Labyrinth'. It has been graphically described by two famous writers of the First World War. One was Henri Barbusse, a comparatively elderly (forty-one when he enlisted in 1914) socialist – some would say communist – whose uncompromisingly subjective book *Le Feu* drew heavily on his experiences of attacks like the desperate one against the Labyrinth. The book was controversial because of its brutality, but it had a profound influence on the realism of Sassoon and Owen when they read it at Craiglockhart. The other writer, also to become controversial for his supposed Nazi sympathies in the 1930s, was Henry Williamson, who described it in the account of his return to the battlefields after the war, *The Wet Flanders Plain*, as the scene of some of the most terrible fighting during the first two years of the war:

> "An underground fortress with access to scores of ferro-concrete blockhouses, held machine-guns under steel cupolas which resisted destruction by all but the heaviest shells. Here a maze of trenches were protected by belts of unpenetrable barbed wire. The Labyrinth spread over thirty acres of chalk. . . . like the web of an immense spider."

In 1915, following almost continuous fighting for Vimy Ridge, thousands of shredded French and colonial uniforms lay on the barbed wire above heaps of bones and skulls. Williamson was appalled by the number of black crosses marking the German graves, concentrated from many areas nearby, that confronted him in 1924. These original crosses remained until the early 1960s when improvement work began. Today there are 37,000 burials here, as well as over 8,000 in one mass grave. In the entrance building is a Calvary and a stone block on which is a *bas relief* map showing all the cemeteries in this area, including Lens. In the centre of the Cemetery is a **Memorial to the German 164th Regt.** On it is inscribed the first line of Ludwig Uhland's famous poem, *Ich hatt einen Kamaraden* ('I had a Comrade') written in 1809.

There is a WC to the left of the entrance and **Information Boards** in three languages which describe the renovation of 1975-1983 by the *Deutsche Kriegsgräbefü rsorge* when it was reopened again to the public.

Opposite is a farm known as La Maison Blanche, the original of which gave its name to this sector. Beneath it is an amazing network of tunnels and chambers known as the **Maison Blanche Souterrain**. Originally a chalk quarry, it was probably used as a refuge in the 19th Century (some graffiti would appear to be c1861) and later as a storage facility for the farmer. Although technically part of the vast Labyrinth system, there is no evidence that it was used by the French or the Germans in the heavy fighting of 1915. It was however certainly used by the Canadian Corps as an underground barracks behind the reserve line in their preparations for the assault on Vimy Ridge of April 1917. (It was later again used as a shelter for Belgian Refugees in May 1940. After WW2 the *souterraine* was used as a dump by the current farmer and rubbish filled the *puit,* almost blocking the entrance.)

The Canadians refer to the 'Maison Blanche Caves' in the *History of the 15th Bn, CEF (48th Highlanders of Canada)* and now they form part of the Canadian *Souterrain Impressions Project*. It started in 2009 when Zenon Andrusyszyn, Canadian founder of CANADIGM saw a TV programme about the Caves and the Canadian carvings in it. They are of an exceptional quality and skill (notably those executed by Pte A.J. Ambler who is understood to have been a stone carver before he enlisted.)

The Project aims to preserve these carvings by documenting, scanning and duplicating them and exhibiting them in travelling exhibitions throughout Canada to commemorate the Centenary of the Battle of Vimy Ridge in 2017. They will then be permanently exhibited in a Canadian museum.

The entrance to the Caves had been rediscovered by a French archaeologist, Dominique Faivre, in 2001. In 2006 Judy Ruzylo, a film researcher, negotiated access to the Caves to film them and at this stage the respected and experienced Durand Group became involved. They formed an agreement with the proprietor to protect access* to the Caves and were permitted to undertake extensive archaeological researches, clearing out the garbage, improving the safety underground, installing lighting etc and mapping the extent of the *souterraine*. They assisted the Canadians in laser scanning the carvings in 3D. A YAP film, *'Vimy Underground'* was duly made in which Ambler's son, Alex, and other family members were shown Pte Ambler's extraordinary work. (Alex died the following year, age 93).

Crosses and Jewish Headstone, German Cemetery, Neuville St Vaast.

Memorial to German 164th Regt, Neuville St Vaast German Cemetery.

15th Can Bn, 48th Highlanders Carving, Maison Blanche Souterrain.

• NOTE. The entrance to the Caves is on private land and may not be visited under any circumstances by individuals who are not part of an authorised group. DO NOT ATTEMPT TO FIND THE ENTRANCE! The only way to see these remarkable Caves is by joining an official tour organised by the Durand Group (Contact: Lt-Col Phillip Robinson (pgrobinson@telco4u.net), sometimes in conjunction with other experienced underground archaeologists, such as Andy Robertshaw (andy@dtsmail.net)

The wonderful work achieved by the Durand Group in the area over many years is detailed in the book Philip wrote with Nigel Cave, *The Underground War. Vimy Ridge to Arras*, Pub Pen & Sword 2011.

Return to La Targette crossroads and turn right. Continue into Neuville St Vaast. Continue to the Mairie.

Extra Visit to SGWs St Laurent Church (Map 14/13a. Lat & Long: 50.35485 2.76055)/Private Museum of M. Browarski, Neuville St-Vaast. Approx time: 30 mins. Lat & Long: 50.35518 2.76418. Round trip: 800 yards. Approximate time: 50 mins

Take the road to the right signed A26 on the rue de la Barre and after 50 yards stop in the car park opposite the Church.

In the Church, unusually rebuilt in 1925 with reinforced concrete, (a technique which was pioneered by a local man, Francois Hennebique, who built the Liver Building in Liverpool), are beautiful **SGWs** which show the sacrifice of soldiers in the war with representations of the Cemetery and Lantern tower at N-D de Lorette, the founding of Montreal and the original church tower of the village etc.

They were made in Limoges in 1932 by F. Chigot. There are also many French Regimental, Divisional and Personal Memorials. After extensive renovations in 2008 this fascinating church with its distinctive white tower is a prominent landmark as you drive around this battlefield.

To the right of the main entrance is a sign directing the visitor to a side door. It is normally open but requires a firm pull!

Continue to No 43.

Through the archway in the wooden gates on the right, is the **Museum of M. Donald Browarski**. This is the most fascinating traditional museum, lovingly maintained by its owner. The exhibits were mainly items found by M Browarski on the battlefield, gradually augmented by gifts from veterans, their families and other collectors with items discovered during various building works. It contains uniforms, superb items of trench art, weapons (including some extremely rare items, such as the rare grenade catapult and trench gun with periscope), personal accounts etc and is well worth a visit.

By appointment only. **Contact** M Browarski on Tel: + (0)3 21 48 84 84, but please call at lunchtime or in the evening.

Rare trench gun, Browarski Museum, Neuville St Vaast.　　　　　*SGW Neuville St Vaast Church.*

N.B. Memorial to Augustin Leuregons & French 53rd Div. (Map 14/13b Lat & Long: 50.34597 2.76505) By continuing 200 yards from the Museum and turning right on the D46E1 signed to Roclincourt, the well-tended Memorial may be found on the right at the top of the hill, some .75 mile further up the road.

This poignant Memorial is to 19 year old **Aspirant (Subaltern) Augustin Leuregons** of the 236 RI who died calling out, 'Come on old Papas. You aren't going to let your child die all alone'.

It also commemorates the bitter fighting for The Labyrinth of May and June 1915 of Gen Berthelot's 53rd Div.

Standing with your back to the Memorial the trees surrounding the German Cemetery at Maison Blanche on the site of The Labyrinth are visible just over half a mile away.

Return to the Mairie and pick up the main itinerary.

Memorial to Augustin Leuregons & French 53rd Div, Neuville St Vaast.

Keep left following signs to Mémorial Canadien to the sign to the right to Lichfield Crater (easily missed).

Extra Visit to Lichfield Crater CWGC Cemetery (Map 14/14). Round trip: 1.4 miles. Approximate time: 15 minutes/Lat & Long: 50.36020 2.77731

Follow the crater sign and continue over the motorway and fork right along a deteriorating cart track (probably not driveable in wet weather) to Lichfield Crater.

This is one of the most unusual cemeteries on the Western Front. It is one of two mine craters (the other being Zivy Crater, see below) used by the Canadian Corps Burial Officer for bodies from the Vimy battlefield from 9 or 10 April 1917. Designed by W.H. Cowlishaw it was originally simply called CB-2A. The grassed circular cemetery is essentially a mass grave and contains only one headstone – to **Pte Albert Stubbs**, 8th S Lancs Regt, age 25, 30 April 1916. The Cross of Sacrifice is on a raised level and below it is a Memorial Wall on which are the names and details of 41 Canadian soldiers buried here. They include **L/Sgt E. Sifton**, 18th Bn, W Ontario Regt C.E.F., who was awarded a posthumous **VC** for his action on 9 April 1917 at Neuville St Vaast where he charged a German machine gun and single-handedly killed all the crew. He then held off an enemy party until his comrades arrived but was killed in the action.

Lichfield Crater CWGC Cemetery.

Extra Visit continued

There are also 11 unidentified Canadians, 4 completely Unknowns and 1 unidentified Russian.

It is thought that a Memorial to the Canadian 2nd Division, which was constructed at the end of the War, lies underneath the Crater. There were at least two other substantial craters beside this track between Lichfield and the T junction, the nearest one called Watling, just 150 yards away.

Return to the main itinerary.

Return to the main road and continue to the Park. Take the first turning right signed to the Tunnels/ Trenches and park.

• *Vimy Ridge Canadian Welcome Centre, National Memorial & Park/ 10.3 miles/90 minutes/Map 14/15, 14/16, 14/17, 14/18*

In 2001 a massive programme of restoration of all Canada's Memorials in Belgium and France began. At $(Can)20 million, Vimy is by far the most important project – 20% of the original stone needed replacing, name panels needed re-engraving, the drainage system needed renewing. Work (which included the renovation of trenches and tunnels) was completed in December 2006 with an official opening date on 9 April 2007, the 90th Anniversary of the Battle. During the extensive work the Welcome Centre was moved to the area near the tunnels/craters/trenches, which is where the visit begins.

On 25 April 1915 allied landings were made in Gallipoli. The ANZAC forces landed in the wrong place and were caught and held by the Turkish defenders on a narrow beach below high cliffs where in essence they were to remain until withdrawn nine months later. The extraordinary courage and resolution of the ANZAC soldiers, depicted mostly in the writings of C.E.W. Bean, the official Australian historian, led to the Gallipoli campaign becoming a focal point in the developing character of that young nation. Here too, at Vimy, was a 'National Army' fighting its first battle, the Canadian. In a way the fighting for, and the capture of, Vimy Ridge, might be seen as Canada's Gallipoli. Their achievement was remarkable and their pride in what they achieved thoroughly deserved. The importance of Vimy to the self-awareness of Canada is evident in that it is at the highest point of the Ridge that they have placed their most important memorial, which is visited next. In the area in front of the Centre is **the Lions Club International Memorial.**

The Vimy Welcome Centre (Map 14/18. Lat & Long: 50.37197 2.76973) has informative panels and photographs, some trench periscopes, a circular audio-visual presentation of the battlefield in English, French and German and a small book stall. Here enthusiastic and well-informed bi-lingual Canadian student guides are based. There is fierce competition in Canada amongst young people who wish to be guides, most of whom are either students or graduates. Each year a new cadre is selected and shared with the Memorial Park at Beaumont Hamel on the Somme.

Open every day (except two weeks around Christmas) 1000-1800 May-Oct, 0900-1700 Nov-April. Guided tours available May-November. Tel: + (0)3 21 50 68 68. E-mail: vimy.memorial@vac-acc.gc.ca Website: www.virtualmemorial.gc.ca. There are WCs next to the Centre.

The underground tour (which must be booked through the Centre – well in advance for groups) goes through part of the Grange Crater tunnel system but for security reasons only in groups accompanied by guides, for which there is no charge. A trip into the tunnel, which begins near the Canadian flag, generally lasts about 25 minutes and should not be taken by anyone who is at all claustrophobic. It is cold underground and often wet and slippery.

Beyond the tunnel, clearly signed, are the preserved trench lines formed with concrete sandbags. Work on preserving this area began in the late 1920s and was still going on in 1936 when the Vimy Memorial was unveiled. The first trenches are the Canadian line, and sniper posts,

The Welcome Centre and Lions Memorial, Vimy National Park.

firesteps and duckboards are plain to see. Just over the top of the Canadian parapet is one of the features that makes Vimy so extraordinary – a huge mine crater.

On one of the tours that we conducted in the 1970s a traveller told us that the preserved trenches brought back many memories. We questioned him about that because he was clearly too young to have been in the First World War. 'Oh', he said, 'we used them as shelter from the Luftwaffe in the Retreat to Dunkirk.'

When the British took over this 'quiet sector' from the French, (after the Artois battles of 1914/15 both sides settled for a mutually uncomfortable existence devoid of set-piece attacks) peace gave way to conflict. Fighting patrols were sent out to take enemy prisoners, raids were launched, 'nuisance' bombardments began and underground too the warfare intensified. Tunnel after tunnel was driven under the enemy trenches, packed with explosives and fired, producing huge craters. The crater immediately beyond the Canadian line is 'Grange'. The effectiveness of the mine warfare is evident in a report from the German 163rd Regiment. 'The continual mine explosions in the end got on the nerves of the men. One stood in the front line defenceless and powerless against these fearful mine explosions.'

Both sides attempted to sabotage each other's mining by burrowing under the other's galleries and blowing them up. Miners had to stop and listen at regular intervals for the sound of enemy digging and then make fine judgements about just where the other's tunnel was and what he was about to do. The tension must have been heart-stopping. Dark cramped conditions, foul air to breathe, hot and probably wet too, trapped mole-like underground – it needed special qualities just to remain sane. Tunnels were frequently dug at different levels. Near Souchez mining went on at 110 ft and 60 ft down, and some tunnels were over 1,000 yards long. One, called 'Goodman', was more than 1,800 yards. Grange was a sophisticated tunnel 800 yards long with side-bays for headquarters, signal offices, water points, etc. and standing room. It was meant for the movement of troops. Six miles or more of such tunnels were dug before the battle. Tunnels to be used solely as a means of reaching the enemy lines in order to place explosives under them were frequently crawling-size only. There is yet another surprise in store for the visitor because just across the crater, on the opposite lip, are the German trenches.

It was a remarkable feat for the Canadians to do so well here. The whole attack had been rehearsed day after day at unit level on a full-scale replica behind the front. Short, reachable objectives were marked on maps as lines – black, red, blue and brown - attacking formations only moving on or through each line was established. The Canadians went in ten battalions abreast, fighting, for the first time as a national contingent, and working steadily forward from objective to objective. Left to right in line the Divisions were – 4th, 3rd, 2nd and 1st. The Canadian 2nd

Division was strengthened by the attachment of 13 Brigade from the British 5th (Imperial) Division the remainder of that Division being left in reserve.

The 0530 hours pre-assault bombardment, which had been started by the firing of a big gun from behind Mont St Eloi, was of such intensity that it was impossible to distinguish the sound of individual explosions. Those present felt that if they could reach up into the air they would touch a wall of sound. The plan was that the guns would lift at intervals and the infantry would then walk forward as if behind a curtain of steel. Gus Sivertz, serving with the 2nd Canadian Mounted Rifles, later recalled, 'We didn't dare lift our heads, knowing that the barrage was to come flat over us and then lift in three minutes. I don't think anyone was scared ... instead one's whole body seemed to be in a mad macabre dance. It was perhaps the most perfect barrage of the war, as it was so perfectly synchronised. Then suddenly it jumped a hundred yards and we were away,' (*Vimy Ridge* – Alexander McKee). Flying over the assault was Major Billy Bishop VC (the Canadian aviator who became an Hon Air Marshal of the RCAF after the war) who wrote,

'The waves of attacking infantry as they came out of their trenches and trudged forward behind the curtain of shells laid down by the artillery were an amazing sight. These troops had been drilled to move forward at a given pace and from this timing the "Creeping" or rolling barrage which moved in front of them had been mathematically worked out', (*Winged Warfare*).

In fact the timing for the infantry was that they should move 100 yards in three minutes. If they were to go too fast then they would run into their own artillery fire, if they were too slow then the barrage would get too far ahead of them and they would lose its protection.

The timing of the Canadian attack went even further. The four Canadian divisions had 35 minutes to reach the Black Line, then 40 minutes there to re-organise, then 20 minutes to get to the Red Line. There the attack was to narrow to a two division front and, after two and a half hours there, reserve brigades of the 1st and 2nd Divisions were to push on to the Blue Line, re-organise there for 96 minutes and then carry on just beyond the crest of the ridge to the Brown Line which in theory would be at 1318 hours. It was an extraordinary plan. A common military maxim is that 'No plan survives contact with the enemy' and the more complicated a plan the more likely it is to go wrong. There are many examples of too complicated plans going wrong particularly when they involve precise timings. A prime instance took place 27 years later on 6 June 1944 at OMAHA beach when American General Huebner's precise instructions did not survive contact with events. However, it worked for the Canadians in 1917 and they deserved it to do so but they had to have had an added factor – luck. Perhaps one does make one's own luck and as President Lincoln apparently said, 'Give me lucky generals'.

The Grange position was defended by companies of the German 261st Reserve Regiment of the 79th Reserve Division. When the fighting was over the 261st Regiment had lost 86 killed, 199 wounded and 451 missing – a total of 736 men. The Canadian assault here was made by 7th Brigade of the 3rd Division and alongside, to the north, 111th Brigade of the 4th Division. One of the Canadians waiting in the Grange tunnel at 0530 hours described the sound of the opening barrage as 'like water on a tin roof in a heavy thunderstorm'. Around the Grange crater area there are many other craters with names like Durand, Duffield, Patricia, Birkin and Commons, as well as paths leading off into the woods.

It was long believed that each of the trees in the park represented one of the 66,655 Canadian soldiers (their dead for the entire war) listed on the Memorial and that they came from Canada. In fact they are Austrian firs, three containers of whose seeds arrived by train after the war as part of Germany's reparations price. Beneath the trees, shell-holes, craters and lines of trenches in the Park are a series of German and allied tunnels which were packed with mines and then exploded. The 100-hectare Park is full of unexploded and highly volatile materiel and most areas are out of bounds. There is a constant threat of erosion to this historic site, presenting great problems of preservation to the Canadian Ministry of Veterans Affairs which administers it. Much dangerous work has been undertaken by the **Durand Group** (qv) to render known unexploded mines harmless to the thousands of visitors who walk and drive over them each year.

Sadly one of the group's founders, **Lt Col Mike Watkins,** was killed in 1998 when one of the tunnels they were excavating collapsed. There is a **Memorial Plaque** to him at the entrance to the Grange subway.

Drive out of the car park area and turn right signed to the Memorial. En route you will pass signs to the following:

Canadian Cemetery No 2, Givenchy Road Canadian Cemetery and Givenchy-en-Gohelle Canadian Cemetery. Map 14/16

Continue to the main car park. It is opposite the **Moroccan Memorial (Lat & Long: 50.37919 2.76990)** see below.

• Canadian National Memorial/Map 14/17/WC

Here are Canadian Guides ready to assist you – and occasionally buggies are available for the disabled. There is a toilet block on the right before you go up the main path.

As you walk towards the Memorial you are looking at the rear of the monument. When the Canadians decided to erect a national Memorial here to replace the divisional Memorials placed after the battle, they invited competitive designs and 160 were submitted. The winner, who said that the design came to him in a dream, was a Toronto sculptor, Walter Seymour Allward (who also designed the Superintendent's house opposite). The two tall pylons symbolize Canada and France and between them at the front, carved from a single 30-ton block of stone, is a figure of Canada mourning for her dead. She overlooks the Douai Plain and the Loos Battlefield.

Below the figure is a sarcophagus carrying a helmet and laurels and a Latin subscription commemorating the 60,000 Canadians who died during the Great War. On the wall of the memorial are the names of 11,285 Canadian soldiers who were killed in France and who have no known grave. The 90 ft high Memorial stands on Point 145, the highest point of Vimy Ridge. The base was formed from 12,000 tons of concrete and masonry and 6,000 tons of Dalmatian stone was used for the pylons and the figures, of which there are twenty, all 12 ft high. Construction began in 1925 and Allward's aim was, he said, to produce 'a structure which would endure, in an exposed position, for a thousand years – indeed, for all time'.

When the Memorial was unveiled on 26 July 1936 (it took four years longer to build than at first estimated) it was in the presence of King Edward VIII, his only overseas official engagement as King. Also present was M. Victor Maistriau, the Burgomaster of Mons, which had been liberated by the Canadian Corps on 11 November 1918. He carried with him the personal flag of Lt General Sir Arthur Currie who had commanded the Corps. The General presented his flag to the town of

The imposing twin pylons of the Canadian National Memorial, Vimy, with detail of Canada mourning for her dead.

The Grange Tunnel, Vimy.

Preserved Trenches, Vimy Ridge.

Some parts are off limits.

Mons and it is now in the Museum there. The area between where you are and the Memorial was estimated to have been filled with 100,000 pilgrims, of whom 8,000 had come from Canada. These had left Canada on 16 July 1936 in five of Canadian Pacific's steamers, sailed to Antwerp, stayed overnight in Armentières and then on to the unveiling ceremony on Sunday 26 July. The pilgrimage, which was organised by the Canadian Legion, continued to London where ceremonies were held at the Cenotaph attended by British Prime Minister Stanley Baldwin.

Return to the car park. Opposite is

The **Moroccan Division Memorial**, commemorating the Division's achievements during the second battle of Artois on 9 May 1915. Bronze panels around the stone monument list the ORBAT of the Division (motto *Sans peur, sans pitié* – without fear, without mercy) and also recognise the contribution of other foreign forces, including the Jews, Greeks, Sudanese and Czechs.

Return past the Canadian Cemetery No 2 signs etc and turn left following signs to Vimy for 1.2 miles to a small track to the left which may – or may not – be signed to the Canadian 3rd Division Memorial.

The Moroccan Memorial, Vimy National Park.

Extra Visit to 3rd 'Canadian' Division Monument (Map 14/19) Round trip 400m. Approximate time: 15 minutes. Lat & Long: 50.36848 2.78247

Walk along a track to the Monument.

This concrete Cross was erected to the men of the Division who gave their lives in defence of the line from October 23rd 1916 to February 15th 1917 and in the attack and capture of Vimy Ridge on April 9th 1917 and in subsequent operations. The Memorial is on the centre line of the Divisional attack which came from the area of the Welcome Centre and was aimed in the direction in which you are driving towards Thélus (the next stop). In the middle of the 1,500 yards wide front was the 2nd Canadian Mounted Regiment who came through this area heading for a German position at la Folie Farm, some 350 yards further on from the Memorial. The Divisional Commander, Major-General Lipsett, had commanded a Battalion during the first German gas attacks around Ypres in April 1915. This same Division would go on to liberate Mons on the last day of the war and they have a Memorial Plaque on the wall of the Town Hall (qv).

Return to your car and pick up the main itinerary.

Continue to the T junction turn right on the N17(N25) signed Arras/A26. Continue into Thélus.

N.B. 1: On the left at the cross roads with the D49 is the **Canadian Artillery Memorial (Map 14/20. Lat & Long: 50.35616 2.78983)** unveiled by General Byng on 9 April 1918 and signed to the right is **Zivy Crater Cemetery (Map 14/21/Lat & Long: 50.35502 2.77732)** about half a mile away on the left hand side. This was used by the Canadian Corps in 1917 as one large grave and contains 50 Canadian and 3 Unknown. The Zivy Crater road, the D49, leads to la Targette, just under 2 miles away, where you were earlier. The D49 was effectively the line of advance of the 2nd Canadian Division which came directly towards you. The Canadians, reaching here on the 9th, took many prisoners including 4 German guns which their gunners turned upon the enemy. Thus it seems an appropriate place for the Artillery Memorial.

N.B. 2: By turning left along the D49 **Bois Carré British Cemetery (Lat & Long: 50.35172 2.80895)** is reached on the right hand side after about .4 mile. The Cemetery was begun by units of the 1st Canadian Division in April 1917, and used until the following June. These 61 graves are in Plot I (a Canadian soldier, accidentally killed in 1919, was also buried in Plot I, Row F). The cemetery was greatly enlarged after the Armistice by the concentration of graves and burial grounds from the surrounding battlefields.

During the 1939-40 War the cemetery was used in April 1940 by No.8 Casualty Clearing Station.

There are now over five hundred 1914-18 and a small number of 1939-45 war casualties commemorated in this site. Of these, nearly 60 from the 1914-18 War are unidentified and there are Special Memorials to one soldier from the United Kingdom and one from Canada known to be buried among them. Other Special Memorials record the names of ten Canadian soldiers and three from the United Kingdom, buried in smaller cemeteries, whose graves were destroyed by shell fire.

By continuing a further .4 miles the **1st (Canadian) Div Memorial (Lat & Long: 50.34997 2.81610)** is reached on the right. The 1st Division had advanced on the right of the 2nd Division, and was the southernmost of the four Canadian

Memorial to 1st (Canadian) Division, Thélus.

Divisions which had advanced in line with the 51st Highland Division on their right. Their direction was that of Farbus Wood, the Brown Line objective, ahead on the left before the railway line. It is probable that the 5th Battalion of the 3rd Brigade of 1st Division moved along this road.

Continue under the motorway

N.B. 3: As the road crosses Rue Pasteur, to the right along the road at the junction with Rue du Saumon (Map 14/23a. Lat & Long: 550.28885 2.780600) is a Plaque to the 56th (1st London) Div. July 1916 the Division took part in the Battle of the Somme and in the September fighting captured Combles, the most successful Fourth Army advance since July.

Memorial to 3rd (Canadian) Division, Vimy Ridge.   *Memorial to Canadian Artillery, Thélus.*

Continue to the centre of Arras following signs to Gare SCNF and park as near as possible to the railway station.

• Arras Centre/Boves/18.6 approx miles/60 minutes/Map 14/23/Lat & Long: 50.28747 2.78166

N.B. From here the mileage may vary depending upon exactly where you can park and if you walk or drive to the Town Hall.

Arras suffered considerable damage from long-range shells – the German front line was only some two miles east of the town. In 1916 the British took over from the French and in the days preceding the April 1917 offensive the war correspondent Philip Gibbs vividly described the scene in the damaged town: the Highlanders playing their pipe bands, the soldiers in their steel helmets and goatskin coats who resembled 'medieval men-at-arms', the dead horses lying thick on the Arras-Cambrai road, the long queues of wounded men waiting for treatment in the old Vauban Citadel – 3,000 of them on one day alone... Men and materiel poured through the town in huge numbers in the preparation for the offensive.

On the wall of the station are **Plaques to Station Workers** (SNCF) killed in the War 1 and WW2 and the **Red Cross** in 1940.

SNCF War Memorial, Arras Station.

Opposite the railway station on the central area is the **Arras War Memorial**, with some fine *bas reliefs* of various aspects of the Great War, which shows scars from the Second World War. All around the square are numerous **Cafés and Hotels** (see **Tourist Information**, page 338). The town has been a centre of trade and population since ancient times. It was fortified by Vauban who built the citadel. It was briefly over-run by the Germans in September 1914 but then held by the French until March 1916 and then the British until the end of the war.

The Town Hall/Boves. This is a five minute walk from the station area (follow signs to 'Les Places', or you may decide to drive and park under the Grand' Place). The Squares have delightful Flemish baroque facades and many restaurants. Through the Town Hall (with its impressive belfry, started in 1463, rebuilt between 1924-1932) is access to the *'Boves'* – the caves and tunnels dating from the fourteenth century that were enlarged and extended during the 1914-18 war. The soft, porous stone underlying Arras was tunnelled in deepest secrecy for 18 months before the April 1917 offensive when narrow-gauge railways were constructed to carry away the spoil. The tunnels, christened after British towns – 'Glasgow', 'Manchester' etc, were reinforced with pine logs supporting the heavy cross timbers of the roof and led to cavernous chambers. Generating stations to produce electricity were installed and miles of wiring were used in the hundreds of yards of tunnels that linked the ancient cellars, crypts and quarries. Not only were the undergrounds used as hospitals and shelters, but also to transport vast bodies of troops and material safely to the start line trenches of the offensive in open country.

The **Tourist Office** in the Town Hall is **open** 21 April-16 September Mon-Sat: 0900 - 1830; Sun: 1000-1300 and 1430-1830. 1 Jan-20 April and 17 Sept-31 Dec: Mon 1000-1200 and 1400-1800; Tues-Sat 0900-1200 and 1400-1800; Sun 1000-1230 and 1430-1830. A visit to the *Boves* and tours of the surrounding battlefields may be booked here. Tel: + (0)3 21 51 26 95. E-mail: arras.tourisme@wanadoo.fr Website: www.ot-arras.fr It will be useful to pick up a town plan here, lists of any commemorative events in the vicinity and more information about accommodation and restaurants.

Return to your car. Take the N17 on Ave du Maréchal Leclerc, direction Bapaume. After crossing over the railway bridge the road then leads into the Ave Ferdinand Lobbedez. Continue almost exactly half a mile after the bridge to the junction with rue Alexandre Ribot to the Memorial on the left.

Arras Memorial to the missing and RAF Memorial.

• *Memorial to New Zealand Tunnellers and Wellington Quarry/ 19.5 miles/45 mins/Map 14/24/Lat & Long: 50.28040 2.78285*

The striking Monument which simulates a section of a tunnel, was designed by Arras artist, Luc Brévart. It is made of white stone and railway sleepers (reminiscent of those used by the NZ tunnellers) with bronze components, such as a NZ tin hat, a pick and a map of New Zealand. It honours the 41 NZ tunnellers who lost their lives here and the 151 who were wounded. They included Maori and Pacific Islanders of the ZN Pioneer Battalion.

Beside the Memorial is the old '*Défence Passive*' building. This was the name for the quarry in which the local inhabitants sheltered during the bombings of May 1940 and the building was used as a power/water supply zone for the underground quarries, originally dug in the Middle Ages. These were the basis for the network of underground quarries linked up by the NZ Tunnellers in preparation for the April 1917 Battle of Arras and which eventually could house 24,000 soldiers as they waited for the surprise offensive to start on 9 April at 05.30. The section underground here is known as '**Wellington Quarry'**.

Its imposing entrance is in the adjacent Rue Delétoile which should be signed from here. There is a large car park. A **Memorial Wall** listing the Regiments of the 1st, 3rd and 5th British Armies involved in the battle leads the visitor to the entrance.

Open: every day from 1000-1230 and 1330-1800 except 25 Dec and the three following weeks. **Contact:** as **Tourist Office** above. This is a fascinating and atmospheric visit. Accompanied by a guide and an audio-guide available in several languages, the visitor descends 20m in a glass lift to the living and administrative quarters. Most poignant are the many examples of signs and carved and painted graffiti (also from the period of WW2), examples of letters and photos. A film sets the scene.

Return to the Place Maréchal Foch and follow signs to the Citadelle/Motorway and on the town ring road, Boulevard Gen de Gaulle, just south of the junction with the N25 to Doullens, is

New Zealand Tunnellers Memorial, Arras.

Wellington Quarry, Arras.

• Faubourg d'Amiens CWGC Cemetery/Memorials to the Missing & RFC/Mur des Fusillés/approx 22 miles/60 minutes/Map 14/22/Lat & Long: 50.28667 2.76048

Despite the name, this is the Arras Memorial. It takes the form of a wall carrying almost 36,000 names of the Missing of the battles around Arras. On it are the names of the First World War poet **Capt. T.P. Cameron Wilson** of the Sherwood Foresters, **Lt Geoffrey Thurlow** of the same regiment – one of Vera Brittain's coterie of friends, and **Captain Charles McKay** and **Private David Sutherland** of the Seaforths. David was the subject of Lt. E. A. Mackintosh's searing poem, *In Memoriam*, which describes his death during a trench raid on 16 May 1916 in which McKay also took part.

Also commemorated here is **2nd Lt Walter Daniel John Tull**, Middx Regt, 25 March 1918, age 29. Tull was one of Britain's first black professional footballers and, despite his poor background, also its first black Army Officer. Tull was admitted to an orphanage in Bethnal Green when both his parents died and was signed up by Tottenham Hotspur in 1908. In 1909 he suffered appalling racial abuse during a match and was transferred to Northampton Town. On the outbreak of war he enlisted in the 17th (1st Football) Bn of the Middx Regt, was promoted to sergeant in 1916, was invalided home with trench fever at the end of the year and went to the officer cadet training school at Gailes in Scotland – despite the fact that 'Negroes' were specifically excluded from commanding as officers. In 1917 he went to the Italian Front as a 2nd Lieutenant in the 23rd (2nd Football) Bn of the Middx Regt and was MiD in the Battle of the Piave. In 1918 he returned to France and was killed in No Man's Land near Favreuil. In the mid-1990s a campaign was started to use Tull's inspiring story to help black recruitment in the British Army and to defuse racial discrimination in the world of football and on 11 July 1999 the **Walter Tull Memorial and Garden of Rest** was opened at Sixfields Stadium, Northampton.

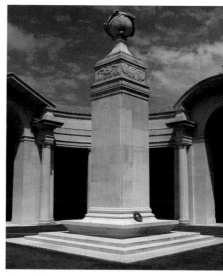

Arras Flying Services Memorial.

The wall encloses the Cemetery, begun in March 1916, and which contains 2,700 burials. At the back are separate small rows for Hindus, Mohammedans and Sikhs. Just within the entrance wall, in a space once occupied by the graves of French soldiers, is the **Royal Flying Corps Memorial**. It takes the form of a column surmounted by a globe. The

The Arras Memorial to the Missing.

Memorial panels and execution post, Mur des Fusillés.

flight of doves encircling the globe is following the path of the sun on 11 November 1918. It carries the names of over 1,000 personnel of the **RNAS, RFC** and **RAF** personnel missing on the Western Front, **including VCs Major Lanoe Hawker and Major E. ('Mick') Mannock**. Also commemorated here is **Lt Donald MacGregor**, the Red Baron's 63rd victim, shot down on 30 November 1917 during the Cambrai battle.

Beyond the memorial the '*Mur des Fusillés*' is signed. This is a 1 mile round trip which leads to a poignant area where between July 1941 and July 1944 the Germans shot over 200 Frenchmen, including some liberated in the 'Operation Jericho' Amiens prison raid of 1944. A concrete marker indicates the Execution Post and Memorial Plaques commemorate those who were killed (many of them Miners, dating from 1942 and June 1944). Entry to the area is controlled by a gate which closes at dusk and you must park before the barrier and walk the last section around the old Citadel walls.

• *End of Notre-Dame de Lorette, Artois/Vimy Battlefield Tour*

THIRD YPRES
Passchendaele

7 JUNE-10 NOVEMBER 1917

'Rain has turned everything into a quagmire and the shell holes are full of water.
Duckboards are everywhere leading to the front line,
but Jerry has these well taped and frequently shells them or sprays them with
indirect machine-gun fire. ... Guns of all calibres are everywhere,
in places wheel to wheel. The debris of war is lying about.
Broken guns, limbers, horses blown to blazes. But very few human bodies,
for they have all been swallowed up in the mud and water of this horrible sector.
It seems madness on the part of Higher Authority
to expect any advance over this indescribable morass.'
The diary of a Sergeant in the Somerset Light Infantry.

SUMMARY OF THE BATTLE

On 7 June 1917 the British attacked and captured the Messines Ridge, a dominant feature that extended northwards to the German-held Passchendaele Ridge. On 31 July, the British attacked again and floundered in mud and rain in an assault that earned General Haig the title of 'Butcher' and won the Passchendaele Ridge after 16 weeks' fighting. British losses were over 300,000 and German losses, never published, variously estimated between 65,000 and 260,000.

OPENING MOVES

Early in May 1917, following the bloody failure of Nivelle's attack on the Chemin des Dames, the French Army began to mutiny until sixteen Army Corps were involved. On 15 May, General Pétain, 'the saviour of Verdun', took Nivelle's place and, by a mixture of personal visits to front line units and summary courts martial, including executions, set about restoring discipline. Richard M. Watt, in his book *Dare Call it Treason*, supposes that at least 100,000 men actively mutinied and even the official figures admit that between May and October 1917, 23,385 men were found guilty of offences. Yet, extraordinarily, the news of the mutinies did not become general knowledge.

Haig therefore realised that the French would have to be left out of any immediate British plans for an offensive and later asserted that Pétain actually asked him to maintain British attacks on the Germans in order to relieve pressure on the French. Haig had fought his first battle as C-in-C the previous year on the Somme and opinions were sharply divided about its outcome – whether it had been a strategic success in the casualties inflicted upon the Germans, or a costly failure because of our own losses. Nevertheless, Haig was still determined to prove himself as a commander. His conviction that the only way to win the war was by frontal assault remained undimmed. If he wanted to win the war alone he had to hurry, because on 6 April 1917 America had declared war on Germany and soon her soldiers would arrive to swing the balance against the Germans.

Thus to 'help' the French, to prove himself and his men, and to do it before the Americans arrived, he set about planning an attack. First though, he had to persuade a reluctant War Committee that an attack was both needed and would have positive results. The War Cabinet, which had to sanction the C-in-C's plans, was led by the Prime Minister, Lloyd George, who was very unhappy at the long British casualty lists for which he held Haig personally responsible. Haig promised that his campaign would be a limited one and proposed that it should be in Flanders in order to capture the German U-Boat bases on the Belgian coast, said by the Admiralty to be the source of the submarine offensive. In fact the U-Boats were coming from Germany and the Belgian theory surprised many people, including the chief of Haig's intelligence staff who later said, 'No one really believed this rather amazing view.'

However, Haig found it useful and when he maintained that 'if the fighting was kept up at its present intensity for six months, Germany would be at the end of her available manpower', the War Committee reluctantly agreed to his plans.

First of all the C-in-C wanted to gain a foothold at the southern end of the Ypres Salient, around a village called Messines. It was to be a remarkably successful battle that by its very success may have doomed General Gough's 5th Army to the seemingly endless slog up the slope to Passchendaele.

WHAT HAPPENED

The high ground at the southern end of the Salient had been occupied by the Germans since the British shortened their lines at the end of Second Ypres. The Messines-Wijtschate area was of particular value to the Germans because from there they could enfilade much of the British trench system. The task of dislodging them was given to General Plumer's 2nd Army. Plumer had already been preparing for an assault for over a year by tunnelling under the German lines and placing 19 huge mines in a ten-mile arc from near Hill 60 via Spanbroekmolen to Ploegsteert Wood. There were over four miles of tunnels and more than a million pounds of high explosives. The attack was planned in great detail and models of the German positions used so that formations down to company level could be quite clear what their objectives were, and those objectives were limited and precise.

At 0310 on 7 June 1917 the mines exploded following more than two weeks bombardment by over 2,000 guns. X (British) Corps and II (Anzac) Corps advanced, assisted by 72 tanks and with complete air superiority. By the end of the day the first objectives were all taken. The 36th (Ulster) Division and the 16th (Irish) Division took Wijtschate and Messines fell to the New Zealanders.

So far so good. So now on to the Passchendaele Ridge while the momentum of success was still warm? No. Now a near 8 weeks delay while preparations were made for the next attack. Why wasn't the Messines attack delayed until it could be followed immediately by the second phase? Were the French in such desperate straights that we had to grasp the Germans' attention in June? Perhaps. Perhaps too we needed to assemble and to reposition our artillery, something not done in a few hours, but the delay was fateful. It saw out the good weather and gave the Germans time to put the finishing touches to their new scheme of defence – defence in depth. Gone now were the old linear lines. Now trenches ran backwards and forwards in great depth and within the grid so formed were disconnected strongpoints and concrete pillboxes. The manning philosophy had changed too. The ground was covered by mutually supporting machine guns and forward positions were lightly held with reserves well back and concentrated ready for counter-attack. On top of all that the Germans introduced mustard gas.

The preliminary British bombardment began on 22 July 1917. Over 3,000 guns hurled almost five tons of shells at every yard of the front. Ten days later, at 0350 hours on 31 July, twelve divisions advanced on an 11-mile front in pouring rain. North of Ypres advances of two miles were made, the Pilckem Ridge was recaptured, but further south and around the Menin Road the attack quickly stuck. The preliminary bombardment had totally destroyed the water table and the rain

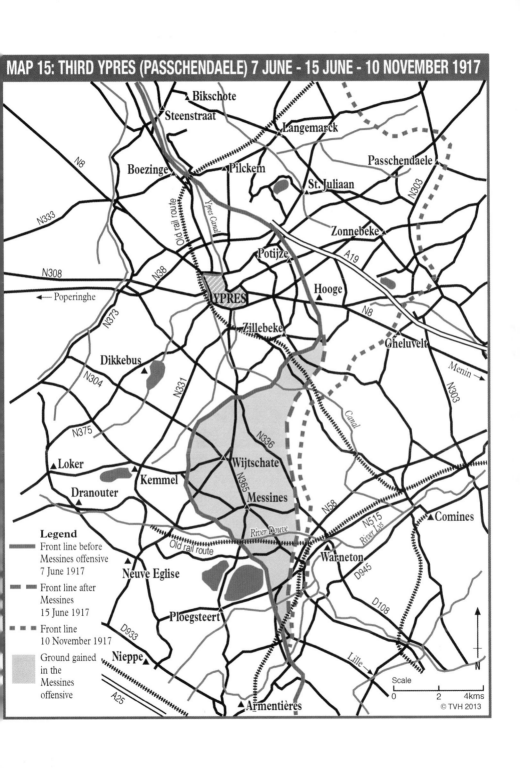

could not run away. Shell holes filled to overflowing with water and the earth turned into a thick glutinous mud, stinking and foul with the decay of dead horses and thousands of corpses. The mud reached out and sucked under any unwary soldier who left the duckboard path. Gough advised Haig that the attack should be stopped, but the C-in-C, falsely buoyant from the success at Messines, perhaps, or determined to demonstrate what Clausewitz called the 'maintenance of the Aim', i.e. steadfastness of purpose, pressed on, through battle after battle and casualty after casualty.

The Official History records the following battles:

Messines	7-14 June
Pilckem	31 July-2 Aug
Langemarck	16-18 Aug
Menin Road	20-25 Sept
Polygon Wood	26 Sept-3 Oct
Broodseinde	4 Oct.
Poelcapelle	9 Oct
First Passchendaele	12 Oct
Second Passchendaele	26 Oct-10 Nov

In the first week of November, 16 weeks after the second phase began, the 1st and 2nd Canadian Divisions occupied the shapeless ruins of Passchendaele village. The mud and blood bath was over. It is said that Lt-Gen. Sir Launcelot Kiggell, Haig's Chief of Staff, visited the battlefield for the first time just after the fighting was over (a terrible indictment in itself) and when he saw the foul swamp in which it had been fought burst into tears saying, 'Good God! Did we really send men to fight in this?'

Whether this story is true or not, it is certainly the case that many officers on the Staff were ignorant about the true conditions in the front line.

THE SALIENT BATTLEFIELD TOUR: 1ST, 2ND, 3RD YPRES

Although the Three Battles of Ypres are normally identified and treated separately as historical bites, it is not possible to tour them in isolation. Therefore the battlefield tour described here is a tour of the Ypres Salient and encompasses all three battles (see **Map 6**, page 103). At its end the tour which concentrates on the Fourth Battle of Ypres could then be followed (see page 300). To tour the Salient in a comprehensive manner requires at least three days and travellers with that amount of time are referred to our guide book *Major & Mrs Holt's Battlefield Guide to the Ypres Salient* with its accompanying detailed Battle Map. The following suggested tour covers the most important and easily accessible points of interest in the Salient.

The Route: The Tour of First, Second and Third Ypres begins at the In Flanders Fields Museum in Ypres, visits St George's Memorial Church and the Menin Gate Memorial by foot. It then moves north and clockwise via Essex Farm; Yorkshire Trench, Boezinge; Pilckem Ridge – Breton Memorial, Artillery Wood CWGC Cem, Ledwidge, Hedd Wyn & Welsh Memorials, Cement House CWGC Cem; Langemarck German Cemetery & Information Centre; Bellew VC Plaque/the Canadian Brooding Soldier Memorial, Vancouver Corner; 48th Highlanders of Canada, Gas Attack Memorial, New Zealand Memorial, 's-Graventafel; Tyne Cot British Cemetery (Passchendaele) & Memorials/Visitor Centre; Passchendaele Memorial Museum, Zonnebeke; Polygon Wood & Buttes New Brit Cemeteries, Australian 5th Div & N Zealand Memorial to the Missing; Black Watch Corner; Sgt Nicholas VC Memorial; Gheluvelt Mill & Memorials; Clapham Junction Memorials; KRRC Memorial; Hooge Crater, Preserved Trenches, Museum & Cemetery; Menin Road Museum; Sanctuary Wood CWGC Cemetery, Museum & Preserved Trenches; Mount Sorrel

Can Monument; Hellfire Corner; Hill 60 & Memorials; St Eloi Tunnellers' Memorial & Craters; Wijtschate – Bayern Wood, Croonaert Chapel CWGC Cemetery, 1st Chasseurs à Pied Memorial, Site of Hitler Painting; Wytschaete Military CWGC Cemetery/16th Irish & 36th (Ulster) Divs Memorials; Spanbroekmolen (Pool of Peace); Lone Tree CWGC Cemetery; Kruisstraat Craters; Messines Ridge British CWGC Cemetery/New Zealand Memorial; Messines Museum & Memorials; Island of Ireland Tower; Ploegsteert Memorial & Interpretation Centre/Berks & Hyde Park Corner Cemeteries.

NOTE: At this point one may return to Ieper or continue with the tour which visits sites of **Fourth Ypres** (see page **300**).

• **Extra Visits:** Lijssenthoek CWGC Cemetery & Information Centre and Talbot House & Walking Tour, Poperinge; The London Scottish Memorial; Plugstreet Wood and St Yvon – Prowse Point CWGC Cemetery, Khaki Chums Christmas Truce Cross, Bairnsfather Memorial Plaque.

• **[N.B.]** Visits are indicated to: CWGC HQ, Ypres; Harry Patch Memorial, Steenbeek Albertina, 20th Light Div Memorial; 34th Div Memorial, Dancox VC Plaque, Langemarck; 'Road to Passchendaele Marker'; French Memorial, Zillebeke Demarcation Stone; Hollandseschuur Craters.

• **Total distance: 45 miles**
• **Total time: 13** hours – best split over two days – it is wise to be selective about the duration of your stops.
• **Distance from Calais to start point: 60** miles. No Motorway Tolls
• **Base towns:** Ieper, Poperinge
• **Maps:** *Major & Mrs Holt's Battle Map of the Ypres Salient* plus best of all are *the Carte de Belgique* 1:25,000 Nos. 20/5-6, 28/1-2, 28/3-4, and 28/5-6. *The Carte de Belgique* No. 28 IEPER 1:50,000 is coloured and covers the whole area and shows the road changes, including the motorway. IGN 2 Lille/Dunkerque 1:100,000 covers the area.

From Calais take the A16/A26 signed Dunkerque. At Grande Synthe take Exit 28 to the A25 to the right signed Lille, Ypres. Take Exit 13 at Steenvoorde on the D948 and follow signs to Ypres (Ieper). Cross the border (no longer manned) and continue on the D948/N38 towards Poperinge to a sign to the right to Lijssenthoek Cemetery.

Extra Visits to Lijssenthoek Military CWGC Cemetery & Visitor's Centre (Lat & Long: 50.82840 2.701661) and Talbot House & Poperinge Walking Tour (Map 6/1b/RWC/Lat & Long: 50.85593 2.72288) Mileage: 2.0 miles. Approximate time: 2.0 hours

Turn right and continue following CWGC signs to the right to **Lijssenthoek CWGC Cemetery.**

At the back of the cemetery was the old railway line. This spur from the Poperinghe line was built to carry supplies to the front and the wounded back to the CCS's. The Sidings were named from the farm owned by Remi (sometimes seen as Remy) Quaghebeur beside the line, whose buildings still remain today. During the war the farm's barns acted as a shelter. As at Godewaersvelde (see Approach Two), there were many air raids at Lijssenthoek. The French first used the farm as an Evacuation Hospital in May 1915 and theirs are the earliest burials in this cosmopolitan cemetery and some of the latest, as they used it again in August 1918. In July 1915 the British established CCSs here and in August 1916 the 2nd Canadian CCS took over from the French. By August 1918 the area had developed into four large Field Hospitals with some 4,000 beds. It was now a virtual village with huts, streets, electricity unit, vegetable gardens, concerts and football pitches. During the June 1917 Messines Battle alone 5,000 casualties had arrived at Remi Siding. It had become the second largest war cemetery in the area.

The post-war cemetery, designed by Sir Reginald Blomfield, remains so today, with a

Extra Visit continued

total of over 10,800 burials - 7,369 known UK plus 23 Unknown, 1,131 Australian, 1,058 Canadian, 21 British West Indies, 3 Indian, 5 Newfoundland, 291 New Zealand, 28 South African plus 1 Unknown, 35 Chinese Labourers, 233 German – including many graves in which more than one soldier is buried, and 1 ex-soldier employed by the CWGC. There are 8 Special Memorials near the Stone of Remembrance to men Known to be Buried in the Cemetery.

There are also two American burials – **Lt James A. Pigue** and **Harry A. King** of the 3rd US Cavalry who died of pneumonia on 20 September 1918, and whose brother, **Private Reginald King** of the ASC, attd 25th Siege Battery RGA, killed on 17 October 1917, is also buried here.

Other burials of interest (although each one, of course, was of immense interest to his friends and family) are: **Staff Nurse N. Spindler** of the QA Imp Mil Nursing Service, killed on 21 August 1917, and **Maj-Gen Malcolm Smith Mercer**, CB, killed on 3 June 1916, commanding the 3rd Canadian Division; **Brig-Gen Hugh Gregory Fitton, CB, DSO,** killed on 20 January 1916, commanding 101st Inf Bde, 34th Div; **Brig-Gen A. F. Gordon,** CMG, DSO, killed on 31 July 1917, commanding 153rd Inf Bde, the 51st Highland Div; **Brig-Gen R. C. Gore CB, CMG,** killed on 13 April 1918, commanding 101st Inf Bde, 34th Div, are also buried here, as is the **Rev Charles Edmund Doudney** (qv) who died of his wounds on 16 October 1915. He was given a full military funeral, the Service being conducted by 6th Div's Senior Chaplain, which was attended by 'five or six of his fellow chaplains'. **Capt James Ernest Studholme Wilson, MC,** RAMC (attd Ox & Bucks), age 51, was the subject of a poem written by surviving comrades during a 1930 Pilgrimage. It describes how this much-loved MO was hit by a splinter during a raid near Wijtschate. He was taken to a Dressing Station– overflowing with the dead and dying – where he died whilst undergoing surgery.

There is a separate register for the 658 French burials.

The trees and shrubs are particularly beautiful in this forbiddingly vast cemetery, especially the willows and wistaria. The CWGC nurseries which adjoined the cemetery for many years have been closed as they were not competitive with local commercial nurseries. .

Visitors' Centre. On 21 September 2012 an unmanned Visitors'/Interpretation Centre, sited parallel to the small north-eastern side entrance to the Cemetery, with parking area and WC block, was opened. The architect Luc Vandewynckel was influenced by the shape of the wartime huts, barracks and hospitals. Its entrance is sunk 1 metre below grass level and it then rises to a glass structure with panoramic views. A path leads to the original entrance to the cemetery, on one side of which is a row of 1,392 poles, representing the days on which at least one person was buried in the Cemetery.

The Centre tells the history of the Field Hospitals, of the CWGC (which has its nurseries adjacent to the cemetery) and of how the Cemetery is a mirror of what was happening at the front, as for every day of the year there is at least one grave. Personal stories and photos etc are being collected on a database system to tell a different 'Daily Story' 365 days of the year of men who are buried in this multinational Cemetery. Visitors will be able to print out a plan of the cemetery showing the location of the subject of the day's story. A 9metre 'Touch Table' gives access to the database and shows archaeological finds discovered during the construction, another shows contributions from relatives. One external wall is a 'Listening Wall' which recounts extracts from letters, diaries, hospital reports etc. Another is a 'Portrait Wall' with more than 1,000 portraits of men buried here. **Open** 0900-1800, free entrance, disabled access., For group visits contact toerisme@poperinge.be. Tel: + (0) 57 34 66 76.

Lijssenthoek CWGC Cemetery.

Headstone of an American Doughboy, James A. Pigue.

Visitors' Centre, Lijssenthoek.

Extra Visit continued

Contact Annemie Morisse at lijssenthoek@poperinge.be if you can contribute any information or need help with research about those buried in the Cemetery or the hospitals, and see also www.lijssenthoek.be Annemie wrote a superbly detailed article about the Cemetery and its history following the research project started at Talbot House (qv) in June 2009 which was published in the WFA *Bulletin* of Oct/Nov 2009.

An interesting App – 'Diary 14-15' is available for download on the App Store and Android Market.

Return to the main road. Continue on the N38, follow signs to Poperinge Centrum and park in the main Market Square.

Known as 'the last stop before Hell', **Poperinghe** (as it was known during WW1) was the BEF's principal town behind the lines and was never taken by the Germans although it suffered occasional heavy shelling. The town teemed with shops, estaminets (segregated for officers and ORs), restaurants, hostels, concert halls, cabarets and cinemas, brothels and other facilities for the troops coming out of the line for rest and refreshment. The YMCA and the Church Army were well-represented. Today it makes a good base for touring the Salient.

In the square is the picturesque Town Hall with the **Tourist Office** (Tel: + (0) 57 34 66 76) in the basement. They have literature on Poperinghe during the Great War. Behind it is the **Execution Post** where at least 5 men were shot during the war and beside it the cells where the men were kept. There is an audio presentation by Chaplain Ray Jones and others. The site was redesigned in 2012.

Walk to the far end of the square.

On the left is the famous **Café de Ranke**, popular with officers during the war, mainly because of the charms of the daughter of the house, 'Ginger', and the liberally flowing champagne.

Walk up Gasthuisstraat.

At No 12 was another popular officer's club, nicknamed Skindles. It is now a pharmacy.

Continue to No 43.

Talbot House. Still hanging outside the elegant building where Padre Philip Byard (Tubby) Clayton started a rest house which inspired the movement which is now world-wide, is a sign which states, 'Talbot House 1915-? Every Man's Club'. This extraordinary club was named after Gilbert Talbot, son of the Bishop of Winchester, who was killed in the Salient and is buried in Sanctuary Wood Cemetery (qv). Tommy shortened the name in Army signallers' language to 'Toc H'. It had the atmosphere of a home, where the men, weary and frightened from a spell in the trenches of the Salient, could come, whatever their rank, and be refreshed physically and spiritually.

Talbot House was officially opened on 11 December 1915, in the empty house of the banker and hop merchant, Maurice Coevoet. It operated on 'the Robin Hood principle of taking from the rich to give to the poor', maintained Tubby, another of whose occasional nicknames was 'Boniface' (after the innkeeper in George Farquhar's *The Beaux Stratagem*). Tubby had a marvellous knack of wheedling supplies, furniture and other domestic items from all and sundry. According to *Tales from Talbot House*, for 5 francs officers arriving from the leave train at one a.m. secured cocoa and Oliver biscuits or before departure at 5 a.m. a cold meat breakfast. Other ranks did not pay until June 1916 when the officers were "thrown out" to Skindles (see above). Until then they (but never other ranks) could get a bed.

Only one soldier was killed in Talbot House during the war. He was Sgt G.J.M. Pegg, ASC CEF, who was mortally wounded by a shell that hit the side of The House on 28 May 1916. He is buried in Poperinghe New Mil Cemetery (qv).

From April 1918 the Germans pressed ever closer to Ypres, Kemmel fell, defensive

Talbot House.

'Tubby' Clayton, the Chaplain.

The Execution Post, Poperinge Town Hall.

Piano exhibit, Talbot House Museum.

Extra Visit continued

lines were hastily built around Poperinghe, great expanses of countryside between Dunkirk and St Omer were flooded. Poperinghe was evacuated of civilians; cinemas, shops and other entertainments closed down. Alone Toc H remained open. But it was heavily shelled and eventually 'imperative orders to leave at once' were received. It closed on Whit Tuesday, 21 May to re-open on 30 September at the end of Fourth Ypres.

In 1919 Tubby founded the Toc H movement and in 1929 Lord Wakefield of Hythe, at the instigation of Major Paul Slessor (who gave his name, to the 'Slessorium' – originally a bath house for post-war pilgrims – built in the garden in 1930 and to whom there is a memorial plaque in the hall), put up sufficient funds to buy the Old House. He also bought the 'Pool of Peace' or Spanbroekmolen crater at Wijtschate (qv) for Toc H.

During World War II the Germans occupied Poperinghe on 29 May 1940. One report, as yet unconfirmed, says they requisitioned Talbot House on 13 July and in 1943 used it as billets for the Kriegsmarine. On 6 September 1944, Polish troops liberated the town and all the precious contents, whisked away by local sympathisers as the Germans moved in, were soon restored. On 10 September the house re-opened, with its original purpose to act as a rest house for British soldiers.

Many original artefacts, pictures (including portraits by one of the ninety-odd official war artists, Eric Kennington) and signs remain to be seen, witness of Tubby's relaxed attitude and the sense of humour which made him so special. 'All rank abandon ye who enter here' was his motto, inscribed over his, the Chaplain's, room.

The chapel on the top floor, with its carpenter's bench which served as an altar, looks much the same as in the days when over 20,000 officers and soldiers received the Sacrament there before going into the trenches. In 1922 Barclay Baron, a founder member of Talbot House, suggested that the form of an early Christian lamp should become the symbol of Toc H ('as dim as a Toc H lamp' was a popular post-war phrase). The lamp was first lit by the Prince of Wales in 1923. In the well-tended, tranquil garden, which gave rest to many a man from the shattered landscape of the Salient, is an obelisk-shaped Mié Tabé Peace Post (qv) inaugurated on 24 September 1988.

On 24 October 1996, the Talbot House Association finally succeeded in purchasing the adjacent old hop store which Tubby had also used. Once more it forms an integral part of the Old House. The Association also owns and runs The House and provides guides and members of staff to look after it. Their Chief Executive is Mrs Annelies Vermeulen, e-mail talbot.house@skynet.be.

The House has had a succession of wardens and guides. Much research has been done by The Secretary, Mr Jan Louagie and his wife, authors of *Talbot House – Poperinghe, 'First Stop After Hell'*.

Talbot House provides clean and comfortable self-catering accommodation at a reasonable price. It makes an excellent base for touring the Salient. It is extremely popular – there is something very special about staying in this Club, so redolent of the Great War and the men who peopled it – and booking well in advance is advised.

Until 2003 The House was entered through the imposing front door in Gasthuisstraat but on 15 May 2004 the new reception area with a shop and toilets and the large exhibition area was opened in the old Hop Store with an entrance in Pottestraat (turn first right after the building on Gasthuisstraat). The old building has been extensively renovated and reinforced for the purpose. The exhibition is based on 'Life in the Poperinge area during The First World War' and is conceived as Tubby's 'photo album' showing the various aspects of life in the British sector. A new glass extension with a lift gives access to the first and second floors of the Hop Store and to the garden (in which there are some informative plaques). The Slessorium houses an audio-visual presentation in which Tubby shows the visitor around Talbot House and Skindles plus some illustrations and

---

Extra Visit continued

documents on Little Talbot House in Ypres. It includes Tubby's original 'hut' which was located at Proven in 'Dingley Dell'. On the first floor of the Hop Store the wartime Concert Hall has been restored to its 1917 aspect and shows a recreation of a wartime concert party (filmed with a live audience in January 2004). The second floor is used as a documentation and archives area and is not generally is part of the regular visitor circuit but can be booked by school parties for lectures and working sessions.

Entrance fee payable. **Open:** daily except for Mondays: 1000-1200 and 1400-1700.

Tel: + (0) 57 33 32 28. Fax: + (0) 57 33 21 83.

E-mail: info@talbot.house.be **Website:** www.talbothouse.be

Visits for groups must be booked in advance.

Walk back to your car and rejoin the N38.

Continue on the N38 and follow signs into the centre of Ieper and park in the Grand' Place (Main Square) in front of the large cathedral-like building (small parking fee from meter).

This is the Cloth Hall. The actual Cathedral (St Martin's) is behind it and there is more parking in front of it. In the Cloth Hall are the **Tourist Office** and *In Flanders Fields* Museum. We suggest a walking tour from here to the following places:-

• In Flanders Fields Museum/Regional Visitors' Centre, Boutique & Cafeteria, Cloth Hall/0 miles/2 hours 15 minutes for complete Ypres Tour/Map 6/1/Lat & Long: 50.85128 2.88683

In the 35 years since we have been visiting the Salient the Museum has undergone a series of metamorphoses. From the simple Museum on the ground floor run by Caretaker Albert Beke, it moved in 1998 to the first floor but retained its 'object-led' type of presentation. Some years later following an important investment from the EC, West Flanders, Ieper and other sponsors, it was totally modernised using up to date technology and fewer 'objects'. At this stage it adopted its current name after John McCrae's 1915 poem (qv).

NOW a major redesign of the **Museum, Tourist Office**, Boutique and Offices opened on June 2012 in time for the series of 100th Anniversaries which start in 2014. The new Museum occupies virtually the entire Cloth Hall (other than municipal offices), after internal walls were knocked down to return it to its original vast, impressive open space.

It incorporates the Documentation Centre (qv) which moved into spacious accommodation from its cramped HQ in the Stedelijke Museum (qv) facilitating easy access to its enormous and important library, collections and archives. An important project is to make cemetery registers for the Belgian, French, German and Missing of the Belgian Front and local historians and schools are working on the fascinating task of superimposing current maps of the area on trench maps of various stages of the battles. Their new address is 3 Sint-Maartensplein. Known as "**The Knowledge Centre**"it is accessible Mon-Fri from 1000 to 1500, with entry on Sint-Maartensplein (Square between Cloth Hall and Cathedral). This is a most impressive research facility, with its many computers for accessing information. **Contacts:** Piet Chielens and Dominiek Dendooven.

The Flemish Chief Architect, heritage experts, local, regional and Government authorities were involved in the Euro 10 million project together with the competition-winning new architects. Cloakroom, elevator and cafeteria facilities are improved and the Museum itself changed from the current linear to a circular format. There is greater emphasis on landscape-related items, such as archaeological evidence, (using models of Hill 60, Bellewaerde Ridge etc), personal histories and encounters with events at specific place at a specific time. Although the latest cutting edge technology is used where appropriate, there is also a return to acknowledging the power of personal possessions, artefacts, ephemera etc. It is considered that as the last human witness of the war, Harry Patch (qv), has now disappeared, the land itself will indeed remain – 'The Last

Witness' and there will be more need for material objects as evidence, as time goes by. The scope of the Museum widens to cover the Belgian WW1 Front from Ostende and Nieupoort, through the Salient, Roeselare and Menin to the French border at Armentières and the Lys. Visitors 'log in' with an ingenious wristband, giving their country and district of origin so that the stories they will see and hear in the various showcases and computer screens will relate to their personal and cultural experience. The stories are told chronologically: one from the home front; one from the opponent's point of view and two chronological histories of the war covering:

1. The area pre-WW1: growing wealth; nationalism and the sensitive Flemish-Walloon situation
2. Visitors then cross over a huge steel plate, following the path of the German invasion through Liège to the Marne.
3. The story of the War on Belgian soil then unfolds.
4. 'Remembrance' is the theme of the final section - the war graves and memorials

There are imaginative displays, such as those of uniforms and weapons, suspended on high boards, some familiar friends from former museums, such as the horse struggling in the mud and some superb contemporary photographs. At the centre is the amazing Belfry Experience. Once again visitors (maximum 20 at a time, and with a small additional fee) are able to mount the 205 stairs (with stops to catch breath at several platforms (including the one from which cats have traditionally been thrown). At the top (provided they are svelte enough to get through the final narrow entrance) they will be rewarded by stunning views over the Salient from beyond the Yser Tower to Cassel. Over 15,000 aerial photos are projected on multi-touch LCD screens which have the capacity of zooming in on monuments, cemeteries and important sites on the map of the entire front - even interesting architectural features of individual buildings.

Tourist Officer Peter Slosse and Museum Director Piet Chielens in the museum boutique.

Activation Wristband, In Flanders Fields Museum.

The horse struggling in the mud, In Fkanders Fields Museum.

Behind the medieval reproduction façade, the Belfry was constructed with then-modern techniques and construction material in the '20s, such as concrete beams, and the carillon will be an interesting part of the story told in it.

Opening times: 1 April-15 November 1000-1800, every day. 16 November-31 March 1000-1700, closed on Mondays, Christmas and New Year's Day and the first three weeks after the Christmas holidays. Ticket sales stop one hour before closing time. Entrance fee payable with special rates for students and groups.

Contact: Cloth Hall, Grote Markt 34, 8900 Ieper. Tel: 57 23 92 20. Fax: 57 23 92 75

E-mail: Flandersfields@ieper.be   Website; www.inflandersfields.be

Entry is through the **Tourist Office**, Visitor's Centre & Boutique, selling souvenirs, books and maps (still occupying their old position but in a much enlarged space). After the **exit** are smart **Cafeteria** facilities.

*Leave the museum on foot via the archway at the corner of the Nieuwerke with the **Kleine Stadhuis Restaurant** and continue left around the building (in which, incidentally, there are good public toilets).*

Opposite is St Martin's Cathedral in which there are several WW1 Memorials, including the standard **Cathedral Tablet by H.P. Cart de Lafontaine**, a **Memorial to the RAF** and to **French Forces** and the **Memorial to King Albert**.

Turn right on Coomensstraat. St George's Church is on the far corner on the opposite side of the road to the cathedral.

CWGC Tablet, St Martin's Cathedral, Ypres.

• St George's Memorial Church/Map 6/2/Lat & Long: 50.85237 2.88288

The idea of having a British Memorial Church or Chapel in Ypres was raised formally as early as 1920 when the Church Army appealed for donations to establish a building fund. In 1924 Sir John French, who had taken the title Earl of Ypres, added his voice to the call and the foundation stone was laid on Sunday, 24 July 1927. On 24 March 1929 the church was dedicated by the Right Reverend Bishop of Fulham. As a tribute to the 342 old Etonians who fell in the Salient the College provided the 'British School' which is next door to the church and is now used as the Church Hall. Services are held every Sunday and on 11 November each year the congregation is swelled by hundreds of people from all over Britain and further afield and spills into the nearby theatre or the Cloth Hall.

Every item in the church is a memorial, from the beautiful stained-glass windows to the chairs, on each of which is a brass plate naming the missing loved one. On the south wall of the church is a bust of Sir John French and on either side of it memorials to Field Marshal Montgomery and Sir Winston Churchill who both served in the Salient. New memorials continue to be erected, for the church now commemorates the fallen of both World Wars. A few minutes contemplation in this home of memory brings gentle pride in the solid beliefs of the men who fought for King and Country and there is sadness too that so many had to suffer, both on the battlefield and left alone at home. It is right to remember the sacrifice and the penalties and here it can be done without pomp or circumstance. The church is usually open and there are postcards available on a table beside the door, a visitors' book to be signed and a collection box. Tel: + (0) 57 21 56 85. Churchwarden email: ricky.beets@orange.fr The current Chaplain is Fr Brian Llewellyn.

Return past the Cathedral and walk up the Menin Road to the Menin Gate.

St George's Church with detail of the colourful kneelers.

• The Menin Gate, Model for the Blind, Indian Memorial, RB Australian Memorial/Map 6/3/Lat & Long: 50.85217 2.89166

Winston Churchill said of Ypres, 'A more sacred place for the British race does not exist in the world', and proposed that the town be left in ruins as an eternal memorial to the million men who fought in the Salient. The townspeople had other ideas and began to rebuild their homes, and it was agreed that on the site of an old Vauban gateway from Ypres on the road to Menin, the road taken by tens of thousands of British soldiers on their way to the trenches, a memorial arch should be constructed. Work under Sir Reginald Blomfield began in 1923. The material used was French limestone and the arch is 80 ft high, 135 ft long and 104 ft wide. It was unveiled on 24 July 1927 by Field Marshal Plumer (the same day that he laid the foundation stone of St George's Church) in the presence of the King of the Belgians and many thousands of veterans and relatives of the Fallen. The whole ceremony was transmitted by wireless by the BBC and the Last Post was sounded at the Gate for the first time. Carved over all the walls of the great gate, inside, up the stairs and around the top on each side overlooking the ramparts are the names of almost 55,000 soldiers who fell in the Salient between the beginning of the war and 15 August 1917. They simply disappeared.

In his address Lord Plumer said, 'It can be said of each one in whose honour we are assembled here today, "He is not missing, he is here".'

Among the 54,000 names recorded on its panels – each important to those who mourn – are the poets **Lt John Collinson Hobson**, MGC, killed on 31 July 1917, **Lt Walter Scott Stuart Lyon** (qv), Royal Scots, killed on 8 May 1915, **Capt the Hon C.E.A. Philipps** (qv), RHG killed on 13 May 1915, and **Lt Gerald George Samuel**, RWK, killed on 7 June 1917.

Also listed are **2nd Lt Henry Anthony Birrell-Anthony**, 1st Bn the Monmouthshire Regt, killed on 8 May 1915, who is mentioned on the Monmouth Memorial at St Julien; **Lt Aidan Chavasse** of the 17th King's Liverpool Regiment, missing in action on 4 July 1917 (youngest brother of Noel Chavasse (qv), the Double VC winner); **Lt the Hon W.A.M. ('Bill') Eden**, KRRC, killed on 3 March 1915, cousin of Anthony Eden; **2nd Lt the Hon Gerald William ('Billy') Grenfell**, Rifle Brigade, brother of the poet Julian Grenfell; **Lt Alexis Helmer**, 1st Bde Field Artillery, inspiration for John McCrae's poem *In Flanders Fields*, killed on 2 May 1915; **2nd Lt Arthur Oscar Hornung**, Attd 2nd Bn the Essex Regiment, killed on 6 July 1915, son of E. W. Hornung, creator of Raffles, the 'Gentleman Burglar' and nephew of Conan Doyle; **L/Cpl Thomas ('Pat') Rafferty** of the R Warwicks, Bruce Bairnsfather's inspiration for 'Old Bill'; three men who were executed: **Driver T. Moore**, of 24 Div Train ASC, shot on 26 February 1916, for murder, **Cpl George Povey** of the Cheshire Regt, shot on 11 February 1915, **Pte W Scotton** of the 4th Middlesex, shot on 3 February 1915.

Victoria Cross Winners commemorated are **L/Cpl Frederick Fisher** of the Quebec Regt, killed on 24 April 1915; **Brig-Gen Charles FitzClarence** of the Irish Guards, killed on 12 November 1914 near Polygon Wood commanding the 1st Guards Brigade (a Boer War VC); **Sgt Maj F.W. Hall** of the 8th Manitoba Regt, killed on 25 April 1915; **2nd Lt Dennis George Wyldbore Hewitt** of the 14th Hampshires, killed on 31 July 1917; **Capt John Franks Vallentin**, 1st S Staffs, killed on 7 November 1914; **Pte Edward Warner**, 1st Beds, killed on 2 May 1915, near Hill 60 and **2nd Lt Sidney Woodroffe** of the Rifle Brigade, killed on 30 July 1915, friend of, and subject of a poem by, the poet Charles Sorley (qv).

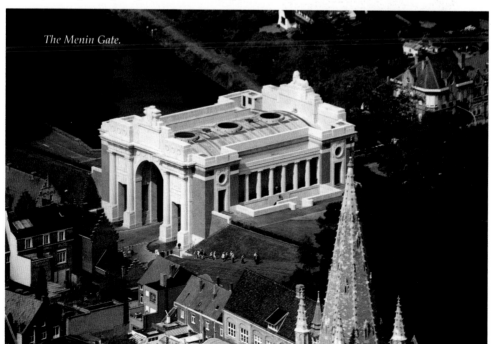

The Menin Gate.

Pte James Smith of the 1st Bn the Black Watch, killed on 31 October 1914, has the Regimental Number '1'. **Capt A.E.B. O'Neill** of the 2nd Life Guards was the first Member of Parliament (for Mid Antrim) to be killed in the war on 6 November 1914. Brothers-in-law of the 1st Life Guards, **Capt Lord Hugh Grosvenor** (son of the Duke of Westminster) and **Lt the Hon Gerald Ward, MVO** (son of the 1st Earl of Dudley) both disappeared in the fighting of 30 October 1914, at Zantvoorde.

Note that the UK names inscribed on the wall are for the period up to 15 August 1917, after which date they were inscribed on the Memorial Wall at Tyne Cot. The names of Australians, Canadians, Indians and South Africans are for the entire duration of the war: they have no names on the Tyne Cot Memorial. There are no New Zealand names on the wall – they have their own memorials throughout the Salient.

On the town side at the top of the arch is a sarcophagus, while looking down the Menin Road is a British lion sculpted by Sir Reid Dick RA. Under each is an inscription by Kipling (after whom the street to the left beyond the arch is named).

At ground level in the pillars are the bronze boxes containing the Memorial Reports with details of those commemorated, first in regimental order and then by name. The ramparts should be visited above the Gate, access being via the stairways to each side of the centre.

Walk up the steps on the left hand side (facing the Cloth Hall). At the top is

Model of the Menin Gate. This 1.9m long, 1.05m wide bronze model stands on a socle of Portland Stone and has a Braille text in 4 languages. It was cast by Dirk de Groeve and funded by the local Kiwanis Club (who also sponsored the Cloth Hall model in the Grand' Place). It was unveiled on 20 September 2003 by the blind Belgian singer, Séverine Doré.

Indian Memorial. Beyond it a white stone **Indian Monument** was unveiled on 10 November 2002 as part of the 'Flanders India 2002 Partnership Year' by Major-General A.J. Bajwa who had come all

The Indian Memorial, Menin Gate Ramparts.

the way from India for the ceremony. It commemorates the 130,000 Indian troops who served in France and Belgium during WW1 in a landscape and culture totally alien to them. By the end of the war 1,100,000 Indians, all of them volunteers, had served overseas, earning 9,200 gallantry awards including 11 Victoria Crosses. Over 74,000 were killed, of whom 447 are commemorated on the Menin Gate. On 12 March 2011 it was replaced, a little further along the Ramparts, by a splendid new Memorial depicting the lion emblems of King Ashoka, the symbol of Peace and Power. It lists the major battles of the Indian Forces, 9,000 of whom were killed in Flanders.

On top of the embankment on the grass beside the right-hand loggia and near the Australian names is a **Ross Bastiaan bronze Australian tablet**, showing a *bas relief* map of the Salient. It was unveiled on 1 September 1993, by the Hon Bill Haydon, the Governor General of Australia.

It is possible to walk around the beautifully renovated ramparts to the Lille (Rijsel) Gate.

Return to your car and leave the Square, driving out round the Cloth Hall and turning left past St George's Church on Elverdingsestraat.

N.B. The HQ of the CWGC (Lat & Long: 50.85149 2.87738) is on the right at no 82, with flagpoles outside. Tel: + (0) 57 20 01 18. Fax: + (0) 57 21 80 14. **E-mail:** neaoffice@cwgc.org

---

Continue to the first roundabout and turn right signed A19, Veurne. Continue to the next roundabout and turn right on the N379 signed Centrum and turn left at the next junction signed Diksmuide on the N369. Continue under the motorway bridge to the British war cemetery on the right with flagpoles. Stop.

• Essex Farm CWGC Cemetery/Albertina Memorial/Dressing Station/ 49th (W Riding) Div Memorial/2.3 miles/25 minutes/Map 6/4, 6/5, 6/6/Lat & Long: 50.87109 2.87276

Outside the cemetery is an Albertina Memorial to the poet John McCrae (qv), unveiled on 15 November 1985 by the Governor of West Flanders and executed by the sculptor Pieter-Hein Boudens of Bruges. Unlike the other Albertina Memorials (qv), McCrae's bears a poppy instead of King Albert's Royal Cipher. To the left of the cemetery is a commercial building and behind it some concrete dugouts. Between 1915 and 1917 these were used as a dressing station. The path to the canal leads to the site of the notorious 'Bridge 4'. Third Ypres casualties from the 51st (Highland) and 38th (Welsh) Divisions were treated here.

Canadian Medical Officer Colonel **John McCrae**, who had served with the Artillery in the Boer War, had written what is perhaps the war's best-known poem, *In Flanders Fields*, when he served in what was then a simple earthen dugout dressing station in the spring of 1915. On 24 April McCrae wrote home with one of the most vivid and moving accounts of the Second Battle of Ypres. He saw the 'asphyxiated French soldiers' and streams of civilian refugees – 'the very picture of debacle'. By 25 April the Canadians had lost 6,000 of their strength of 10,000. The shelling was unremitting and the small cemetery beside the dressing station grew daily. On 2 May, one of McCrae's patients and a friend, Lt Alexis Helmer, was virtually blown to pieces by a direct hit by an 8in shell. McCrae was touched by the last words in Helmer's diary, 'It has quieted a little and I shall try to get a good sleep'. McCrae said the committal service over Helmer's body. 'A soldier's death,' he commented. A wooden cross was put over Helmer's grave and the Colonel was moved to write his famous lines,

In Flanders fields the poppies blow
Between the crosses, row on row,
That mark our place...

The poem was published in *Punch* on 8 December 1915, and became an instant popular success. In 1918, Moira Michael who worked with the American YMCA, suggested that a poppy be worn 'in honour of our dead', following which Earl Haig decided to use the poppy as the symbol of the newly formed British Legion.

Helmer's grave was lost in the subsequent fighting over the ground and he is commemorated on the Menin Gate.

In the early spring of 1995 extensive restoration began in the concrete bunkers of the dressing station at the joint initiative of the Ieper Town Council, Talbot House and local school children. It was completed in time for the eightieth anniversary of the writing of McCrae's poem on 3 May 1995, when an impressive ceremony was held. Now the various chambers which housed the Officers' Mess, the wards for walking cases and stretcher cases, the latrines, the mess kitchen, the area for the wounded to be evacuated, the stores and offices – all built in 1916/17 – can once again clearly be seen. At the entrance are bronze plaques placed by the Historic Sites & Monuments Board of Canada with a brief summary of McCrae's career and his famous poem.

The sheer volume of visitors to this site was overwhelming it and in spring 2003 extensive landscaping was undertaken, leading visitors on gravel paths to the 49th Div Memorial and to the canal bank 'to spread the load' with Information Boards along the way.

The Cemetery contains 1,088 UK, 9 Canadian, 102 Unknown, 5 German prisoners and 19 special memorials. They include **15-year-old Private V.J. Strudwick** of 8th Bn the Rifle Brigade, killed on 14 January 1916, and **Pte Thomas Barratt, VC,** of the 7th Bn the S Staffs Regt who on 27 July 1917, acted as the scout to a successful patrol, killing two German snipers and covering the patrol's withdrawal, but was killed by a shell on his return. Also buried here is **Lt Frederick Leopold Pusch,** DSO, of the 1st Bn Irish Guards, age 20, killed on 27 June 1916. A silver memorial cup, inscribed to Lt Pusch – 'M. H. 1908-

Heeadstone of 15-year-old Pte Strudwick, with student tributes, Essex Farm CWGC Cemetery.

1910', was found by the authors in the shop at Delville Wood Museum on the Somme. His 19-year-old brother, 2nd Lt E. J. Pusch of the 11th Bn the Royal Warwickshires, was killed on 19 August 1916, and is buried in Flatiron Copse CWGC Cemetery on the Somme. **Lt Donald Campbell** of the Coldstream Guards, killed on 19 July 1916 is buried here and is the son of Capt the Hon John B Campbell, DSO, age 48, of the same regiment, who had been killed on 25 January 1915, and is commemorated on the Le Touret Memorial.

Behind the cemetery on the canal bank is the **Memorial Column to the 49th (West Riding) Division.** The 49th, a Territorial Division, came out early in 1915. It had the dubious distinctions of being, together with 6th Division, one of the first to face a phosgene attack when the two divisions suffered over 1,000 casualties from the gas alone and in the winter of 1915 having more than 400 cases of trench foot in just one battalion. Trench foot was the result of prolonged standing in water in flooded trenches. The feet swelled to football-sized proportions and became painfully sensitive to the extent that the sufferer found it virtually impossible to walk and hence became unfit for duty. The memorial was inaugurated in 1924.

Continue on the N369 past the turn off to the village of Boezinge and take the first turning to the right signed Langemark. Continue over the canal and take the second right signed Ieper. Continue along the canal bank to the left turn on Bargiestraat at the Biovita buildings with flags and follow the road to the left to the site.

Essex Farm Bunker Dressing Station.

McCrae Albertina marker, Essex Farm.

Memorial to 49th (West Riding) Division, Essex Farm.

• Boezinge Archaeological Battlefield Site-Yorkshire Trench/5.5 miles/15 minutes/Map 6/7/Lat & Long: 50.88778 2.87403

This is the site, first explored by the 'Diggers' (a team of amateur archaeologists) in February 1992 of an important trench and dugout system known as Yorkshire Trench. The incredibly well-preserved 'A' frames and other original elements discovered in the retentive Flanders blue clay mud have been incorporated in a representation of the system in the In Flanders Fields Museum. At the site itself the Town of Ieper have recreated the trench and entrance to the dugout, with realistic looking sandbags and duckboards, with several explanatory panels, inaugurated in May 2003.

Turn round and return to the Langemark-Poelkapelle road and turn right on Langemarkseweg.

Yorkshire Trench Preserved Trenches, Industrial Estate, Boezinge.

• Pilckem Ridge Memorials and Cemeteries/Travel time if stopping at each stop: 40 minutes

You are now travelling along the **Pilckem Ridge** and will pass the following places of interest:
Breton Memorial/ 6.9 miles (Map 6/8, Lat & Long: 50.89724 2.87429).
Artillery Wood CWGC Cemetery/7.00 miles (Lat & Long: 50.89967 2.87256), where the poets 'Hedd Wyn' and Francis Ledwidge are buried. It is signed to the left and the Irish flag flies over the **Ledwidge Memorial (Map 6/8a)** on the corner to the left as you turn.

Plaques to the poet 'Hedd Wyn' (Ellis Humphrey Evans)/8.3 miles (**Map 6/9, Lat & Long: 50.90328 2.90097)**. The Plaques are on the house on the right just before the crossroads (Iron Cross) where Ruisseau Farm CWGC Cemetery is signed to the left. **Welsh National Memorial. (Lat & Long: 50.90304 2.90010)**. Plans are now well underway to recognise the success of the Welsh with a Memorial, not only to the 38th Welsh on the Pilckem Ridge, but (as with the Scottish Memorial at Frezenburg), to all Welsh Forces who made the ultimate sacrifice during WW1. As at Mametz it will take the form of a Welsh Dragon, but this time in bronze, painted red, on a Cromlech of Welsh stone from the Graig yr Hesg Quarry, Pontypridd (the stones actually arrived in July 2013). The Memorial will be on land donated by the Langemarck Council at the corner of the field just before the buildings. It is planned to be unveiled on 16 August 2014, subject to the raising of some £40,000 required. It will be surrounded by a Garden of Remembrance.
The project is supported by and donations may be made via:
1. The Welsh Memorial in Flanders Campaign. **Contact:** Co-ordinator, Peter Jones, Tel: 01639730838 E-mail: p.carterjay@gmail.com or Patron, Lt Col Ian R Gumm, Tel: 01989 565599.
2. The Passchendaele Society. **Contact:** Chairman Freddy Declerck, Tel: + (0) 474 913 246, or Erwin Ureel, e-mail: erwin.ureel@gmail.com
3. Dedicated enthusiast Marc Decaester, owner of the Feestzaal Caracas and Sportsman Pub opposite (where he always has an interesting display) and his brother-in-law Mario Liva, who made the Hedd Wyn Plaque above. On the first Monday of each month they raise the Welsh flag and hold a commemorative event. See also "STOP PRESS" on page 333 for an illustration.

Cement House CWGC Cemetery on the right/8.5 miles. (**Map 6/10, Lat & Long: 50.90497 2.90682)**. The name originates from a nearby fortified farm building. The cemetery was started in August 1917, during Third Ypres, and used until April 1918. After the war burials from over 15 other cemeteries were concentrated here. There are now almost 3,600 burials of whom 67% are

Plaques to Hedd Wyn, Decaestecker (left) and Mario Liva.

Memorial to Irish poet, Francis Ledwidge, Artillery Wood.

unidentified, a measure of the severity of the fighting. The cemetery remains open for new burials of bodies discovered on the battlefields.

Continue to the road junction.

N.B. By, turning left and then right again along a track (just before the '100m/Cycle Path/Bend' sign) to a rather difficult-to-spot low memorial to the left on the bank of the stream, you will reach the

Memorial to Harry Patch (Map 6/12a/Lat & Long: 50.90979 2.90864)

In March 2008 the then-Poet Laureate Andrew Motion wrote a poem entitled, *The Five Acts of Harry Patch*, to honour Harry, the only surviving veteran of the Passchendaele battle and whose 110th birthday was on 17 June.

Later that year Harry decided to erect, at his own expense, this small Memorial. The inscription explains his desire:

"Here at dawn on 16 August 1917 the 7th Bn DCLI 20th (Light) Division, crossed the Steenbeek prior to their successful assault on the village of Langemarck. This stone is erected to the memory of fallen comrades and to honour the courage, sacrifice and passing of 'The Great War Generation'. It is the gift of former Private and

Harry Patch's memorial, the Steenbeek and Langemarck church beyond.

Lewis Gunner, Harry Patch, No 29295, C Coy, 7th DCLI. The last surviving veteran to have served in the Trenches of **the Western Front. September 2008."**
Harry died on 25 July 2009, age 111 years, 1 month, 1 week, 1 day, then verified as the third oldest man in the world.

Continue straight over at the road junction.

N.B. On crossing the Steenbeek, on the bridge (known as Piccadilly Bridge during the war) to the left is an **Albertina Memorial (Map 6/11)** to mark the end of the Steenbeek Offensive.

Just beyond, on the left is
The **20th Light Division Memorial (Map 6/12, Lat & Long: 50.90836 2.91564).** The Division took the village from the Germans on 16 August 1917 during the Third Battle of Ypres.
Continue to the Langemark crossroads (once known as Trafalgar Square). Turn left (the restriction only applies to heavy vehicles) and follow signs to Diksmuide and 'Deutsche Soldaten Friedhof' over the old Ypres-Tourhout railway line and drive past the cemetery, turn left and park next to the Information Centre.

• *Langemarck German Cemetery & Information Centre/10.1 miles/30 minutes/Map 6/13/WC/ Lat & Long: 50.92164 2.91675*

This area was captured by the British 20th (Light) Division on 16 August during the Third Ypres offensive of 1917. It had been defended by the French in 1914 and lost on 22 April 1915 (Second Ypres) during the gas attack. In continuing operations in October 1917 the 4th Bn Worcester Regiment were ordered to push further north from here. On the evening of 7 October the battalion had marched out from Ypres following the route you have driven, turned right at Boezinghe and along the Pilckem Ridge via duckboards to the front line at the northern end of the cemetery. They were in position by dawn on 8 October and spent the day preparing for their assault. In the engagement that followed the next day a famous **VC** was won by **Private Frederick George Dancox**, a solid old soldier who captured a pillbox, taking 40 prisoners and the machine gun which was pinning the Worcesters down.

20th Light Division Memorial, Langemarck.

Dancox was due to go on leave to receive his award in December 1917 and his family and dignitaries of Worcester waited at Shrub Hill Station to greet him. Dancox never arrived. He had been killed at Masnières near Cambrai on 30 November. His body was never found (nor were the bodies of his brother and two step-brothers, all like Fred, of the Worcestershire Regiment) and he is commemorated on the Louverval Memorial.

Dancox Memorial Unveiling, Namur Crossing.

N.B. By turning left out of the car park and continuing some .7 mile to Galgestraat, a small road to the right, turning along it and continuing .6 mile, past a house on the right ,you arrive at a cycle path (at the old railway Line, Namur Crossing.) Here, (**Lat & Long: 50.92777 2.93660**), on 9 September 2006, a commemorative stainless steel **Plaque to Dancox,** designed by Sam Eedle (ex-London Scottish), was unveiled by his grandson, also called Fred Dancox (whose own son and grandson are also called 'Fred'). It is an initiative of the Worcestershire & Herefordshire WFA (notably Stephen Moorhouse), supported by the Dancox family, Worcester City Council, the Worcestershire Regt, the local commune and others. Representatives of all were present at the simple but moving inauguration ceremony at the 'Namur Crossing' on the disused railway line which is now a cycle path in the Langemark district of Madonna. The Plaque overlooks the site of the bunker – in a dip behind the bushy-topped tree - where Dancox's act of valour took place (see Map 6/13a).

The Cemetery is maintained by the *Volksbund Deutsche Kriegsgräberfürsorge* (qv) – and is the only German cemetery in the actual Salient. It is one of the largest German cemeteries in Belgium, with 44,292 bodies, and has an impressive entrance with two chambers, one with the names of the missing carved in oak, and the other bearing a relief map showing the past and present German cemeteries in Belgium and containing the Visitors' book and Cemetery Register. The cemetery is planted with oak trees, the symbol of German strength, and in the communal grave rest the remains of 25,000 soldiers – half of whose names are known. The four dramatic sculptures which overlook the cemetery were executed by Professor Emil Krieger and around the mass grave are the Regimental insignia of the student brigades who fought in this area. In the north wall of the cemetery are the remains of some massive German block-houses, doubtless similar to the one that Private Dancox captured.

In December 2004 a small bronze Plaque was attached to the end of the left hand column surrounding the mass grave. It commemorates **Pte A. Carlill**, Loyal North Lancs, 4 November 1918 and **Pte L.H. Lockley**, Seaforth Highlanders, 30 October 1918, both now known to be buried in the mass grave. Their names were located on the bronze panels (to be found by searching alphabetically, noting that Carlill is spelt 'Carhill' and Lockley is listed as 'Lookley') by researchers Michel Vansuyt and Michel Van den Bogaert. Carlill was originally recorded by the CWGC as being buried in Louvain Communal Cemetery, German Plot and listed on the Loos Memorial, while Lockley was listed in Jemappes Communal Cemetery.

On 26 August 2006 an Information Centre was unveiled on land adjoining the cemetery to the north – a joint initiative of West Flanders, the Commune of Langemarck and the *Kriegrsgräbefürsorge*. In a black tunnel which is precisely the same length as the mass grave in the

Langemarck German Cemetery mass grave, with grieving figures behind and personal tribute.

The Information Centre, Langemarck German Cemetery.

cemetery are video screens which explain the work of the *Kriegräberfürsorge* and the creation of the cemetery; the First Battle of Ypres; the Gas Attack of April 1915 and the landscape today as it related to the battle. Each screen uses superb contemporary still photographs and movies. Slits on the opposite wall look to the bunkers in the cemetery wall and between is a Poppy Field.

On 15 September 2006 the remains of 11 German soldiers, found in the Boezinge excavations (qv), were buried in the cemetery.

Langemarck Cemetery was on the route of Adolf Hitler's June 1940 tour of the Salient.

> **N.B.** By turning left from the car park and taking the first turning left along Beekstraat a **Bunker** and **the Memorial to 34th Division, RE and RA (Lat & Long: 50.9242.0 2.91335)** may be reached.

Drive back to Langemarck traffic lights and continue straight over to the next crossroads with the N313 at which there is a tall memorial column. Stop in the car park on the left.

• Bellew VC Plaque/The Brooding Soldier, Vancouver Corner/12.1 miles/10 minutes/Map 6/14/Lat & Long: 50.89916 2.94044.

Walk over the road to the long red brick building.
On the wall is a **Plaque to Lt Edward Donald Bellew VC**, 7th Bn CEF, who won his VC near this site. It was unveiled on 8 September 2008.

34th Division memorial and bunker, Langemarck.

Bellew was born in Bombay in 1882, educated at Blundells School and Sandhurst, emigrated to Canada in 1903 and enlisted in the British Columbia Regiment when war broke out.

THIS·COLUMN·MARKS·THE
BATTLEFIELD·WHERE·18,000
CANADIANS·ON·THE·BRITISH
LEFT·WITHSTOOD·THE·FIRST
GERMAN·GAS·ATTACKS·THE
22-24 APRIL 1915·2,000·FELL
AND·LIE·BURIED·NEARBY

The Brooding Soldier, Vancouver Corner.

As machine-gun officer, Bellew held two guns with his sergeant (who was killed in the attack) when attacked from the front and rear. Bellew continued firing until he ran out of ammunition. He then smashed his machine gun and was taken prisoner and remained in captivity until 1919. He died on 1 February 1961 and sadly his VC medal was stolen from the Royal Canadian Military Institute in the 1970s. Bellew was the second cousin of Maj-Gen Sir Robert Adams KCB, who won the VC on 11 August 1897 in India.

It is intended that this Plaque should be moved over the road near the Brooding Soldier and placed on a plinth.

Return to the Brooding soldier.

This remarkable, dramatic Memorial, represents a soldier standing with 'arms reversed', the traditional stance at a funeral. When the Canadian government decided to erect memorials in Europe to their war dead they initiated a competition to find the most appropriate design. This was the runner-up. The winning design was erected on Vimy Ridge. The architect here was Chapman Clemesha, from Regina, who had fought in the war and had been wounded. The 35-ft high central column of Vosges stone rises out of a circular pavement on which are marked direction indicators to other parts of the battlefield. The bowed helmeted head was carved in Brussels. At the back of the memorial is the bronze box containing the visitors' book. The inscription on the column in French and in English reads. 'This column marks the battlefield where 18,000 Canadians on the British left withstood the first German gas attacks the 22nd-24th April 1915. Two thousand fell and lie here buried."Here buried' does not literally mean on this spot, but over the battlefield. The memorial was unveiled on 8 July 1923 by the Duke of Connaught in the presence of Marshal Foch. The Canadian cedars are trimmed to represent shells.

The German gas attack launched in the afternoon of 22 April 1915 caught the Allies by surprise. The French Colonial troops on the left side of the allied line broke before the gas and the Canadians, with British county regiment reinforcements – the Buffs, Middlesex, York and Lancs, Leicesters – moved into the gap and held both that attack and the second on 25 April. The soldiers had no gas masks but discovered that, by soaking handkerchiefs in water and stuffing them into their mouths, they could get some relief. This road junction is also known as Vancouver Corner, Triangle Corner and Kerselaere.

Continue past the Brooding Soldier towards Zonnebeke. After some 200m take the small road, Vrouwstraat, to the left, past the glasshouses. This leads to the mill.

On turning, look right down the road towards Zonnebeke. Three tall chimneys are visible. One is taller than the other two. They are on the Western edge of Zonnebeke and provide an excellent reference point.

• *Totemühle (Death Mill)/12.5 miles/Lat & Long: 50.89740 2.94828*

The original mill on this site earned its title during its use by the Germans as an observation post. In such flat countryside even a few metres of additional height greatly increased visibility and Forward Observation Officers directing artillery fire often carried their own step ladders to climb upon. When you are sitting in a coach you are roughly at the height of a man on horseback.

Near the *Totemühle* served Erich Maria Remarque, author of the German classic *All Quiet on the Western Front*. The mill may be visited and opening times are posted outside.

Continue to the right of the mill. Pass a small junction to the left and stop just before the next junction to the right opposite a calvary. The British gave the farm buildings up the track to the left the splendid name of 'Von Tirpitz Farm'.

The Totemüle.

• *Observation Point/12.9 miles/5 minutes/OP (crops permitting)/Lat & Long: 50.89460 2.95418*

You are in the middle of the battlefields of Second and Third Ypres. Take 12 o'clock to be your direction of travel. At 10 o'clock is the rectangular shape of Passchendaele water tower and at 11 o'clock the spire of Passchendaele Church. The Passchendaele-Messines Ridge runs from 11 o'clock to 2 o'clock. The three chimneys are at 1 o'clock. The bulk of Kemmel Hill may be seen on the horizon just to the left of Ypres which is at 3 o'clock, with the other Flanders hills behind it and Langemarck Church can be seen past the mill at 6 o'clock. On a clear day the tops of a group of four poplars may be seen between 11 and 12 o'clock through the buildings beyond the near horizon. That is Tyne Cot Cemetery. Before the beginning of Second Ypres the Germans held the ridge, the British the area you can see between Ypres and some 3km to your left. Following the success of the chlorine gas on 22 April 1915, the Germans released their next cloud at 0400 hours on 24 April in the area to your left. It swept across the road on which you are now standing, while German artillery kept up a continuous assault on British positions in the Salient. The German forces involved here were part of the 51st Reserve Division and, in particular, the 4th Marine Brigade which advanced through here on the following day. Map 8 page 114 shows the extent of the German advance when the assault ended on 25 May. At the beginning of Third Ypres in June 1917 this spot was just to the rear of the German third main trench line.

Continue along the road to the memorial on the left.

• Memorial to 15th Bn, 48th Highlanders of Canada, Gas Attack, 's-Gravenstafel/13.4 miles/ 5 minutes/Map 6/15a/Lat & Long: 50.89303 2.96507

On a clear bronze Plaque with badge the **Memorial** tells the story of the **22 April 1915 Gas Attack** (the first major engagement of 1 Can Div) in considerable detail. It was inaugurated on 24 April 2010. The 15th also has a memorial at Loos.

Continue along the road to the next crossroads.

• s-Graventafel Crossroads, New Zealand Memorial/Bunker/14 miles/10 minutes/Map 6/15/Lat & Long: 50.89067 2.97855

Memorial to 15th Battalion 48th Highlanders of Canada, Gas Attack, 's-Gravenstafel.

The column on the left commemorates the men of the New Zealand Division in the battle of Broodseinde of 4 October 1917. On a front extending from around Geluveld to just short of Houthulst, an attack began at 0600 on 4 October in which Australian, New Zealand and English divisions took part. By chance the attack went in 10 minutes before the Germans planned to launch their own assault and the Germans thus suffered severely from artillery fire, much of the fighting then being finished off with the bayonet. The task of taking the Zonnebeke/'s-Graventafel spur was given to the 2nd Anzac Corps and the stiffest opposition was faced in this area which was taken by the New Zealanders under Maj-Gen Sir A. H. Russell. By the end of the day the division had taken over 1,100 prisoners and 59 machine guns. Among the dead was **Sgt David Gallaher** (also known as Gallagher), 2nd Bn Auckland Regt, age 41, former Captain of the New Zealand All Blacks rugby team. He is buried in Nine Elms Brit Cemetery near Poperinge.

Bunker, s-Graventafel.

New Zealand Memorial, s-Graventafel.

On 12 October a further attack by the New Zealanders was not as successful and resulted in 2,700 casualties in 4 hours, the blackest day in the young country's history so far. See http://passchendaelesociety.org/ for details of the New Zealanders' extraordinary contribution to WW1 in terms of percentage of casualties relative to the then-1 million population.

To the right at the crossroads and some 100m down is a **bunker** in the right-hand bank now cleared and visitable.

Continue straight over the crossroads onto Schipstraat (which runs over Abraham Heights). *Continue and turn left along Vijfwegenstraat then follow signs to the parking area behind the cemetery in which there are toilet facilities* (for which you will require 50 cents) *and from which one enters the Visitor Centre.*

• Tyne Cot CWGC Cemetery & Interpretative Centre/New Zealand, KOYLI & Sherwood Foresters Memorials/15.3 miles/1 hour/Map 6/16/OP/Lat & Long: 50.88771 3.00113

On the 90th Anniversary of the Battle, on 12 July 2007, the unmanned **Interpretative Centre** was inaugurated by HM Queen Elizabeth II, as was the **KOYLI Memorial**, the initiative of the Leeds City Council and the Community of Zonnebeke. The Regiment was awarded Battle Honours for the Battles of Langemarck, Menin Road, Polygon Wood, Broodseinde, Poelcapelle and the Passchendaele Ridge. **Pte Wilfred Edwards** of the 7th Bn won the **Victoria Cross** at Langemarck on 16 August 1917 and **Lt-Col Harry Moorhouse**, DSO, MiD, *Légion d'Honneur,* and his son, **Capt R.W. Moorhouse**, also of the Regiment were both killed on 9 October 1917 during the attack on Belle Vue Spur, the ground behind the Memorial. They are both commemorated on the Tyne Cot Memorial, Panels 108-111. Rupert Forrester, age 17, great-great grandson of Harry Moorhouse, was present at the unveiling. The Memorial pays tribute to all members of the Regiment who served in the Great War, 9,447 of whom were killed in action. In 1927 Queen Elizabeth, the Queen Mother, was appointed Colonel-in-Chief of the Regiment, her first such appointment. Sited to the right of the path to the Information Centre, the Memorial is now joined by a **Sherwood Foresters (Notts & Derby Regt) Memorial,** the first WW1 Memorial to the Regiment in France or Belgium. Made of Derbyshire stone it was inaugurated on 24 October 2009. Sadly the memorial stones have not weathered well and inscriptions are hard to read. These memorials were all constructed behind the cemetery so as not to obstruct the fine vista of the approach. This area is now designated as the site for new memorials, which should all conform to the same size.

The low building of the Centre does not obtrude above the cemetery wall. The panoramic windows offer superb views over the Passchendaele Battlefield and *Tables d'Orientation* point out all the salient features in 4 languages. On the remaining black-painted walls are the history of the cemetery and its construction, the Battle of Passchendaele and the contribution of the Australians on 4 October 1917. A database with access to the CWGC and Passchendaele Archives sites and an Australian CD ROM for 3rd Ypres available.

Follow exit signs and walk along the elevated path around the cemetery wall to the original cemetery entrance.

On this forward slope of the Passchendaele Ridge are both the largest British war cemetery in the world and a Memorial Wall designed by Sir Herbert Baker on which are commemorated the almost 35,000 soldiers missing with no known grave for whom room could not be found on the Menin Gate, i.e. those killed after 15 August 1917. In the centre of the wall is a **Memorial to the New Zealanders**.

The local name for this area is Keerselaerhoek, but, according to received legend, British soldiers of the Northumberland Fusiliers, seeing on the ridge square shapes which they thought resembled Tyneside cottages called it 'Tyne Cot'. Recent research prefers the theory that contemporary trench maps show the use of river names in this area – such as Thames, Alma, Rhine, Marne and Tyne – in use well before 1917. In actual fact the square shapes were those of 5 or 6 German pillboxes and inside the cemetery on each side of the central path two of them can still be seen, now surrounded by poplar trees and at the end of the path is the Cross of Sacrifice which has been built on top of a third pillbox. Pillboxes 4 and 5 were under Plot LXV and the northern pavilion.

On his Pilgrimage in 1922 King George V suggested that the Cross of Sacrifice be placed where it now is – on top of the third German pill box. A small patch of that pill box is visible within a bronze wreath below the Cross. Beyond the Cross are the irregular burials made at the time of the fighting and in front are almost 12,000 later burials whose headstones are standing in rows as if on parade. The Cemetery Report is in the entrance porch and that for the Memorial wall in the left hand loggia.

Looking back from the cross to the lower entrance, the chimneys of Zonnebeke should be visible well to the left and to their right on the near horizon the spires of the Cloth Hall can be seen on a clear day. The battle of Third Ypres surged up to here for three months from the direction of Ypres, the Germans holding this ridge, defending it with pill-boxes, machine guns, barbed wire and mustard gas. It was an Empire battle, the graves bearing witness to the team effort – some 8,900 from the

The New Zealand Memorial in the Tyne Cot Memorial Wall.

UK, 1,350 from Australia, almost 1,000 from Canada and over 500 from New Zealand.

At the end of October 1917 the ridge in this area was taken by the Australians and the empty village by the Canadians. On 12 October the 34th AIF attacked two German pillboxes at Hamburg Farm, some 400yds north-west of the Cross of Sacrifice. **Captain Clarence Jeffries** led one attack taking 35 prisoners and capturing 4 machine guns, he then took another machine-gun emplacement and was killed tackling a third, actions for which he was awarded the **VC**. He and five other **VCs** are buried or commemorated here including **Sgt Lewis McGee** who was killed in the same attack.

Graves and Memorial Wall, Tyne Cot CWGC Cemetery.

This is truly a 'Silent City', each headstone representing not just a life lost, but a family bereaved and generations unborn. Standing beside the white sentinels on this now peaceful hillside in Flanders, it is difficult to believe that all the suffering was worthwhile — and yet, simply to be able to stand here is a privilege won and paid for by many thousands who lost everything they had, including their name, and whose headstone reads only 'A Soldier of the Great War Known Unto God' — a phrase chosen by Kipling who accompanied the King on his Pilgrimage.

NOTE. The Old Railway Line. The cemetery is now linked by a walking/cycling path to Zonnebeke along a section of the disused Ypres-Roulers railway line – 'The Road to Passchendaele' (qv). Logically it should be followed from Zonnebeke - a visit to the Passchendale Museum is first advised, as one then follows the path of the Australian attack of 4 October 1917. Excavations along the route have revealed dugouts, tunnels and other interesting features that are marked by well-researched Information Plaques. A fascinating programme is available for students who can don the persona and clothing of a particular soldier, eventually finding his grave in Tyne Cot Cemetery.

Follow signs to the junction with Passendalestraat and turn right. Continue to the next roundabout and turn right on the N332 to Zonnebeke.

N.B. The French Memorial to the 9th Army Corps, Broodseinde **(Lat & Long: 50.87563 3.00172)** is on the left at the roundabout. In 1917 there were cemeteries on both sides of the road here.

French memorial, Broodseinde.

Continue into Zonnebeke.
Zonnebeke. From April 1915 Zonnebeke remained in German hands until July 1917 but was lost again in Spring 1918.
Continue past the church on the left and the old entrance to the Museum with flagpoles.
To the right is the **Café-restaurant De Volksbund.** Tel: +(0) 51 77 98 38 (closed Tues), with special 'Tucker-Tommy' menu.
This entrance is still available to pedestrians and houses the changing room for the Platoon Experience (qv).
Turn first left and follows signs to the Museum and car park.
This will take you to the rear of the Château, with the renovated Public Library and toilet facilities to the right and to the left the pleasant **Bistro Koklilo,** Tel: +(0) 51 72 574 13 (closed Mon & Tues).

• Passchendaele Memorial Museum, Zonnebeke/17.1 miles/1 hour /Map 6/17/Lat & Long: 50.87207 2.98683

The old Streek Museum (in the 1924 Château with its lovely grounds) was refurbished to house the splendid Passchendaele 1917 Memorial Museum, and opened on 23 April 2004. Notable is 'The Dugout Experience', a realistic and authentic recreation of life underground – a trench/dugout/tunnel system, complete with sound effects and vividly executed dioramas (e.g. HQ, first aid, dormitories).

This is an extremely well conceived Museum, with sensitive use of modern technology – well worth a visit. Franky Bostyn, the original enthusiastic and knowledgeable curator (who left the Museum in spring 2013) and his dedicated team have also been instrumental in the development of many WW1 sites in the region e.g. the Tyne Cot Information Centre, and with the ABAF (Association for Battlefield Archeology in Flanders), Bayernwald, Cryer Farm and most recently 'The Road to Passchendaele', the physical link recently opened up between Zonnebeke and Tyne Cot along the old Ypres-Roulers railway (qv). Student programmes and guided battlefield visits with knowledgeable guides available, notably 'The Road to Passchendaele and Platoon Experience' (qv). Many enterprising WW1-related events are organised throughout the year. One of the Museum's most ambitious projects is the Passchendaele Archives – the progressive recording of the data of men who fought at Passchendaele, complete with personal details and photographs, many used in the Tyne Cot Information Centre. Relatives are encouraged to contribute information. A large reference library of books and documents has been built up here. The Museum also works with the Belgian War Graves when human remains are discovered, especially when identifiable artefacts are involved. Many interesting events organised throughout the year.

Open: Every day except December and January: 1000-1800, Sat/Sun:1400-1800. Groups any time by appointment. Entrance fee payable. Tel: + (0) 51 77 04 41. Fax: + (0) 51 78 07 50. E-mail: info@passchendaele.be Website: www.zonnebeke.be

Refurbished and enlarged Museum.

A completely redesigned and much enlarged Euros 2 million Museum was opened on 12 July 2013 in the presence of dignitaries from all the major sponsors (see below) in time for the 100th Anniversary commemorations. It has been designed to blend sympathetically with the grounds of the Château. The main Château building has been beautifully restored – inside and out - with the exterior painted in an exuberant cream and terracotta. The large salon to the right of the entrance has been redecorated in period-sympathetic decor and houses the boutique and **Tourist Office**, with access to computers for research purposes and a comfortable rest area. This area was opened on **1 Sept 2012**, when the **new trench line** also became visitable.

Work had gradually started from winter 2010/2011 onwards. The new sections were due to open April 2012 but horrendous flooding problems were encountered when the foundation work started, causing serious delays.

The Dugout Experience area extends (to twice its present size) underground into the wooded grounds. A running presentation of the 1917 battles is shown on a vast model of Passchendaele. There are three main themes:

1a. **The Landscape:** The WW1 heritage research project has so far located 800 bunkers, 40 subterranean structures, old military cemeteries etc in Zonnebeke and Passchendaele alone.

1b. **The Nations and the International Dimension**: 15mm projections (in English with Dutch translation) with wartime footage and a series of exhibitions will give an atmosphere of the contribution of the Australians, Canadians, British, N Zealand, N & S Irish, Scots, Welsh… with testimony from the last veterans. Major sponsorship came from the Australians and New Zealanders, with additional sponsorship from the CWGC and the Americans.

2. **The Artillery**: featuring a private collection (purportedly the largest in existence).

The Engineers: trench and light railway etc construction.

3. **Aerial**, including many aerial photos.

The Trench Experience. Visitors emerge into replicas of the different types of WW1 trenches, original dugouts and shelters (removed from their original sites in the surrounding area), including an American 'emergency' wooden house built by their servicemen after the war. Originally erected in Wevelgem where it was damaged by a WW2 bomb but otherwise survived to this day, it was dismantled, transported here and rebuilt with a grant from the US Embassy in Brussels. When complete it will house an exhibition of the AEF in the Salient and Herbert Hoover's Commission for Relief in Belgium..

Remembrance: 1919-Today. They will then go back into an underground gallery which concentrates on the theme of Remembrance – the cemeteries, the iron harvest, veterans' memories etc.

Allow two hours for the comprehensive visit - there is also a disabled circuit and there is a lift for disabled people round the corner to the left of the Museum entrance and beside it is a fine Derbyshire Stone *bas relief* **Plaque**, presented to the Commune of Zonnebeke when the **Sherwood Foresters** Western Front Memorial (qv) was unveiled at Tyne Cot on 24 October 2009.

A 2014 Master Plan will co-ordinate all the WW1 sites in Passchendaele for visits by foot, bike, car and coach and the many commemorative events that will be held.

Sculptor extraordinaire Rik Ryon with one of his emotive figures ('A letter from home") made from original copper shell driving bands in the Passchendaele Memorial Museum. Contact: Tel: + (0) 57 30 10 67. e-mail:rik.ryon@yucom.be

Section of Trenches, Passchendaele Memorial Museum, Zonnebeke.

Passchendaele Memorial Museum, Zonnebeke.

Return to the main road and take the first turn to the left and follow signs to Buttes New &
Polygon Wood Cemeteries.

• Polygon Wood CWGC Cemetery/Buttes New British CWGC Cemetery/NZ Memorial/Australian 5th Div Memorial/18.6 miles/35 minutes/Map 6/18, 6/19, 6/20/Lat & Long: 50.85703 2.99089

This area is 1.5 miles due north of Gheluvelt (the next stop but one on the itinerary) where the Worcesters distinguished themselves in 1914. You are at the north-eastern end of the wood which in November 1914 (First Ypres) was held by 1st Kings with just 450 men and 6 officers strung along the 1 mile long southern edge and two companies of the Black Watch in the south-west corner.

On 11 November 1914, the Prussian Guard attacked along the axis of the Menin Road moving east to west. This is described at Black Watch Corner, the next stop. The 1st Kings had originally entered the wood (a complicated feature containing a musketry butte from the 1870s and an oval Cavalry training track) during the first week in November and were told to hold it at all costs. They came under shell-fire almost immediately and that, combined with heavy rain, turned the ground into a quagmire. Trenches, such as they were, were knee deep in water and it was impossible to get warm because a fire straightaway brought down German artillery. Hand pumps were used both to draw water and to clear the trenches. Yet, despite their discomfort, the casualties which mounted steadily and being outnumbered, the Kings held on to the wood. Following the German gains made after the gas attacks of April 1915 (Second Ypres) the wood was evacuated and the Germans constructed a number of pillboxes in it as well as tunnelling into the high mound of the butte.

During 3rd Ypres the wood again featured in a named battle – the 'Battle of Polygon Wood', 26 September to 3 October 1917. The British offensive opened at 0550 on 26 September being a rolling barrage with seven divisions in line on a 6-mile front. In the centre were the Australian 4th and 5th Divisions attacking west to east. The wood here and the butte were the objectives of the 14th Australian Brigade, the Australian line stretching north from here to Zonnebeke (from where you have just come).

The New Zealand Memorial, Polygon Wood.

*Australian 5th
Division Memorial,
Polygon Wood, plus
detail.*

The barrage was overwhelming. Immediately behind the Australians were the 2nd RWF and Private Frank Richards recalled the experience:

'I entered one pillbox during the day and found 18 dead Germans inside. There was not a mark on one of them. One of our heavy shells had made a direct hit on top of it and they were killed by concussion, but very little damage had been done to the pillbox'.

By the end of the day the wood was taken but the two Australian divisions had 5,500 casualties.

On top of the butte is a **Memorial to the Australian 5th Division** and below are over 2,000 headstones of the Butte cemetery. This was made after the Armistice by concentrating graves from the Zonnebeke area, almost all of them from 1917. More than four-fifths are unknown, a testimony to the savagery of the fighting. At the far end of the cemetery is a **Memorial to the officers and men of New Zealand** who fell in this area and have no known graves. It has its own Cemetery Report book. It was designed by Charles Holden in his distinctive, somewhat severe, style.

The small cemetery opposite Buttes is Polygon Wood Cemetery, begun in August 1917 in the front line, which has some 100 burials, mostly of New Zealanders. There was at one time a German cemetery at the back of it, but the graves have been moved, probably to Langemarck.

Continue along the side of the wood (in which there are still some important Bunkers, notably '**Scott's Bunker**'. **Lat & Long: 50.85348 2.98750**).

To the right just before the junction is the **Café-Bar. De Dreve** (also known as **ANZAC Rest**). Tel: + (0) 57 466235. E-mail: dedreve@hotmail.com Website: www.dedreve.com It is owned by the well-known archaeolgist of WW1 underground in the Salient, Johan Vandewalle (qv), co-author with Peter Barton of *Beneath Flanders Fields* (qv) who has been associated with such projects as Beecham Dugout, Vampire etc. It provides snacks (even breakfast with prior notice), has many interesting photos and a projection on a large screen of Johan's many discoveries.

Turn left on Lotegatsestraat until you reach the road bridge over the motorway. Turn left and immediately stop by the gate into the wood.

• *Black Watch Corner/19.6 miles/5 minutes/Map 6/21/OP/Lat & Long: 50.84850 2.98175*

On 11 November 1914 began the battle known as 'Nonnebossen" ('Nun's Wood'). Polygon Wood was at the northern edge of the German attack. Crown Prince Rupprecht ordered the Prussian Guard to take Polygon in co-operation with the 54th Reserve Division. Just after 0630 the German guns opened fire and at 0900 the assault began on a nine-mile front in mist and rain. The barrage had reduced the woods to a tangle of broken trees and undergrowth which impeded the German advance. On almost all of the front the attack faltered but at the southern end of Polygon Wood, between it and Nonnebossen (where the motorway now is) was a gap in the British line for which the German 3rd Foot Guard Regiment headed. At this south-west corner of the wood, the 23rd Field Company RE under Major C. Russell-Brown had completed a strong point just an hour before the assault, and in it were forty men of the Black Watch commanded by Lt F. Anderson. The position consisted only of a trench inside the hedges of a cottage garden and a few strands of barbed wire but it provided shelter from the artillery. Anderson's party opened such an effective fire on the Guards that they broke formation and were eventually stopped and beaten back by the guns of 2nd Division. In recognition of the role that the Black Watch played here the corner was named after them. Only one officer of the Black Watch remained unwounded. His name was Capt Fortune. It was during this period of fighting that Captain Brodie (who has a Private Memorial in Nonnebossen) of the Cameron Highlanders was killed. He is commemorated on the Menin Gate.

The Brigade formation which had taken the brunt of the attack was the 1st (Guards) Brigade under Brigadier-General FitzClarence (qv) and, having stopped the German assault on 11 November, the Brigadier decided to mount a counterattack to recover trenches lost to the Germans. While reconnoitring forward of Black Watch Corner he was killed. A farm to the south of the wood near Black Watch Corner is named FitzClarence Farm in honour of this popular old soldier who was affectionately known as 'GOC Menin Road'.

OP. Stand with your back to the gateway to the corner of the wood and look along the motorway. The church spire on the horizon to the right of the motorway, partly obscured by trees, is that of Geluveld. It was from this corner, on 31 October 1914, at the height of the crisis of First Ypres, that Major Hankey led off the 2nd Worcesters in an advance that would end in their famous bayonet charge into the grounds of the château. They used the church spire as their marker. See 'STOP PRESS' on page 333.

Continue on Oude Kortrijkstraat/d'Hekschscheure to the memorial on the right.

• Memorial to New Zealander Sgt H.J.Nicholas, VC, MM, 1891-1918/20.1 miles/5 minutes/Map 6/21a/Lat & Long: 50. 84841 2.99427

The Memorial, unveiled on 14 September 2008, is near the site of the pillbox taken by the then Pte Nicholas, 1st Bn Canterbury Regt. He was killed on 23 October 1918 in Beaudignies, 2 miles south-west of le Quesnoy. A road in the village is named after him. He is buried in Vertigineul Churchyard.

Continue to the first crossroads then turn right on Reutelhoekstraat. Continue to the the T junction, turn left and at the next T junction turn right over the motorway.

As you drive uphill you are skirting Geluveld Château and its grounds on the right.

Continue to the church on the right and stop in the car park.

Behind the church and in front of the Château gates is an **Information Board**.

Walk towards the site of the mill (now unrecognisable as such) *on the left.*

Memorial to H.J. Nicholas VC, Oude Kortrijkstraat.

• Geluveld Mill/Memorials to S Wales Borderers & 2nd Worcesters/ 22.6 miles/10 minutes/Map 6/22/Lat & Long: 50.83455 2.99447

At the foot of the old windmill is an Information Panel and memorials to the 1st South Wales Borderers and to the 2nd Bn Worcestershire Regiment which commemorate a famous action of 31 October 1914. The German attacks astride the Menin Road towards Ypres began on 29 October 1914, urged on by the Kaiser, certain that he would soon address his victorious army from the Cloth Hall in Ypres. So confident was the Kaiser that he moved nearer to the front line in order to be on the spot for the triumphal entry into the town. The German Order of the Day read,

'The break through will be of decisive importance. We must, and therefore will, conquer, settle for ever the centuries long struggle, end the war, and strike the decisive blow against our most detested enemy. We will finish with the British, Indians, Canadians, Moroccans and other trash, feeble adversaries who surrender in mass if they are attacked with vigour.'

The Germans, in overwhelming strength, pushed hard against the thin line of defenders. This area was the responsibility of the British 1st Division under General Lomax (qv). At midday on 31 October Geluveld fell and shortly afterwards Lomax was killed by a shell in his headquarters at Hooge (nearer to Ypres). The game was in the balance. General Haig, the Corps Commander, was somewhere along the Menin Road at this time, but unaware of the true tactical situation. However, he did issue orders to the effect that if his Corps could not hold on where it was, it should fall back to a line just in front of Ypres. Meanwhile local commanders took matters into their own hands. The commander of the Menin Road front was Brigadier-**General C. FitzClarence** (qv), late of the Irish Guards, who had won a **VC** as a Captain in the Boer War at Mafeking for 'extraordinary spirit and fearlessness'.

A counter-attack by the 1st South Wales Borderers had made the Germans pause just past Geluveld and at 1300 on 31 October FitzClarence called upon the Worcesters, gathered at the southern end of Polygon Wood, to regain the village. The Worcesters were actually part of

Memorial to 2nd Worcesters, Geluveld Mill.

2nd Division, but General Lomax had arranged that in an emergency they could be detached to 1st Division. They had been in continuous action for ten days and were down to about 500 men, little more than half of their original strength. Major Hankey, commanding the Worcesters, sent one company to cover the Menin Road itself, lined up his three remaining companies side by side, fixed bayonets and doubled across the open ground between Polygon and the village. Just short of the village was Gheluveld Château and here the Worcesters found gallant remnants of the South Wales Borderers still hanging on.

Together they pushed forward to the village, now burning furiously and under bombardment from both German and British artillery. Brigadier FitzClarence decided to withdraw to a firmer position and at 1800 the Worcesters and Borderers began a move backward to Veldhoek, just under a mile from here along the Menin Road). The German tide had been stopped, but it had cost the Worcesters dear – 187 of the 500 had been killed or wounded. The chase across the open field with bayonets may have saved Ypres, may have saved the BEF, may have saved the war. The British Commander-in-Chief, Sir John French, said that the moment of the counter-attack was 'the worst half-hour of my life'. Sadly, on 12 November, less than two weeks later, Brigadier FitzClarence was killed. His body was never found and he is commemorated on the Menin Gate.

Drive to the Menin Road and turn right towards Ypres. Continue to a crest with a garage complex on the right and the turning to Pappotstraat on the left.

• Clapham Junction/ Gloucestershire Memorial/18th Division Memorial/24.2 miles/10 minutes/Map 6/23, 6/24/Lat & Long: 50.84347 2.96192

This was a meeting point for roads and tracks, hence its name. The 1st Battalion of the Gloucestershires saw heavy fighting here during First Ypres and the 2nd Battalion during Second Ypres. Their memorial obelisk is on the right. Opposite on the left is a similar one for the 18th (Eastern) Division which has others in Trones Wood and Thiepval on the Somme.

For his unstinting care of the wounded around this area between 31 July and 1 August 1917, **Capt Harold Ackroyd**, RAMC of 18th Div, was awarded the **VC**. He was killed on 11 August 1917 and is believed to be buried in Birr Cross Roads CWGC Cemetery.

Memorial to the 18th Division with 1st Gloucesters Memorial behind, Clapham Junction, with detail of plaque.

To the left is the area known as Stirling Castle, named by the Argyll & Sutherland Highlanders after their garrison town and described in 1917 by Col Seton Hutchison in his book *Pilgrimage* as a 'treacherous heap of filth'.

Continue downhill along the Menin Road, to the memorial by the entrance to the car park for Bellewaerde Leisure Park on the right.

• KRRC Memorial/24.8 miles/5 minutes/ Map 6/25 /Lat & Long: 50.84575 2.94966

The memorial, which is similar to one on the Somme at Pozières and another in Winchester, is placed here in acknowledgement of the Regiment's part in the battle of 30/31 July 1915 at Hooge Château (qv) and the later battle of Sanctuary Wood (qv) on 2 June 1916. During the war the Regiment grew to twenty-two Battalions. The complex of German trenches between here and Hooge Crater Museum below, had been given the collective name of 'Ignorance', e.g. 'Ignorance Trench', Ignorance Row' etc. and may well have reflected the state of mind of the Staff Officer who thought them up.

Memorial to KRRC, Hooge.

• Site of Hooge Château/Crater

The leisure park is on the site of the original Château whose destruction began on 31 October 1914, when a shell fell on Maj-Gen Monro's Divisional Headquarters and several staff officers were killed. Others were wounded, including Gen Monro (qv) and Lt Gen Samuel Holt Lomax (qv), CB, of 1st Division, age 59, who was mortally wounded and eventually died on 10 April 1915. He is buried in the Aldershot Military Cemetery. Several of the casualties are buried in Ypres Town CWGC Cemetery. The crater itself was filled in during the 1920s. It was formed by a mine sprung by 3rd Division on 19 July 1915. The gallery leading to the charge of 3,500lb of ammonal was 190ft long and was prepared by 175th Tunnelling Company RE. When new the crater measured 120ft across and 20ft deep. (For those who know the Lochnagar crater on the Somme, that took 60,000 lbs of ammonal.)

Continue to the Hotel Kasteel to the right.

• Front Line Hooghe Crater/Preserved Trenches/Bunkers/25.0 miles/10 minutes/RWC/Map 6/26/Lat & Long: 50.84639 2.94624

To the left of the hotel, three adjoining water-filled craters (blown by the Germans in June 1916 during the attack on Mount Sorrel) and blockhouses, both in and out of the water, have been excavated and may be visited. There is no formal entrance fee but there is a box by the entrance of the site for donations to its maintenance. The area where the path runs between the craters and the fenced border of the theme park is where, in a surprise attack at 0315 on 30 July 1915, the Germans are said to have first used the flame thrower against British troops. At that time the crater and its immediate surroundings were held by the 8th Rifle Brigade and the 7th Bn KRRC, and jets of flame were sent against both sides of the crater from the direction of today's theme park. The Flammenwerfer equipment that the Germans used was carried by one man and looked rather like a portable fire extinguisher. The liquid was ignited at the nozzle and produced a jet of flame some 25yd long accompanied by thick black smoke.

Both battalions were forced back beyond what is now the rear wall of Hooge Crater Cemetery. Despite further flame attacks that night the line was stabilised some 200yd beyond the other side of the Menin Road and in the two days of fighting the 7th KRRC lost 12 officers and 289 other ranks and 8th Rifle Brigade 19 officers and 462 other ranks.

Bitter fighting had taken place earlier in this sector in 'The Battle of Hooge' (or Bellewaerde) of 16/17 June 1915, and the Royal Fusiliers, the Royal Scots Fusiliers and the Northumberland Fusiliers, followed by the Lincolns and the Liverpool Scottish, assaulted enemy trenches between the Menin Road and the Ypers-Roulers railway line. An account of this action, which practically wiped out the Liverpool Scottish, appears in Ann Clayton's biography of **Noel Chavasse** (qv). For it was here that their Medical Officer, who was to go on to win the **VC and Bar**, won the **MC** for 'untiring efforts in personally searching the ground between our line and the enemy's [for which] many of the wounded owe their lives'.

This area is noted for another innovation. It is said that here the first experimental use of portable wireless was attempted between division and brigade HQ. It is to be hoped that the army radios worked better then than they seemed to do at Arnhem in 1944 or even in 21st Century conflicts such as in the Gulf.

The adjoining **Hotel Kasteelhof 't Hooghe and Restaurant**, Tel: + (0) 57 46 87 87, **e-mail:** kasteelhof.thooghe@belgacom.net website: www.hotelkasteelhofthooghe.be owned and run by the Loontjens family offers not the usual 'sea views' but 'crater views'!

Continue to the Hooge Crater Museum on the right.

• Hooge Crater Museum/25.2 miles/20 minutes/RWC/Map 6/27/Lat & Long: 50.84634 2.94338

This is truly an atmospheric, traditional, enjoyable, classic style museum. It is housed in the old Chapel at Hooge, built as a memorial to those who fell in the Salient, and was opened at Easter

Liverpool Scottish soldier, Hooge Crater Museum.

Exterior and SGW of Ypres in flames, Hooge Crater Museum.

1994 by Roger de Smul using his own collection and that of Philippe Oosterlinck. There are some well-interpreted dioramas, clear commentaries and a dramatic stained glass window of the Cloth Hall on fire and outstanding displays of German helmets and decorated shell cases. There is a 1917 German Fokker DR1 and an authentic British 1916 Ford 'T' ambulance, audio-visual presentations, a section dedicated to the finds of 'The Diggers' (qv). British sculptor John Bunting created a statue of Madonna and Child for the museum in memory of Pte Joseph P. Bunting, killed 1 July 1916 on the Somme. It stands in a niche above the doorway. A Liverpool Scottish display and other improvements have been added by the enthusiastic Niek and Ilse Benoot-Wateyne who have now taken over the complex. Attached to the Museum, on the site of a former small school, is a pleasant modern **Café** with clean WCs. Excellent value, appetising sandwich lunch.

Open daily: 1000-1800. **Closed** Mondays and January. Tel: + (0) 57 46 84 46. E-mail: info@hoogecrater.com Website: hoogecrater.com A small entrance fee is payable, with the option of a combined entry fee/lunch.

Walk carefully over the road to the cemetery.

• *Hooge Crater CWGC Cemetery/25.2 miles/10 minutes/Map 6/28*

The cemetery was begun during Third Ypres by the 7th Division's Burial Officer on land that had been heavily fought over in 1915 and 1916 and extended by concentration burials from the surrounding battlefields after the Armistice. There are 5,892 graves registered here, including 2 from the British West Indies and 45 Special Memorials. Over 60% are 'Known Unto God'. The cemetery was designed by Sir Edwin Lutyens assisted by N.A. Rew.

The stone wall that encircles the Stone of Remembrance and which leads to the Cross of

Sacrifice at the front of the cemetery is said to be reminiscent of the crater blown across the road on 19 July 1915.

Private Patrick Joseph Bugden, VC, of the 31st Battalion, AIF, who won the medal for his heroic actions at Polygon Wood on 26-27 September 1917, and who was killed on his fifth mission to rescue wounded men under intense fire, is buried here. In the area of the cemetery **2nd Lt Sidney Clayton Woodroffe** of the 8th Bn The Rifle Brigade won his **VC** on 30 July 1915, for gallantly defending his position against the German attack and for leading a counter-attack under intense fire, during which he was killed. His body was lost in subsequent fighting and Woodroffe is commemorated on the Menin Gate. The VC was gazetted on 6 August and on 8 August Woodroffe's friend, the poet Charles Sorley (qv), wrote:

> In Memoriam S.C.W., VC
> There is no fitter end than this.
> No need is now to yearn nor sigh.
> We know the glory that is his,
> A glory that can never die.

Also buried here is **Lt Wilfrid Evelyn Littleboy** of the 16th Bn R Warwicks, killed on 7 October 1917, to whom there is a plaque in Geluveld Church (qv).

Continue down the hill for 500m to the Canada Café on the left

Menin Road Museum/25.6 miles/15 minutes/Map 6/28a/Lat & Long: 50.84693 2.93479

Behind the **Canada Café** is the small **Museum** owned by Gregory Florissoone. A typical private collection museum, it has realistic dioramas, some interesting and unusual items such as displays of enlistment posters (including one on Exemption From Military Service) and old private memorial plaques. **Closed** Tues. Tel: + (0) 57 20 11 36. E-mail: info@feestzaalcanada.be Small entry fee payable. Visitors' own food may be consumed here provided a drink is bought and the Museum visited.

Turn left up Canadalaan (Maple Avenue) by the Canada Café to the cemetery on the right.

• Sanctuary Wood CWGC Cemetery, Lt Rae Memorial/26.5 miles/10 minutes/Lat & Long: 50.83838 2.94439

The cemetery contains 102 UK, 41 Canadian and 1 German burial. Here is buried Lt Gilbert Talbot of the Rifle Brigade, after whom Talbot House (qv) was named. Son of the Bishop of London and brother of the Rev Neville Talbot, Senior C of E Chaplain of 6th Division, Gilbert was educated at Winchester (where he became friendly with A. P. Herbert) and Christ Church, Oxford, where he was President of the Union and a brilliant debater. In the afternoon of 30 July 1915 he fell, near Zouave Wood, leading a counter-attack with what remained of his men after the brutal liquid fire attack of that morning. Near him as he was shot in the neck cutting the old British barbed wire was his servant, Rifleman Nash, who was shot through the finger as he lay Gilbert's body down. Later attempts by him to return with stretcher bearers to recover Gilbert's body failed, but Nash was later to receive the DCM for his 'devoted care and courage'. Neville Talbot crawled out through the dead of the Rifle Brigade two days later, first finding Woodroffe's body and then Gilbert's. He took his pocket book, prayer book, wrist watch and badge and gave his brother the benediction. A week later he brought the body in and buried it. Killed in the same attack, but whose body although buried and marked, could not be found after the war, was 2nd Lt the Hon G.W. ('Billy') Grenfell, younger brother of Julian Grenfell (qv), the poet. Like Woodroffe, he is commemorated on the Menin Gate. Near to Talbot's grave is that of Hauptmann Hans Roser, Iron Cross holder, who was the observer in an Albatross of Field Flying Section 3 which on 25 July 1915 was shot down by a Bristol Scout piloted by Captain Lanoe Hawker. Many British soldiers watched the action, including, it is said, General Plumer. Hawker won the VC for his victories that day. He brought down two other planes in the same action.

The cemetery was designed by Sir Edwin Lutyens with N.A.Rew and its fan-shaped layout is typical of Lutyens' originality.

Outside the cemetery is a **Private Memorial** to **Lt Keith Rae**, also of the Rifle Brigade, killed on the same day. He was last seen at a spot near Hooge Crater in the *Château* grounds and after the war his family erected this memorial to him on that site. When the last member of the Vink family to own the *Château* felt that the memorial could no longer be cared for it was moved here and is maintained by the Commonwealth War Graves Commission.

Continue to Sanctuary Wood Museum car park.

• *Sanctuary Wood Museum/Preserved Trenches/26.7 miles/30 minutes/ Map 6/29/RWC /Lat & Long: 50.83698 2.94606*

The wood in which the museum is sited is on the forward slopes (Ypres side) of the last ridge before the town. At the top of the road is Hill 62, where a Canadian memorial in the form of a small garden and Stone of Remembrance commemorates the Dominion's efforts in the Salient and in particular the presence in 1914 of the first Canadian troops – Princess Patricia's Light Infantry – to fight against the Germans. During the First Ypres battle the wood still had trees, not yet destroyed by artillery, and it housed a few reserves, medical facilities and dozens of stragglers. Brigadier General Bulfin, of 2nd Division, ordered that the stragglers be left 'in sanctuary' until he instructed what should be done with them – and the wood got its name.

The museum here is owned by Jacques Schier and it is in two parts – the building and the preserved trenches. The building houses the **Café/bar** and bookstall, with various military souvenirs on sale, and a museum. The souvenirs are not exclusively from the First World War, although many of the artefacts on sale were actually found in the Salient. It is always sensible to be cautious about remnants of bullets and shells and collectors should *never* pick up anything on the battlefield itself. People are still occasionally killed or maimed by First World War explosives. Every year farmers plough up what is called the Iron Harvest and the Belgian Army collects it at regular intervals and blows it up in controlled explosions.

Exterior Sanctuary Wood.   *Jacques Schier in his Museum.*

At the heart of the collection are the dozen or so 3-D wooden viewing cabinets. They are a *must*. Each one has different glass slides that when viewed with persistence focus dramatically into sharp 3 dimensions. Here in this atmospheric environment is the true horror of war – dead horses, bodies in trees, heads and legs in trenches and, everywhere, mud, mud, mud. The history of the pictures is obscure. Jacques maintains that they are Belgian, others say that they were once owned by the Imperial War Museum and disposed of during a clean-out in the 1950s. There are similar, if not identical, cabinets and slides at the Armistice Carriage Museum at Compiègne and in a stationer's shop in Verdun. They may well be of French origin.

At the back of the museum, past hardware so rusty that is difficult to see how it keeps heart and soul together, are the trenches. They are original in the way that George Washington's axe, with three new heads and two new handles, is original. Yet they follow the shape and nature of the original trenches, which were designed to twist and turn so that invaders were always isolated in a short length of trench and could not set up machine guns to mow down the defenders in lines. They smell, but not with the stench of death that hung over the Salient for four long years. They are damp, probably with water underfoot, and in the middle is a concrete tunnel, passable to the wellie brigade. It defies the imagination to conjure up a picture of trenches in belts up to a mile or more wide joined in chicken-wire patterns and stretching from the North Sea to Switzerland – but that was how it was. The 'original' trenches were almost certainly British as this ground was only temporarily taken by the Germans and they may have been part of the 'Bydand Avenue' line of defences. 'Bydand' is sometimes a word used to describe a Newfoundland dog and in Scots is thought to mean, 'Stand and Fight'. As the 42nd Regiment, the Royal Highlanders of Canada were involved in the battle, the latter seems most likely. See cover for picture of the preserved trenches.

Open all year round during daylight hours. Entrance fee payable. Tel: + (0) 57 46 63 73.

Continue up the road to a turning circle which is some 300 yards further up the road.

Here is the **Canadian Memorial at Hill 62 ('Mount Sorrel', Map 6/29a Lat & Long: 50.83515 2.94721).** It marks the Canadian response to the German offensive that began on 2 June 1916 which led to the greatest of all Canadian battles up to that time. Also involved in the fighting was the KRRC whose memorial you visited earlier. Despite an excessive amount of 'the fog of battle' the Canadians held on and stopped the German advance, the lines settling around here until the start of the allied Passchendaele offensive a year later.

Drive up the hill, around the roundabout and return to the Menin Road, turn left and drive to the first roundabout.

The first turning to the right marks what was the route of the Ypres-Roulers railway line and along the Menin Road a light railway ran from the Western edge of Gheluvelt into the city. This roundabout marks what was Hellfire Corner.

Canadian Memorial, Hill 62.

• Hellfire Corner Demarcation Stone/28.7 miles/Map 6/30/Lat & Long: 50.84893 2.91586

This is Hellfire Corner. It was under constant observation by Germans on the high ground and anything that moved across it was shelled. Canvas screens were erected beside the road in an attempt to conceal movement.

By the roadside on the third exit as you drive round the roundabout is a **Demarcation Stone** (one of twelve surviving in the Salient) to mark the Germans' nearest point to Ypres. It now bears an explanatory plaque. The metre-high stones, made from pink Alsace granite were designed by the sculptor Paul Moreau-Vauthier who had been seriously wounded while serving as a machine gunner at Verdun and who first conceived the stone at the *Salon des Artistes Décorateurs* in 1919. It was made by the stonemason Léon Telle and had three patterns: the Belgian, surmounted by a *Jass's* casque, with, on its sides, a typical Belgian water bottle and gas mask; the British, surmounted by a Tommy's tin helmet, with a British water bottle and small box respirator, and the French, surmounted by a *Poilu's* casque, with on its sides a typical French water (or wine!) bottle and gas mask. Beneath the helmet was a laurel wreath. All bore inscriptions in the three languages: 'Here the invader was brought to a standstill 1918'; *'Hier werd de overweldiger tot staan gebrackt 1918'* and *'Ici fut arrêté l'envahisseur 1918'* (preferred to a proposed *'Ici fut brisé l'élan des Barbares'!* 'Here the thrust of the barbarian was broken') and the name of the appropriate sector. At each corner was a palm emerging from a hand grenade.

They were erected by the Touring Club of France, supported by the Belgian Touring Club and the Ypres League and erected in the early 1920s, their sites having been decided by Marshal Pétain and his staff. They were to mark the length of the Front Line from the North Sea to the Vosges. Accounts vary wildly as to how many actually were erected – from 119 (Rose Coombs) to 280 (Swinton's *Twenty Years After*). The history of the stones is being researched by Rik Scherpenberg,: bornesdufront. blogspot.co.uk. He reports that the last stone was put up in 1927, that there were 118 official stones, plus one private one making 119. Rose was right.

Hellfire Corner Demarcation stone.

Take the fifth exit signed Zillebeke.

Perth China Wall CWGC Cemetery (Lat & Long: 50.84184 2.92087) is passed on the left.

Continue through the village of Zillebeke, turning left at the T junction after the church following signs to Maple Copse CWGC Cemetery, but before reaching it turn right just before the woods following signs to Hill 60. Stop at the restaurant on the right.

• Hill 60 Memorials/30.8 miles/20 minutes/RWC/Map 6/31, 6/32/Lat & Long: 50.82468 2.92975

Here is a Memorial to the Queen Victoria's Rifles, plus small craters, a blockhouse and across the road a café. It replaces the museum run for many years by a member of the Schier (qv) family, thus ending a long tradition at Hill 60. It was originally maintained by the Queen Victoria's Rifles. Today the smart **Hill 60 Tearoom/Restaurant** with its bright modern décor is run by the Comyn family. Snacks and a more substantial menu available. Tel: + (0) 57 20 88 60.

The 'Hill' was formed by the spoil taken from the cutting through which the railway runs (200 yards further up the road) and gets its name because the resultant feature is 60 metres above sea level and forms an extension to the Messines Ridge. In 1915 the hill was effectively on the German Front line and the British line between 50 and 200 yards away towards Ypres. At this place it was named 'Immovable'. The French lost the Hill to the Germans in 1914 and when the British took over from them following the Race to the Sea, it was then decided that the feature must be retaken.

Much of the fighting here was underground and it was probably here that the first British mine of the war was blown by Lt White, RE on 17 February 1915 – though the tunnelling had actually

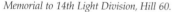

Memorial to 14th Light Division, Hill 60.

Memorial to 1st Australian Tunnelling Company, Hill 60.

been taken over from the French. It was decided that a major mining operation should be undertaken and the job was given to 173rd Tunnelling Company, RE. Work began early in March 1915 and three tunnels were begun within 50 yards of the German line, a pit having first been dug some 16 ft deep. Almost immediately the miners came upon dead bodies and quick-lime was brought up to cover them and the bodies were dragged out. It was hot, unpleasant and dangerous work. Apart from the constant threat that the tunnel would collapse and bury the miners alive, there was the possibility of poison gas and not least that the enemy might break into the tunnel or explode a mine of his own below it. By the time that the digging was finished the tunnels stretched more than 100 yards, and dragging the ninety-four 100 lb bags of gunpowder to the mineheads, winching them down the shafts and then manoeuvring them along the tunnels was a Herculean task. On 15 April all the charges were ready and on 17 April at 1905 hours the mine was fired.

The explosion built up over 10 seconds throwing volcano-like debris nearly 300 ft high and for 300 yards all around. Simultaneously British, French and Belgian guns opened an artillery barrage and encouraged by regimental buglers the Royal West Kents fixed bayonets and charged the dazed Germans of the 172nd Infantry Regiment, killing about 150 for only seven casualties of their own. The Hill was won.

Three days later **Lt Geoffrey Harold Woolley** won the **first Territorial Army** VC in resisting a German counter-attack. His citation reads, 'For most conspicuous bravery on Hill 60 during the night of 20-2l April 1915. Although the only officer on the hill at the time, and with very few men, he successfully resisted all attacks on his trench and continued throwing bombs and encouraging his men till relieved. His trench during all the time was being heavily shelled and bombed, and was subjected to heavy machine-gun fire by the enemy.' Woolley was a member of the 9th London Regiment, Queen Victoria's Rifles who had, with the Royal West Kents and King's Own Scottish Borderers, taken part in the initial assault on 17 April. Underground warfare went on here for another 10 months until the beginning of Third Ypres. Many of the men who worked and fought in those black corridors in the clay died there and are there still. Hill 60 is a cemetery.

Beyond the enclosed area on the left are **Memorials to the 14th (Light) Division and the 1st Australian Tunnelling Company.**

The hitherto inaccessible path to **Caterpillar Crater,** to the left beside the railway, is now open. *Continue over the railway and turn right towards Ypres at the T junction. Continue past the sign to Larchwood Cemetery to the right and take the first left turn (Vaartstraat) with a signboard to several CWGC Cemeteries.*

Ahead Kemmel Hill can be seen in the distance.

N.B. By continuing some 400 yards to the next junction you would reach the **Zillebeke Demarcation Stone (Lat & Long: 50.83095 2.91211)** with a Belgian Helmet, in the centre of the road. Its 'objectional' inscription concerning 'The Invaders' was erased by the Germans during WW2.

Turn left and continue.

CWGC Cemeteries Chester Farm and **Spoilbank** are passed on the right.

Continue to the T junction and turn left. Continue to the roundabout. Ahead is

• *Monument to St Eloi Tunnellers/Craters/33.5 miles/15 minutes/Map 6/33, 6/34/Lat & Long: 50.81002 2.89206/50.80910 2.89348*

This Memorial was erected on 11 November 2001 to **172nd Tunnelling Coy 3rd Br Div, 2nd Can Div and 7th Belg Fld Arty.** T. E. Hulme (qv) served in the trenches at St Eloi 27/3-16/4 1916 and wrote a poem *Trenches: St Eloi*, which expresses the mind-numbing emptiness and apparent futility of trench warfare:

"... Behind the line, cannon, hidden, lying back miles.
Before the line, chaos:
My mind is a corridor. The minds about me are corridors.
Nothing suggests itself. There is nothing to do but keep on."

Hulme was wounded in the arm here on 14 April 1915, with a 'Blighty one'. An extract from his poem is inscribed on the memorial. The British flag flies beside it and in 2003 a Krupp gun was added.

Two of the **craters blown here on 27 March 1916 and 7 June 1917** are now visitable by taking the fork to the left of the memorial. They are then one on each side of the road. On the right is an Information Board about the 7 June 1917 mine and a wooden path leads to the impressive water-filled crater where there is a seat and more Information Boards. A trail round the crater leads to a well-preserved bunker. **NOTE.** To enter you must ring the **Tourist Office** in Ieper (+ (0) 57 23 92 20) giving your name and mobile phone no. You will then be given a key code to enter the complex. Well worth the effort.

Walk over the road to the small road to the left, keeping left by the telephone exchange tower to the second crater.

The crater is up the small path to the left and easily accessible. It was created by one of six mines blown astride the old German front line at 0415 hours on 27 March 1916. Shafts dug to position the mines were up to 55ft deep and took more than 8 months to prepare. The mines were blown as part of an assault by 9th Brigade, after which most of the 4th Royal Fusiliers' objectives were still in enemy hands. Casualties were forty officers and 809 other ranks. On 3 April, 76th Brigade was brought in to reinforce a new attack. During the assault the Brigade Major, Capt Billy Congreve (qv), reached the rim of one of the craters. He wrote in his diary:

"Imagine my surprise and horror when I saw a whole crowd of armed Boches! I stood there for a moment feeling a bit sort of shy, and then I levelled my revolver at the nearest Boche and shouted, 'Hands up, all the lot of you!' A few went up at once, then a few more and then the lot; and I felt the proudest fellow in the world as I cursed them."

St Eloi, 7 June 1917 Crater.

Bunker near St Eloi Crater.

Memorial to St Eloi Tunnellers with Krupp Kanon.

Congreve brought in four officers and sixty-eight men – though other accounts make it five officers and seventy-seven men – for which he was recommended for the **VC** (which he was not to receive until July 1916 and then posthumously after further acts of bravery on the Somme) and awarded the DSO.

Today the water-filled crater is stocked with fish.

Take the N365 signed to Armentières and continue to Wijtschate.

• *Wijtschate & Miner's Statue/35.4 miles/5 minutes/Lat & Long: 50.78594 2.88240)*

Nicknamed 'Whitesheet' by the Tommies, fighting began around here in the first year of the war. The Germans held this area of high ground despite efforts by both the British and the French to take it. In the first, Messines, phase of the Third Battle of Ypres, the village was taken by the 36th (Ulster) Division and the 16th (South of Ireland) Division. On 3 July 1917 General Plumer presented King Albert of the Belgians with the bell of the church which had been dug out of the ruins.

Serving near Wijtschate from 6 June 1917 with 224th Siege Battery RGA was the vorticist artist, writer and philosopher, **Wyndham Lewis**. On 14 June he wrote to Ezra Pound, 'Imagine a stretch of land one mile in depth sloping up from the old German first-line to the top of a ridge, stretching to right and left as far as you can see. It looks very large, never-ending and empty. There are only occasional little groups of men around a bomb-dump, or building a light railway: two men pushing a small truck on which a man is being brought back lying on his stomach, his head hanging over the side. The edge of the ridge is where you are bound for, at the corner of a demolished wood. The place is either loathesomely hot, or chilly according to the time of day at which you cross it. It is a reddish colour, and all pits, ditches & chasms, & black stakes, several hundred, here & there, marking the map-position of a wood.' Later in June Lewis contracted trench fever and was hospitalised in Boulogne.

On entering Wijtschate take the right turn signed Kemmel. Continue into the main square and keeping to the right of the bandstand turn right direction Dikkebus/Sporthaal.

Immediately on the right is a **Statue of a Miner** by Jan Diensaert, inaugurated on 31 October 2008 and **Information Boards** on the **Battle for Wijtschaete/Bayernwald & Tunnelling**.

Continue to a right turn signed to Croonaert Chapel Cemetery. Continue to the path (which is 200m long) to the left leading to the cemetery.

• *Memorial to 1st Chasseurs à Pied/Croonaert Chapel CWGC Cemetery/36.6 miles/15 minutes/Map/6/42, 6/41/Lat & Long: 50.80150 2.87510*

At this point there is a grey stone **Memorial to Lt Lasmer**, 11 'Sous Officiers' and 174 Corporals and Chasseurs of the **1st Bn Chasseurs à Pied** who fell here in the defence of Belgium and France in the fighting of 3-15 November 1914. It was unveiled on 9 June 1935 when 90 veterans of the regiment came from all corners of France to pay homage to their old comrades with their old commanding officer, General Somon.

In **Croonaert Chapel Cemetery** there are 75 burials, seven of which are unknown. After the Armistice 51 German graves from 1917 were removed. The grave of **Chang Chi Hsuen** of the Chinese Labour Corps, 23 January 1919 lies in a separate plot just within the entrance. The cemetery, which was designed by W.C Von Berg, was begun in June 1917 by 19th Division and used until the following November. Two later burials were made in April 1918 and January 1919.

It is on the site of the original chapel painted by Adolf Hitler who fought in this area in the 16th BRIR.

Turn round and return towards Wijtschate.

• *Bayernwald Trenchlines and Mine Shafts/36.7 miles/20 minutes/ Map 6/43*

To the left is the area known to the Germans as Bayernwald, also known as Bois Quarante, a site owned for many years by M. Becquaert (Senior) who operated an idiosyncratic museum here. After his death the site was left to deteriorate but it has now been sold and the present owner has granted permission to the ABAF (qv) to excavate the interesting network of trenches, dugouts and the Bertha 4 and 5 mineshafts. Together with the Commune of Heuvelland they have restored 4 exceptional concrete bunkers made of pre-cast blocks, 2 deep German counter-mine shafts constructed to listen for British workings, about 100m of the trench system from the main German line of resistance 1916-17, recreating with A-frames and wickerwork 320m of trenches and constructing a wooden shelter with Information Boards. Entry is controlled by combination-lock gates and to make a visit contact the Heuvelland Tourist Office at Kemmel, 11 Reningelsstraat, Tel: +(0) 57 45 04 55 for the code. There is a small entrance fee.

Turn first right along Hollandseschuur (ignoring the restriction sign) to the T junction.

> **N.B.** By turning right here and continuing some 250m to the right the **Hollandseschuur Craters** are seen to the right (**Map 6/40/Lat & Long: 50.79772 2.86842**).

Turn left onto Vierstraat. Continue to the farm on the right and pull in at the end of the farm buildings. (These had been given the ambitious name of 'Red Château').
Ahead in the meadow to the right is a distinct dip leading up to 5 tall poplar-like trees. This is the site of the **Sunken Road painted by Adolf Hitler in 1914.**
Return to Wijtschate Square. Keeping right past the bandstand, turn right following signs to Kemmel. On the right is

• Wytschaete Military CWGC Cemetery/ 16th Irish & 36th (Ulster) Div Memorials/ 38.1 miles/10 minutes/Map 6/44, 6/45/Lat & Long: 50.78452 2.87673 & 50.78196 2.86568

Containing 486 UK, 31 Australian, 19 Canadian, 7 New Zealand, 11 South African, 1 German, 25 special memorials and 673 unknown burials, the cemetery was created after the Armistice by concentration of graves from the surrounding battlefields. Here are the graves of Drummer

Bayenwold reconstructed trenches showing plank and wattles.

James Etak McKay, 1st/4th Gordon Highlanders, 19 March 1915 age 20 and 2nd Lt John Victor Ariel, 45th Sqn RFC, age 20 who 'Died of wounds received in aerial combat 7 July 1916'. The cemetery was designed by Sir Edwin Lutyens with W.H. Cowlishaw. Just beyond it is the **Memorial to the 16th Irish Div** who captured Wijtschate on 7 June 1917. There is a similar

Memorial to 36th (Ulster) Division.

Memorial to 16th Irish Division with Wytschaete Military CWGC Cemetery behind.

monument to the Division at Guillemont on the Somme. Kemmel Hill is visible on the horizon ahead. **Memorials to the 16th (Irish) Division (on the right) and the 36th (Ulster) Division** (on the left) were inaugurated on 10 June 2007 some 800m further on down the road.

Continue to a green CWGC sign to the left to Spanbroekmolen Cemetery.

A short distance up the road to the left (and only visible from that road) is the large water-filled **Peckham Farm Crater (Lat & Long 50.77967 2.86301)**.

Continue along the road (which was known as Suicide Road) to the CWGC sign to Lone Tree Cemetery to the left and turn left along Kruisstraat. Stop on the left at the entrance to the Spanbroekmolen crater.

• *Spanbroekmolen (Pool of Peace)/39.2 miles/10 minutes/Map 6/46/Lat & Long: 50.77658 2.86124 /OP*

Named for the windmill that stood here for three centuries until it was destroyed by the Germans on 1 November 1914, this is the site of what was probably the largest mine explosion of the nineteen blown on 7 June 1917, at the start of the Messines phase of the Third Battle of Ypres. It consisted of 91,000lbs of ammonal.

Following a seven-day bombardment the battle opened with nine divisions of infantry advancing on a 9-mile front. They came towards you from the west. They had been told to advance at zero hour, 0310, whether the mines had blown or not. Spanbroekmolen went up 15 seconds late, killing a number of our own soldiers from the 36th Ulster Division, some of whom are buried in the cemetery ahead. The war diary of the 3rd Bn Worcester Regiment, that attacked a little south of here, records for that day, 'Battalion casualties were heavy and difficult to account for – a fair proportion must have been caused by our own barrage'.

Sir Philip Gibbs (qv), the war correspondent, described the scene thus, 'Suddenly at dawn, as a signal for all of our guns to open fire, there rose out of the dark ridge of Messines and "Whitesheet" and that ill-famed Hill 60, enormous volumes of scarlet flame from nineteen separate mines, throwing up high towers of earth and smoke all lighted by the flame, spilling over into fountains of fierce colour, so that many of our soldiers waiting for the assault were thrown to the ground. The German troops were stunned, dazed and horror-stricken if they were not killed outright. Many of them lay dead in the great craters opened by the mines.'

On 12 March 1915 an attack on the mill (coming from the direction of Kemmel) then in German hands, was used by the British as a diversionary action during the Neuve Chapelle battle as a means of drawing away enemy reserves. The 1st Wiltshires and 3rd Worcesters achieved little and incurred heavy losses.

In September 1929 Tubby Clayton wrote to *The Times* to point out that the last of the big craters at St Eloi, now 'a pool of rare perfection', was in danger of being lost in plans to extend the village. Two major craters, however, still remain visible in the village today (see page 232). Tubby's letter prompted discussions which led to Lord Wakefield buying the Spanbroekmolen Crater. It was renamed 'The Pool of Peace' and then left untouched as a memorial. On 22 April 1985 (the seventieth anniversary of the inauguration of Talbot House) Princess Alexandra visited the Pool and planted two mountain ash trees. She was due to be accompanied by her husband, the Hon Angus Ogilvy, who was Patron of Toc H, but he was ill and could not travel. Nevertheless he was mentioned on the commemorative plaque that was erected at the time at the entrance. However on 2 June 1992 the site was listed as an area 'of outstanding natural beauty' and therefore subject to the attendant rules and regulations. This included the removal of this plaque. (It is planned in the future to erect one plaque which will tell the history of the Pool of Peace.) After the listing a new wooden gate and fence were erected and the perimeter cleared. Visitors can walk all the way round the original borders. Just inside the gate was a tubular metal sculpture erected in 1998 and designed by the then 16-year-old Aline Overbergh. It symbolised two timeless people reaching out to each other with the Dove of Peace between them. Sadly this memorial has twice been badly vandalised and has had to be removed for repair.

The path to Spanbroekmolen Crater (Pool of Peace).

Continue a few yards to the path on the right to the cemetery.
From this point a superb view over the Messines battlefield can be seen. Looking back down the road the bulk of Kemmel Hill is clearly visible and looking forward along the road Messines Church can be seen on the Ridge. To the left on the skyline is Wijtschate Church.

• Lone Tree CWGC Cemetery/29.3 miles/10 minutes/Map 6/47

The cemetery contains 88 UK burials and 6 unknown, many of them of the RI Rifles (36th) Division, killed on 7 June 1917, some by our own mine.
Continue, to the next crossroads and turn right along Wulvergemstraat (once known as Pill Road).
On the crest of the hill, before the house on the right are some large craters. Stop.

• Kruisstraat Craters/39.9 miles/10 minutes/Map 6/48/Lat & Long: 50.77014 2.86491/OP

You are now standing on the German front line at the beginning (7 June 1917) Messines Phase, of Third Ypres. The attack came from the direction of Kemmel Hill (which can be seen just beyond the craters) passed over the area where you now are, down into the valley and up onto the Messines Ridge where the distinctive shape of Messines Church can be seen.

These two craters are legacies of the mines blown at the start of Third Ypres. The digging was begun by 250th Tunnelling Coy in December 1915, handed over to 182nd Company at the beginning of January 1916, and to 3rd Canadian at the end of the month. In April, 175th Tunnelling Coy briefly took charge and when the gallery reached 1,051ft it was handed over to 171st Coy who were also responsible for Spanbroekmolen.

At 1,605ft a charge of 30,000lb of ammonal was laid and at the end of a small branch of 166ft to the right a second charge of 30,000lb was placed under the German front line. This completed

Kruisstraat Craters.

the original plan, but it was decided to extend the mining to a position under the German third line. Despite meeting clay and being inundated with water underground which necessitated the digging of a sump, in just two months a gallery stretching almost half a mile from the shaft was completed and a further charge of 30,000lb of ammonal placed. This tunnel was the longest of any of the Third Ypres mines. In February 1917 enemy counter-measures necessitated some repair to one of the chambers and the opportunity was taken to place a further charge of 19,500lb making a total of four mines all of which were ready by 9 May 1917.

The two craters that remain, probably the first two charges, are favourite fishing spots for licence holders.

Return to the crossroads and turn right towards Mesen (Messines). At the next T junction turn left and stop immediately on the right.

• Messines Ridge British CWGC Cemetery/New Zealand Memorial/ 41.3 miles/10 minutes/ Map 6/49, 6/50/Lat & Long: 50.76532 2.89085

Created after the Armistice, the cemetery contains 986 UK, 332 Australian, 1 Canadian, 115 New Zealand, 56 South African, 954 unknown and a large number of special memorials. At the entrance to the cemetery is the New Zealand Memorial, listing 840 men killed in the Salient and who have no known graves, following their policy not to list their missing on the Menin Gate. The New Zealand Memorials are all in cemeteries chosen as appropriate to the fighting in which the men died. This cemetery and memorial were designed by Charles Holden (who also designed the New Zealand Memorial at Polygon Wood).

On 7 June 1917, during the Messines action which was the prelude to Third Ypres, one of the war's most beloved Padres was awarded the Military Cross for his work on the Messines Ridge. The citation which was published in the London Gazette of 16 August reads,

> "For conspicuous gallantry and devotion to duty. He showed the greatest courage and disregard of his own safety in attending wounded under heavy fire. He searched shell holes for our own and enemy wounded, assisting them to the dressing station, and his cheerfulness and endurance had a splendid effect upon all ranks, whom he constantly visited."

This brave Padre was the **Rev Geoffrey Anketell Studdert Kennedy, Chaplain to the Forces**, then serving with 17th Bde of 24th Division and better known as 'Woodbine Willie'. This unconventional Padre endeared himself to the men for his habit of doling out Woodbine

The New Zealand Memorial, Messines Ridge Brit Cemetery.

cigarettes, for using their own strong language when he felt it necessary, and because he questioned his own faith when confronted by the cruel carnage around him. His *Rough Rhymes of a Padre* expressed his love for his fellow soldiers and his understanding of their love of each other, as exemplified in the poem, *His Mate,* which describes the burial of a soldier and whose last verse is,

> "There are many kinds of sorrow
> In this world of Love and Hate,
> But there is no sterner sorrow
> Than a soldier's for his mate."

Studdert Kennedy was not so popular with the Establishment. General Plumer walked out half-way through one of his sermons in ire and had Woodbine Willie removed from the 2nd Army. After the war Studdert Kennedy continued his tireless ministry, speaking on many themes that were then considered to be avant-garde – divorce, contraception and abortion. At his funeral in 1929, the two-mile cortège from Worcester Cathedral to the cemetery was lined by crowds of his old comrades and the coffin was showered with packets of Woodbines.

Buried here is **Usko Leonard Salonen** 'of Finland' serving with the 39th AIF, killed 8 June 1917 aged 29.

From the top of the cemetery the Island of Ireland Tower can be seen.

Continue along Nieuwkerkestraat. On the right is **The Messines Peace Village, International 'Rural' Hostel.** This smart. attractively laid out, 128-bed facility is fully equipped for conferences and seminars with restaurant and bar facilities and is ideal for student groups, clubs etc. Access for wheelchairs. Helpful and knowledgeable Wardens. Tel: +(0) 57 22 60 40. E-mail: info@peacevillage.be Website: www. peacevillage.be

Continue to the to the crossroads with the N365.

Extra Visit to the London Scottish Memorial (Map 6/51, Lat & Long: 50.77256 2.89303) Round trip: 1.5 miles. Approximate time: 10 minutes

Turn left and continue to the memorial on the right.

The inscription on the grey granite Celtic Cross records how near this spot on Hallowe'en 1914 the London Scottish came into action, being the first territorial Battalion to engage the enemy. The battalion lost 394 of their 700 strength in the action. It was erected to the memory of all the Officers, NCOs and men of the Regiment who fell in the Great War, 1914-1919 and shows its Battle Honours year by year.

Turn round and return to Nieuwkerkestraat and pick up the main itinerary.

Turn right at the crossroads along the N365 into Mesen and first left following signs to Bethleem Farm CWGC Cemetery. Park near the bandstand.

• Messines (Mesen)/Museum & Cultural Centre/RB/N Zealand & Frickleton Memorials/41.7 miles/20 minutes/ Map 6/35, 6/36/OP/Lat & Long: 50.76541 2.89808

On the left is the old Town Hall of this,'the smallest city in Belgium'. It contained a small Museum which closed in 2011 until the Town Hall is restored to its original 1926 state to house the brand new Museum, WW1 Information Point and Cultural Centre (Tel: + (0) 57 22 17 14. E-mail: info@mesen.be) which is due to open on 25 April (ANZAC Day, 2014, at the beginning of the Centenary commemorations in 2014. (The restored'Adele House' opposite now contains the new local administrative centre.) The old Town Hall will also contain the town library and a small theatre. The project is being funded by the EEC, the Flemish Government and the Province of West Flanders. The Interpretative Centre on the ground floor will feature an unmanned exhibition area and concentrate on Messines and its environs during the Great War, detailing the New Zealand contribution and the liberation of the town during the Battle of the Messines Ridge on 7 June 1917. On the first floor exhibitions (with guides available) will change every six months, planned topics include the Maori Pioneer Battalion, Sportsmen in the Battle of Messines and personal accounts of the battle.

From this 'Information Point' visitors will be encouraged to visit the 'Satellites' at the St Nicholas Church, the Irish Peace Tower and the New Zealand Memorial (qv). At each of these will be interactive tablets giving the history of the monuments.

To the right is a small group of Memorials including a New Zealand Kowhai tree, planted on 11 November 1993 (the 75th Anniversary of the Armistice). The New Zealand Ambassador comes to Messines each year to celebrate ANZAC Day and Messines is associated with the New Zealand town of Featherston, where some 8,000 NZ soldiers trained before coming to the Western Front. There is also a Ross Bastiaan Australian bronze relief memorial tablet and a Japanese International Peace Post (qv) unveiled on 17 September 1989 by the artist, Miss Mié Tabé, and given to Messines by the Japanese Peace Movement. Its message says 'May Peace Rule the World'.

Turn right before the bandstand to the Church.

This was the subject of a painting by Cpl Adolf Hitler when he was posted in the area with the 16th Bavarian Reserve Infantry from November 1914 to March 1915 and when he was wounded in the arm purportedly treated in the crypt which served as a German Field Hospital. It now contains an extraordinary carillon whose bells were contributed by many Belgian and Allied organisations.

On 7 June 2007, as part of the Messines commemorations of the 90th Anniversary of Passchendaele, a Memorial was unveiled to the left of the church door to **L/Cpl (later Captain)**

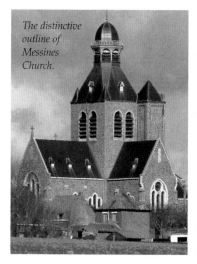

The distinctive outline of Messines Church.

Memorial to Samuel Frickleton VC, outside Messines Church.

Samuel Frickleton, VC, of the 3rd NZ (Rifle) Bde in the presence of two of his grandchildren and his great-grandson. The bronze plaque bears his photo.

Two days before Anzac Day (25 April) 2011 the remains of a New Zealand soldier were found during archaeological investigations along the track of the new Messines pipeline system beside an old German trench, on farmland a few hundred metres from Messines Ridge CWGC Cemetery.

Continue back to the main road and continue on the N365 direction Armentières. After some 400m turn right following signs to the New Zealand Memorial. Park at the entrance.

• New Zealand Memorial and Park/Bunkers/42.2 miles/15 minutes/ Map 6/52/Lat & Long: 50.76076 2.89098/OP

This memorial is identical to that at s-Graventafel (qv). It was unveiled on 1 August 1924 by King Albert I of the Belgians and overlooks a memorial park at the foot of which are two large, well-preserved German pill boxes.

It was well known that the Germans were constructing numbers of pill boxes on the Messines Ridge and prior to the opening of Third Ypres frequent patrols were made into German lines in order to find out more about the defences. The New Zealanders maintained daily intelligence summaries on the current state of the defences and their engineers blew up concrete dugouts half a mile south of here at Petite Douve Farm (qv) barely two days before the offensive opened. These two pill boxes appear identical, but the one on the left was made in situ while the other was put together with concrete blocks, probably to a pre-fabricated design.

On 7 June the attack here was led by the 3rd New Zealand Rifle Brigade advancing broadly from the direction of Nieuwkerke and the bunkers were taken in the first hour. They stood exactly on a major German trench system known to the New Zealanders as 'Uhlan Trench'.

From the seat between the bunkers a good view of the Messines battlefield can be had provided trees do not obscure the view. The British front lines here were 700 yards away beyond the Steenbeek below. Take straight ahead as 12 o'clock. At 1 o'clock the church on the skyline is Nieuwkerke. At 11 o'clock on the horizon are the spires of Armentières and at 10 o'clock in the middle distance is Prowse Point Military CWGC Cemetery (**Map YP R26**).

Memorial and bunkers, New Zealand Memorial Park, Messines.

Standing outside the park, with one's back to the entrance, look straight towards the hills ahead and take that as 12 o'clock. At 10 o'clock in the middle distance is the spire of Wulvergem Church roughly 1,500 yards away. Moving towards 12 o'clock is the tall wireless mast of Mont des Cats, then Mont Noir and next to it, the tallest hill, Kemmel, with a smaller radio mast. At 12 o'clock on the horizon are the bushes which surround Spanbroekmolen.

A well-constructed duckboard path from the adjacent football pitch links the park to the Irish Park.

Return to the N365 and follow signs to Ploegsteert and Armentières. Continue downhill to the tower on the right.

• Island of Ireland Peace Park and Tower/42.6 miles/15 minutes/Map 6/37/Lat & Long: 50.75979 2.89572

For many years following the Armistice, during the turbulent period leading to the formation of the Irish Free State, men from Southern Ireland who fought with the British in the Great War were often considered as 'traitors' and their sacrifice deliberately forgotten. This imposing grey stone tower is dedicated to the memory of all those from the Island of Ireland who fought and died in the First World War in an overdue gesture of remembrance and reconciliation between nationalists and unionists. The Tower was the brainchild of Catholic Nationalist MP Paddy Harte and Protestant Unionist Glen Barr who visited the area together in 1996 and conceived the project as 'A Journey of Reconciliation'.

The Park, which stands on the same Uhlan Trench line as the New Zealand Park, was unveiled on 11 November 1998 by President Mary McAlease and Queen Elizabeth II in the presence of the King and Queen of the Belgians. This site was chosen as it stands on the Messines Ridge where men from the north and the south of the Island fought almost shoulder to shoulder in June 1917.

As one passes through the entrance in the grey stone walls there are polished granite Information Plaques in Belgian, French, English and Gaelic leading up to the tower itself. They include some moving quotations from the poets Francis Ledwidge (qv) and Tom Kettle, from the Official War Artist, Sir William Orpen, Chaplain Francis Gleeson of the R Munster Fusiliers and others who served with Irish Regiments. Other plaques salute the memory of the 10th (Irish) Division which lost 9,363 men, the 16th (Irish) Division which lost 28,398 and the 36th (Ulster) Division which lost 32,186. In the room at the base of the slim Tower, a traditional Irish form which has been built in Ireland since the 8th Century, are beautiful bronze boxes made to contain the names of the Irish casualties and a Visitor's Book.

Island of Ireland Peace Park and Tower.

The park surrounding the tower includes four gardens for the four Provinces with four different types of tree representing the Irish soldiers marching towards the tower. Owing to financial difficulties experienced by the originators, the park is now maintained by the Commonwealth War Graves Commission.

Continue downhill.

Just before the bottom of the hill on the right hand side is La Petite Douve Farm. Under this farm many experts believe is one of the powerful remaining unexploded mines set to fire on 7 June 1917.

Continue to a left turn to the group of CWGC signs to Mud Corner, Prowse Point and Bairnsfather Memorial etc.

On the slope to the right is the site of the old Château de la Hutte on Hill 63 under which the British built large subterranean shelters. At one time it was planned to build the Ploegsteert Memorial here. From this point you will begin to see examples of the 19 well-researched and illustrated three language **Information Panels** outside the war cemeteries, memorials and remaining sites of WW1 interest in this area. They have been erected by the Commune of Comines-Warneton. In this vicinity are: 1. The Ploegsteert Memorial; 2. The Last Post; 3. The Catacombs of Hyde Park Corner; 4. The Château de la Hutte; 6. Prowse Point CWGC Cemetery. 7. Christmas Truce. 8. Bruce Bairnsfather. 16. Mud Lane from Hyde Park Corner. A leaflet proposing a route is available at local **Tourist Offices**/Town Halls.

Extra Visit to Prowse Point CWGC Cemetery (Map 6/53), St Yvon Christmas Truce Cross (Map 6/54) and Bairnsfather Plaque (Map 6/55) Round trip: 1.4 miles. Approximate time: 30 minutes.

Turn left and continue along the Chemin du Mont de la Hutte to the cemetery on the right.
Prowse Point Military CWGC Cemetery. (Lat & Long: 50.74427 2.89883)
Designed by W.H.Cowlishaw, this lovely cemetery with an unusual irregular layout was named after **Brig-Gen C.B. ('Bertie') Prowse**, DSO, who fell on 1 July 1916, and is buried at Louvencourt on the Somme. It was begun by the Dublin Fusiliers and the 1st Warwicks

Extra Visit continued

and was used from as early as November 1914 until April 1918 and contains 159 UK, 42 New Zealand, 13 Australian, 1 Canadian and 12 German prisoner burials. At the front of the cemetery is a rectangular pond with water lillies. The roof of a small bunker that existed during the war can still be seen in the lawn to the right of the graves area.

Also buried in Louvencourt CWGC Cemetery is the poet, **Lt Roland Aubrey Leighton,** probably best known for being the fiancé of Vera Brittain, author of *Testament of Youth*. On 12 April 1915, Leighton's battalion, the 7th Worcesters, reached trenches in Plugstreet Wood. Here he wrote the poem to Vera entitled *Villanelle*,
"Violets from Plug Street Wood,
    Sweet, I send you oversea."
(*Violets from Oversea*, the first line of the last verse, gave us the title of the first edition of our book on twenty-five poets of World War I). Leighton was killed on 23 December 1916.

Another poet was **Charles Sorley** (qv) of the 7th Suffolk Regt serving to the south of Ploegsteert Wood in July 1915. In his letters Sorley describes a bombing raid on a 'redoubt of some kind' the Germans were making and upon which the battalion did not have enough shells to fire. Although some bombs (grenades) were thrown, the Germans soon raked the ground 'with an absolute hail of rifle and machine-gun fire'. Many of the raiding Suffolks were wounded. Nevertheless the officer leading the raid, described only as 'C' by Sorley, was noticed the next day on trench patrol, 'dressed in summer get-up; gum boot, breeches, shirt-sleeves, sambrown belt and pistol. He had a bandage round his head, but only a very slight scratch from a fragment of bomb. He was walking along, reading from his German pocket edition of *Faust*.'

In the Cemetery, on 31 October 2001 was buried, with full military honours, the body of **Private Harry Wilkinson**, of the Lancashire Fusiliers, killed on 10 November 1914, discovered at the archaeological site at Boezinge (qv). Present at the funeral were three generations of the family, including his grand-daughter, great grand-daughter and great, great grandson, who wore Private Wilkinson's medals.

On 22 July 2010 **Pte A.J. Mather**, 33rd Bn AIF, died 8 June 1917 age 37, was also buried here, his remains having been found in Ploegsteert Wood in August 2008. He was identified through painstaking DNA matching (using his tooth enamel) with a 97-year-old cousin. He was buried with full military honours in the presence of 7 family members and Lt-Gen Ken J. Gillespie, chief of the Australian Army.

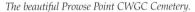

The beautiful Prowse Point CWGC Cemetery.

Extra Visit continued

To the right just beyond the Cemetery is a path which leads to **Mud Corner**, **Toronto Avenue**, **Ploegsteert Wood Mil** and **Rifle House** CWGC Cemeteries. It would take about an hour to walk to all of them and back to the road. They are in what was the infamous 'Plugstreet' Wood. The Wood is about 2,000 yards wide, east to west, and about 1,000 yds, north to south. Critical fighting for possession of it took place in 1914, between mid-October and the beginning of November – known as the Battle of Armentières. It ran, therefore, concurrently with First Ypres and this point, of Ploegsteert, marks the bottom end of the Salient. A fine bayonet charge by the 1st Somersets (their '1st in France', as the Regimental History puts it – although they were in fact in Belgium) stopped one German attack on the village of le Gheer at the south-east corner of the wood. Conditions in the wood were abominable. The Somerset History records,

"On 25 October ... the trenches were absolute quagmires ... the water and mud were ankle deep in the front lines; by the beginning of November the trenches were knee-deep in slime and filth. The stench from dead bodies often partially buried in the soggy, slimy ground, just as they had fallen, was awful. Unwashed, caked with mud, clothes sodden... aching with rheumatism and the early symptoms of trench feet, verminous and generally in a deplorable condition [the Somersets] held the line with a degree of staunchness, determination and cheerfulness of spirit never surpassed in the whole glorious history of the Army."

Although they made excursions into the eastern edge, the Germans never took the wood. *Continue to the cross in the bank on the left.*

• *Khaki Chums' Christmas Truce Cross/ Lat & Long: 50.744438 2.90257*

Khaki Chums Christmas Truce Cross with football tributes, St Yvon.

A simple wooden cross was erected here by the Khaki Chums Association for Military Remembrance when they spent a cold Christmas in the area to commemorate the 85th Anniversary of the Truce. On 13 December 2003 a more substantial Cross was dedicated.

You are now in the village of St Yvon. Here the cartoonist **Capt Bruce Bairnsfather** (qv), then a Lieutenant, was billetted and created his immortal character, 'Old Bill'. Bairnsfather, a trained artist who had previously served in the Royal Warwickshires before the war, rejoined the colours in August 1914 and by November was with the 1st Battalion here in the trenches at Plugstreet Wood. Possessed with sharp powers of observation and a quick pencil he began to draw cartoons to amuse his men – on anything that was to hand, from ammunition boxes to walls. Just behind the regiment's lines in this village he and a fellow officer called Hudson took over the ruins of a cottage with a more or less intact cellar, which they converted into a dugout for living quarters. On the dugout's walls Bairnsfather amused himself by sketching the situations that he was experiencing in the area. *Continue, past a pond at the bend to the right, to the first house on the right.*

• *Commemorative Plaque to Capt Bruce Bairnsfather on House No. 12 Chemin du Mont de la Hutte/Lat & Long: 50.74298 2.90404.*

This house has been built on the very site of that billet. On one occasion when several of them were in the cottage, the Germans began to shell the village and, knowing that the

Extra Visit continued

enemy would have ranged his guns on the buildings, they dashed outside and took cover in a nearby ditch. At last when the shelling seemed to be over they went back into the cottage and just as they did so a heavy shell landed close by and to a man they rushed to the broken doorway and with one voice exclaimed, 'Where did that one go to?' Bairnsfather turned the situation into a cartoon of that title. It was an action that was to lead to a lifetime career built around the archetypal Tommy, 'Old Bill', that emerged from his cartoons, collectively called *Fragments from France*. [It is a story that we examine in our biography *In Search of the Better 'Ole, The Life, the Works and the Collectables of Bruce Bairnsfather*.]

On 13 December 2003 the authors unveiled a bronze Plaque on the cottage wall to commemorate the birth of Bairnsfather's inspired creation and the seeds of his extraordinary career.

Plaque on the cottage on the site of the dugout when Bairnsfather drew his first cartoon.

Bairnsfather also decided to try his hand at sniping, considered an 'officer's sport', and climbed onto the roof of another cottage. He had hardly done so when another German barrage began and he had to beat a hasty retreat, an experience that he turned into the cartoon, *They've evidently seen me*, which shows a startled soldier clinging to a chimney as a huge shell whistles by. This is the cartoon that we chose to illustrate on the memorial plaque.

It was in this area that men participated in that curious phenomenon, 'The Christmas Truce' on 24/25 December 1914. The 1st Battalion the Warwickshire Regiment in Plugstreet Wood took part in the truce and 2nd Lt Bruce Bairnsfather, in his book, *Bullets and Billets*, gives a full and humorous account of what happened. After singing and shouting 'a complete Boche figure suddenly appeared on the parapet and looked about itself. This complaint became infectious. It didn't take Our Bert long to be up on the skyline. This was the signal for more Boche anatomy to be disclosed and this was replied to by all our Alfs and Bills until in less time than it takes to tell, half a dozen or so of each of the belligerents were outside their trenches and advancing towards each other in no-man's-land.' He goes on to describe how he joined in the fraternisation and how eventually everyone returned to their trenches. 'The last I saw of this little affair was a vision of one of my machine gunners, who was a bit of an amateur hairdresser in civil life, cutting the unnaturally long hair of a docile Boche who was patiently kneeling on the ground whilst the automatic clippers crept up the back of his neck'. The experience may well have led to one of his *Fragments* cartoons entitled *Coiffure in the Trenches* where a soldier (either Alf or Bert) is having his hair cut by Old Bill as a large shell sails by. Bill is saying 'Keep yer 'ead still or I'll 'ave yer blinkin' ear off'.

Sir John French reacted quickly to the news of the truce. Units that had participated were moved out of the lines and hostilities immediately recommenced. Christmas Day 1914 was not without its official pleasures, however. Every officer and soldier in the field was given two gifts. The King and Queen sent a postcard bearing pictures of themselves, the King in service dress, and on the reverse in a facsimile of the King's hand the message, 'With our best wishes for Christmas 1914. May God protect you and bring you home safe. Mary R. George R'. Princess Mary, following a tradition that Queen Victoria had begun in

---

Extra Visit continued

the Boer War, sent an embossed brass tin containing a mixture of cigarettes, pipe tobacco and chocolate together with a small folded card wishing the recipient a Happy Christmas.

> **N.B.** By continuing along the small road to the T junction, the St Yvon craters of Trench 127 (Ultimo) to the left (**Lat & Long: 50.74359 2.88699),** and Trench 122 (Factory Farm) to the right (**Lat & Long: 50.74200 2.91347)** can be visited.

Turn round and return to the main road, turn left and rejoin the main itinerary.

Continue downhill to the large memorial on the right.

Note that this is a French-speaking (Walloon) area of Belgium.

Opposite the Memorial is the l'**Auberge** owned by Claude & Nellie Verhaeghe, the HQ of the Last Post Committee. Local WW1 expert Claude offers guided tours. Interesting WW1 exhibits, menus and local beers. Groups by prior reservation. Tel: + (0 56 58 84 41. E-mail: restaurant@ auberge-ploegsteert.be Website: www.auberge-ploegsteert.be

• *Ploegsteert Memorial/Berkshire CWGC Cemetery Extension and Hyde Park Corner CWGC Cemeteries/Interpretation Centre/Last Post/ 44.3 miles/30 minutes/Map 6/39, 6/38/RWC/Lat & Long: 50.73772 2.88234*

Here, since 7 June 1999, the Last Post has been played on the first Friday of the month at 1900 hours by local buglers. The event was organised by the Comité du Mémorial de Ploegsteert with the assistance of Ted Smith of the WFA. Special ceremonies may be requested. Tel: l'Auberge - see above.

Guarded by two lions, one baring his teeth, the other looking benign, designed by Sir Gilbert Ledward (who was to do work in the World War II Reichswald Cemetery on the Dutch-German border) is the Berkshire Cemetery Extension which was begun in June 1916. The rotunda structure is the Ploegsteert Memorial to the Missing bearing the names of 11,447 officers and men from nearby battles for every year of the war and has its own Reports, separate to those for the adjoining cemetery.

There are **three VCs** commemorated on it: **Sapper William Hackett** of 254th Tunnelling Coy, RE, for helping to rescue men entombed with him in a mine shaft at Givenchy (qv) in June 1916, after an enemy counter-explosion which created Red Dragon Crater. He was killed four days later (a Memorial was inaugurated to Hackett and the Tunnellers at Givenchy on 19 June 2010); **Pte James Mackenzie** of the 2nd Bn Scots Guards for on 19 December 1914, at Rouges Bancs, rescuing a severely wounded man under very heavy fire and who was killed later that day attempting the same act; **Capt Thomas Tannatt Pryce** of the 4th Bn Grenadier Guards for on 11/12 April 1918, at Vieux Berquin leading an attack on the village, beating off 4 counter-attacks and driving off a fifth with a bayonet charge, who was last seen, with only 17 men and no ammunition, leading another bayonet charge. The Report for the memorial shows the continuing work of the Commission. Several entries have been amended as men whose names are inscribed on the memorial have been identified in cemeteries, e.g. **Serjt J. B. Coutts**, now in Tournai Cemetery, and **Pte T. Gordie** buried in Le Grand Beaumont British Cemetery.

The memorial was originally planned to stand in Lille, but the French were becoming 'disquieted by the number and scale of the Memorials which the Commission proposed to erect'. When the number of Imperial Memorials in France was reduced from the planned twelve to four (Soissons, La Ferté, Neuve-Chapelle and the Somme) extra land was acquired from the Belgians here at Ploegsteert. The names of the missing destined to be inscribed on other cancelled

Ploegsteert Memorial.

memorials were inscribed on memorial walls built inside the land assigned to a cemetery, e.g. Vis-en-Artois and Pozières. The disappointed architects of the aborted memorials were given other assignments. Thus Charlton Bradshaw, who had won competitions for his designs for Lille and Cambrai (another memorial which was cancelled) was allotted Ploegsteert and Louverval. This explains why the memorial commemorates the Missing of the Battles of Armentières, 1914, Aubers Ridge, Loos and Fromelles, 1915, Estaires, 1916 and Hazebrouck, Scherpenberg and Outtersteene, 1918. It was inaugurated on 7 June 1931, by the Duke of Brabant, later to become King Leopold III.

In 1981 a ceremony was held at the Memorial to celebrate the 50th anniversary of the inauguration. It was attended by Winston Churchill, grandson of Sir Winston Churchill. His illustrious grandfather had served with the Royal Scots Fusiliers in the Ploegsteert sector after the humiliating end to the imaginative concept of the Dardanelles campaign, from 26 January to 3 May 1916. A **Plaque, showing Churchill** in his WW2 attire of Homburg hat and large cigar, can be seen on the wall of the Ploegsteert Town Hall (**Lat & Long: 50.72617 2.87991**).

The Eden Family in the Salient.

The future Prime Minister **Anthony Eden** served during the winter of 1916/17 as Adjutant of 21st Bn, KRRC in the village of La Clytte [present day De Klijte]. When in reserve Eden - known as 'Boy' by fellow officers - 'lived in Hunter's Avenue' (see above), where 'the rats were a plague in the trenches'. Coincidentally he was not far from where another future Prime Minister, Winston Churchill, served in 1915/1916 (see above).

Anthony's older brother 'Jack' had been killed in the Salient in October 1914, his cousin 'Bill' (the Hon W.A.M) Eden, also of the KRRC, had been killed on 3 March 1915 and his younger brother, Nicholas, was killed as a 16 year old Midshipman when the *Indefatigable* went down in the Battle of Jutland. Anthony's sister Marjorie served on a hospital train in France. As Lady Marjorie Brooke she donated a considerable sum of money to build a church at Kruiseke (there had previously been no church in the village), in memory of Jack, near where he was killed. He is buried in Larch Wood (Railway Cutting) CWGC Cemetery. A **Memorial Plaque** on the church wall records her generosity (**Lat & Long: 50.815703 3.021219**). It was unveiled on 11 November 1998 by Lady Clarissa Eden, Anthony Eden's widow, and Lord John Eden, his nephew.

To complete this aristocratic family's contribution to the war, Eden's maternal Uncle, Robin Grey, a pilot with the RFC, was shot down, taken prisoner and suffered solitary confinement as he was a cousin of the Foreign Secretary, Sir Edward Grey. The family seat, Windlestone, in County Durham, was used as a war-time VAD hospital.

• *Ploegsteert Plugstreet Interpretation Centre. (Lat & Long: 50.7369 2.8809)*

The Centre will adjoin the Memorial (near the site of the catacombs where Australian forces took shelter in 1917), with an entrance on rue de la Munque, the first turning right after the Memorial. The work is being done in collaboration with the CWGC, the Commune, together with the *Région Wallonne*, the European Regional Development Fund and the *Commissariat Général au Tourisme, Deulys* (an association of 7 nearby cities) and some 20 other partners (including a considerable contribution from the Australian Government). It is part of a European project, **'The Great War Remembered'**, with a budget of nearly €3million. Official opening in September 2014. The foundation Stone was laid on 3 May 2012 and it was inaugurated on 9 November 2013.

The original design was by Comines-Warneton Architect, Isabelle Delforge and the main building are covered by a grassy mound, with a glass pyramid over the entrance hall. It charts the various battles which took place on this land, such as three phases of the Australian campaign – the Battle of Mesines, the Catacombs and Winter 1917-18. It will show the human face of the War, how the local population lived throughout it in relation to the various armed forces who occupied their region (co-operation, evacuation, destruction and rebuilding after the War – including that of the Ploegsteert Memorial - etc). Contemporary newspaper accounts, photos, postcards, personal accounts etc, will illustrate these facets. The visitor will be encouraged to enter a war-time character's 'living space'. Frequent temporary exhibitions will also feature, including the opening one on Cartoonists and Bairnsfather's Old Bill, who will form an important role in the story line and on which the authors are pleased to co-operate.

A series of commemorative activities is planned, including Special Last Posts to commemorate particular events, some followed by a torchlight march to the Christmas Truce Cross, where on 25

The newly opened Plugstreet Interpretation Centre.

December 2014 there will be a re-enactment of the Christmas Truce Football Match and an encampment by British and German re-enactors in a recreated trench; a showing of films featuring Bruce Bairnsfather and 'Old Bill'; Anzac Day (25 April) ceremony; Carol concerts in the Centre...

A special issue of '14-'18 will be published by the Tourist Office showing the human and military effects of the War in the Region and a variety of guided Battlefield Tours will be offered. The sites of the Chateau Breuvart (Mont de la Hutte) and the 1917 mines (including ULTIMO qv) will be developed.

In the adjoining **Berkshire Cemetery Extension** are 295 UK, 51 Australian, 3 Canadian and 45 New Zealand burials, among them Anthony Eden's **Platoon Sergeant, 'Reg' Park.**

Over the road **is Hyde Park Corner CWGC Cemetery** which was begun during Second Ypres by the 1st/4th Royal Berkshires, remained in use until November 1917 and contains the grave of **16-year-old Pte Albert Edward French,** the subject of a BBC Radio 4 documentary in 1983. He was killed on 15 June 1916, a week before his seventeenth birthday. Apparently the War Office refused the family a war pension as Albert had lied about his age on joining up and was under the official enlistment age when he was killed. The local Member of Parliament took up the case and eventually Albert's father received 5 shillings a week. His brother George spoke the words that gave the title to the radio programme about Albert, *He shouldn't have been there, should he?*

Behind the cemetery is the edge of the infamous 'Plugstreet Wood' which is about 2,000 yards wide, east to west and about 1,000 yards north to south. It marks the bottom end of the Salient. In it are the remains of several well-preserved British machine-gun posts and bunkers and the wood was intersected by several well-defined paths – the main one being 'Hunter's Avenue.' Although they made excursions into the eastern edge of the wood, the Germans never took it.

• End of 1st, 2nd & 3rd Ypres Battlefield Tour
OR Return to Ieper for RWC
OR Continue with 4th Ypres Battlefield Tour (page 301).

FOURTH YPRES: BATTLE OF THE LYS

7-29 APRIL 1918

'The enemy has exerted all his strength in men and guns in the battle
now raging from the river Lys to Wytschaete and our troops have been fighting
without respite to hold him on our main defensive positions...
Once again our men are outnumbered – the same men who fought
until they could hardly stand in the week that followed March 21.'
Philip Gibbs, *Open Warfare. The Way to Victory.*

'There was no nobler or more decisive stand than that of the
BEF in front of Ypres in April 1918.'
Brigadier General S.L.A. Marshall, American historian.

SUMMARY OF THE BATTLE

Despite the extraordinary initial success of the Kaiser's Offensive, Ludendorff did not make the gains that he had desired and when the next – Lys – phase of his plan, 'Operation George', opened on 7 April, he had to reduce the troops involved and the frontage of his attack to such an extent that one of his staff officers suggested that the offensive be renamed 'Georgette'.

After three weeks of desperate fighting as the Germans drove towards the Flanders Hills, Ludendorff's supply line became too stretched and he was exposed on three sides. April 29 became the most bloody day of all for many tired German regiments who were swept back on all sides. Fourth Ypres ended in the Allies' favour.

OPENING MOVES

Following two days of concentrated gas attacks around Armentières, nine full-strength divisions drove directly at Neuve Chapelle where a solitary Portuguese Division in the process of being relieved was no match for the Germans and the town fell, hence their memorial and cemetery (qv) there.

By the evening of 9 April the Germans had reached the Lys (see **Map 16**, page 250) and the next day they drove north of Armentières, taking the Wijtschate and Messines Ridges and Ploegsteert village, despite determined resistance by the South African Brigade. The British 34th Division just escaped encirclement in Armentières and by the end of that day the Germans had driven a 10-mile salient into the British lines and were just 4 miles south of Ypres.

WHAT HAPPENED

Below Armentières the 51st Division was saved from near disaster by the 61st, another Territorial force, and frantic phone calls from London by the Prime Minister and others called for help from the French and the Americans. Both in London and at GHQ the view was forming that the

Germans were on the edge of splitting the Allies and that Ypres could well fall. Haig wrote a 'Special Order of the Day' which ended, 'With our backs to the wall, and believing in the justice of our cause, each one of us must fight to the end.' It was meant to stiffen the resolve of his troops, but it unintentionally revealed the level of his concern about the situation. The message, which reached very few of the front line soldiers, is popularly connected with the near rout of Gough's 5th Army on the Somme but it was more likely prompted by the situation in Flanders.

On 12 April General Plumer assumed command of General Horne's 1st Army (responsible for Ypres) in addition to his own, the Third (responsible for the area south of the Lys) as the British attempted to co-ordinate their response to what was becoming a very confused struggle. Haig brought up the Australians from the Somme, his reserves dwindling. Formations and units fought for every inch of ground, often reduced to bullet and bayonet. Rear areas were prepared for defence and civilians and non-combatants were evacuated from Poperinghe. Ludendorff drove north-west, straight for Neuve Eglise en route for the Flanders Hills – Kemmel, Mont Noir, Mont Rouge and Mont des Cats – knowing that if he had them the British and Belgian positions between Ypres and the sea would become untenable and that the way to the Channel Ports would be open. The tired troops of 34th Division struggled backwards and the 2nd Worcesters held the Germans for a while in Neuve Eglise before the village fell.

But Ludendorff was confused too and, short of the hills, changed the direction of his attack towards Langemarck and then switched again this time towards Kemmel which fell on 25 April, the French who had taken over the hill just nine days earlier from the British, putting up little resistance. Meanwhile Plumer, in order to shorten his line, withdrew from the hard-won Passchendaele Ridge in the first phase of a movement that called for the evacuation of the Ypres Salient – Foch vetoed it. The protagonists were like two tiring boxers, ducking and weaving, looking for gaps in the other's defences, but Ludendorff was now at a disadvantage. His lines of supply were longer and his deep salient into the Allied lines left his troops open to fire on three flanks. Back at home dissatisfaction with the conduct of the war had spawned endless strikes, food riots and the beginnings of armed revolution. Ludendorff himself was worn out and had never recovered from the death of his youngest son, Erich, in March. Finally, on 29 April, once again a finger's touch from success, the German commander ended the campaign. Ypres and the Channel Ports had been saved.

THE BATTLEFIELD TOUR

[Inevitably the route goes through some sites of 1st, 2nd and 3rd Ypres as well.]

• **The Route:** The tour begins at Ploegsteert, visits Underhill Farm CWGC Cemetery; Neuve Eglise Churchyard and CWGC Plot, Capt Crowe VC Plaque; Dranouter Churchyard and CWGC Plot, Dranoutre Mil CWGC Cemetery; Locre No 10 CWGC Cemetery, Locre South Demarcation Stone, Hospice CWGC Cemetery & Redmond Memorial, Locre Churchyard and CWGC Plot, French Plaques; Mont Noir Mil Cemetery & 34th Div Memorial; Westouter Churchyard & Churchyard Extension CWGC Plots, Westoutre Brit Cemetery; Locre East Demarcation Stone; Kemmel Hill: French Ossuary, French Memorial, Belvedere; Kemmel Château Mil CWGC Cemetery; La Laiterie CWGC Cemetery; American Memorial; Vierstraat Demarcation Stone; Suffolk CWGC Cemetery; Godezonne Farm CWGC Cemetery; French 32nd Div Memorial; Kemmel No 1 & Klein Vierstraat Brit CWGC Cemeteries; Dickebusch Group of Cemeteries and Dikkebus Lake; Menin Gate. If possible travellers should return to the Menin Gate by 2000 hours (any and every day of the year) for the Last Post ceremony.

• **[N.B.]** : The following sites are indicated: Meteren Village (Montgomery); Klijte (La Clytte) (Anthony Eden).

MAP 16: FOURTH YPRES (BATTLE OF THE LYS) 7-29 APRIL 1918

Legend

1. Hyde Park Corner CWGC Cem
2. Ploegsteert Mem & Berkshire CWGC Cem
2a. Ploegsteert Information Centre
3. Underhill Farm CWGC Cem
4. Neuve Eglise Churchyard CWGC Plot
4a. Capt Crowe VC Plaque
5. Dranoutre Churchyard CWGC Plot
6. Dranoutre Mil CWGC Cem
6a. Locre No 10 CWGC Cem
7. Demarcation Stone Locre South
8. Locre Hospice CWGC Cem
9. Willie Redmond Mem
10. Locre Churchyard CWGC Plots
11. French 17/18th Cavalry, 4/12th Dragoons & 23rd Inf Regt Mems
12. Mont Noir CWGC Cem
13. 34th Div Mem
14. Westouter Churchyard & Extension CWGC Cems

15. Westouter Brit CWGC Cem
16. Demarcation Stone Locre East
17. French Nat Cem & Ossuary, Kemmel
18. French April 1918 Mem
19. Belvedere Kemmel
20. Kemmel Château CWGC Cem
21. Demarcation Stone Kemmel
22. La Laiterie CWGC Cem
23. American 27th & 30th Div Mem
24. Suffolk CWGC Cem
25. Godezonne Farm CWGC Cem
26. French 32nd Div Mem
27. Demarcation Stone Vierstraat
28. Kemmel No1 CWGC Cem
29. Klein Vierstraat CWGC Cem
30. Dickebusch Group Cems

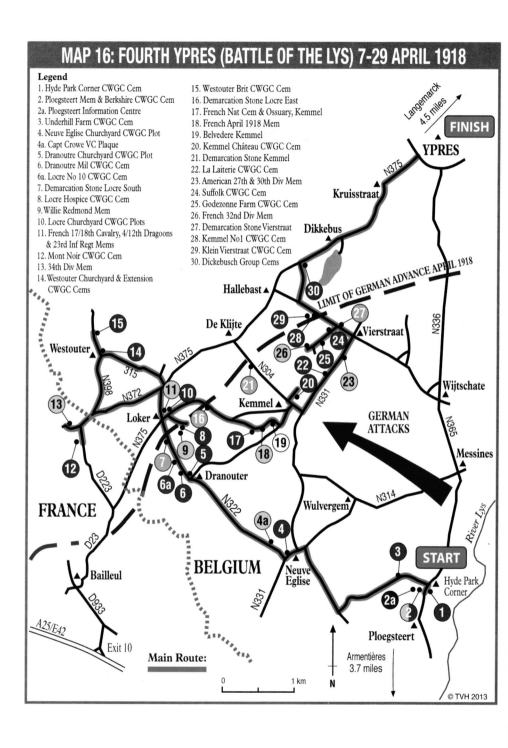

© TVH 2013

- **Total time:** 5 hours 40 minutes
- **Total distance: 28.5** miles
- **Distance from Calais to start point:** See 1st, 2nd and 3rd Ypres Tour
- **Base town:** Ieper
- **Maps:** Major & Mrs Holt's Battle Map of the Ypres Salient plus best of all are *the Carte de Belgique* 1:25,000 Nos. 20/5-6, 28/1-2, 28/3-4, and 28/5-6. *The Carte de Belgique* No. 28 IEPER 1:50,000 is coloured and covers the whole area and shows the road changes, including the motorway. IGN 2 Lille/Dunkerque 1:100,000 covers the area.

Set your mileometer to zero.

From the Ploegsteert Memorial drive in the direction of Ieper to the first turning to the left signed to Underhill Farm CWGC Cemetery.

This was **Hyde Park Corner**. To the right is a small track known as 'Mud Lane' which leads eventually to St Yvon (qv) and is part of one of the walking tours suggested by the Comines-Warneton Tourist Office.

Turn left. Continue past the wooded area to the left (the 'Bois de Boulogne') *to the cemetery on the right.*

• *Underhill Farm CWGC Cemetery/.7 miles/10 minutes/Map 16/3/Lat & Long: 50.74103 2.870145*

Started in June 1917 during the Battle of Messines and used until 1918 when it fell into German hands in the spring (it was recovered in September 1918), this cemetery at the foot of Hill 63 (Rossignol, or Nightingale, Heights) contains 102 UK, 47 Australian, 1 Canadian, 39 New Zealand, 1 unknown burial and 5 Special Memorials. The Cemetery was designed by G.H. Goldsmith. From the back of the cemetery Niewkerke (Neuve Eglise) Church spire can be seen. Here is **Comines-Warneton Information Panel No 19** re Underhill Farm and the Château de Rosenberg (shown on several trench maps as 'Rosemberg'. By 1918 this area was covered with a lattice work of light railways, one branch of which ran past the left hand edge of the cemetery.

The area of the old Château de Rosenberg some 350 yards behind the cemetery was defended by the 19th Hussars and 1st Dorsets in 1914. In 1918, 25th Division held the position.

Continue along what was known as 'Red Lodge Road' to the T junction and turn right along 'Leinster Road' (Zuidlindestraat). After entering Nieuwkerke (Neuve Eglise), turn left at the T junction and continue to the car park by the church.

• *Neuve Eglise Churchyard, CWGC Plot/3.6 miles/10 minutes/Map 16/4/Lat & Long: 50.74567 2.82554*

On the morning of 13 April 1918, the Germans pushed the tiring troops of 34th Division back towards Neuve Eglise broadly from the direction of Hyde Park Corner and in response to their pleas for help 100th Brigade sent forward their 'Battle Reserve', the 2nd Worcesters. By late afternoon the Worcesters were forced northwards up the N331 into the village, the CO, Colonel Stoney, losing contact with A, C and D Companies. He set up his HQ in the *Mairie* and with help from two rifle platoons of B Company barricaded the windows, made improvised loopholes and prepared the area for defence. (The *Mairie* has been rebuilt opposite the church. At the time of the action described, it was on the right hand side 200 yards up the Dranouter Road from the junction ahead.)

Belgian Veterans' Plaque, Neuve Eglise Churchyard.

At dawn the *Mairie* was surrounded and mortar shells were falling on it, causing many casualties. Machine guns were firing at it on three sides, from the church where you now are, from the crossroads to the south and from the open high ground to the west. Something drastic had to be done and 26-year-old **2nd Lt Anthony Johnson**, who in the previous two days had carried messages between the companies, volunteered to set out for help, but was killed, winning a **bar to his MC** for his bravery. He is buried in Kandahar Farm CWGC Cemetery. What happened next is described at the following stop.

At the entrance to the Churchyard is an impressive local War Memorial. The CWGC plot, with its Cross of Sacrifice, contains 69 UK, 5 Australian, 1 Canadian, 1 Indian, 1 New Zealand and 1 unknown burials from WW1 from 1914, 1915 and 1918 and a World War II plot of 11 UK, 3 Belgian and 1 French burials. The Cemetery which had been used by fighting units and field ambulances at intervals during the war was captured by the Germans on 14 April 1918 and retaken by the 36th (Ulster) Division on 2 September and there is a row of 7 RIR burials from 2/3 September 1918 along the side.

Continue to the junction and turn right direction Dranouter on the N322.

•*Plaque to Captain J.J. Crowe, VC, Nieuwkerke/3.8 miles/10 minutes/ Map 16/4a/Lat & Long: 50.74662 2.82223*

Continuing the story from above, the adjutant of the Worcesters, **Captain J. J. Crowe,** asked for volunteers to go with him to silence one of the machine guns, which was successfully done, CQMS Trotman joining him. However, enemy reinforcements continued to enter the village and the ammunition at the *Mairie* was running out so, at about 1330, Colonel Stoney gave the order to withdraw. Under covering fire from Private F.R. Bough the whole force retired safely along the Dranouter Road. For this action Private Bough and CQMS Trotman were awarded the DCM, Lt Colonel Stoney the DSO and **Captain Crowe** the **VC.**

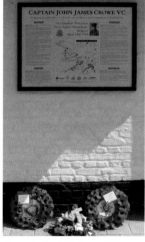

While this was going on, the other companies of the Worcesters were engaged in isolated actions with the enemy. Just beyond Neuve Eglise to the north east, about half a mile on the N331 past the church in the area of the T Junction where you turned into the village, **Lt C.S. Jagger** (qv) rallied the remnants of D Company and held up the German advance from the east. Gathering stragglers of other regiments he set up defensive positions in the buildings at La Trompe Cabaret (now called Trompe) and held on until relieved. As they were moving back, Jagger was badly wounded, but survived, both to receive the MC and to become a famous sculptor.

Plaque to Capt J.J. Crowe VC, Nieuwkerke Hospice.

On 16 April 2011 an **Information Plaque** in a wooden frame was erected on the white wall of the Hospice (opposite the fire station on the Dranouter Road) to commemorate **Capt Crowe's action.** Over 30 members of his family and representatives of the Mercian Regiment attended. It describes Crowe's action in detail, complete with photo, clear sketch map and text in English, French Dutch and German. Capt Crowe, age 41, was awarded his VC by King George V in the field on 6 August 1918. He died, age 88, in 1965, when the Rev Tanner (see above) assisted at his funeral.

Continue on the N322.

Before the Kaiser's Offensive of March 1918 this area was well behind the lines with many camps dotted each side of the road – Wildy, Alexander, Inkerman, Ayrshire, Lurgan etc to which light railways provided access.

Continue to the T junction, turn left and continue to the church.

Memorial to Kapt-Vlieger B. De Hemptinne,
Dranouter Churchyard.

Headstone of 2nd Lt G. Staniland,
Dranoutre Churchyard CWGC Plot.

• *Dranouter Churchyard Cemetery and CWGC Plot/6.0 miles/15 minutes/Map 16/5/Lat & Long: 50.76603 2.78340*

This contains 19 UK burials and 2 unknowns who still lie in this small plot, 19 graves having been moved in 1923 to the nearby Military Cemetery. The churchyard was used for burial by the British from October 1914 until the Military Cemetery was opened in July 1915. In the far left corner is a Memorial in the form of a Belgian soldier, erected by the Flemish Old Soldiers' Association with the Joe English 'AVV-VVK' (qv) insignia. Beside it is a World War II memorial in the shape of an aeroplane tail to **Capt Flyer Baudouin de Hemptinne**, 5 May 1942, inaugurated in May 1992. Hemptinne was shot down in his Spitfire in the Operation known as *Circus 157*, an RAF bombing mission on the electricity power station at Lille. It was aborted due to cloud cover but 4 Spitfires were shot down in this area while returning to the UK. See www.lestweforget.vpweb.be There is an Information Panel outside the Cemetery which describes the Operation.

In the right-hand British plot (all burials from 1914) is the grave of Norbert D'Huysser, age 9, an innocent victim of the war. His headstone is non-standard. Just inside the hedge to the right is a long row of 1915 headstones in single file. At the front is the grave of **2nd Lt Geoffrey Staniland**, Lincolnshire Regt, 13 April 1915, age 31. Three months later the body of his brother, **Capt Meaburn Staniland**, 29 July 1915, was brought here for burial in the nearest space – the third from the end of the row. [The remarkable story of the brothers is told in Martin Middlebrook's, *Captain Staniland's Journey*].

Continue round the church to the right and then turn left on Vierstraat following signs to Dranoutre Mil Cemetery.

Dranoutre Military CWGC Cemetery.

• *Dranoutre Military CWGC Cemetery/6.2 miles/10 minutes/Map 16/6/Lat & Long: 50.76749 2.78025*

This was the area of Lurgan Camp and is approached by a track that passes alongside the local timber yard where you should park and walk up the grass path to the left. The Cemetery, was in use from July 1915 until the German assault of March 1918. There are 421 UK, 17 Australian, 19 Canadian, 1 New Zealand, 3 unknown and 1 German burials. Many of those from April-June 1916 were of the 72nd Bde of 24th Division. The entire back row is from September 1918. Buried here is a member of the Australian YMCA, the **Rev Thomas George Trueman,** attd 5th Bn Australian Inf, killed on 22 March 1918, age 30, and **Pte Frederick Broadrick** of the Royal Warwickshires who deserted from his billets in Locre on 1 July 1914. He was arrested in Calais five days later and, as he was already serving a suspended death sentence for a previous desertion, was executed on 1 August at Dranoutre.

The Cemetery, designed by Charles Holden, has a most pleasing lay-out. A beech hedge surrounds the area and one enters onto a generous lawn then ascends a few steps cut into a fine low grey dry stone wall to the graves area and Cross of Sacrifice. In mid-summer there is a joyous mixture of flowers.

Dranoutre was captured by the Germans under the Crown Prince of Bavaria on 25 April 1918. The depth of the German advance in this area during Fourth Ypres was formidable and can be readily seen by using a pencil to join the marker stones K13, L1, L5 and L13 on the Holts'Ypres Map.

Continue to the cemetery on the left.

• *Locre No 10 CWGC Cemetery/6.6 miles/10 minutes/Map 16/6a/Lat & Long: 50.77178 2.77698*

This Cemetery, with a most unusual layout has a large lawn with the headstones against the walls and with an extra plot at right angles on the left (mostly with German graves) - was originally started by the French during the German offensive of April 1918. After the Armistice the French graves were removed (probably to the Kemmel Ossuary) and British and German dead were reburied here from the surrounding battlefield. There are 55 UK burials, mostly of the 2nd London Scottish and the 2nd S Lancs, and some 150 Germans lie under a number of headstones with multi-burials, some with flat tops, some with pointed. There are 14 Unknowns. There are many burials from 21-23 August 1918, among them, Pte J. Pickup, S Lancs, 21 August 1918, age 20, whose headstone bears the message, 'Some day we'll understand.' The Cemetery was designed by W H Cowlishaw.

Continue to the Demarcation Stone on the left.

Locre No 10 CWGC Cemetery.

• *Locre South Demarcation Stone/6.9 miles/Map 16/7/Lat & Long: 50.77597 2.77497*

Unusually this Demarcation Stone does sit pretty precisely on the limit of the German advance of 1918. Often the stones have been placed at the 'nearest' or 'safest' point. The line here ran at right angles across the road and the German advance had come up the road as you have done

Continue into Loker and turn right just before the Church and right again in about 100m. Continue to the sign to the right to Locre Hospice Cemetery and park. Walk up the grass path beside House No 34.

• *Locre Hospice CWGC Cemetery & Private Memorial to Major Redmond/7.8 miles/20 minutes/Map 16/8, 16/9/Lat & Long: 50.77961 2.78108*

This was opened in June 1917 (during the Battle of Messines) and used until April 1918 when the Germans attacked. It lies near the Hospice, now also a school and a convent, and was the scene of fierce battles in 1918. The Germans took the area in April and the French counter-attacked on 20 May 1918. They failed to retake the position, which was only regained in July.

The Cemetery contains 238 UK burials, amongst them 28 year old **Pte Denis Jetson Blakemore** of the 8th N Staffs, who was arrested in Boulogne 18 days after he deserted whilst already serving a suspended sentence for the same offence. He was shot on Mount Kemmel on 9 July 1917, and his grave bears the inscription, 'Thy will be done'. Also buried here is **Pte William Jones** of the 9th RWF, a stretcher bearer who absconded whilst taking a wounded man to a dressing station on 15 June 1917. Jones gave himself up to the assistant Provost-Marshal at Bristol on 4 September and was shot on Kemmel Hill on 25 October. He, too, was already under a suspended sentence for desertion. Who now can blame these men for reaching the end of their tether under unspeakably horrific conditions? Tragically their supposed 'crimes'were committed in an age when there was little understanding of the reasons why. Their sentences were imposed 'For the Sake of Example' and in his forthright book, *A Brass Hat in No Man's Land*, Brig-Gen F.P. Crozier wrote, 'I should be very sorry to command the finest army in the world on active service without the power behind me which the fear of execution brings.' [See the Introduction for news of a blanket Pardon in 2006.] There are also 2 Australian, 1 British West Indies, 1 Canadian, 1 New Zealand and 2 German burials with 12 unknown. The Cemetery was designed by W H Cowlishaw.

Beside the Cemetery entrance a path leads to the **Private Memorial** grave of **Major William (known as 'Willie') Hoey Kearney Redmond** (now maintained by the CWGC). Redmond was the Irish Nationalist MP for Wexford, then for North Fermanagh and finally for East Clare. Born in 1861 he was a fervent Irish nationalist and was imprisoned as a nationalist 'suspect' in 1881. With his brother   John, the MP for Waterford, who was Charles Parnell's successor as leader of the Nationalist Party 1890-1916, he went on a political mission to Australia and America in 1883. He joined the Royal Irish Rifles and was a well-loved officer. Wounded in the attack on Messines on 6 June, the 54 years old Redmond's injuries proved fatal. He was taken to the 36th (Ulster) Division Dressing Station at Dranouter where he subsequently died. His body was originally buried in the Nuns' garden, in a spot personally chosen by Colonel Rowland Feilding (qv) who had described him as 'a charming fellow'. On 20 October the Mayor of Wexford, accompanied by'a red-hot Sinn Feiner', came from Dublin to visit the grave.

The 'Hospice' of the title was on the other side of the road about 100 yards up towards the church.

Turn round and return to Loker Church. Turn right past the local War Memorial and stop.

Private Memorial to Major Redmond with Kemmel Hill behind.

• *Locre Churchyard CWGC Plot & French Plaques /8.4 miles/15 minutes/Map 16/11, 16/10/Lat & Long: 50.78179 2.77234*

In the churchyard are the two plots of Locre Churchyard Cemetery, one either side of the church. Here are 184 UK burials, including the sad graves, side by side, of two young Privates of the 1st Royal Scots Fusiliers: **Andrew Evans** and **Joseph Byers** (the first Kitchener Volunteer to be executed and who was not represented at his trial). Both were shot at Locre on 16 February 1915, for'attempting to desert'. In the next row lies 20-year-old **Pte George Collins** of the 1st Lincolns, shot on 15 February for desertion – also undefended at his trial. Also buried here is **2nd Lt C. Hawdon,** Yorkshire Regt, age 20, 27 June 1916, two of whose brothers fell in the war. There are 31 Canadian and 2 unknown burials.

Beyond the main entrance to the Church, past the children's playground and by the bus stop, is a large stone Memorial which bears Plaques to French units who succeeded in repulsing the Germans from the village in April 1918: the **17th & 18th Light Cav of 2nd Bde, the 4th & 12th Dragoons** and the **23rd Inf Regt**. (They were moved here when the churchyard wall was replaced with a hedge.)

In the church on Sunday 17 December 1916, Col Rowland Feilding, commanding the 6th Connaught Rangers, arranged a special Church Parade and High Mass for his Irish troops. The men marched through the village with pipes and drums and three priests officiated.'All was very impressive,' wrote Col Feilding to his wife, 'and, considering that they are only out of the trenches

Plaque to French 17th &18th Light Cavalry, Locre.

Headstone of Pte J. Byers, Locre Churchyard CWGC Plot.

for a few days' rest, the smart and soldierly appearance of the men was very remarkable.' Rowland Feilding was the very best kind of Regimental officer. He had a genuine love of and respect for his men and commanded the same in return. In a typical gesture, Feilding got his wife to obtain miniature crucifixes, have them blessed by the Pope and brought back from Rome by a Cardinal. They were presented to the men (each of whom kissed the crucifix as he received it) at another splendid Church Parade on 22 April 1917. The Mass was conducted by Father O'Connell 'for Mrs. Feilding's intention'. 'I may admit that the devout reverence of these soldiers, redolent of the trenches, as they filed towards the altar, affected me, too, very deeply,' reported the Colonel.

Continue to the acute junction on the left with the N372.

This is **Canada Corner**.

Turn left on the N372, signed Zwarteberg and Rodeberg, and continue uphill over Rodeberg.

You are now driving through the most scenic and popular tourist area of Flanders, with many **hotels, hostels and restaurants**, including the basic **Hotel Kosmos** (Tel: +(0) 57 44 44 55) catering for student groups.

Continue to the junction with the D223 just over the French border.

You are driving through the bustling and busy area of souvenir shops, **restaurants, snack bars and hotels**.

Turn first left and continue to the sign to Mont Noir Mil Cemetery to the right. If it is not too wet and muddy the final track is negotiable by car, but there is no turning area at the end.

• Mont Noir Military CWGC Cemetery/11.0 miles/ 15 minutes/Map 16/12/Lat & Long: 50.77663 2.73821

The Cemetery was started in April 1918 during the First Battle of the Lys and used again in the Second Battle of September 1918. At the Armistice it contained 96 British and 33 French graves (all of the 26th Dragoons or the 88th Infantry Regiment). It was enlarged afterwards by the concentration of 57 more British graves (including some from November 1914) from the surrounding battlefields and more French graves (from March-May 1915 and April-May 1918), one Australian and two Newfoundlanders. There are 2 graves from WW2. The traditional CWGC Cross of Sacrifice is mirrored by a French Cross to the *Morts Pour La Patrie* 1914/1915 /1916/1917/1918. The Cemetery lies in a disused sandpit.

Turn round and return to the junction with the D318/N372. Turn left and continue uphill to the Memorial on the right past the old Hotel du Mont Noir.

Grave of Foilleret, Mont Noir CWGC Cemetery.

• 34th Division Memorial, Mont Noir/11.5 miles/5 minutes/Map 16/13/Lat & Long: 50.77915 2.73481

Mont Noir was captured by the Cavalry Corps on 13 October 1914. In November 1914 3rd Division set up their HQ in Mont Noir Château (about 650 yards further on the left in what is now a Park area) and 'Billy' Congreve (qv), ADC to General Haldane, reported in his diary on 25 November 'We are going to keep the Château as our night headquarters and use the Scherpenberg Hill (about 2½ miles north east of here) as a day headquarters'. It was held throughout the 1918 Battles of the Lys (Fourth Ypres) but there were anxious moments when it looked as if the Germans were going to break through. The advanced HQ of 34th Div came to Mont Noir on the afternoon of 12 April and on 15 April General Nicholson, the divisional commander who was having trouble maintaining contact with his brigades in the confusion of the battle, brought the brigade HQs together in a large dugout on the hill and co-ordinated his artillery support from there. On 21 April the fighting in the immediate area died down and the division was relieved by the French 133rd Division while 34th Division went back to Abeele. In the period 8-21 April 1918, the division lost almost 200 officers and over 4,700 soldiers. A New Army division, the 34th had as its first commander Major General E.C. Ingouville-Williams (Inky Bill) who was killed on 23 July 1916, and is buried in Warloy Baillon CWGC Cemetery on the Somme.

This handsome Memorial of a victorious female figure, the Angel of Victory, is similar in style to the Division's memorial at La Boisselle on the Somme, but there the figure no longer holds her laurel wreath. On the base is the Division's black and white checkerboard insignia and the Division's ORBAT. The memorial commemorates the officers and men 'who fought near this spot October-November 1918 and is on the site of the Divisional Headquarters during the Battles of the Lys' when the Germans captured Kemmel Hill, little more than 5km ahead, just over the Belgian border.

34th Division Memorial, Mont Noir.

It bears the legend, 'On the eastern slopes of this ridge the 34th British Division finally stopped the German advance from Armentières 9-21 April 1918.'

Behind the large building adjacent to the Memorial, on **private ground**, is a **Bunker** dating from 1938 with a Maginot Line style metal cupola.

Turn round and continue downhill, passing a well-preserved, ivy-covered Bunker on the right.

N.B. Some 3 miles to the southwest lies the village of Meteren. In this village on 13 October the 1st Bn the Royal Warwickshires made an attack on the enemy. One platoon was led by its lieutenant with drawn sword, who ran it through 'a large German' and then took him prisoner. He was then shot through the chest and saved by one of his soldiers who ran to put a field dressing on the wound. The soldier was then shot in the head by a sniper, collapsing over his officer, and thereby saving him. The lieutenant was taken back to an ADS, where he looked in such bad shape that a grave was dug for him. He survived, however, to be transported back to base hospital and thence to the UK, returning to the front in early 1916 as a brigade-major. That 26-year-old lieutenant, who had joined the regiment in 1908, was none other than **Bernard Law Montgomery**, who led the British to victory at El Alamein in 1942, and was promoted to Field Marshal on 1 September 1944. There is little doubt that Monty's horror at the loss of life in World War I led to the cautiousness that was sometimes criticised by his American colleagues in World War II.

Cross the border into Belgium and take the first (sharp) left signed Westouter on the D398 and continue into the town.

Westouter. This was another behind-the-lines area where tired troops went to get some rest before being sent into the front line once more. The 3rd Division rested here for four days from 22 November 1914, exhausted from their participation in the First Battle of Ypres.

Continue to the church and park.

• *Westouter Churchyard & Churchyard Extension CWGC Cemeteries/13.3 miles/10 minutes/Map 16/14/Lat & Long: 50.79778 2.74634*

The local churchyard and then the extension were used by the British from November 1914 until April 1918. The extension contains 64 UK, 1 Australian, 15 Canadian, 1 New Zealand and 3 German burials.

Continue, direction Poperinge. On the right is

• *Westoutre British CWGC Cemetery/13.3 miles/10 minutes/Map 16/15/Lat & Long: 50.80048 2.74535*

This was begun in October 1917 during the Third Battle of Ypres. It contains 166 UK, 4 Canadian, 3 New Zealand and 3 Chinese burials. There is one French WW2 burial. **Maj Eric Stuart Dougall VC, MC, 'A'** Bty 88th Bde RFA, 14 April 1918, age 32, is 'known to be buried' here. Dougall won his VC on 10 April at Messines when he managed to maintain his line of gunners throughout the day, under intensive fire, thereby delaying the German advance. Among many moving inscriptions in this cemetery, Dougall's says, 'A man greatly beloved.'

Turn round and return to Westouter. Turn left after the church signed Ieper and continue on the N315 to the N375. Turn right signed to Armentières and continue to Loker. Immediately after Loker Church turn left onto Kemmelbergweg and continue straight on to the first crossroads, keeping to the right. Continue to the Demarcation Stone on the right.

Headstone of Maj E.S. Dougall, VC, MC, Westoutre British CWGC Cemetery.

• Locre East Demarcation Stone/16.5 miles/Map 16/16/Lat & Long: 50.78371 2.79167

The stone sits where a light railway crossed the road. It linked a considerable number of rest camps in the area, the one immediately left being 'Bulle Camp'. Pronounce it as you wish!

Continue uphill, over the next crossroads following signs to Kemmelberg and French Ossuary, to the Cemetery on the right.

• French National Ossuary, Kemmel/17.3 miles/10 minutes/Map 16/17/OP/Lat & Long: 50.77883 2.80838

The cockerel (emblem of France) standing on an elongated pyramid marks the ossuary where 5,294 officers and soldiers lie buried, most of whom fell in the April 1918 battle of Mount Kemmel. Of these only fifty-seven have been identified. The bodies were concentrated here between 1920 and 1925. On the right of the pyramid are inscribed the French units which fought in Belgium and on the left the names of their commanders. Standing in front of the Memorial and taking the cockerel as 12 o'clock, the wireless aerial of Mont des Cats can be seen at 11 o'clock on the horizon. To the right of it the abbey is visible in the

French National Cemetery, Kemmelberg.

dip between Mont Noir to the left and Mont Rouge to the right – trees permitting! There are Information Boards giving the history of the French 4th Army in the battles of April-19 October 1918 with a plan of the 1918 Flanders Battles with some interesting contemporary photos..

Continue uphill on a cobbled road, evocative of '14-'18, to the memorial on the right.

• Memorial to French Soldiers 1918/17.4 miles/ 5 minutes/Map YP L4 and Map 16/18/Lat & Long: 50.77820 2.81064

This 60ft high column with its winged figure commemorates those who fell in the battles on the Flanders Hills during the German assault of April 1918. Until 1970, when it was struck by lightning, the column was capped with a French casque. It was unveiled by General Pétain in 1932. The French plaque on the Cloth Hall commemorates in general the French who fell in the Salient. This Monument commemorates the units who fought in this sector and whose names are inscribed around the column.

Continue uphill.

To the right is signed the 3-star **Hostellerie Kemmelberg** with 16 bedrooms, gourmet restaurant and superb views from its terrace. Closed Sun night and Mon. Tel: + (0) 57 45 21 60. E-mail: info@kemmelberg.be. During the war the building on this site was known as the *Belle View Cabaret*.

Continue to the tower and car park on the right.

French Memorial, Kemmelberg.

• *Kemmel Hill and Belvedere/17.6 miles/15 minutes/Map 16/19/RWC/ OP/Lat & Long: 50.77915 2.81555*

The tower, which is a rebuilt and different version of the original which was destroyed during the war, is open from the end of April to the end of September and may be climbed for a small fee. On a clear day it provides superb views over the Salient to Ypres and beyond as well as south to Armentières. The pleasant **Restaurant** has a bar and can offer snacks or full meals during the season. Tel: + (0) 57 44 54 13, closed on Tuesday except by prior appointment.

The hill was in Allied hands until Fourth Ypres. The French had taken it over on 17/18 April 1918, by which time the Germans had stormed through Armentières and pushed the front to a line running from Dranouter to Wijtschate. On 25 April, preceded by a savage artillery barrage of high explosives and gas that one French soldier described as 'worse than anything at Verdun', three and a half German divisions attacked the six French regiments holding the hill. By 0710, the Alpine Corps, leading the assault, reached the summit taking 800 prisoners. Before 0730 Kemmel village fell to the German 56th Division which took 1,600 prisoners. French infantry tumbled in confusion down the far side of the hill, their failure to hold the height adding to the distrust that was growing between the Allied politicians as to what each others' true defence priorities were – Paris or the Channel ports. However, German faith in victory and a determination to carry on had reached their zenith and commanders and soldiers began to lose heart. Early in August there were rearward movements in the south and the Allies kept up a

The Belvedere, Kemmel Hill.

constant pressure so that, on the night of 29 August, withdrawal began along the whole front, the British 34th Division retaking Kemmel on 31 August.

Continue downhill.

As you turn right out of the car park there is an unreadable concrete and brick **Memorial** on the bank to the right to a **French Regiment.**

Continue to the bottom of the hill, turn left downhill into Kemmel past the bandstand and turn left again on the N304 signed to Poperinge and then immediately right following signs to Kemmel Château Mil Cemetery on the right.

• *Kemmel Château Military CWGC Cemetery/18.8 miles/10 minutes/ Map 16/20/Lat & Long: 50.78667 2.82888*

An early cemetery, begun in December 1914, it was used until the German offensive of March 1918 and again from September of that year when the village was retaken. It contains 1,030 UK, 24 Australian, 80 Canadian, 1 New Zealand, 21 unknown and 21 World War II burials from May 1940. Many men from the Sherwood Foresters and from Irish Regiments lie here. Also buried in the cemetery is **Lt Col Guy Louis Busson du Maurier, DSO**, of the 3rd Bn the Royal Fusiliers, killed on 9 March 1915, brother of the novelist Gerald du Maurier. A professional soldier, who had fought in the Boer War, (where, so sensitive a man was he that his hair had turned white when the man next to him had been killed) du Maurier went out to the front in January 1915. Guy was the uncle of George Llewelyn Davies (the original 'Peter Pan'), also newly out.

Nothing of the Château, which was badly damaged in August 1918, now remains but Sir Edwin Lutyens' elegant design retains some of its grace and its grandeur is reflected in the two arches at the entrance. The area was known as 'Kemmel Camp'.

Return to the N304 turn left and at the roundabout turn left on the N331. Continue to the cemetery on the left.

*Headstone of Lt
P. Lightbourn, La
Laiterie CWGC
Cemetery, with
moving personal
message.*

*Entrance with Report
Box, Kemmel
Château Military
Cemetery.*

• La Laiterie CWGC Cemetery/20.0 miles/15 minutes/Map 16/22/Lat & Long: 50.79123 2.84207

The cemetery, named for the Dairy Farm here and designed by Sir Edwin Lutyens assisted by G. H. Goldsmith, contains 468 UK, 7 Australian, 197 Canadian, 1 Newfoundland and 78 unknown burials. It was used throughout the War and enlarged with concentrations after the Armistice. Against the right hand hedge is a row of April/May 1918 graves. L/Cpl J.G. Munro, KO Scottish Borderers, age 19, 25 April 1918, has the message, 'Gone to meet his mother.' Lt P. Lightbourne, Gloucestershire Regt, has the message, 'I cannot say and will not say that he is dead. He is just away.'

Continue to the Memorial on the right.

• American 27th and 30th Divisions Monument/20.5 miles/5 minutes/ Map 16/23/Lat & Long: 50.79763 2.84908

When the war began America was firmly neutral, but the activities of the belligerents at sea began to interfere with American maritime trade and when, on 4 February 1915, Germany declared that she would regard the waters around Great Britain and Ireland as part of the war zone in which even neutral vessels could be targeted, America protested. The stories of German atrocities in Belgium (many, if not all, the products of the Allied propaganda machine), their use of poison gas which was considered an 'evil' weapon, and patently false German propaganda being produced by the Washington embassy, contributed to an atmosphere in which America became sympathetic to the Allied cause. The event that more than any other prompted American entry into the war was the torpedoing of the liner *Lusitania* on 7 May 1915, with the loss of 1,100 lives, some American, although it was two years before war was declared – on 6 April 1917.

Urged on by the Allies, whose armies were hard pressed and anxious for fresh troops, the Americans created the 1st Division from existing formations and sent it to France, the first units landing at the end of July 1917 at St Nazaire. General Pershing established his HQ at Chaumont on the Marne and was soon visited by Clemenceau, the French Prime Minister, who as a schoolmaster had been in Richmond, Virginia, during the American Civil War when General US Grant marched into the city. Clemenceau wanted the Americans to be under the total command of the Allies. Pershing would have none of it. Nevertheless, to accustom the Americans to the 'new' European type of war, some were attached to different Allied formations. The divisions commemorated here, the 27th and 30th, arrived in Europe in May 1918 and served with the British until the Armistice, initially as small units and finally as divisions. In August 1918 the 27th Division took over the sector from, but excluding, Kemmel to here, the 30th Division from here to the area of Lankhof, the front lines being roughly parallel to this road and 700yd west of it (i.e. to the left of the road – the memorial area was behind the German lines). On 31 August 27th Division attacked towards where you are now standing and the following day the 30th followed suit. Both the villages up ahead, Vierstraat and Voormezele, were taken with advances of up to 2,000 yards. Some of the American casualties from the operations here are buried in the Flanders Field cemetery near Wareghem (qv). By the time that the two divisions were relieved three days later the 27th had suffered nearly 1,300 and the 30th some 800 casualties.

The Memorial is a rectangular white block with a soldier's helmet in front resting on a wreath. The architect was George Howe of Philadelphia.

Taking your direction of travel as 12 o'clock, Mont Kemmel and its Belvedere (which you have recently visited) are on the horizon at 7 o'clock.

Continue to the large Goudezeune Prefab building on the left and a group of CWGC signs on the right. Immediately turn left along Vierstraat. Continue to the next small crossroads. Just before it on the left is

The American Memorial, Vierstraat.

• Vierstraat Demarcation Stone/21.1 miles/Map 16/27/Lat & Long: 50.80371 2.84595

This stone once stood alongside the Kemmel No 1 French CWGC Cemetery and before that at the American Memorial and there are still disputes as to its rightful location. A September 1918 trench map shows a German front line to be about 300 yards further on but …

> *Turn left and left again following CWGC signs to the cemetery on the right.*

• Suffolk CWGC Cemetery/21.2 miles/10 minutes/Map 16/24 /Lat & Long: 50.80310 2.84509

This tiny cemetery, approached up a grassy path, containing 47 UK and 8 unknown burials, was begun by the 3rd Suffolks in March 1917. There is a row of York & Lancs burials from April 1918.

> *Continue* (the road was known as 'Cheapside') *to the next cemetery on the left.*

• Godezonne Farm CWGC Cemetery/21.5 miles/10 minutes/Map 16/25/Lat & Long: 50.80059 2.84036/French 32nd Division Memorial/22.1 miles/5 minutes/Map 16/26, Lat & Long: 50.79853 2.83447

Suffolk CWGC Cemetery.

The Cemetery, named after the farm on the site, was made between February and May 1915 by the 2nd R Scots and the 4th Middlesex. It contains 79 burials and in the back row are graves from April/May 1918. Also buried here is **Capt the Hon Douglas Arthur Kinnaird**, son of Baron & Baroness Kinnaird, killed on 24 October 1914. His brother, Lt the Hon A.M. Kinnaird, was killed on 27 November 1917 and is buried in Ruyaulcourt Mil Cem, Pas de Calais. The Cemetery was designed by W.H. Cowlishaw.

> *Continue to the junction ahead.*

Just beyond is the **French 32nd Division Memorial** commemorating the battles of Wytschaete 1914, Kemmel 1918 and the Canal de Charleroi to Dunkerque 1940. Its insignia is in the form of a bunch of grapes.

> *Turn round and return to Vierstraat and turn left, signed Dikkebus. As you drive along here the Flanders Hills are clearly visible to the left. Continue following signs to Dikkebus to the cemetery on the left.*

Monument to French 32nd Division, Vierstraat.

• *Kemmel No 1 French CWGC Cemetery/23.0 miles/15 minutes/Map 16/28/Lat & Long: 50.80546 2.84079*

Originally started by the French, who later removed their burials to the Ossuary at Kemmel or the French National Cemetery at St Charles de Potijze, the plot was taken over by the British. It contains 277 UK, 12 Australian, 3 Canadian, 3 New Zealand, appproximately 250 German in a mass grave and 1 unknown burial. It is approached by an imposing, but fairly steep, flight of stairs. Behind it is

• *Klein Vierstraat British CWGC Cemetery/ Map 16/29*

The cemetery contains 777 UK, 8 Australian, 1 British West Indies, 8 Canadian, 7 New Zealand, 1 South African, and 1 Chinese Labour Corps burials. It was begun in January 1917. All of this area was involved in the fierce fighting during the German April 1918 assault of Fourth Ypres.

Continue and at the next junction keep right up Kerkstraat towards the church. Stop by the cemetery on the right.

• *The Dickebusch Group of CWGC Cemeteries /24.1 miles/20 minutes/Map 16/30/Lat & Long: 50.81833 2.8324*

The cemeteries were designed by Sir Edwin Lutyens, assisted by W.C. Von Berg.

• *Dickebusch New Military Cemetery Extension*

This was begun in May 1917 in succession to the other Dickebusch cemeteries and used until January 1918. It contains 520 UK, 24 Australian, 2 Canadian, 1 South African and 1 German burials.

On the right is

• *Dickebusch New Military Cemetery*

The cemetery, begun in 1915 and used to May 1919, contains 528 UK, 11 Australian and 84 Canadian burials, including the poet and classic scholar Lt R.W. Sterling of the 1st Royal Scots Fusiliers. He was killed on 23 April 1915, after holding a trench all day with fifteen men in the Second Battle of Ypres in 'the storm and bitter glory of red war', to quote from one of his short poems, *Lines Written in the Trenches, 1915.*

Beside the church is

• *Dickebusch Old Military Cemetery*

A front-line cemetery from January to March 1915, it contains 41 UK, 2 Canadian and 1 German burials.

Turn right and after approx 0.8 miles right again following signs to Dikkebus Vijver/Etang (Lake). Stop in the restaurant car park.

• *Dikkebus (Dickebusch) Lake/25.4 miles/10 minutes/RWC/Lat & Long: 50.82188 2.84752*

The name Dickebusch means 'thick forest' and dates from the era when this area was dense woodland. On the right of the path leading, until recently, from the car park to the lakeside **restaurant**, which had a bar and offered snacks, is an old Vauban watchtower and from it around the edge of the water are ramparts dating from 1678 which may be walked. The lake has been artificially enlarged and is a leisure resort for fishing and boating. The patio railings posts are shells and behind them over the water is Kemmelberg. The future of the restaurant is in some doubt.

Dikkebus Lake.

Neither the village nor the lake were ever taken by the Germans, although in the May 1918 fighting they reached the edge of the water. Rest camps (Bristol, Vauban, Maida, Liverpool) of temporary huts and tent lines were set up here and T. E. Hulme (qv), serving with the 1st Bn, the HAC, was billeted here in March/April 1915. The Liverpool Scottish were also here and stayed through May. In 'the Black Hut' in Dickebusch their MO, Noel Chavasse (qv), held his sick parade and he sent home for sweet pea, nasturtium and other seeds to brighten up the huts area (Ann Clayton *Chavasse Double VC*).

Return to the main road and turn right following signs to Ypres.
This whole area was covered by a complex of light and heavier gauge railways. After some 1.5miles the sign to **Belgian Battery Corner Cemetery (Lat & Long: 50.83930   2.86146)** is passed on the left. The 'Corner' is the one where the CWGC sign is.

Continue to the Ieper Ring Road and turn left signed Andere Richtingen, then turn right signed Centrum and park in the Grand' Place. Walk up Meensestraat.

• *The Last Post Ceremony, Menin Gate/28.4 miles/Map 6/3/Lat & Long: 50.85217 2.89166*

This is where the echoes still remain, under the Menin Gate at 2000 hours every evening when the call of the Last Post rings out under the impressive arch. Just before 2000 hours two policemen arrive, stop the traffic and stand guard at each end of the gate. The buglers, sometimes just two, or as many as six in uniform on special occasions, stand at the side of the road by the north-east pillar and, as the Cloth Hall clock strikes eight, they march together into the centre of the road, face the town and play the Last Post.

It is the very simplicity of the occasion that makes it poignant, the absence of martial organisation. Here are people gathered together in an orderly and respectful manner to remember, not because they have been told to do so but because they wish to do so. Now and again a particular regiment may bring a colour party to the occasion, a Legion branch or school cadet force may come, and so the ceremony may be extended by the laying of wreaths, the recitation of Binyon's words of Exhortation, the playing of the Reveille. There are, too, the growing number of conducted battlefield tours groups, but each bows to the Gate's tradition. This is not a ceremony extolling the glories of war. This is remembrance, acknowledgement of a debt by those that remain to those who sacrificed, together with the hope that knowledge of war's legacies might increase the chance of future peace. It is not appropriate to applaud. When the ceremony is over, do thank the buglers. They are dedicated people from the local fire brigades and, often, Commonwealth War Graves gardeners. They take it in turns to play the nightly ceremony with pride. The longest serving was Maurice Barattoo, MBE, who played before and after World War II, followed by Daniel Demey, MBE, who played from 1945 until his death in 1995. Next was Anton Verschoot, MBE, followed by Albert Verkouter MBE, who is now retired from his job with the CWGC. They were joined by the twins, Rik and Dirk Vandekerckehove and later by Tonny Desodt, Raf Decombel, Filip Top, Christophe Wils and Jan Callemein. The organisation behind this unique act of tribute is known as the Last Post Association. Anyone wishing to participate in the ceremony can send a request for an extended Ceremony to the Association via its website, www.lastpost.be E-mail: info@lastpost.be

The original idea for the ceremony was that of Pierre Vandenbroembussche, Commissioner of Police in 1927. From 1 May 1929 the Last Post was sounded every day until interrupted by the Second World War, when the ceremony was continued at Brookwood cemetery near Pirbright. Twenty-four hours after the liberation of Ypres in September 1944 by the Poles the ceremony recommenced. On 8 October 1960 the Last Post was played for the 10,000th time. On 12 July 1992, the 75th Anniversary year of the Battle of Passchendaele, the 65th anniversary of the Menin Gate was celebrated, once more by the presentation of new bugles. For one year, from 1 November 2001 to 31 October 2002, to mark the historic 25,000th playing of the Last Post on 31 October 2001, one soldier was featured each night at the ceremony to represent all his companions who were killed on that date. A book entitled *At the Going Down of the Sun* was produced to commemorate the event, the proceeds of which go to the perpetuation of the Last Post ceremony. It features short biographical details of each soldier chosen – some famous, some hitherto unknown.

• End of Fourth Ypres Battlefield Tour

The Last Post Buglers with the authors.

ALLIED AND GERMAN WARGRAVES & COMMEMORATIVE ASSOCIATIONS

THE AMERICAN BATTLE MONUMENTS COMMISSION (ABMC)

'Time will not dim the glory of their deeds.' Gen John J. Pershing

The Commission was established by Congress in March 1923 and has been responsible for commemorating members of the American Armed Forces where they have served overseas since 6 April 1917 (the date of the US entry into WW1). Its task was to erect suitable memorials and cemeteries. It now administers 24 permanent burials grounds (in which there are 30,921 WW1 burials, in 8 cemeteries, of a total of 116,516 killed in the war), 21 separate monuments and three 'markers', as well as 4 memorials in the USA.

Its first chairman was Gen John J. Pershing who served until his death in 1948. The current Chairman is Retired Air Force Gen. Merrill McPeak, who was chief of staff of the U.S. Air Force from 1990 to 1994. He was elected in June 2011 on the retirement of Gen. Frederick M. Franks, Jr.

After WW1 families were allowed to choose to have their loved ones repatriated (at Government expense) or to be buried near where they fell by the War Department for the Dead. In each of the 8 beautifully landscaped WW1 cemeteries at Brookwood, Surrey; Flanders Field, Waregem; Somme, Bony; Aisne-Marne, Belleau; Oise-Aisne, Fère-en-Tardenois; Meuse-Argonne, Romagne; St Mihiel; Thiaucourt and Suresnes, near Paris, there is a non-denominational chapel (although the atmosphere is predominantly Christian). The land for the cemeteries was given free of charge by the various host countries. The graves are surmounted by brilliant white marble crosses, interspersed by Stars of David for Jewish servicemen. There is no appropriate symbol for men and women of other denominations or for atheists and when the authors queried how a Star of David came to be placed on the grave of an Unknown in Flanders Field the Superintendent explained that the percentage of Jewish servicemen was known and the Unknowns were deemed to be Christian or Jewish in that same proportion. Unknown graves bear the legend, 'Here rests in honored glory an American soldier known but to God.' Identified graves bear the name, unit, date of death (but not of birth), and the home State. Headstones of Medal of Honour winners bear a gold star and the wording is picked out in gold. The pristine grave markers are laid out in perfectly symmetrical lines on immaculately manicured emerald green grass. There are no flower beds in front of the rows but the graves areas are surrounded by beautiful shrubs and trees. Each cemetery contains a luxuriously appointed Visitor's Room with a Superintendent's office where information about the burials may be obtained and in which there is always a Visitor's Book, an example of the Purple Heart medal and photographs of the current President of the USA and of other American cemeteries.

The American flag flies proudly and is lowered when the cemetery closes (now a standard 1700 hours in each cemetery throughout the year, opening time 0900) when *Taps* (the American equivalent of the Last Post) is played. There are rest rooms and good parking. The overall impression is one of pride and glory, with gilded seals and mosaics much in evidence giving the feeling that no expense should be spared to honour the dead.

A progressive programme of installing carillons with pealing bells and a sequence of patriotic and wartime songs in ABMC Cemeteries is underway and is funded by the McCormick Tribune Foundation (www.rrmtf.org) who donate the necessary funding to AmVets National Service Foundation (www.amvets.org). The first carillon was installed in 1985 in the Manila Cemetery. Of the WW1 Cemeteries the Meuse-Argonne, Oise-Aisne, Aisne- Marne, St Mihiel and Somme (Bony) already have their carillons.

As well as the cemeteries the AMBC maintains the impressive WW1 memorials at Audenarde, Kemmel, Bellicourt, Château-Thierry, Cantigny, Sommepy, Montfaucon, Montsec and Brest (Naval). There are also some 700 Private American Memorials in Europe which are presently being located

In Flanders Field ABMC Cemetery.

Headstone of an Unknown American Soldier.

and listed, often by the Superintendents in the nearest ABMC Cemetery. Many of them are in a neglected state but local authorities are being encouraged to help maintain them (see American War Memorials Overseas Inc below).

Memorial Day programmes are held on different days near to the actual Memorial Day date at the end of May in each ABMC Cemetery. Then each grave is decorated with the flag of the United States and that of the host nation (who donated the ground for the cemetery). There are speakers, usually including the appropriate American Ambassador, and the laying of wreaths with ceremonies that include military bands and units.

The American dead of the Salient are buried in Flanders Field Cemetery at Waregem (off the A19 motorway, direction Kortrijk). It contains 368 burials, the majority being of the 37th and 91st Divisions, 21 of which are unknown. Here is buried **Lt Kenneth MacLeish**, USNR, 15 October 1915, brother of the American Pulitzer Prize-winnning poet, social critic and educator, Archibald MacLeish. Tel: + (0) 56 60 11 22.

Head Office: Courthouse Plaza II, Suite 500, 2300 Clarendon Boulevard, Arlington, VA22201, USA. Tel: + 703 696 6897. Fax: + 703 696 6666. Website: www.abmc.gov.

European Office: 68 rue du 19 janvier, 92380 Garches, France. Tel: + (0)1 47 01 19 76. Fax: +(0)1 47 41 19 79.

BELGIAN WAR GRAVES

All Belgian war graves are now administered by the Belgian Institute for Veterans & Casualties, resulting in a much higher standard of maintenance and restoration. The nearest Belgian Military Cemetery to Ieper is in the Forest of Houthulst, (to the north of Poelkapelle on the N301) with 1,704 Belgian, 146 French and 81 Italian burials. It has recently been beautifully renovated.

There is also a Belgian Military Cemetery at Westvleteren. From the road which passes the church in the direction of Poperinghe is a sign *Militaire Begraafplats* leading to the cemetery up a narrow road. This concentration cemetery contains 1,100 graves. Other Belgian Military Cemeteries are at Keiem, to the north of Diksmuide, with 628 burials, and Ramskapelle near Nieuwpoort, with 623 graves, 400 of which are unknown.

Headstone at Houthulst
Belgian Cemetery.

Contact: Didier Pontzeele, Belgian War Graves Institute for veterans, Regentlaan 45046, Brussels, Belgium. Tel: + (0) 22 27 63 34. E-mail: oorlogsgraven@lv-niooo.be

A database giving Belgian military casualties (as well as a yet incomplete list of French casualties in the Salient) may be accessed through www.inflandersfields.be

Individual Belgian graves, with their distinctive yellow, black and red enamelled flag roundel, are to be found in several CWGC and French cemeteries on the routes in this book.

CANADIAN VIRTUAL WAR MEMORIAL/ MAPLE LEAF PROJECT

This database contains information about the more than 116,000 Canadians and Newfoundlanders who have lost their lives since 1884 in major conflicts. It is searchable by family name and gives, where available, service number, age, date of death, unit, force, rank and regiment, citations, honours and awards, burial details and any additional information known. It has been created with the support of Canada's Digital Collections, a programme of Industry Canada. Veterans Affairs Canada are also calling on Canadians to provide photos, documents and other memorabilia to help build up the Virtual War Memorial.

Contact: www.virtualmemorial.gc.ca

The Maple Leaf Project is an all-volunteer registered charity which aims to create an online photographic archive of every Canadian War Grave. **Contact**: Steve Douglas, E-mail: fa516609@ skynet.be Website: www.mapleleaf@legacy.ca In December 2012 Steve was awarded the Queen's Diamond Jubilee medal for services to Canada.

COMMONWEALTH WAR GRAVES COMMISSION (CWGC)

'Their name liveth for ever-more' *Ecclesiasticus 44.14*
[Many detailed and different aspects of the origins and work of the CWGC
have been covered in other *Major & Mrs Holt's Battlefield Guidebooks.*]

Many detailed and different aspects of the origins and work of the CWGC have been covered in other *Major & Mrs Holt's Battlefield Guidebooks*. This information is now readily available on the comprehensive website: www.cwgc.org which covers the Debt of Honour data base, the services, publications and products provided to the public, detailed information about plans for the WW1 Centenary and other news.

In this edition we are very pleased to include the following:

SUMMARY OF THE COMMISSION'S WORK
BY MR COLIN KERR, DIRECTOR OF FINANCE

Part of the landscape of any of your tours will be the Commission's war cemeteries. Large or small, on open plains, or on high peaks, these cemeteries provide a form of reassurance that these men are not forgotten and that, by maintaining sites in a condition of quiet beauty, we somehow see our own values reflected back on us. The sheer scale of a Tyne Cot or a Bayeux can be, literally, shocking to the first time visitor, but any quick scan through the visitors' books will tell you that these sites still retain the power to move people.

Origins
Traditionally, the Commission has kept a very low profile (although this is changing); so, who or what is this organisation, recently described by Sir Max Hastings as a "national treasure"?

Prior to 1914, the military practice after a battle was to place all of the dead into a large pit. This was still the practice in 1914. However, a young officer in the Ambulance Corps, Fabian Ware, working in France in 1914, began to establish a more formal "graves registration unit"and, with Government support, a comprehensive process of recording and tracking was put in place, which continued until the end of the war. By 1917, the scale of the losses was such that an Imperial War Graves Commission was established by Royal Charter, with the Prince of Wales as the patron, managed by Ware.

Russian Headstone,
Mons General Cemetery.

In the aftermath of the war, cemeteries were constructed on land donated"in perpetuity"to Britain, with a"cross of sacrifice"and a"stone of remembrance". In some cases, bodies were exhumed and brought into more central locations. Headstones (of Portland stone) replaced the wooden crosses and families were given the option of adding personal lines at the bottom of each headstone. Major figures worked with the Commission, including Lutyens and Kipling. After impassioned national debate, important decisions were taken: there would be no repatriation of bodies and there would be no distinctions of rank: a general's headstone would be identical to a private's headstone. Of the 1 million dead of the Empire, some two thirds were identified, but the balance were not. Of that remaining one third, memorials would be erected, showing the names of the missing: these would include the massive memorials at Ypres (the Menin Gate), the Somme (Thiepval) and Arras, all designed by Lutyens. Of these men, the bodies of many were found, but could not be identified: they too were buried and Kipling created the phrase"a soldier of the Great War, known unto God". When the Menin Gate was opened by General Plumer in 1926, he declared that "they are not missing, they are here". The words were Kipling's. Churchill, in a speech to Parliament, talked of"periods as remote from our own as we ourselves are from the Tudors, when the graveyards in France shall remain an abiding and supreme memorial to the sacrifices made in the great cause".

This had been *a world* war. Beyond the western front, cemeteries and memorials were erected in Palestine, in Mesopotamia, in Macedonia, in Gallipoli, in Italy and in a host of far flung sites from China, to Kenya, to northern Russia, to the Falkland Islands. The Commission established itself in headquarters in London and was funded by the main countries of the Empire, proportionate to the losses (which were 80% British). The Commission hired skilled gardeners to

Rumanian Headstone, Mons
General Cemetery.

CWGC Employee Headstone,
Mons General Cemetery.

Australian Jewish Headstone, Mons
General Cemetery.

Hooge Crater CWGC Cemetery entrance, reminiscent of the original crater.

bring a sense of tranquillity to the sites and skilled craftsmen to maintain the walls and the headstones. A couple of myths to dispel: the gardens were not designed by Gertrude Jeykll (although she participated in some initial thinking) and they were not supposed to be an"English country garden". The design guidance, drafted by Frederick Kenyon in 1918, talked only of "a sheet of grass and occasional beds of flowers".

Naval casualties were a different matter. Although a specifically naval cemetery was built at Scapa Flow, in the Orkneys, most men went down with their ships. Accordingly, three huge memorials were constructed at Portsmouth, Plymouth and Chatham, to record the names of the missing, most of which were lost at the Battle of Jutland. A further memorial was built at Tower Hill, in London, for the Merchant Navy seamen lost during the war (including the huge losses from the *Lusitania*).

In the UK, the situation was also different. Some 250,000 men from World War 1 are buried in the UK, mostly as a result of dying in hospitals, from their wounds (but also from the influenza epidemic). They will be found, mostly, in big city cemeteries, where the local Councils allocated space for the war dead to be buried. Go to any British town today, and you will see, in the main cemeteries, a section with a cross of sacrifice and the neat rows of headstones, with the high standards of maintenance and gardening which you would find in France. British people are generally unaware of what is on their doorstep.

So, the Commission settled down to complete its cemeteries and memorials and then to maintain them as millions of families made their pilgrimages to these resting places.

World War 2

The end of World War 2 brought a further aspect to the work of the Commission, with a further 700,000 casualties of that conflict. Some of the geography was similar (which is why you will find men from both wars in the cemeteries in France and Belgium), but new cemeteries had to be built

'Roses are blooming' in Dud Corner Cemetery.

in the Netherlands, in Germany, North Africa, Italy, Norway, Singapore and Burma. The other significant change was that the major losses of aircrew resulted in scattered graves literally all over the world and to a new memorial to missing aircrew at Runnymede, in England. The existing naval memorials in England were extended to record the names of the missing from this war.

In the 1960s, the Commission changed its name to the Commonwealth War Graves Commission.

The Commission today

Nearly 100 years on, the Commission continues to go from strength to strength.

With Headquarters now in Maidenhead, England, the Commission comprises the Governments of the UK, Australia, Canada, India, New Zealand and South Africa. It runs its operations from offices in Leamington Spa (UK), Arras (France), Ypres (Northern Europe), Larnaca (Mediterranean) and Delhi (Africa, Asia, Pacific) with smaller offices in Rome, Malta, Cairo, Tel Aviv, Salonica and Gallipoli.

Every year, another 20 to 30 men are found, identified (frequently) and buried with full military honours.

The Arras office contains a headstone production unit, where 22,000 new headstones each year are shipped from the quarries (no longer Portland, but Italy and Bulgaria) and engraved on five machines using computerised images which link back to databases in England. Headstones - particularly in coastal areas - can deteriorate badly over the years. Every five years, the Commission grades every one of its headstones to ensure that, above all else, they are readable.

Details of all 1.7million casualties are stored on the Commission's database, which is accessible through the website (cwgc.org), where as long as you know the name, they will tell you where he is buried (or his name commemorated) and how to get there. They also keep records of foreign nationals (mainly German and French) who are buried in the Commission's cemeteries.

With the imminent centenary of World War 1, the Commission is taking active steps to engage more with the public. Five hundred information panels are being prepared for sites all over the world (although predominantly on the western front) which tell you what happened here, who is buried here and also uses QR code technology to provide stories (often personal letters) about some of the men in the cemetery. The website will also include features on aspects of interest to the public (the war poets, VC holders, sons of famous men, famous sportsmen). Six remembrance trails are being created (including the first day of the Somme, Messines Ridge and the Mons to the Marne retreat). The Commission's sites will host most of the major State events which are planned for the centenary, and the Commission's staff are working closely with British and Commonwealth Governments to ensure that everything goes as planned.

If you were to ask the Commission's staff for a view, they would ask you to think about three things:
• please don't forget the sites in the UK: just go to your local cemetery
• visitors will always go to the Menin Gate and to Thiepval, but please go a bit off the beaten track and visit the lesser known sites: they are every bit as beautiful and they all have their own stories to tell
• if you are going on holiday, see if there is a site near your destination: they are all over the world.

Colin Kerr, Director of Finance

CONTACTS: Head Office: Commonwealth War Graves Commission, 2 Marlow Road, Maidenhead, Berks SL6 7DX, UK. Tel: + (0) 1628 634221. Fax: + (0) 1628 771208. E-mail Casualty & Cemetery Enquiries: casualty.enq@cwgc.org.
Area Office in France: rue Angèle Richard, 62217 Beaurains, Tel: + (0)3 21 21 77 00. Fax: (03) 21 21 77 10. E-mail: france.area@cwgc.org
Area Office Northern Europe: Elverdingsestraat 82, B-8900 Ieper, Belgium. Tel: + (0) 57 20 01 18. Fax: + (0) 57 21 80 14. E-mail: neaoffice@cwgc.org
Interesting and informative Newsletter: newsletter@cwgc.org
19-18 Project Manager. Andrew Stillman: E-mail: Andrew.stillman@cwgc.org

JOINT CASUALTY & COMPASSIONATE CENTRE

In April 2005 the Army, Navy and RAF amalgamated in the Joint Casualty & Compassionate Centre (based at RAF Innsworth), part of Service Personnel and Veterans' Agency, to deal with any remains of service personnel (principally from WW1 and WW2) that are found. The Agency replaced the MOD PS4(A) Compassionate Cell.

They liaise with local embassies and the CWGC when remains are discovered and, if there is sufficient evidence with the remains to give hope for an identification, use historical case files and other appropriate means in their research. In addition and contrary to the long-held policy of the CWGC, even use DNA matching techniques. Once an identification has been made they use the media to trace any family. The wishes of the family are then paramount as to the form of burial (e.g. quiet or formal).
Contact: Sue Raftree, Tel: 01452 712612 ext 6303. Email: historicso3.jccc@innsworth.afpaa.mod.uk Any news will be reported on the general MOD website, www.mod.uk

PARLIAMENTARY ALL-PARTY WAR GRAVES & HERITAGE GROUP

Chairman: Lord Faulkner of Worcester. **Contacts:** Joint Secretaries Peter Barton (e-mail: pb@parapet.demon.co.uk) and Peter Doyle (e-mail: doyle.towers@virgin.net) www.wargraves heritage.org.uk/.

FRENCH MINISTERE DES ANCIENS COMBATTANTS ET VICTIMES DE GUERRE

On 29 December 1915 a law was passed to guarantee a perpetual grave at State expense to every Frenchman or ally 'mort pour la France'. On 25 November 1918 a National Commission of *Sépultures Militaires* was formed to create cemeteries with standard concrete markers (Christian crosses, shaped headstones for Muslims, rounded headstones for Jews and non-believers) on graves laid out in plots, ossuaries, monuments, enclosures and gateways. On 31 July 1930 the cemeteries were declared 'national' and the Service des Restitutions de Corps' was created. The *Tricolore* flies in every French cemetery. Many of the damaged wartime cemeteries were concentrated into larger graveyards. On 29 June 1919 each signatory to the Versailles Treaty agreed to respect and maintain the graves of foreign soldiers on their land. On 11 July 1931 generous finances were allocated to the cemeteries and memorials, permitting the rapid completion of important sites such as Notre-Dame de Lorette, Douaumont etc. After the defeat of 1940 the burial of victims of war was left to municipalities, to private individuals or to the enemy. Once WW2 was over new cemeteries were created, several inaugurated by Gen de Gaulle. Between 1983 and 1990 many of the cemeteries were planted with flower beds (in most case with pinky-red polyanthus roses) and in recent years a programme of erecting Information Boards at the cemetery entrances has been undertaken, describing the combats in the region.

As the Ossuary at Verdun is the focus of French remembrance in the Western Front – South, so the Basilique, Tower and Cemetery at Notre-Dame de Lorette is in the North.

On French soil there rest 997,000 Germans, 450,000 British and Commonwealth, 56,000 Americans, 5,719 Italians, 3,450 Belgians, 21,836 Poles, 1,060 Portuguese, Rumanians, Russians, Serbians etc.
Head Office: 37 rue de Bellechasse, 75007 Paris 07 SP. Tel: + (0)1 48 76 11 35. Website: www. defense.gouv.fr/onac

The Basilique and Graves, Notre-Dame de Lorette.

VOLKSBUND DEUTSCHE KREIGSGRÄBERFÜRSORGE (VDK)

The German War Graves Organisation provides a similar service to that of the ABMC and the CWGC in looking after the German war dead and in assisting relatives to find and, in many cases, visit the graves. In 1925 a treaty was signed between Germany and Belgium to organise care of the German dead from the Great War and from 1929 the Germans replaced the Belgians who had taken over the responsibility from the British, who had been in charge of all exhumations from 1919-1922. Until then the German dead lay scattered in 678 burial places, with one vast cemetery of 8,000 near the CWGC Aeroplane Cemetery near Ypres.

In Belgium many were exhumed and concentrated in cemeteries at Langemarck and Roeselare. In 1954 a new convention granted more land and the dead from the remaining 128 small cemeteries were transferred to Langemarck, Menin and Vladslo. Hooglede remained as it was. Langemarck (the only German cemetery which is actually in the Ypres Salient) contains 44,294 burials, 25,000 of which are in the communal grave surrounded by bronze panels bearing the names of the missing. Hooglede (on the Roeselare-Ostende road) contains 8,247 burials. Menin (on the Franco-Belgian border) contains 47,864 burials. Vladslo (on the Diksmuide-Beerst-Torhout road) contains 25,664 burials and the famous statuary group of Grieving Parents by Käthe Kollwitz. Further landscaping work was undertaken between 1970 and 1972, mainly by volunteer students during their vacations. Work in Langemarck was finally completed in the late 1980s.

The German cemeteries present a stark contrast to those of the ABMC or CWGC. The predominant colours are dark and sombre and a strong feeling of grief for the dead is present. The grave markers are not standard like those in American and British cemeteries and vary from stark black metal crosses, to grey or reddish stone crosses or panels, sometimes laid flat as in Langemarck. They bear, when known, only the soldier's name, rank and dates of birth and death. Usually there are several burials beneath each marker, symbolising comradeship in death as well as in life and because less space was available to the vanquished nation. Most cemeteries contain mass graves for the unidentified with tablets listing the missing. Sometimes there is a small chapel, an entrance/reception chamber with a WC and a dramatic piece of mourning sculpture is often present. Also symbolic is the presence of oak trees, which signify strength but there are no flower beds in front of the rows of graves (although flowering shrubs are sometimes planted on the mass graves).

Similar programmes of progressive concentration and landscaping took place in the German cemeteries in France visited on the battlefield tours in this book. The German plots in St Symphorien Cemetery at Mons and the Le Cateau International Cemetery are particularly diverse and interesting, and also contain German monuments. A list of several thousand German casualties discovered at the CWGC HQ, Maidenhead is being researched by the Passchendaele Museum (qv).

Contact: *Volksbund Deutsche Kriegsgräberfürsorge,* Werner Hilperstrasse 2, D-34112 Kassel, Germany. www.volksbund.de/graebersucherhtml

Belgian Office: Col Yvan Vandenbosch, Zwanebloemenlaan 36, 2900 Shoten, Belgium. Tel: + (0) 36 46 08 75. E-mail: yvan.vandenbosch@tenet.be   www.volksbund.de

French Office: Monsieur le Directeur Technique, Hubert LEHMÜLLER, Service pour l'Entretien des Sépultures Militaires Allemandes, 48 rue de Nesle Prolongée, 80320 Chaulnes. Tel: + (0)3 22 85 27 57. Fax :+ (0)3 22 85 45 66.

THE NATIONAL MEMORIAL ARBORETUM

This site which stands on 150 acres of land reclaimed from gravel workings at Alrewas near Lichfield was the brainchild of its director, David Childs, influenced by conversations with Gp Capt Leonard Cheshire, VC. It was envisaged as a tribute to the war-time generations of the

German Memorial and Graves, Wicres Route de la Bassée Cemetery.

German Plot, St Symphorien Cemetery, Mons.

twentieth century, a gift in their memory for future generations to reflect upon and enjoy and in order that the debt that was owed to those who died in the wars should not be forgotten. It was officially opened on 16 May 2001 by the Duchess of Kent. This site is playing an ever-increasing role in National commemoration.

Financially the project was supported by Redland (who donated the original land), the armed services and veterans' organisations and a grant from the National Forest and the Millenium Fund. Enough money was raised to build the Visitor Centre and the Millenium Chapel (the country's only one). The Chapel contains some beautiful wood carvings and at 1100 each day the Last Post is played inside it and a minute's silence observed.

Since March 1977 over 40,000 trees have now been planted and the site is divided into dedicated plots (plans can be obtained from the Visitor Centre), such as 'The Garden of the Innocents', a tribute to all the young lives lost in the wars; 'War Widows' Wood'; The Dunkirk and Normandy Veterans; 'The Beat', an avenue of chestnuts funded by the Police Force and many more regimental and non-military plots. The 'Shot at Dawn' section where stark stakes laid out in the form of a Greek amphitheatre surround the blindfolded statue by Andy DeComyn of Pte Herbert Burden, age 17 of the 1st Northumberland Fusiliers, executed at Ypres on 21 July 1915, is particularly moving. He is commemorated on the Menen Gate. There is a stake for every soldier executed in the First World War other than for the crime of murder. Stakes can be 'adopted' at a cost of £20.

Contact: National Memorial Arboretum, Croxall Road, Alrewas, Staffs, DE13 7AR. Tel: + (0) 1283 792333. Fax: + (0)1283 792034. E-mail: nmarboretum@btconnect.com
Website: www.thenma.org.uk
Open daily: 1000-1700 (or dusk if earlier). Closed Mon Nov-March. Admission fee payable. Group guided visits by appointment. Allow 90 minutes to cover the whole area. Parking, shop, pleasant restaurant and WCs.

American War Memorials Overseas Inc

Non-profit-making charitable organisation whose mission is to document, raise awareness of and care for, private American gravesites and memorials where the US government has no responsibility, liaising with local, national and international organisations.
Contact: Lil Pfluke, 6 rue du Commandant de Larienty 92210, St Cloud, France. Tel: (0)6 1173 1332. E-mail: info@uswarmemorials.org Website: www.uswarmemorials.org

Antiq'Air Flandre-Artois

Research on and erection of memorials to wartime pilots brought down in the area.
Contact: Jocelyn 'Joss' Leclercq, 51 Route de Fromelles, 59249 Aubers, France. Tel: + (0)3 20 50 27 25.
E-mail: JossLeclercq@orange.fr Website: www.aubers.fr

Association Paysages et Sites de Mémoire de la Grande Guerre

See also INTRODUCTION on page 10. Founded in Paris in 2011 to undertake the enormous task of preparing an inventory and plan for UNESCO recognition of WW1 memorial sites on the Western Front. This involves 12 French Départements from Nord-Pas de Calais to the Haut Rhin, plus sites in Belgium Flanders and Wallonia with a total of 45 major sites, including bunkers, craters, trenches, monuments, cemeteries, chapels, archaelogical sites etc. This is being done in collaboration with the CWGC, ABMC, VDK and French organisation for sites of national memory (PSGHLMN).

Paysages et sites de mémoire de la Grande Guerre

The authors are proud to be '*Partenaires*'. Relevant sites mentioned in this book include the Mons, Ypres Salient, Neuve Chapelle, Vimy/N-D de Lorette and Fromelles.

The Association's logo.

Contact: Secrétaire général Serge Barcellini, Controleur général des Armées. E-mail: paysageset sitesdememoire@gmail.com. Website: heritage-grandeguerre.fr

Aubers Cercle Historique

Founded by respected historian Pierre Descamps. Tel: + (0)3 20 50 22 48. E-mail: aubers.mairie@wanadoo.fr Website: www.aubers.fr

Association des Musées et Sites de la Grande Guerre

A grouping of museums and preserved sites of the Western Front from Ieper in the north, through Notre-Dame de la Lorette, Vimy, the Somme, Compiègne, Blérancourt, Chemin des Dames, the Champagne, Meuse-Argonne, Verdun, St Mihiel and into the Vosges in the south-east. The VDK, CWGC, AMBC and WFA are associates. The aim is to preserve and promote international sites of the '14-'18 War.
Contact: Historial, B.P. 63 – 8201 Péronne Cedex. Tel: + (0)3 22 83 14 18. E-mail: df17@Historial.org

Durand Group

Organisation for historical research into subterranean military features run by well-qualified military, ex-military and other professional members (surveyors, archaeologists, engineers etc.). They have done a great deal of work in the tunnels at Vimy Ridge and its surrounds – see Vimy battlefield Tour also at Loos in the Ypres Salient.
Contact: Via website: www.durandgroup.org.uk

Friends of In Flanders Fields Museum

Formed in October 2001, the Hon President is Governor Paul Breyne, the Chairman Gilbert Ossieur and the Secretary Johan Van Duyse. Benefits include free entrance to the Museum, organised tours and an interesting magazine.
Contact: E-mail: Johan.vanduyse@sd.be Website: www.vriendeninflandersfields.be
Tel: +(0) 57 23 94 50.

Friends of St George's Church

From 1933 the Old Comrades of the Queen's Own Royal West Kent Regiment were encouraged by ex-CQMS Len Dawson to support the upkeep of the Church and to make an annual pilgrimage to it which continued until 1939. In 1945 the Royal British Legion restored the slight damage that St George's Memorial Church had suffered during World War II, but it was soon apparent that on-going funds would be needed to provide for the maintenance of the church. In 1955 the Association of the Friends of St George's Memorial Church was formed under Les Dawson, Col Donald Dean, VC and Maj-Gen Raymond Biggs, CB, DSO. Its objects were to promote interest in the life and work of the church, to provide a link between members in the UK and overseas and the local community, to co-operate with bodies such as the RBL and the CWGC for the benefit of the church and to provide funds to help maintain the fabric of the church and its life.

Contact: the Hon Sec Dr. D. F. Gallagher, e-mail: derek@thegalls.demon.co.uk website: www. stgeorgesmemorialchurchypres.com

Fromelles *Association Souvenir de la Bataille de Fromelles*

Contact: M. Francis Delattre, 42 rue Lammeries, 59249 Fromelles, France. Tel: + (0)3 20 50 64 26.

Guild of Battlefield Guides

Launched on 28 November 2003 the Guild aims to provide a 'kite-mark' for Battlefield Guides in the form of a badge which the public can trust and which it will be deemed an honour to wear. Mission Statement: "To analyse, develop and raise the understanding and practice of battlefield guiding." The Guild is an inclusive organisation, not a regulatory body and aims to engender a 'Club' environment with a magazine and educational and social meetings. The popular and well respected founder Patron, Prof Richard Holmes, sadly died in 2011. The authors are Founding Hon Members.

Experienced Guild Guides are supporting STS in the Governments' Centenary scheme to conduct a teacher and two pupils from every State school to the WW1 battlefields.

Contact: The Secretary, e-mail: secretary@gbg-international.com Website: www.gbg-international.com

The coveted and respected badge of an accredited Guide of the Guild of Battlefield Guides.

The Knowledge Centre, In Flanders Fields Museum

This was the Ieper Documentation Centre, now moved to the restored Cloth Hall and spacious new quarters. See page 247 for more details of this wonderful facility.

Open: Mon- Fri from 1000 - 12.30 and 13.30- 1700. Sint-Maartensplein 3 (opposite the Cathedral). **Contact**: Dominiek Dendooven. Tel: + (0)57 239 450 E-mail: kenniscentrum@ieper.be Website: www.inflandersfields.be

Last Post Association

Inaugurated in 1928 (see page ???) to maintain the nightly ceremony 'In perpetuity'. The long-serving and dedicated M. Guy Gruwez is now Hon Chairman and the acting Chairman Benoit Mottrie. For ceremonial assistance: **Contact**: Jackie Platteeuw, Boterstraat 4, 8900 Ieper. Tel: +(0) 57 48 66 10. E-mail: info@lastpost.be Website: www.lastpost.be

Rick Scherpenberg: WW1 Demarcation Stones

For many years this dedicated Belgian Researcher has been discovering information about the history of, and working hard to discover 'lost' examples and ensure the maintenance of, the Demarcation Stones that run along the old Front line at the sites of the furthest German advance. **Contact**: Rik.Scherpenberg@mil.be http://paul-moreau-vauthier.blogspot.co.uk/

Ross Bastiaan Commemorative Plaques

A series of beautifully designed, durable and informative plaques erected by Australian, Ross Bastiaan, on sites where Australian Forces were engaged with distinction. We met Ross and became friends when he installed his first plaque – in Gallipoli. We tell his story in our Somme Battlefield Guide.

Contact: Website: www.plaques.satlink.com.au

Ross Bastiaan Plaque to Cpl Leggett, VC, Geluwe.

Royal British Legion (RBL)

The UK's foremost Association for the welfare of ex-servicemen, formed in 1921 through the energetic efforts of Earl Haig, received its Charter in 1925 and its 'Royal' prefix in 1971. Amongst its functions is the organisation of pilgrimages to battlefields. Now also runs battlefield tours.

Contact: Website: www.remembrancetravel.org.uk E-mail: info@remembrancetravel@org.uk
National HQ, 199 Borough High Street, London SE1 1AA. Tel: + (0) 20 3207 2100
Ypres Branch: Sec - Rene Declercq. E-mail: RBLYpres@gmx.com Website: britishlegion.org.uk/branches/ypres

Souvenir Français

An Association founded in 1872 after the Franco-Prussian War and revived after WW1. Its aim is to keep alive the memory of those who died for France, to maintain their graves and memorials in good condition and to transmit 'the flame of memory' to future generations.

Head Office: 9 rue de Clichy, 75009 Paris. http://www.souvenir-francais.fr

Souvenir Français Roundel

Western Front Association (WFA)

Formed by John Giles in 1980 to further the interest in WW1 to perpetuate the memory, courage and comradeship of all who fought in it. Two excellent publications: *Stand To* and *The Bulletin.*
Contact: Hon Sec Stephen Oram, Spindleberry, Marlow Road, Bourne End, Bucks SL8 5NL
Website: www.westernfrontassociation.com

www.greatwar.be/ www.wo1.be/www.greatwar.be

An initiative of the Province of West-Flanders it lists all military cemeteries, monuments, memorials, and bunkers, craters and other sites of interest with thousands of photographs, also tourist information.

Contact: vzw Westhoek, c/o Jan Matsaert, Markt 10, B-8957 Mesen. E-mail: info@westhoek.be
OR Robert Missinne. Tel: + (0) 57 48 72 69. Mobile: + (0) 478 572 317. E-mail: wo1@westhoek.be

STOP PRESS

Since submitting the draft for the new edition of this book, plans and projects for the WW1 100th Centenary have progressed apace. We describe some of the most important ones that affect the areas covered by this book.

1. LOOS BATTLEFIELD
a. In February 2013 it was announced that a wind farm with 12 immense turbine windmills ('each twice as high as Big Ben') was proposed to be erected right across the Loos Battlefield (one of which would stand on the site of the Lone Tree) between Vermelles, Auchy-les-Mines and Hulluch. Windmills 4, 5 and 6 would be very close to St Mary's ADS Cemetery. A protest is being mounted by local inhabitants and by those who care about these important battlefields, such residents of Derbyshire and Leicestershire from where many men who lie here came.

b. On 20 September 2015 an important Airshow will be held at Lens commemorating The Battle of Loos, with WW1 aircraft. **Contact:** a.villieu@wanadoo.fr

2. BLACK WATCH CORNER MEMORIAL (Lat & Long: 50.84839 2.98195)
On 3 May 2014 a fine, larger-than-life (4.5metres) bronze statue of a kilted WW1 Black Watch soldier in fighting uniform on a plinth, by Edinburgh sculptor, Alan Herriot, will be inaugurated in a field over the road to commemorate the more than 8,000 officers and men killed and 20,000 wounded in WW1. It will be the only Regimental Memorial specific to the Black Watch of WW1. **Contact:** For information and donations, Maj Ronnie Proctor, Black Watch Assocation. Tel: 01738 623 214 .

Maquette of Black Watch Memorial, Black Watch Corner.

3. WELSH MEMORIAL, PILCKEM RIDGE (Lat & Long: 50.90304 2.90010)

For more details see page 256 Here is a rough artist's impression of how the Memorial will finally look when a bronze Welsh Dragon, which will be painted red and stand in a garden of daffodils in springtime, is added.

4. WAR HORSES "AGONY 1914-18" MONUMENT, Poperinge-Ieper Ring Road Nr Vlamertinge (Lat & Long: 50.84986 2.82085 – at the lay-by)

This striking and very moving Memorial was inaugurated on 11 May 2013.   It was commissioned by the Ieper Town Council and is designed by local artist Luc Coomans. The two skeletal horses (reminiscent of the realistic puppet horses in the stage version of Michael Murpurgo's *War Horse*) rear in pain and agony from a ruined building. The forged steel horses are between 3.5-4.0 metres high on a 2.5 metre base. They symbolise the suffering of the thousands of horses that were killed during the Great War. The site was chosen as

Rough artist's impression of the Welsh Memorial on the Pilckem Ridge.

it is on the border between the behind-the-line area around Poperinge and the hell of the front line around Ieper. The artist commented "Man dragged into war the whole of nature. My work is an indictment against war and any form of violence."

Dramatic War Horses Statue, "Agony", nr Vlamertinge.

5. ADVERT FOR EARL HAIG HOUSE, YPRES, on House No. 65 Poperingeseweg, nr Ieper (Lat & Long: 50.84904 2.87083)

In early 2013, during renovation on the house, the sign, covered (and therefore protected) since the late 1940s by tiles, was exposed and therefore became vulnerable to the elements. It advertises the British Legion (before it gained the word 'Royal') Earl Haig House on the corner of the Grand' Place, Ypres, where Poppy wreaths, Luncheons and Tea were available, giving the Telephone and Telegram numbers. Now the Military Upkeep Preservation Society (Committee Members –

Genevra Charnsley, Chris Lock, Iain McHenry, Lorezo Mylle and Jacques Ryckebosch) have a mounted a campaign to preserve it. Ieper Town Council, Province and Flemish heritage are funding 40% of the costs. To donate to the 60% still required **Contact:** Genevra on E-mail: info@ypres-fbt, www.militaryupkeep.com and Military Upkeep Preservation Society, KBC Bank, IBAN: BE75 738037891151. BIC: KREDBEBB.

Advert for Earl Haig House, Ypres, under restoration.

6. RWF 1st BN MEMORIAL, ZANDVOORTE, by local War Memorial in village centre.

The Memorial, in the form of a classic obelisk, will be inaugurated on 26 October 2014. It is to commemorate the Battalion's costly battles of 19-30 October 1914, in the final battle of which (fought some 500m on the slope to the east of the village) they lost some 6 Officers and 400 men. On 31 October only the Quarter Master and 89 men reported for duty. It also remembers the 10,000 men of the Regiment killed in WW1. The Battalion, comprising mainly of regulars and excellent reservists, was commanded by Lt-Col Henry Osbert Samuel Cadogan, who was among the dead of 30 October. He was aged 46, twice MiD and is buried in Hooge Crater CWGC Cemetery.

Impression of new RWF Memorial, Zandvoorte.

7. CHRISTMAS TRUCE EXHIBITION/COMMEMORATIVE FOOTBALL MATCHES.

An exhibition on the 1914 Christmas Truce between the Saxons and the 2nd RWF at Freilinghien will start in Dresden in August/September 1914, move down to Armentières, then to Ploegsteert and after Christmas to Wales.

Contact: Lt-Gen Jonathon Riley: jr.23@hotmail.co.uk

The football matches played during the truce between the adversaries at various sites along the front will be recreated in Frelinghien, Ploegsteert and on the football pitch at the Peace Village, Messines (qv). There are unconfirmed plans there to involve David Beckham and Franz Beckenbauer. **Contact:** simon.louagie@peacevillage.be

8. WW1 CENTENARY. USEFUL WEBSITES

Plans for commemorating the 100th Anniversaries of the 1914-18 War are constantly changing. Some ambitious projects have had to be abandoned or modified due to the effect of the recession throughout Europe as budgets are reduced; plans for erecting new memorials are hurried through as Regimental Associations and other organisations realise that this is probably the last important opportunity to do so; new multi-media 'Heritage' or 'Remembrance' Trails are developed etc. etc. The following websites will help you to keep up to date with developments (see also Introduction).

Australia. www.awm.gov.au/1914-1918; www.remembrancetrails-northernfrance.com
Canada. http://www.veterans.gc.ca/
Belgium.www.greatwarcentenary.be; www.greatwar.co.uk/events/french-flanders-events.htm; www.accessibleflanders.be
France. http://centenaire.org
Imperial War Museum. www.1914.org
New Zealand. www.ww100.govt.nz
USA. www.ww1-centennial.org
WFA. www.greatwar.co.uk/events/2014-2018-centenary-events.htm

9. 15th Bn 48th CAN HIGHLANDERS MEMORIALS.
In addition to the Memorials described in the main text there is another at Observatory Ridge, erected in 2011, commemorating the role of the 15th Battalion in the battle for Mount Sorrel, June 1916. Lat & Long: 50.832817 2.938717.

10. FIELDS OF BATTLE - LANDS OF PEACE 14-18 (see also page 178 for pic.)
Launched on 6 November 2013 in the Great Hall of Westminster, this stunning selection from the 16,000 WW1 photographs taken over a period of 7 years by GBG Member Michael St Maur Shiel will form a touring exhibition as a 'Street Gallery'. This "gateway to the battlefields' will be complemented by a giant walk-on map of the European area of conflict in its global context and an 'Education Station'. Prestigious sponsors include the CWGC, IWM, Flanders Fields 2014-18 and GBG. **Contact:** Jonathan Price, Chief Executive, Tel: 01689 858877.
E-mail: j.prince@fieldsofbattle1418.org Website: www.fieldsofbattle1418.org

11. PLUGSTREET '14-'18 EXPERIENCE INAUGURATION. 9 NOV 2013.
During the splendid opening ceremony a fine new Bas Relief Memorial was unveiled to the Australian Mining Corps 1916-1919 (see also page 298). For opening times and more information, see www.rememberplugstreet.com

L to R - Ross Thompson (donator), Michael Meszaros (creator), Bourgmestre Gilbert Deleu, beside the Bas Relief Memorial to the Australian Mining Corps 1916-1919.

12. MAJ-GEN SIR CHARLES FERGUSSON HQ PLAQUE, REUMONT. (See also page 45.)
On 29 September 2013 the plaque stolen in 1987 was replaced by the Heart of England WFA.

13. QUEEN'S OWN ROYAL WEST KENT REGIMENT MEMORIAL, TERTRE, MONS. Lat & Long: 50.4604 3.807701
This Kent ragstone memorial was unveiled in situ (at the Y junction of Rue Defuisseaux and Rue Des Herbieres approximately 1000m north of the Mons Canal) on 23 August 2013. It will be officially inaugurated in a grand ceremony on 23 August 2014, surrounded by a memorial rose garden and with informative slate plaques around the memorial.
For more details, contact: nigel_bristow@sky.com
Website: www.thequeensown.com/tertre%20memorial.html

Instigator of the QORWK Memorial at Tertre, Nigel Bristow, beside the Memorial.

TOURIST INFORMATION:
WHERE TO STAY AND EAT

It is the ironic fate of a guide book that some information given in it will inevitably become out of date as soon as it is published. For instance, and perhaps somewhat surprisingly after nearly 100 years since the Armistice of 11 November 1918, new memorials and museums are still being erected on the battlefields. Established ones are often dramatically altered by new roundabouts or landscaping by the Commonwealth War Graves Commission or to make way for new motorways or high-speed trains which have completely altered navigation across the battlefields of Belgium and France over the past quarter century.

Print a direction using road numbers and the authorities may decide to alter the system of numbering or send the pilgrim on interminable diversions *(déviations)*, which often abandon the driver part way along. Recommend a restaurant and the brilliant chef may have departed in a huff. Advise on a hotel and the *patron* may have done a moonlight flit. Give opening hours for tourist offices and they may well have invented new, rare 'off season' times.

The information and advice we will, therefore, give here will mostly be of a general and somewhat subjective, nature – with the inclusion of a few favourite haunts we cannot resist mentioning which are conveniently sited close to the battlefield and are sometimes mentioned in the actual itineraries rather than in the section below. But please do not blame us if you should be faced with the dreaded 'Under New Management' sign.

The very best advice if you are well organised is to go carefully through the itineraries that you intend to follow in this book, then **contact your national tourist offices or the appropriate local ones listed in this section, well before you leave.** Give them, if possible, at least one month, list all the major towns you intend to visit, and request the following information, with relevant brochures (tourist literature is now of a generally high and helpful standard):

1. Addresses and phone numbers and emails of local tourist offices with likely opening times. In smaller towns or villages these can be erratic, and we have found that whatever the information you may be given about them, the optimum time for getting in is 1000-1200 and 1400-1600 during the summer time. The most reliable and helpful offices in the battlefields areas are listed below.
2. Listings of local hotels, bed-and-breakfast homes, self-catering lets, restaurants, museums, camping sites, etc, also maps and town plans. Staff are often discouraged from giving personal recommendations, but you can smile and try.
3. Specific information about battlefield routes: in both France and Belgium there are well-marked *circuits,* signed *Route '14-18',* or *Circuit de Souvenir,* etc., often with useful accompanying literature and, increasingly, audio-guided routes or trailsusing your smart phone, ipad etc for information.
4. General tourist information/local attractions/cultural events/festivals, etc. The serious student of the battles may well wish to avoid the latter – the area will be congested, local hostelries full.

Beware of missing lunch – especially in France and on the more isolated areas of battlefields, lunchtime restaurants are few and far between. Several that you pass in high hopes will prove to be firmly shut and in the majority of those that are open (even in fairly major towns) the chef will leave and the kitchen will **close,** in theory **at 1400** hours, but in practice anything up to 15 minutes before this if business is slack. Pathetic pleadings will not wash. We have indicated in the text of the itineraries some fairly reliable restaurants. But even these may be on their *Fermeture annuelle* in mid-summer or in January. The solution is to take with you a basic picnic kit and stock up at local shops with crispy baguettes, delectable cheese or ham, tomatoes, some fruit, your beverage of choice and find a picturesque spot to enjoy the feast – delicious.

Hotels/Restaurants/Tourist Offices en route are distinguished by a **special typeface** throughout the book.

BELGIUM

Note: When phoning Belgium add the following prefix: ex-UK and USA 00 32, indicated by '+' in the phone numbers listed.

FLANDERS: The Flemish-speaking area of Belgium

TOURIST OFFICES

They produce some attractive and helpful booklets – but not one composite one like the French – with details of how to get to Belgium, on local museums and attractions – and hotels (a new list every year). **Beware** – the French and Belgian versions of place-names are very different. You can be driving through France heading for Lille and when you cross the border into Belgium it disappears from the signposts to be replaced with Rijsel. Other traps are: Ypres-Ieper; Anvers-Antwerpen; Courtai-Kortrijk; Tournai-Doornik; Warneton-Waasten. Flemish is generally spoken in the main tourist areas of Flanders today, but English is widely understood and spoken.

UK: Tourism Flanders-Brussels, 1a Cavendish Square, London E149RW, UK. Tel: 0800 954 5245. Fax: 020 7458 0045. E-mail: info@visitflanders.co.uk website: www.visitflanders.co.uk
Canada: Belgian Tourist Office /Office du Tourisme Belge, P.O.Box 760, Succursale N.D.G., Montreal, Quebec, 4A 3S2, Canada. Tel: +1 (514) 484-3594 Fax: +1 (514) 489-8965 website: http://www.visitbelgium.com/
USA: Belgian Tourist Office, 220 East 42nd Street, Suite 3402 New York, NY 10017. Tel: 00 1 212 758 8130. E-mail: info@visitbelgium.com website: www.visitbelgium.com/

THE WESTHOEK. Provincial Tourist Office, Esenkasteel, Woumensweg 100, 8600 Diksmuide. Tel: + (0) 51 51 93 65, Fax: + (0) 51 51 93 51. **Contact:** Frederik Demeyere. E-mail: frederik. demeyere@ west-vlaanderen.be Websites: www.west-vlaanderen.be www.1418herdacht.be The northern region of the battlefields covered in this guidebook is in the Westhoek.

Battlefield tourism is a vital part of the economy of West Flanders - with visits by the British still among the most important - and the Westhoek, which covers the three 'Front Towns' of Ieper, Diksmuide and Nieuwpoort, has undertaken an important study, 'War and Peace in The Westhoek' of the remaining battlefield sites in the Province which has taken several years to complete. The aim is to preserve the battlefield heritage and make more people aware of it. Some of the results are published in a remarkable magazine, *In de Steigers*, with wonderful photos and descriptions of well-known and almost-forgotten sites alike. Unfortunately it is only published in Flemish. There is, however, a booklet entitled *The Great War in Flanders* listing all the battlefield-related annual events to take place and booklets covering two battlefield routes – The Yzer Front (79km around Diksmuide by car) and In Flanders Fields Route (82km around Ieper by car). They are available for a small fee from the appropriate **tourist offices.**

In this age when people are becoming conscious of their 'carbon footprint' visitors may wish to park their cars and visit the battlefields on foot or on bicycle. Walking and cycling battlefield routes are now available from the **tourist offices**, notably the publication by Dominiek Dendooven (qv), *Tales For on the Road*, which has three routes (long, medium and short walks) with historical notes through the Provincial Domein of The Palingbeek (qv); The Messines Ridge Peace Path (3.2km walk); three thematic

Walking the battlefields - they can be muddy!

cycling routes round Ypres – 'Gas', 'The Ypres Salient' and '14-18' (30km). There is a new edition of the 'Pop' (Poperinge) Route and 'The Peace Route', a 45km long, signed cycling route which starts and ends in Ieper.

LOCAL **TOURIST**/INFORMATION OFFICES/**ACCOMMODATION/ RESTAURANTS**

Ypres. The Ieper/Westhoek Tourist Office is handily situated in the Cloth Hall (Stadhuis), attached to the new In Flanders Fields Museum, Grand Place, B-8900 Ieper. Tel: + (0) 57 23 92 20. Fax: + (0) 57 23 92 75. E-mail: toerisme@ieper.be

The staff are very helpful; and they produce their own booklet of tourist information in English, which is very comprehensive. They also sell guidebooks, maps, cycle routes, and souvenirs in an attractive and well-stocked boutique. There is a separate leaflet **for hotels, restaurants, b&bs, camping sites**. It is difficult to have a bad meal in the cafés and restaurants around the Grand' Place, but if you choose an environment with starched tablecloths, gleaming cutlery and glass, it can take a long time.

Around the square are to be found the following: the 3-star **Regina Hotel**, reopened under new ownership on 11 November 2002 with 17 refurbished bedrooms, and two restaurants (one of which is 'gourmet'). Tel: + (0) 57 21 88 88, E-mail: info@hotelregina.be Nearest to the Cloth Hall is the **In't Klein Stadhuis**, Tel: + (0) 57 21 55 42 and next is **The Anker** restaurant where a fine meal can be had, Tel: + (0) 57 20 12 72, but allow plenty of time. **The Trompet** (which serves a superb mixed salad and chips), Tel: + (0) 57 20 02 42, is very convenient and popular, especially for lunch. **The Kolleblume** Tel: + (0) 57 21 90 90, and the **Café Central**, Tel: + (0) 57 20 17 60, are reasonably priced and serve snacks as well as full meals. **The Vivaldi** tearoom/restaurant has undergone a major enlargement but still provides the same mix of snacks and full meals, Tel: + (0) 57 21 75 21. **The Old Tom** (1-star, Tel + (0) 57 20 15 41) has some rooms as well and the **Sultan** (Tel + (0) 57 20 01 93) has been renovated but no longer has hotel rooms.

The magnificent Cloth Hall at night.

The superb **Hostellerie St Nicolas** restaurant is at 532 Veurnseweg, Elverdinge, Tel: + (0) 57 20 06 22.

Local specialities are on offer in most of these restaurants. There are several hundred varieties of beer to choose from to wash them down, from thick dark brown almost treacly black concoctions like that brewed by the Trappist monks to light (*blonde*) lagers or even raspberry flavoured! A few hundred grammes of the renowned Belgian hand-made chocolates – on sale in half a dozen or so outlets in the square – make a perfect end to a calorific spree. You must not leave Belgium without sampling some of their legendary *frites* – quite irresistible with mayonnaise. Mussels are very popular – especially for family treats at lunchtime on Sunday. Pepper steak is also a favourite and the pancakes are yummy, as are leek flans and chicken stew. In fact Belgian cuisine is very good indeed.

Karel Vandaele in the Chocolaterie, No. 9 Grote Markt.

If really pressed for time, buy a carton of those crisp *frites* and a sausage from one of the *frituur* windows and eat them on the hoof. If you want the maximum time on the battlefields, then there is a choice of shops/supermarkets around the square, along Coomansstraat or Meninstraat to buy the makings of a picnic. Along Coomansstraat/A Vandenpeereboomplein is the **'t Ganzeke** (Goose) restaurant with a varied menu. Worth a visit to see the superb posters of Ypres from post-World War I to the 1950s. Tel: + (0) 57 20 00 09. Further along, if you want a change, is the large, Chinese Restaurant, **Shanghai City**, where the food is copious! Tel: + (0) 57 20 06 52.

Continue past the Theatre (by which there is a **Mié Tabé Peace Post**) *on your right opposite St George's Church to the right-hand corner of the square and continue along the small Boezingestraat and Veemarkt.*

Ahead is the 4-star, **Hotel Ariane,** Tel: + (0) 57 21 82 18. E-mail: info@ariane.be. Website: www. booking.com/**Ariane-Hotel** It is within an easy stroll of the Menin Gate and the Grote Markt and the best hotel in Ypres for battlefield tourers. It has a smart new wing with spacious rooms, a superb restaurant, covered and open terraces, and an attractive foyer with WW1 exhibits and book stall, bar, and a warm welcome by owners Natasja and chef Johann and their staff. There is a large car park.

The **Novotel** group has a smart, 122 bedroom modern 3-star hotel in Sint-Jacobsstraat just off the Grote Markt and near the Menin Gate. It has underground parking, fitness room and sauna. Tel: + (0) 57 42 96 00. E-mail: H3172@accor-hotels.com Opposite the **Novotel** is **The Old Bill Pub** whose pub sign, a Bairnsfather cartoon, originally hung outside the **Regina Hotel** in whose cellar a pub and private club

The Bairnsfather cartoon on the Old Bill Pub sign.

was opened on 8 March 1969. The distinguished historian Dr Caenepeel made a speech about Bruce Bairnsfather and his links with the Salient on the occasion.

Opposite the rear of the Novotel in St Jacobsstraat is the attractive **Albion Hotel**, 20 rooms, bed and breakfast, pleasant lounge area. Tel: + (0) 57 20 02 20. E-mail: info@albionhotel.be

On Meensestraat as you walk to the Menin Gate is the **Poppy Pizzeria and Steakhouse**. Tel: +(0) 57 20 55 50.

'T Klein Rijsel. This is a welcoming pub for all battlefield tourists – they even stock 'Peace Beer' served in special peace pots. Behind it is the excellent **Ramparts War Museum** with life-like scenes of trench life and original artefacts. By the Lille Gate. **Open** 1030-2200 (closed Wed & Thurs). Tel: + (0) 57 20 02 36.

At 5 D'Hondestraat (off the Grote Markt and on the site of the old **Shell Hole** b & b is the renovated **Ambrosia Hotel** with 10 ensuite rooms. Tel: + (0) 57 36 63 66. E-mail: info@ ambrosiahotel.be Website: www.ambrosiahotel.be

The industrial estate in the northern is served by a modern hotel, the 3-star **Best Western Flanders Lodge** (formerly the Rabbit), Tel: + (0) 57 21 70 00. E-mail: bw-ieper@skynet.be. It is built in wood like a Swiss Chalet, with thirty-nine rooms with en-suite bathrooms, jacuzzi, restaurant and attractive bar.

The **Protea B&B** near 'Clapham Junction' is very popular with battlefield tourists. 5 simple rooms with ensuite facilities. Tel: +(0) 57 46 63 39. E-mail: info@theprotea.be website: www.the protea.be

Local Guided Battlefield Tours/Military Bookshops/Research Facilities

In addition to the tours by qualified guides offered by the Ieper Tourist Office there are some commercial Ieper-based organisations which run regular English-speaking tours in comfortable mini-buses or in your own transport. The first two are also well-stocked book/map/souvenir etc shops.

• **Salient Tours**. Based in **The British Grenadier Shop**. Run by Canadian Steve Douglas, with a battlefield resource centre and computer facilities for looking up burials. A magnificent database of Canadian casualties, www.mapleleaflegacy.ca 5 Meensestraat. Tel: + (0) 57 21 46 57. E-mail: tours@salienttours.com or fa516609@skynet.be Website: www.salienttours.be/

• **Over the Top Tours.** Run by André and Carol de Bruin from their attractive shop at 41 Meensestraat. Tel: + (0) 57 42 43 20. Email: tours@overthetoptours.be Website: www.overthe toptours.be

• **Flanders Battlefield Tours** . Run by the popular ex-TOC H guide, Jacques Ryckebosch with Genevra Charsley. Tel: + (0) 57 36 04 60. E-mail: info@ypres-fbt.be Website: www.ypres-fbt.com

• **Trench Map Tours.** Run by ex-RMP Iain McHenry. Tel: + (0) 57 48 61 31. Mobile: + (0) 473 762 710. E-mail: tours@trenchmaptours.com Website: www.trenchmaptours.com

• **LEST WE FORGET BATTLEFIELD TOURS (Flanders)**
Director/Owner: Milena Kolarikova BA (Tour management), Principal Guide (& Member of GBG): Chris Lock. Tel: +(0) 478355265. E-mail: info@lestweforgettours.com Website: www.lestweforgettours.com

• **The Ieper Documentation Centre**, which incorporates the Rose Coombs and Dr Caenepeel (founder of the Salient Museum) libraries, contains much fascinating information about the Great War in the Salient. **NOTE.** It has moved from the Stedelijke Musea, opposite St Martin's Cathedral at 9 Janseniusstraat, into the North Wing of the renovated Cloth Hall in the major reorganisation of 2012, with the name 'In Flanders Fields Museum – **Knowledge Centre.** Open for scholars and visitors from Mon-Fri, 100-1700. Its research facilities and on-going projects are exceptional. New address is 3 Sint-Maartensplein with doors both on Sint-Maartensplein (Square between Cloth Hall and Cathedral) and in the new museum café.

Contact: Dominiek Dendooven (qv) who can arrange specialist tours. By appointment. Tel: + (0)57 239 450 E-mail: kenniscentrum@ieper.be

In Ieper there are a series of interesting events to attract the visitor throughout the year. It seems there is always something going on in the Grote Markt Place (which can make parking difficult, especially during the bustling Saturday morning market). The Flemish have a capacity for enjoyment of their festivals and fairs which belies their somewhat dour image and these events are fun to attend. The medieval custom of throwing live cats from the Cloth Hall Belfry (the symbolic killing of evil spirits as personified by the cat) has been revived – with toy cats – in the Festival of the Cats, a colourful and popular carnival which takes place on the second Sunday in May every third year. Other regular events are the 100 Kilometres Ieper March on the weekend after Ascension, the 24 Hours Ieper Automobile Rally on the last weekend in June, the Thuyndag Fair, on the first Saturday and Sunday of August, the four days of the Ijzer March in mid-August, the Tooghedagen Craft and Antiques Fair on the second weekend in September and The Procession of St Martin on 10 November. Armistice Day is always celebrated on 11 November, whatever day of the week it falls on (not the nearest Sunday as happens in Britain) and it is a public holiday. On that day there is a Belgian Memorial Service in St Martin's Cathedral and an English one in St George's Church, a 'Poppy Parade' and special ceremony at the Menin Gate. Hundreds of pilgrims come from the UK and other parts of the world for this event and it is as well to apply early for tickets in the church – if particularly busy there will be a spillover service nearby with TV relay. This commemorates the sacrifice of all those who fought and, in particular, those who gave their lives, many willing and proud volunteers, in the Great War in Flanders.

Diksmuide Tourist Office, Grote Markt 28, 8600 Diksmuide, Tel + (0) 51 51 91 46. Fax: + (0) 51 51 91 48. E-mail: toerisme@diksmuide.be Market day is on Monday, the Cheese and Butter Fair is on Whit Monday, Ijzer Tower Pilgrimage, last Sunday in August, Flemish 'Day of Peace' 11 November. You can hire a canoe or a small motorboat for trips up the Ijzer or hire a pedal cart to explore this attractive town and helicopter flights can also be made to get a bird's eye view over the battlefield – details from the tourist office. The picturesque Grote Markt, with its statue of Jacques of Diksmuide in the centre is the best bet for a lunch break with a good choice of restaurants and snack bars from Chinese to frituur and the 2-star hotel – restaurants **Polderbloem** with 8 rooms, Tel: + (0) 51 50 29 05 and **De Vrede** with 17 rooms, Tel: + (0) 51 50 00 38. At Heilig Hartplein 2 is the 4-star Best Western **Hotel Pax** with 378 rooms, Tel: + (0) 51 50 00 34, Fax: + (0) 51 50 00 35, e-mail: pax.hotel@skynet.be On the Ijzer bank opposite the Peace Tower (qv) is the 3-star Hotel-restaurant **Sint Jan** with 10 rooms, Tel: + (0) 51 50 02 74.

Koksijde Tourist Office, 24 Zeelaan, 8670 Koksijde. Tel: + (0) 58 53 30 55. Fax: + (0) 58 52 25 77, e-mail: toerisme@koksijde.be.
End June Shrimp Festival. Flower Parade 4 August.
Accommodation: A range of 3-star to modest 1-star and B & Bs. List from Tourist Office.
Langemark-Poelkapelle Tourist Office, Kasteelstraat 1, Tel: + (0) 57 49 09 41. Fax: + (0) 57 48 55 89. E-mail: toerisme@langemarck-poelkapelle.be

Mesen. Tourist Office. Markt 22. 8957 Mesen.Tel: +(0) 57 22 17 14. E-mail: toerisme@mesen.be Website: www.mesen.be/website-en/119-wwwhtml
Accommodation: **Peace Village International Hostel**, Nieuwkerkestraat 9A. E-mail: info@peacevillage.be Website: www.peacevillage.be
Great for student groups. 32 en-suite studios (128 beds), 8 with disabled facilities. Conference room, bar, restaurant. Guided tours available. Specialises in peace projects like international matches football matches on the adjoining pitch, including a WW1 100th Anniversary commemorative football match in December 2014.

Entrance to the International Peace Village, Mesen.

Nieuwpoort. Tourist Office, 7 Marktplein, 8620 Nieuwpoort. Tel: + (0) 58 22 44 44. Fax: + (0) 58 22 44 28, e-mail: nieuwpoort@toerismevlaanderen.be
End March-beginning April, The Fourteen French-Flemish Days. 20 May, Blessing of the Fishing Fleet. On 4 August is the Day of Honouring King Albert I and the Heroes of the Yser.
Accommodation: A range of 3-star to B & Bs. List from the Tourist Office.

Poperinge. Tourist Office, Stadhuis, B-8970 Poperinghe. Tel: + (0) 57 33 40 81, Fax: + (0) 57 33 75 81, e-mail: poperinge@tourismevlaanderen.be
The annual Hop Festival is in September, and there is a signed, 54km 'Hop Route' around the area. Market day is on Friday (as it has been since the Count of Flanders granted permission for a market in 1187). They produce a leaflet called Poperinge in the First World War as well as the POP.Route booklet (for which there is a fee).
Accommodation etc:
Talbot House (qv), 43 Gasthuisstraat. Self-catering, clean and simple accommodation in this marvellously evocative setting. Tel: + (0) 57 33 32 28.
Hotel Amphora, 3-star, attractive décor, Market Square. Tel: + (0) 57 33 88 66.
Hotel Belfort, 3-star, good restaurant, Market Square. Tel: + (0) 57 33 88 88.
Hotel Palace, 3-star, good restaurant, 34 Ieperstraat. Tel: + (0) 57 33 30 93.
Hotel Recour, Luxe, gourmet restaurant **Pegasus**, 7 Guido Gezellestraat. Tel: + (0) 57 33 57 25.
There are several good restaurants and cafés around the main square which are convenient for a lunch break, including the old WW1 favourite the De Ranke.

Zonnebeke Tourist Office in the Passchendaele Memorial Museum (qv), Château Zonnebeke, 7 Ieperstraat. Tel: + (0) 51 77 04 41. Fax: + (0) 51 78 07 50. E-mail: toerisme@zonnebeke.be Details of guided battlefield tours by the Museum's expert guides and local accommodation and eateries available. Many fascinating WW1-related events are organised by the Museum throughout the year and absorbing educational packages for students are available. The grounds of the Château are quite delightful to stroll or to take your picnic in. Another attraction in Zonnebeke is the Old Cheese Factory.

Vlamertinge. Cherry Blossom B + B, now moved to Casselstraat 27, Vlamertinghe. Tel: + (0) 57 30 15 55: + (0) 57 30 15 55. E-mail: cherryblossom@telenet.com.be Website|: www.cherryblossom.be
Welcoming and popular with battlefield tourists (tours available). Great English breakfast.
Contact: Liz & John Millward.

WALLONIA. PROVINCE OF HAINAULT:
The French-speaking area of Belgium

UK. BELGIAN TOURIST OFFICE BRUSSELS & WALLONIA.
217 Marsh Wall, London E14 9F. Tel: 0207 537 1132 info@belgiumtheplacetobe.be
www.belgiumtheplaceto.be
USA. 220. East 42nd Street, Room 3402 NY. www.visitbelgium.com

Comines-Warneton Tourist Office: 21 Chemin du Moulin Soete – 7780 Comines. Tel: + (0) 56 55 56
00. Fax: + (0) 56 55 56 08. E-mail: office.tourisme.comineswarneton@belgacom.net. Website:
www.villedecomines-warneton.be
This covers the area of Ploegsteert/St Yvon and Warneton.
Lists of *gîtes* and *chambres d'hôte* in the area. The region is showing an increasing interest in
developing its historical WW1 sites (see Last Post at Ploegsteert Memorial and new Interpretation
Centre) with 19 well-researched and illustrated Information Panels at cemeteries and sites of
historical WW1 interest in the area. These were written by Ted Smith (co-author with our dear
friend Tony Spagnoly - who sadly died in 2008 - of books about the area) and Claude Verhaeghe
(qv) of the Tourist Office.
There are several ideas for lunch breaks in Ploegsteert: **Café des Touristes,** beside the Ploegsteert
Memorial. Tel: + (0) 56 55 60 66. Brasserie style. **L'Auberge**, opposite the Memorial. Closed Wed. Tel:
+ (0) 56 58 84 41. E-mail: restaurant@auberge-ploegsteert.be. Variety of menus. Can take groups
on prior reservation. HQ of Last Post Committee. Owned by Claude & Nelly Verhaeghe. **Hostellerie
de la Place**, next to the Town Hall. Tel: + (0) 56 58 86 77. Good for a quick lunch.

Mons Tourist Office in the Grand Place, No. 20, 7000 Mons. Tel: + (0) 65 33 55 80. **E-mail:**
info@tourisme@ville.mons.be **Website:** www.monsregion.be

They produce literature, available in English, on the
battlefield, hotels, restaurants, B & B., Gites, Youth Hostels
and Camping sites and local events (see also **Mons
Battlefield Tour** above).

Typically, the beautiful Grand' Place has a huge variety of
restaurants and cafés serving good, hearty Belgian cooking.
Mons is very proud of its gastronomic tradition and is fond of
folkloric pageants, parades and festivals, e.g. the Lumecon (le
Doudou') – the Combat between St George and the Dragon
on Trinity Sunday; St Waudru, Mons' Patron Saint, who has
her own procession when a relic is carried through the streets
in a golden carriage, normally housed in the St Waudru
Church's Treasury. The proximity to **SHAPE,** with its mixture
of nationalities, gives Mons a cosmopolitan flavour.

Every year at the end of August/beginning of September
there is a Mons – 'Operation "Tanks in Town"' tank rally to
commemorate the Liberation of Mons by the US 1st (Big Red
1) Div on 3 September 1944.

Also an annual highlight is the International Festival of
Military Music in June.

*The 'Grande Garde; good luck
monkey, Mons.*

Mons's status as European Capital of Culture for the year
2015 will engender much renovation and new build in the town, with many ambitious projects
and events planned. The 100th Anniversaries of all the WW1 battles in the area from 1914-1918
will also be commemorated with new initiatives. See the Mons website for latest details.

Accommodation

Some hotels are mentioned as they are passed en route during the Mons battlefield tour. Also – the 4-star Best Western **Lido Hotel**, 112 rue des Arbelestiers (at the bottom of the hill leading to the Grand' Place) is very smart and conveniently placed. 72 rooms. Tel: + (0) 65 32 78 00, e-mail: info@lido.be Website: www.lido.be

Near the station is the 3-star **Ibis Centre**, 27 Bvd Charles Quint, Tel: + (0) 65 84 74 40, e-mail: info@ibismons.be Website: www.ibismons.be

On the Route d'Ath at Nimy are the attractive 3-star **Le Monte Cristo**, Tel: + (0) 65 36 42 99, E-mail: lemontecristo@hotmail.be 12 rooms and the 3-star **Château de la Cense au Bois**, Tel: + (0) 65 31 60 00, 10 rooms. Also nearby is the 4-star **Hotel Mercure Mons-Nimy**, Rue des Fusillés, Tél: +(0) 65 72.36.85

E-mail: hotel.mercure.mons-gm@skynet.be   website: http://www.mercure.com 53 rooms. All three have excellent restaurants.

FRANCE

Note: When phoning France add the following prefixes: ex-UK and USA 00 33, indicated by '+' in the phone numbers listed.

FRENCH GOVERNMENT TOURIST OFFICES

UK. 300 High Holborn, London WCIV 7JH. Information line, Tel: 09068 24 4123. Open Mon-Fri 0830-2000 (calls charged at 60p per minute), http://uk.franceguide.com/ **USA.** 825 3rd Ave, NY 10022. Tel: 00 1 212 838 7800. www.franceguide.com/

The French produce a marvellous booklet, *The Traveller in France: Reference Guide.* This is updated every year. It contains just about all the basic information you need to know before going to France: on currency, passports/visas, medical advice, electricity, metric measurements and sizes, banking and shopping hours, phoning, motorways, driving, caravanning, camping, hotels, self-catering, *Gîtes de France,* local tourist offices *(syndicats d'initiative)* signed 'i' for information, maps, food and drink, etc., how to get there by car, ferry, rail and air, car hire, with relevant phone numbers. It is absolutely essential. Please send **a large SAE and £1 in stamps.**

LOCAL INFORMATION/TOURIST OFFICES/
ACCOMMODATION IN FRANCE

The largest group serving the whole area is the Accor Group. This includes the 4/5-star **Sofitel**, the 3/4-star **Mercure**, the 3/4-star **Novotel**, the 2-star **Ibis** and the 1/0-star **Etap** and **Formule 1**. They are reliable, if somewhat predictable, with well-equipped bedrooms (usually standard and identical throughout the hotel) and bathrooms, restaurants, parking (some with swimming pool). Size of room decreases with the star rating. The ambience and quality of food in the restaurants of the 3/4-star hotels has greatly improved of late. They are conveniently sited on motorway access roads, with a few in city centres. Central booking: www.accorhotels.com/

UK Tel: 0870 609 0961. N America Tel: 1 800 221 45 42 Toll Free.

The 2-star **Campanile Hotels** are to be found near many of our battlefields. Usually run by a husband and wife team they have small but well-equipped rooms and specialise in good value buffet style meals. Central booking: Tel: 0 825 003 003. UK Tel: 0207 519 5045. www.booking.com/Campanile

New hotels are springing up in France like mushrooms – especially in the 2 and even 1 or 0-star category: chains like **Balladins, Fasthotel, Mister Bed, Première Classe**, 1-star Plus. Often conveniently sited on access roads to main towns, they are functional, with private bathrooms – the lower the star rating, the tinier the space – and the basic essentials; usually very clean, and good value for money but with little atmosphere or personality. Most are listed in *The Traveller in France*.

For something more individual, with character and personality, often privately owned, the hotels grouped under the banners **Relais & Châteaux** (Central booking UK Tel: 0207 630 7667), *Logis de France* (**Central booking:** Paris Tel: + (0)1 45 84 83 84), **Relais du Silence** (Central booking, Paris Tel: + (0)1 44 49 90 00) and those marketed under the **Best Western** group (**Central booking: UK** Tel: 0800 39 31 30. **N AMERICA** Tel: 800 528 1234) are worth investigating. Not all have restaurants, but when they do they are normally very good. Not all rooms have en-suite bathrooms (although this is becoming far more prevalent) and may vary in size and furnishing – check carefully when you book. Because of this non-standardization they vary from 2 to 4 stars. More hotel groups are listed in the *Traveller in France Reference Guide*.

The words *auberge* or *hostellerie* often indicate a patron-run establishment with superb restaurant but more basic accommodation.

Self-catering accommodation can be booked through the reliable **Gîtes de France**. Central booking UK Tel: 0990 360360.

A selection of **Bed and Breakfast** *(Chambres d'Hôtes)* establishments are listed in the *Traveller in France*. Lists of Camping Sites can be obtained from local tourist offices.

Lille Area

Comité Departmental de Tourisme du Nord, 15-17 rue du Nouveau Siècle, 59800 Lille. Tel: + (0)3 20 57 00 61. Fax: + (0)3 20 57 52 70. www.tourisme-nord.fr/cdtnord_fr This has full hotel, restaurant and attractions listings.

Lille and its surroundings make an alternative base for touring the Ypres Salient and even Mons, and the Nord-Pas de Calais-Artois group of battlefields. It is an interesting, lively, garrison city, with many WW1 associations too, and some superb restaurants. But beware, navigation is complicated and the traffic heavy and fast-moving.

There is a variety of hotels in the Accor group (qv) in the Centre and at the Airport and the more distinctive, centrally situated Best Western **Grand Hôtel Bellevue** (Tel: + (0)3 20 57 45 64) and **Hôtel Arts Deco Romarin** (Tel: + (0)3 20 14 81 81).

Maubeuge

There are a **Campanile** (Tel: + (0)3 27 64 00 91) and **Formule 1**(Tel: + (0)8 91 70 53 04) which are convenient for the Mons tour.

Region of Nord-Pas-de-Calais-Artois

Most of the French battlefields in this book are in this region. Many of them are in old mining and industrial districts and if you are unfamiliar with the area, firstly you will be amazed at just how close these battlefields are, the one to another, so that you can segue quite easily from one Itinerary to the next.

Secondly you probably have a preconception of flat featureless landscapes interspersed with slagheaps and winding gear and dreary, drab towns and villages. The reality is quite different. It is an area where much civic pride is evident. Trees are abundant, new community buildings are bright, with railings and lamp-posts colour-coordinated, gardens at their approaches and exits, hanging baskets (a great many of the towns and villages have '*fleuri*' awards) joyfully exuberant roundabouts with imaginative sculptures and representations of old local industries and crafts, or dreams of holidays by the sea. Water towers may be painted like lotus flowers, the winding gear has been dismantled, the slagheaps covered in vegetation or converted into ski-slopes...

The charming Estaminetde l'Ermitage, Bois l'Evêque.

Here there is an immense sense of heritage and history and an awareness of the importance of the phrase that you will be hearing with increasing frequency, '**Remembrance Tourism**'. In most districts where WW1 and/or WW2 battles took part there are strong Historical Associations with extremely knowledgeable amateur historians who have charted their history with meticulous research and record-keeping. Their members give generously and freely of their time in maintaining local museums, sites, trails, and generally in assisting the pilgrim, historian and tourist in discovering 'their' battlefields. If we have not given a specific contact for the particular area that interests you, the *Mairie* is always the first place to try and then any small **Tourist Office**. But beware – their opening times may be infrequent.

One hazard, however, is the total lack of restaurants open at lunchtime in some of the more isolated areas, as already described. Be prepared.

Béthune Tourist Office: 3 rue Aristide Briand, 62400 Béthune. Open every day 0930-1230 and 1400-1830. Closed Tues a.m. except July/August. Tel: + (0)3 21 52 50 00.
This delightful town would make an ideal base. The picturesque main square is everything you imagine a northern French *Place* should be. After the almost total destruction of the war it was rebuilt with style and verve in a mixture of architectural styles, incorporating the new *Art Deco* fashion with the traditional Flemish. It has the statutory belfry tower (originally dating from 1346, twice burned and thrice rebuilt) with bells that ring out each hour. Béthune is famous for its beer CH'TI (nickname for the people of Northern France). Nearby at 1098 rue de Lilliers, 62350 Busnes, Tel: + (0)3 21 68 88 88, Website: www.lechateaudebeaulieu.fr in the 4-star **Hotel. Le Château de Beaulieu** (with its somewhat quirky modern decor) is the 2-star Michelin restaurant (the only one in the Nord Pas de Calais), **le Meurin**, with chef Marc Meurin, and its less formal Restaurant **Le Jardin d'Alice**. There are several other excellent restaurants and a variety of cheap and cheerful eateries around the square – pick up a restaurant guide from the Tourist Office. There is an equal array of hotels and the 4-star **Chartreuse du Val St Esprit** at nearby Gosnay, Tel: + (0)3 21 62 80 00, Website: www.lachartreuse.com – is an elegant château with 53 rooms and gourmet restaurant. In the old château grounds, 1 rue Fouquières, are also the 3-star Best Western **La Métairie,** Tel: + (0)3 91 80 11 20, Website: www.hotel-lametairie.com and two restaurants, the **Vasco** and the

Distillerie. There is a **Campanile Béthune-Fouquières** (near near the A26 on the ZA Actipolis) Tel: + (0)3 21 56 98 50 and the nearby Première Classe with 87 rooms as well as conveniently situated hostelleries like the 3-star **Hôtel L'Eden**, Place de la République, Tél. + (0)3 21 68 83 83. E-mail : hotel-eden@tiscali.fr and the **Hôtel du Vieux Beffroi** in the Grand' Place. Tel: + (0)3 21 68 15 00 (more details from the Tourist Office).

There are 4-star **Novotel Hotels** (Website: www.novotel.com) at **Noyelles-Godault (formerly Hénin Douai)** Tel: + (0)3 21 08 58 08, in the Centre Commercial, Ave de la République, A1-E15), with swimming pool and pleasant restaurant, ideally situated without having to move and a similar **Novotel** at **Valenciennes Aerodrome,** rue de Maugre Parc Activités l'Aerodrome, 59220 Rouvignies, off the A1, also convenient for Le Cateau (Tel: + (0)3 27 21 12 12, E-mail: H0456@accorhotels.com)

There are also 2-star **Campaniles at Valenciennes Airport** (Tel: + (0)3 27 47 87 87. Fax: + (0)3 27 28 95 25 off the A23) and **Lens** (Tel: + (0)3 21 28 82 82 (off the A23).

La Bassée. Tourist Information: Mairie. Tel: + (0)3 20 29 90 29. Fax: + (0)3 20 29 21 40. Here an annual guide to la Bassée with useful telephone numbers and listings of restaurants is available. There are no hotels in la Bassée, but it is a useful lunch stop, with a selection of restaurants and brasseries with local, North African, oriental and Italian specialities.

Arras. Tourist Office: Hôtel de Ville, Place des Héros, 62000 Arras. Tel: + (0)3 21 51 26 95 . Fax: + (0)3 21 71 07 34. E-mail: arras.tourisme@wanadoo.fr Website: www.arras.fr/tourisme/ arras
This makes the best base for Vimy, and is convenient for N-D de Lorette and le Cateau and too, if you prefer not to move and don't mind a bit of daily motoring. You could even do the Somme from Arras. It is also an ideal place to eat. All around the station square is a variety of **restaurants** and **cafés** – from 'quick snack' (and what better for lunch than a *Croque Monsieur* or half a *baguette* with *jambon de Paris* or *Camembert*) to gourmet. The **'Astoria'**, 10-12 Place Maréchal Foch, is a good compromise. Highly recommended is **La Coupole**, 26 Boulevard de Strasbourg, Tel: + (0)3 21 71 88 44, with a great Parisian brasserie atmosphere and décor and fine seafood specialities. The only 4-star hotel in Arras is the **Hotel d'Angleterre**, Place Maréchal Foch, Tel: + (0)3 21 51 51 16. Fax: + (0)3 21 71 38 20. A Conference Centre has been built in the square with a 3-star **Mercure Hotel**, Tel: + (0)3 21 23 88 88. E-mail: h1560@accor.com. Also near the station at 3 rue Docteur Brassart is the **Holiday Inn Express**, Tel: + 0871423 4917. The 3-star **Hotel Moderne**, Bvd Faidherbe Tel: + (0)3 21 23 39 57. Fax: + (0)3 21 71 55 42 is opposite the station. There is a 2-star **Ibis**, 11 rue de la Justice, Tel: + (0)3 21 23 61 61. Fax: + (0)3 21 71 31 31, and on the outskirts there is a **Campanile, ZA les Alouettes**, Tel: + (0)3 21 55 56 30. Fax: + (0)3 21 55 46 36. The *Places* (squares) with their picturesque Flemish baroque arcades also offer a variety of eating possibilities. Beneath the Grand' Place is a huge car park. Beneath the Gothic Town Hall and Belfry Tower are the *Boves* (qv) – underground tunnels and chambers much-utilised in the First World War and visited from the Town Hall.

Lens-Liéven Tourist Office, 26 Rue de la Paix, 62300 Lens. Tel: + (0)3 21 67 66 66. E-mail Info@villedelens.fr Website: www.villedelens.fr Has details and local maps showing of hotels, gîtes, camping sites etc.
This covers Loos, N-D de Lorette and Vimy. Several restaurants are mentioned during the battlefield tour. There are several **restaurants in Lens** and handy for Loos is the 2-star **Campanile**, 282 Route de La Bassée, 62300 Lens. Tel: + (0)3 21 28 82 82. Signed off the road but quite difficult to find on the edge of the Parc d'Activités.
The Lens-Liéven *Communauté d'Agglomeration* has taken part in the '14-'18 Remembered' (qv) project.
Somewhat out on a limb is -
Le Cateau. Tourist Office: Opposite the Matisse Museum. 9, place Commandant Richez, 59360 Le Cateau-Cambrésis, Tel: + (0)3 27 84 10 94. They have a list of the small local hotels and variety of restaurants from friteries and pizzerias to traditional fare. Accessible from the Valenciennes hotels described above and all the numerous **Cambrai Hotels**. Nearby is the 4-star **Château de Ligny**, 2 rue

Pierre Curie, Ligny. Tel: + (0)3 27 85 25 84. E-mail: contact@chateau-de-ligny.fr, Website www.chateau-de-ligny.fr In the town is the **Relais Fénélon** at 21 rue du Maréchal Mortier. Tel: + (0)3 27 84 25 80. Website: www.hotel-restaurant-relais-fenelon.fr
Near The Forester's House, Bois l'Evêque, is the **Estaminet de l'Ermitage**. Tel: +(0) 3. 27 77 99 48.

ACKNOWLEDGEMENTS

During our long 'recce and research' phase of this updated version of the book we renewed many old friendships and made many new ones who were generous with their knowledge and their time.

As always we express our admiration for the dedicated work of the **CWGC** and for the assistance we have had from staff at Maidenhead, Ieper and Beaurains. In **Ypres** Piet Chielens, coordinator of the new In Flanders Fields Museum, Peter Slosse, Tourist Officer and Dominiek Dendooven from the Documentation (now the Knowledge Centre have been helpful as always, as have Natasja and the Staff of the Ariane Hotel who looked after us extremely well during 'recces. Steve Douglas, Chris Lock and Milena, Jacques Ryckebosch and Genevra Charsley, Iain McHenry and Liz Millward have kept us posted of new developments. In **Zonnebeke** we have received much help from Franky Bostyn and his successors. For permission to reproduce the poem *The Next War* from *Selected Satires and Poems*, Osbert Sitwell and Macmillan. We would like to thank Martin Stoneham for info about Lt Philip Neame VC, at **Neuve Chapelle**. At **Loos** Brig-Gen Gregory Young gave us information on the 15th Bn, 58th Highlanders of Canada Memorial Project, the indefatigable Gilles Payen cheerfully responded to query after query, as did Jack Thorpe at **Erquinghem-Lys**. Our thanks to Members of the *Association Souvenir de la Bataille de Fromelles* and to Lt-Col Phillip Robinson for information about the astonishing work of the **Durand Group** throughout the region, Peter Barton for information about the Tunnellers' Memorial at **Givenchy** and other projects and Patrick Vanleene for information about **Pervyse**. Horst Howe, retd rep of the *Deutsche Kriegsgrabefursorge*, has as always been generous with his time and information. In **Comines-Warneton** the enthusiastic team at the Archives and the Tourist Office have supplied us with information on the Interpretation Centre at Ploegsteert. The **Mons** Tourist Office personnel have also answered several queries. Finally our thanks to Elaine Parker who maintains the Home HQ.

PICTURE CREDITS

Our thanks go to: the Ville de Mons for the photo of Germans in Mons and the site of the new Museum, page 32; www.greatwar.be for the photo of Coppens Memorial on page 71; De Klaproos, publishers of Patrick Vanleene's book *Op Naar de Grote Oorlog* (qv) for the picture of 'The Two at Pervyse' on page 84; the Domein Raversijde (Ostende) for pictures of the Atlantic Wall Museum on pages 96 & 97; Peter Slosse for the picture of the IFF interior on page 248; Foto Daniel for the pictures of the Menin Gate Buglers on page 319; the Passchendaele Museum for the picture of the trenches on page 268; Jessica Wise for the Le Cateau picture on page 53 and Dud Corner Cem on pages 324 & 325; Lt-Col Phillip Robinson and Pen & Sword Books for the photo of carving in Maison Blanche Caves, page 222; Living Museum, N-D Lorette for picture of diorama, page 214; ©AAPP/Artefactory for the picture of the 'Circle of Death, N-D de Lorette, page 212; Luc Mignotte for the picture of L'Estaminet de Lorette on page 214; Veterans' Affairs, Canada for the pictures of Grange Tunnel on page 229; Steve Douglas for the pictures of the Vimy Memorial on page 228; Iain McHenry for the aerial photo of the Menin Gate on page 251 and the Kruisstraat Craters on page 287; Brig-Gen Gregory Young for the 15th Bn, 58th Highlanders of Canada Memorial Project Memorial and Gilles Payen for the pictures of 'Tower Bridge', Loos, page 173; Jack Thorpe for the picture of the Pte Poulter, VC Memorial, page 198 & Railton Memorial page 196; Serero Architect for the impression of the new Museum at Fromelles, page 186; Alan Herriot (sculptor) for the Black Watch Highlander on page 333; Peter Jones for the sketch of the Welsh Memorial on page 334 and Lt-Col H.O.S. Cadogan for the new RWF Memorial on page 335; Michael St Maur Shiel for the Loos picture on page 178; Jean-Michel Van Elslande for the pic on page 336 of the Australian Memorial, Plugstreet '14-'18 Experience.

INDEX

FORCES

These are listed in descending order of size, i.e. Armies, Corps, Divisions, Brigades, Regiments... then numerically and then alphabetically. Many more units are mentioned in the Cemetery descriptions throughout the book.

MEMORIALS

MUSEUMS/INFORMATION CENTRES

WAR CEMETERIES

GENERAL INDEX